Fashioning Adultery

This book provides the first major survey of representations of adultery in later seventeenth- and early eighteenth-century England. Bringing together a wide variety of literary and legal sources – including sermons, pamphlets, plays, diaries, periodicals, trial reports and the records of marital litigation – it documents a growing diversity in perceptions of marital infidelity in this period, against the backdrop of an explosion in print culture and a decline in the judicial regulation of sexual immorality.

In general terms the book explains a gradual transformation of ideas about extra-marital sex, whereby the powerfully established religious argument that adultery was universally a sin became increasingly open to challenge. The book charts significant developments in the idiom in which sexually transgressive behaviour was discussed, showing how evolving ideas of civility and social refinement and new thinking about gender difference influenced assessments of immoral behaviour.

DAVID M. TURNER is Lecturer in History, University of Glamorgan.

Past and Present Publications

General Editor: LYNDAL ROPER, *Royal Holloway, University of London*

Past and Present Publications comprise books similar in character to the articles in the journal *Past and Present*. Whether the volumes in the series are collections of essays – some previously published, others new studies – or monographs, they encompass a wide variety of scholarly and original works primarily concerned with social, economic and cultural changes, and their causes and consequences. They will appeal to both specialists and non-specialists and will endeavour to communicate the results of historical and allied research in the most readable and lively form.

For a list of titles in Past and Present Publications, see end of book.

Fashioning Adultery

Gender, Sex and Civility in England, 1660–1740

DAVID M. TURNER

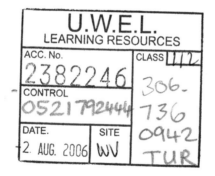

CAMBRIDGE
UNIVERSITY PRESS

PUBLISHED BY THE PRESS SYNDICATE OF THE UNIVERSITY OF CAMBRIDGE
The Pitt Building, Trumpington Street, Cambridge, United Kingdom

CAMBRIDGE UNIVERSITY PRESS
The Edinburgh Building, Cambridge CB2 2RU, UK
40 West 20th Street, New York, NY 10011-4211, USA
477 Williamstown Road, Port Melbourne, VIC 3207, Australia
Ruiz de Alarcón 13, 28014 Madrid, Spain
Dock House, The Waterfront, Cape Town 8001, South Africa

http://www.cambridge.org

First published 2002
Reprinted 2005

Printed in the United Kingdom at the University Press, Cambridge

Typefaces Times 10/12 pt and Plantin   *System* LaTeX 2$_\varepsilon$ [TB]

A catalogue record for this book is available from the British Library

Library of Congress Cataloguing in Publication data

Turner, David M., 1972–
Fashioning adultery: gender, sex, and civility in England, 1660–1740 / David M. Turner.
    p.   cm. – (Past and present publications)
Includes bibliographical references and index.
ISBN 0-521-79244-4
1. Adultery–England–History.   2. England–Social life and customs.   I. Title.
II. Series.
HQ806 .T87 2002
306.73′6′0942–dc21   2002022277

ISBN 0 521 79244 4 hardback

To my parents and sister

Contents

Acknowledgements

In writing this book, I have benefited from the advice and support of many people and institutions. My greatest academic debt is to Martin Ingram who meticulously supervised the Oxford University doctoral thesis from which this book developed and has continued to provide a constant source of inspiration, encouragement and support. My postgraduate research was largely funded by a British Academy studentship with additional financial support provided by a Scouloudi Research Fellowship at the Institute of Historical Research, University of London and a Hulme Continuation Grant awarded by the Principal and Fellows of Brasenose College, Oxford. In 1998 I was awarded the first Past and Present Society Postdoctoral Research Fellowship, held at the Institute of Historical Research, which enabled me to undertake additional research for this book. I am also indebted to the staff of all the libraries and archives I have used in the course of my research for their patience and assistance. I would like to thank in particular Melanie Barber and her staff at Lambeth Palace Library for their help with using the records of the Court of Arches.

In turning my doctoral thesis into a book I have benefited from the suggestions of my examiners, Ian Archer and Anthony Fletcher, and the anonymous readers at Past and Present Publications. Joanna Innes has been particularly supportive of this project and has offered much encouragement. Tim Hitchcock and Faramerz Dabhoiwala also generously took time to read my thesis and suggested ways in which it might be developed. In producing the final version, the incisive comments of Matthew Kinservik and (especially) Sharif Gemie and Elizabeth Foyster have assisted me greatly – any errors that remain are my own. I must also thank Philip Carter, Chris Chapman, Karen Harvey, Paul Mitchell, Kevin Stagg and Dinah Winch for discussing ideas with me at various stages, asking many searching questions and sharing the insights of their own research and academic interests. I must also thank my colleagues in the history field at the University of Glamorgan for creating such a stimulating and good-humoured academic environment in which to work.

My energy for this project has been sustained by the support of many friends. Henrice Altink, John Beynon, Andy Croll, Elizabeth Foyster, Matthew Kinservik, Norry Laporte, Romita Ray, Susi Schrafstetter and Kevin Stagg all offered valuable encouragement when the going got tough. Rosemary and Fred Marcus deserve special thanks for their kindness and generosity. Finally I must thank my sister, Kathryn, and my parents, Maurice and Margaret, for their love and unwavering support throughout. I dedicate this book to them.

Note on the text

Quotations from original sources retain the original spelling, grammar and punctuation. In quoting from legal manuscripts, i/j and u/v have been distinguished and 'th' substituted for 'y' where appropriate, and the contractions used by court clerks have been expanded. Occasional clerical or printer's errors in the original sources have been silently corrected. Dates follow Old Style, but the year is taken to begin on 1 January.

Abbreviations

AM	*The Athenian Mercury*
Etherege, *Man of Mode*	Sir George Etherege, *The Man of Mode, Or, Sir Fopling Flutter* (1676), in *The Dramatic Works of Sir George Etherege*, ed. H. F. B. Brett-Smith (2 vols., London, 1927), II, pp. 181–288
Etherege, *She Would if She Could*	Sir George Etherege, *She Would if She Could* (1668), in *The Dramatic Works of Sir George Etherege*, ed. H. F. B. Brett-Smith (2 vols., London, 1927), II, pp. 89–179
LMA	London Metropolitan Archives
LPL	Lambeth Palace Library
OED	*Oxford English Dictionary* (Oxford, 1989 edn)
Pepys, *Diary*	Samuel Pepys, *The Diary of Samuel Pepys*, ed. Robert Latham and William Matthews (11 vols., London, 1970–83)
PP	*Past and Present*
Ravenscroft, *London Cuckolds*	Edward Ravenscroft, *The London Cuckolds* (1682), in *Restoration Comedy*, ed. A. Norman Jeffares (4 vols., London, 1974), II, pp. 435–552
Review	*Defoe's Review*, ed. Arthur Wellesley Secord (9 vols., New York, 1938)
Spectator	*The Spectator*, ed. Donald F. Bond (5 vols., Oxford, 1965)
Tatler	*The Tatler*, ed. Donald F. Bond (3 vols., Oxford, 1987)
TRHS	*Transactions of the Royal Historical Society*
Wycherley, *Country Wife*	William Wycherley, *The Country Wife* (1675), in *The Plays of William Wycherley*, ed. Arthur Friedman (Oxford, 1979), pp. 245–355

Introduction

On 4 February 1674 Herbert Croft, Bishop of Hereford, delivered a Fast Day sermon to the assembled House of Lords. In keeping with the spirit of gloomy self-reflection and calls for repentance and reform that such occasions demanded, his text offered dire warnings of the spread of debauchery and vice. 'Fornication and Adultery', Croft lamented, were 'not only frequently acted in private but publickly owned', their perpetrators openly bragging about their conquests. Although he conceded that sexual sins were no new thing, they were now conducted in a particularly scandalous manner. While adulteries had once been committed in the 'dark' and men had 'formerly skulkt into lewd houses, and there had their revellings', nowadays, 'men, married men, in the light, bring into their own Houses most lewd Strumpets, feast and sport with them in the face of the sun'. In the meantime, their 'neglected, scorned, disconsolate wives' were 'forc'd to retire to their secret closets, that they be not spectators of these abominations'. Rippling out from the court, where the debauches of 'grandees' set a bad example copied by their inferiors, the forces of 'lewdness and atheism' threatened to engulf the land. Wherever one looked, concluded the bishop, it was as though civilised Englishmen had 'metamorphosed themselves into lascivious goats'.[1]

Invectives against the depravity of the times are a feature of many societies at many historical moments. Croft's picture of an epidemic of sexual sin fits a tradition of moral complaint that had been a persistent feature of English pulpit oratory since the Middle Ages. Yet there was a distinctive shrillness and urgency to this rhetoric in the later seventeenth century. The Restoration project of enforcing moral unity and returning to an antediluvian order after the mid-century upheavals was perceived to be under threat from a number of inter-related forces: from the much-publicised adulteries of King Charles II and his courtiers, from the open scoffing at religion by 'wits' and 'atheists', and from the

---

[1] Herbert Croft, *A Sermon Preached before Right Honourable the Lords Assembled in Parliament, Upon the Fast-Day Appointed February 4 1673/4* (London, 1674), pp. 22–3.

fragmentation of religious allegiances marked by the rise of Protestant dissent and the insidious threat of Roman Catholicism.[2] Embedded in the rhetoric of Croft's sermon, and the writings of other later seventeenth-century churchmen, appeared to be a growing recognition that the moral hegemony and unity of moral vision which they had striven so hard to preserve was becoming seriously undermined. The core value that underlay Croft's vision of adultery, that it was a sin for which all who committed it were considered equally guilty and deserving of punishment, was increasingly tested. Over the course of the late seventeenth and early eighteenth centuries a variety of factors – including a burgeoning print culture, the slackening of censorship, a changing urban environment, shifting patterns of sociability, civility and sensibility, and legal innovations – were to lead to the proliferation of a wide range of opinions and angles of vision on adultery and other moral issues. By the 1730s and '40s boundaries were being redrawn and assessments of adultery depended on a wider variety of social and cultural circumstances. This book charts and explains this process of debate and displacement and explores how, in the process, the meanings of extra-marital sex were significantly altered.

Although great advances have been made in recent years in our understanding of the sexual mores of early modern England, little is known in detail about the period from the Restoration to the mid-eighteenth century. Studies of divorce, prostitution and sexual slander have begun to make good this neglect, but many gaps remain in our understanding of the changing social, cultural and intellectual context in which illicit sexual activity was viewed and discussed.[3] Studying adultery has provided valuable insights into the myriad social and sexual relations in early modern English society, shedding light on such matters as the sexual double standard, codes of male and female honour and reputation, and power relations within the household.[4] Conjugal infidelity has also been studied as an offence punished by the courts or by popular shaming rituals and as an event which might set husbands and wives on the 'road to divorce',

---

[2] John Spurr, 'Virtue, Religion and Government: the Anglican Uses of Providence', in Tim Harris, Paul Seaward and Mark Goldie (eds.), *The Politics of Religion in Restoration England* (Oxford, 1990), p. 35; Spurr, *The Restoration Church of England, 1646–1689* (New Haven, CT and London, 1991), p. 238 and ch. 5 *passim*.

[3] For instance: Lawrence Stone, *Road to Divorce: England 1530–1987* (Oxford, 1990); Tim Meldrum, 'A Women's Court in London: Defamation at the Bishop of London's Consistory Court, 1700–1745', *The London Journal*, 19 (1994), 1–20; Faramerz Dabhoiwala, 'Prostitution and Police in London, *c*.1660–*c*.1760', DPhil thesis, University of Oxford (1995); Randolph Trumbach, *Sex and the Gender Revolution, Volume I: Heterosexuality and the Third Gender in Enlightenment London* (Chicago, IL and London, 1998).

[4] Keith Thomas, 'The Double Standard', *Journal of the History of Ideas*, 20 (1959), 195–216; G. R. Quaife, *Wanton Wenches and Wayward Wives: Peasants and Illicit Sex in Early Seventeenth-Century England* (London, 1979); Susan Dwyer Amussen, *An Ordered Society: Gender and Class in Early Modern England* (Oxford, 1988), ch. 4; Laura Gowing, *Domestic Dangers: Women, Words and Sex in Early Modern London* (Oxford, 1996), ch. 6; Elizabeth A. Foyster, *Manhood in Early Modern England: Honour, Sex and Marriage* (London, 1999).

whether through formal legal proceedings or private separation or desertion.[5] However, relatively few studies have explored the cultural representation of adultery in early modern England as a topic in its own right, despite the visibility of marital breakdown as a theme of a wide variety of texts. Though historians are increasingly aware that patterns of moral regulation and ideas about the family and domestic relations were undergoing significant changes in later seventeenth- and early eighteenth-century England, the meanings of adultery in this period await detailed attention.

This book attempts to fill this lacuna by analysing how marital infidelity was represented in a variety of literary and legal contexts. Drawing on a broad range of sources, including sermons, treatises, periodicals, comic plays, jokes, social documentary, pamphlets reporting on crimes of passion, journalistic trial reports and the records of marital separation in the church courts, it explores the multiple strategies of 'fashioning' or constructing the experience of marital breakdown and adultery and analyses the languages through which infidelity was conceptualised. It views these texts not as passive 'reflectors' of 'attitudes' towards infidelity, but rather as elements of a dynamic process of communication, not only describing but also constituting and shaping changing perceptions and understandings of conjugal disintegration. Four themes underpinning Croft's message on sexual morality are given special attention in this survey. In the first place, it examines the ways in which representations of adultery were influenced by concepts of 'public' and 'private', set against the backdrop of significant changes in the theory and practice of public regulation of sexual morals. Second, drawing on Croft's singling out for special comment the sexual behaviour of 'grandees' whose conduct seemed to be beyond the reach of conventional moral teaching, it examines the effects of social differentiation on understandings of sexuality and the ways in which morals were used as a tool of class demarcation, in particular between the increasingly powerful middling sort and their social superiors, at a time when status was increasingly expressed in cultural form. Third, this book explores how changing ideas about masculinity and femininity bore on perceptions of marital breakdown. Particular attention is paid to the neglected question of how men's sexual behaviour threatened domestic relations and damaged the patriarchal household – a danger clearly of concern to Croft and, as we shall see, many other commentators. Finally, Croft's attack on the bad sexual manners of Restoration England, and his recourse to distinctions between the civilised and the bestial in conceptualising

---

[5] Martin Ingram, *Church Courts, Sex and Marriage in England, 1570–1640* (Cambridge, 1987), ch. 8; Ingram, 'Ridings, Rough Music and the "Reform of Popular Culture" in Early Modern England', *PP*, 105 (1984), 79–113; Stone, *Road to Divorce*; Stone, *Uncertain Unions and Broken Lives: Marriage and Divorce in England 1660–1857* (Oxford, 1995); Joanne Bailey, 'Breaking the Conjugal Vows: Marriage and Marriage Breakdown in the North of England, 1660–1800', PhD thesis, University of Durham (1999).

illicit sexuality, points to another relatively neglected area explored in this survey – the ways in which concepts of civility and polite manners influenced discourses of sexual behaviour. The remainder of this introductory chapter develops the objectives of this book in more detail and explains its methodological approach. At the outset, it reviews the changing social, cultural and judicial context in which perceptions of infidelity were formed.

AIMS AND CONTEXT

Since the Middle Ages, adultery had been subject to judicial sanction.[6] However, during the later seventeenth century, the questions of how far the civil and ecclesiastical authorities should intervene in regulating sexual morality, and the forms such intervention should take, were becoming increasingly contested issues. The ecclesiastical courts, which had long functioned as a kind of flagship of acceptable morality, resumed their business of policing adultery and fornication after the Restoration following a mid-century hiatus brought about by the Civil War and temporary disestablishment of the Church of England during the Interregnum. During that time, infidelity had carried the death penalty under the 1650 Adultery Act, but this draconian, largely unworkable, statute lapsed at the Restoration.[7] However, in spite of an initial influx of business caused by a backlog of cases that had built up over the previous decades, the Restoration church courts found their ability to regulate public morals increasingly compromised. The growth of Protestant dissent placed a significant number of people beyond the pale of the Anglican church, eroding the religious consensus on which the courts had operated. The position of the courts was undermined still further by the granting of limited freedom of conscience by James II's Declaration of Indulgence in 1687 and the Toleration Act of 1689.[8] The expense and tedious procedure of the church courts also began to seriously undermine their effectiveness.[9] At the same time, growing prosperity and relative political stability in later seventeenth-century England removed some of the impetus on the part of authorities, especially in rural areas, to routinely intervene to uphold the social, moral and gender order by punishing adulterers and other sexual offenders.[10] The result was a general decline in the business of the church courts in the later seventeenth and early eighteenth centuries.

---

[6] James A. Brundage, *Law, Sex and Christian Society in Medieval Europe* (Chicago, IL, 1987); Richard Wunderli, *London Church Courts and Society on the Eve of the Reformation* (Cambridge, MA, 1981).

[7] Keith Thomas, 'The Puritans and Adultery: the Act of 1650 Reconsidered', in Donald Pennington and Keith Thomas (eds.), *Puritans and Revolutionaries: Essays in Seventeenth-Century History Presented to Christopher Hill* (Oxford, 1978), pp. 257–82.

[8] Ingram, *Church Courts*, p. 373.   [9] Dabhoiwala, 'Prostitution and Police', p. 94.

[10] Amussen, *An Ordered Society*, p. 186.

The dynamics and characteristics of this process have yet to be charted in detail for the whole of the country, and there may have been significant regional variations.[11] The decline of ecclesiastical jurisdiction over sexual offences seems to have been particularly rapid in London owing to the high proportion of dissenters residing in the capital.[12] There was also a well-established system of regulating sexual offences under common law, which meant that in the 1680s much of the criminal business of the church courts in moral regulation was being transferred to Quarter Sessions and other local courts.[13] Control of vice remained high on the political agenda into the eighteenth century, evinced by the activities of the Societies for the Reformation of Manners, established in the capital and a few provincial cities in the 1690s with the aim of creating a new moral order in the wake of the Glorious Revolution. These organisations prosecuted adulterers alongside fornicators, sabbath breakers and other offenders.[14] However, public policy was increasingly becoming reoriented towards dealing with the social problem of prostitution rather than regulating family relationships. By the 1730s, prosecutions for adultery in London had virtually ceased, as marital infidelity came to be viewed by the legal authorities as a 'private vice', no longer subject to public prosecution.[15] Though adultery may not have become quite so rapidly 'decriminalised' in other parts of the country, there is no doubt that by 1740, the terminal date for this study, prosecutions were increasingly rare.[16]

The cultural dimensions of these changes, and their impact on how extramarital sex was viewed, await detailed historical attention. Yet their implications

---

[11] In some areas correction of morals may have increased as a proportion of the church courts' overall business in the century after the Restoration as other matters, such as the enforcement of religious uniformity, disappeared in the wake of the Toleration Act. See M. G. Smith, *Pastoral Discipline and the Church Courts: the Hexham Court 1680–1730*, Borthwick Papers, 62 (York, 1982); Mary Kinnear, 'The Correction Court in the Diocese of Carlisle, 1704–1756', *Church History*, 59 (1990), 191–206; John Walsh and Stephen Taylor, 'Introduction: the Church and Anglicanism in the "Long" Eighteenth Century', in John Walsh, Colin Hayden and Stephen Taylor (eds.), *The Church of England c.1689–c.1833: From Toleration to Tractarianism* (Cambridge, 1993), pp. 5–6.

[12] On the strength of nonconformity in Restoration London see Tim Harris, *London Crowds in the Reign of Charles II: Propaganda and Politics from the Restoration until the Exclusion Crisis* (Cambridge, 1987), esp. ch. 4.

[13] Dabhoiwala, 'Prostitution and Police', pp. 130–1.

[14] Dudley Bahlman, *The Moral Revolution of 1688* (New Haven, CT, 1957); T. C. Curtis and W. A. Speck, 'The Societies for the Reformation of Manners: a Case Study in the Theory and Practice of Moral Reform', *Literature and History*, 3 (1976), 45–64; Tony Claydon, *William III and the Godly Revolution* (Cambridge, 1996); Tina Isaacs, 'The Anglican Hierarchy and the Reformation of Manners', *Journal of Ecclesiastical History*, 33 (1982), 391–411; David Hayton, 'Moral Reform and Country Politics in the Late Seventeenth-Century House of Commons', *PP*, 128 (1990), 48–91; Robert B. Shoemaker, *Prosecution and Punishment: Petty Crime and the Law in London and Rural Middlesex, c.1660–1725* (Cambridge, 1991), pp. 238–72; Dabhoiwala, 'Prostitution and Police', ch. 5.

[15] Ibid., p. 61; Trumbach, *Sex and the Gender Revolution*, p. 29.

[16] Bailey, 'Breaking the Conjugal Vows', p. 125.

were profound, not just for how adultery was regarded in official and religious circles, but also for questions of personal choice and moral responsibility. The church courts upheld the principle that all extra-marital sex was considered equally sinful and deserving of punishment and there can be no doubt that their declining efficiency dealt a serious blow to the religious ideal of a moral consensus – thus explaining why Herbert Croft was so concerned about adulterers shamelessly flouting their behaviour in public. Stone has argued that, among the elite in particular, there was a shift in sensibilities during the later seventeenth century 'away from regarding illicit sex as basically sinful and shameful to treating it as an interesting and amusing aspect of life'.[17] Trumbach has also suggested a widespread toleration for men's sexual relations with women outside marriage in the wake of the emergence of a distinct male homosexual subculture in the early eighteenth century, as men became increasingly anxious to prove their heterosexuality.[18] However, this framework of interpretation is open to question. Illegitimacy rates, admittedly a crude indicator of sexual conduct, were low during the later seventeenth and early eighteenth centuries, although they were to rise significantly after 1750.[19] Given the variety of contexts in which the meanings of illicit sexuality were formed, and the complex emotions it raised, the notion of a rising 'toleration' for adultery needs to be treated warily. Just because adultery was becoming less liable for routine prosecution does not necessarily mean it was becoming more 'acceptable'.[20] But whatever this meant for actual behaviour, the decline of the church courts marked an important watershed for the ways in which adultery was talked about and represented in print. As we shall see, the question of whether adultery was a matter for public regulation or a matter of personal conscience was a key topic of debate from the late seventeenth century.

Changing patterns of moral regulation have been viewed as one aspect of a wider 'privatisation' of domestic relations in this period.[21] In the late sixteenth and early seventeenth centuries, the regulation of vice by the church courts and magistrates, together with a host of informal community-based shaming rituals against sexual offenders, had been underpinned by an organic conception of society that had viewed the well-governed patriarchal family as a microcosm of the state.[22] Over the course of the seventeenth century these patriarchal ideals became internalised, but analogies between familial and political order began

---

[17] Stone, *Road to Divorce*, p. 248.   [18] Trumbach, *Sex and the Gender Revolution, passim.*

[19] Peter Laslett, *The World We Have Lost: Further Explored* (London, 1983), pp. 158–62; cf. Tim Hitchcock, 'Redefining Sex in Eighteenth-Century England', *History Workshop Journal*, 41 (1996), 73–90.

[20] Cf. Bailey, 'Breaking the Conjugal Vows', p. 125.

[21] The fullest analysis of this phenomenon, albeit largely from a French perspective, remains Roger Chartier (ed.), *A History of Private Life, Volume III: Passions of the Renaissance* (Cambridge, MA and London, 1989).

[22] Amussen, *An Ordered Society*, ch. 2.

to break down. The experience of the Civil Wars, which had divided family members and resulted in the execution of the king, challenged this harmonious political vision. After the Restoration, the connection between political and familial authority was increasingly scrutinised as the well-publicised adulteries of Charles II ushered in visions not of familial order but of domestic tyranny.[23] Finally, the direct analogy between the power of magistrates and the power of fathers over children and husbands over wives was dealt a serious blow by the contractual arguments used by Whig political theorists to justify the Glorious Revolution. To support the deposition of James II by his subjects, they argued that the power of the magistrate over the people was distinct from the authority a father had over his children or a husband over his wife. The result was that order in the household receded from theories of the state. Among the middling sort in particular, the family was increasingly cast as a private sphere, a refuge of intimacy distinct from the public world of politics, and it was considered increasingly improper for external forces, whether the state or community, to interfere in its relationships. Harsh strictures on relationships of power and subordination within the family, which had dominated puritan conduct literature of the sixteenth and seventeenth centuries, gave way to a more marked emphasis on married love. This has been seen as the start of a gradual separation of the public political and private domestic spheres that would reach its fullest expression in the cult of domesticity that dominated the ideology of the respectable classes in the late eighteenth and early nineteenth centuries.[24]

There can be no doubt that the events of 1688 changed the terms of reference in which family relations were viewed. However, notions of a rising cult of 'domesticity' or a privatisation of the family ignore the complexity of the debate on the public or private nature of marriage and adultery in the late seventeenth and early eighteenth centuries. This book argues that the 'privatisation' of adultery was something too complex to be taken for granted. The notion that the family was becoming a less 'political' institution needs to be set against what is now known about the continuing importance of gender, the family and sexuality to political debate in this period.[25] Moreover, as Margaret Hunt and others have shown, during the eighteenth century there was a growing

---

[23] Rachel Weil, 'Sometimes a Scepter is Only a Scepter: Pornography and Politics in Restoration England', in Lynn Hunt (ed.), *The Invention of Pornography: Obscenity and the Origins of Modernity 1500–1800* (New York, 1993), pp. 125–53.

[24] Amussen, *An Ordered Society*, pp. 64–5; Leonore Davidoff and Catherine Hall, *Family Fortunes: Men and Women of the English Middle Class, 1780–1850* (London, 1987); cf. Amanda Vickery, 'Golden Age to Separate Spheres? A Review of the Categories and Chronology of English Women's History', *Historical Journal*, 36 (1993), 383–414; Robert B. Shoemaker, *Gender in English Society, 1650–1850: the Emergence of Separate Spheres?* (London and New York, 1998); Trumbach, *Sex and the Gender Revolution*, ch. 12.

[25] Rachel Weil, *Political Passions: Gender, the Family and Political Argument in England, 1680–1714* (Manchester, 1999).

interest in the relationship between private virtue and political probity, marked by increased attacks on aristocratic vice by a middling sort anxious to assert its social, economic and political worth.[26] Such attacks did not run contrary to the cult of bourgeois domesticity; rather they were of its essence. Recent work has also shown that for the middling sort in particular, the household remained important in the public world of business dealings in a financial world still dominated by credit.[27] As Houlbrooke has pointed out, the history of early modern family life is best seen in terms of structural continuity, punctuated by changes in the 'media of expression'.[28]

The notions of a 'privatisation' or 'de-politicisation' of the family become still more problematic in the context of a much greater visibility of sex and marriage in the burgeoning public sphere of later seventeenth-century England.[29] Cultural innovations and new genres of print, by revealing details of 'private' life, were making marriage and adultery more 'public' than ever before. The climate of relative social stability in the later seventeenth century created the conditions for a more questioning approach to traditional meanings of sexual behaviour and morality, which found an outlet in a variety of cultural forms. The introduction of actresses on stage after 1660, together with the growing use of moveable scenery, which allowed adulterous couples to be 'discovered' *in flagrante delicto*, increased the vogue for plays dealing with all aspects of marital relations and the battle between the sexes.[30] Sex and marriage were topics of consuming interest in an increasingly eclectic mix of publications – from sermons and works of religious devotion to pamphlets describing domestic homicides, from periodicals answering questions on matrimonial issues submitted by their readers, to scandalous 'secret histories' serving up tales of the sexual adventures of the *beau monde*, which allowed their readers to experience the thrills of clandestine affairs vicariously.[31]

[26] Margaret R. Hunt, *The Middling Sort: Commerce, Gender and the Family in England 1680–1780* (Berkeley and Los Angeles, CA, 1996), ch. 8.

[27] Jonathan Barry, 'Bourgeois Collectivism? Urban Association and the Middling Sort', in Jonathan Barry and Christopher Brooks (eds.), *The Middling Sort of People: Culture, Society and Politics in England 1550–1800* (Basingstoke, 1994), pp. 84–112; Craig Muldrew, *The Economy of Obligation* (Basingstoke, 1998); Hunt, *The Middling Sort*; Bailey, 'Breaking the Conjugal Vows'.

[28] Ralph Houlbrooke, *Death, Religion and the Family in England 1450–1750* (Oxford, 1998), p. 2.

[29] John Brewer, '"The Most Polite Age and the Most Vicious": Attitudes towards Culture as a Commodity, 1660–1800', in Ann Bermingham and John Brewer (eds.), *The Consumption of Culture 1600–1800: Image, Object, Text* (London and New York, 1995), pp. 341–61.

[30] Robert D. Hume, *The Rakish Stage: Studies in English Drama 1660–1800* (Carbondale, IL, 1983), pp. 152–4; Elizabeth Howe, *The First English Actresses: Women and Drama 1660–1700* (Cambridge, 1992), p. 62 and *passim*; Derek Hughes, *English Drama, 1660–1700* (Oxford, 1996), p. 3.

[31] Frances E. Dolan, *Dangerous Familiars: Representations of Domestic Crime in England, 1550–1700* (Ithaca, NY and London, 1994); Helen Berry, '"Nice and Curious Questions": Coffee Houses and the Representation of Women in John Dunton's *Athenian Mercury*', *The Seventeenth Century*, 12 (1997), 257–76; J. J. Richetti, *Popular Fiction Before Richardson: Narrative Patterns 1700–1739* (Oxford, 1969).

These changes in cultural production and consumption are central to this study. The proliferation of plays, pamphlets and periodicals discussing sex and marriage was part of a much broader expansion of the realm of public debate in the later seventeenth century, marked by an increasing volume of printed output, improving levels of literacy and a developing infrastructure of communication. James Raven has calculated that printed output grew from around 400 titles published in the first decade of the seventeenth century to 6,000 in the 1630s, and 22,000 by the 1710s.[32] This growth was particularly spectacular during the lapses of censorship that occurred during the Civil War and Interregnum, between 1679 and 1685 and in the wake of the permanent lapsing of the Licensing Act in 1695.[33] Conservative estimates of reading skills, based on the ability to sign one's name,[34] suggest that in the mid-seventeenth century around 30 per cent of men and 10 per cent of women had acquired basic literacy. By 1700 the proportion of literates had risen to 50 per cent of men and 25 per cent of women, and by 1750 some 62 per cent of adult males were literate compared with 38 per cent of women.[35] Literacy levels were higher in London than the rest of society, due to greater educational opportunities and the development of metropolitan trade, which necessitated the acquisition of reading and writing skills.[36] A flourishing network of coffee houses and taverns in the later seventeenth-century metropolis encouraged the flow of ideas and acted as a forum for the interchange of ideas. At the same time, improved roads and transport links with the provinces enabled the spread of printed materials produced in the capital, and with them the values and opinions of London society, to reach a wider audience.[37]

This proliferation of genres prompted greater questioning of how and why marriages failed and what motivated men and women to be unfaithful to their spouses. Aimed first and foremost at a metropolitan audience, print was used by urban dwellers to explore the moral boundaries, tensions and contradictions

[32] James Raven, 'New Reading Histories, Print Culture and the Identification of Change: the Case of Eighteenth-Century England', *Social History*, 23 (1998), 275.

[33] Donald Thomas, *A Long Time Burning: the History of Literary Censorship in England* (London, 1969), ch. 1; John Feather, *History of British Publishing* (London and New York, 1988), p. 67.

[34] The actual levels of reading ability may have been higher as writing was taught after reading: Margaret Spufford, 'First Steps in Literacy: the Reading and Writing Experience of the Humblest Seventeenth-Century Spiritual Autobiographers', *Social History*, 4 (1979), 407–35; Keith Thomas, 'The Meaning of Literacy in Early Modern England', in Gerd Baumann (ed.), *The Written Word: Literacy in Transition* (Oxford, 1986), pp. 97–131.

[35] David Cressy, 'Literacy in Context: Meaning and Measurement in Early Modern England', in John Brewer and Roy Porter (eds.), *Consumption and the World of Goods* (London and New York, 1993), pp. 313–14. For more details see Cressy, *Literacy and the Social Order: Reading and Writing in Tudor and Stuart England* (Cambridge, 1980), ch. 7 *passim*.

[36] Hunt, *The Middling Sort*, ch. 7.

[37] John Brewer, *The Pleasures of the Imagination: English Culture in the Eighteenth Century* (London, 1997), pp. 34–9; Gilbert D. McEwen, *The Oracle of the Coffee House: John Dunton's Athenian Mercury* (San Marino, CA, 1972).

of their world, putting traditional ideas and modes of thought to the test. Though vice was never represented as an exclusively urban or metropolitan phenomenon, there was an increasing cultural interest in the place of illicit sexuality in urban society, set against the expansion of opportunities for elite sociability in the capital (later copied by provincial towns) such as playhouses, assemblies, pleasure gardens like Vauxhall and Ranelagh, parks, balls and masquerades, all of which seemed to offer new opportunities for adulterous assignations.[38] Interest in urban vice was, of course, no new thing – it had featured regularly in satires comparing 'country' and 'city' living, dating back to classical times, and in 'city' comedies performed on the Renaissance stage.[39] Over the course of the early modern period, there was a growing awareness that London, as a complex, urbanising society sustained by high levels of migration, followed different rules for living than more stratified rural communities. The perception of London as a separate moral universe, where rules for conduct needed to be reconsidered to cope with the variety of its social scene, became sharper during the late seventeenth century as an increasing proportion of the population (perhaps one in six people) spent part of their lives residing in the metropolis.[40] The result, as we shall see, was increased public debate about how new forms of social and spatial organisation altered the perception of social and moral issues, including adultery. Inevitably, focus on these issues gives a metropolitan bias to this survey. While acknowledging the need to recognise the diversity of regional cultures, and being aware that outside London changes in thinking may have followed different trajectories and that 'rustic' societies could have been more resistant to 'urbane' culture, the urban focus of many of the printed sources nevertheless raises a series of interesting questions and therefore deserves study.[41]

The development of new arenas of urban sociability or 'polite society' gave new cultural prominence to ideas of refined behaviour and virtuous interaction

[38] Brewer, *Pleasures of the Imagination*, pp. 3–55; David H. Solkin, *Painting for Money: the Visual Arts and the Public Sphere in Eighteenth-Century England* (New Haven, CT and London, 1993), pp. 106–56; Peter Borsay, *The English Urban Renaissance: Culture and Society in the Provincial Town, 1660–1700* (Oxford, 1989), ch. 6.

[39] Lawrence Manley, 'From Matron to Monster: Tudor-Stuart London and the Languages of Urban Description', in Heather Dubrow and Richard Strier (eds.), *The Historical Renaissance: New Essays on Tudor and Stuart Literature and Culture* (Chicago, IL and London, 1988), pp. 347–74; Theodore B. Leinward, *The City Staged: Jacobean Comedy, 1603–1613* (Madison, WI and London, 1986).

[40] Roger Finlay and Beatrice Shearer, 'Population Growth and Suburban Expansion', in A. L. Beier and Roger Finlay (eds.), *London 1500–1700: the Making of the Metropolis* (London, 1986), p. 48; Peter Borsay, 'The Restoration Town', in Lionel K. J. Glassey (ed.), *The Reigns of Charles II and James VII and II* (Basingstoke, 1997), p. 173; Lawrence Stone, 'The Residential Development of the West End of London in the Seventeenth Century', in Barbara C. Malamant (ed.), *After the Reformation: Essays in Honor of J. H. Hexter* (Manchester, 1980), pp. 168, 183.

[41] For an ambitious study of cultural diversity see Carl B. Estabrook, *Urbane and Rustic England: Cultural Ties and Social Spheres in the Provinces 1660–1780* (Manchester, 1998).

between the sexes. London's emergence as the social hub of the nation after the Restoration stimulated the production of guides to courteous social relations and prescriptions for manners.[42] This book examines the impact of concepts of civility and politeness – codes of refined conduct and virtuous social engagement – on the understanding of marital relations and their breakdown. In doing so, it provides a bridge between historiographies that have tended to develop in isolation from one another: on the one hand the burgeoning early modern historiography of popular values and opinions concerning sex and marriage and, on the other, an eighteenth-century historiography that is dominated by the rise of 'politeness'. The terms 'civil' and 'civility' carried a number of meanings in the early modern period. In the first place, there was a close association, well established by the sixteenth century, between 'civility' or 'civil' behaviour and civilised conduct. The terms were used in particular to distinguish between 'civilised' Christian nations and more 'barbarous' or heathen peoples, and, more generally, between the human and the bestial. 'Civility' was also used in a variety of guides to conduct or 'courtesy' books, appearing from the Elizabethan period, to refer to rules of form and precedence and various rules of bodily deportment relating to such matters as urination, defecation, blowing the nose, spitting and table manners. Thomas Hobbes later contemptuously dismissed these rules as 'small morals', yet Anna Bryson has recently shown that, as important symbols of hierarchy and precedence, they were more than mere 'etiquette'. By the seventeenth century, the ideal of 'civility' embodied a powerful notion of accommodating oneself to others, of 'complaisance' or being pleasing in company. 'Civility' was also closely associated with 'civic' values, translating more generally into the assumption that towns and cities were ideal places for establishing a more refined, ordered and polite mode of behaviour.[43]

After the Restoration, concepts of civility and refined conduct gradually coalesced into new notions of politeness. Although there were strong continuities with existing prescriptions for manners, chiefly the values of propriety and decorum, which were at the heart of older concepts of civility, the orientation of politeness was subtly different. Taking as their ideal the 'urbanity of ancient Romans', architects of polite manners sought to develop a complete system of behaviour necessary to perform 'the reasonable duties of society'.[44] Good manners were ideally cultivated in mixed company, in the developing sphere of urban social life. There was less emphasis on matters of form and precedence

---

[42] Fenela Childs, 'Prescriptions for Manners in English Courtesy Literature 1690–1760, and their Social Implications', DPhil thesis, University of Oxford (1984); Paul Langford, *A Polite and Commercial People: England 1727–1783* (Oxford, 1989), ch. 3; Philip Carter, *Men and the Emergence of Polite Society: Britain 1660–1800* (London, 2001).

[43] Anna Bryson, *From Courtesy to Civility: Changing Codes of Conduct in Early Modern England* (Oxford, 1998), ch. 2 and *passim*. See also the contributions to Peter Burke, Brian Harrison and Paul Slack (eds.), *Civil Histories: Essays Presented to Sir Keith Thomas* (Oxford, 2000).

[44] *The Monthly Miscellany: Or, Memoirs for the Curious* (2 vols., London, 1708), I, pp. 314–15.

than in earlier guides to courteous manners, and an increasing premium placed on genteel modes of expression and the display of benevolent generosity and accommodation to one's companions. This meant that a person's behaviour should vary according to sex, rank, occupation, age, circumstances and surroundings. Deriving from a variety of impulses, including the writings of Whig journalists such as Joseph Addison and Richard Steele, French manuals of 'politesse' and religious pressures for improved standards of behaviour, politeness became a pre-eminent social ideal for anyone claiming respectability.[45] Manners became an important tool of cultural differentiation both between urban and country dwellers and between the 'genteel' and 'vulgar' sorts in an age of sharpening social differentiation.[46]

The rise of polite society dominates the cultural history of the period post-1660, but marriage and sexuality have seldom featured in these historical debates. Although recent studies have illustrated the importance of social interaction between the sexes in the formation of polite manners and have shown the significance of polite ideals in the formation of gender roles and identities, much of this work has concentrated on the display of polite behaviour in arenas of public display such as the coffee house, the assembly or the pleasure garden rather than in the more intimate space of the bedroom or household more generally.[47] Anna Bryson's recent study of early modern conduct books has little to say on sexuality outside the context of the studied 'anti-civility' practised by the rakes and libertines of Restoration drama and has even less to say about marriage, in spite of its social and moral importance for taming or civilising the sexual passions in this period.[48] The classic attempt to incorporate sexuality into analyses of civility remains Norbert Elias's *Civilizing Process* (1939), which observed a growing secrecy and concealment of sexual activities (including adultery), concomitant with a more general rising threshold of shame concerning the body, its functions and display in early modern Europe. However, it now seems clear that many of these developments pre-dated the explosion of courtesy literature that formed the basis of his study.[49] Furthermore, Elias had little to say about the impact of ideas of civility on moral discourse in the early modern

---

[45] Brewer, *Pleasures of the Imagination*, pp. 3–55, 102–7; Amanda Vickery, *The Gentleman's Daughter: Women's Lives in Georgian England* (New Haven, CT and London, 1998), p. 197; Carter, *Men and the Emergence of Polite Society*, ch. 1.

[46] Anthony Fletcher and John Stevenson, 'Introduction', in Fletcher and Stevenson (eds.), *Order and Disorder in Early Modern England* (Cambridge, 1985), pp. 1–15; E. P. Thompson, *Customs in Common* (Harmondsworth, 1991), pp. 16–96.

[47] See, for example, Michele Cohen, *Fashioning Masculinity: National Identity and Language in the Eighteenth Century* (London and New York, 1996); Carter, *Men and the Emergence of Polite Society*. But cf. Vickery, *Gentleman's Daughter*, ch. 6; G. J. Barker-Benfield, *The Culture of Sensibility: Sex and Society in Eighteenth-Century Britain* (Chicago, IL and London, 1992).

[48] Bryson, *From Courtesy to Civility*, ch. 7.

[49] Norbert Elias, *The Civilizing Process: the History of Manners*, trans. Edmund Jephcott ([1939], Oxford, 1978), pp. 180–90; cf. Bryson, *From Courtesy to Civility*, p. 101.

period. More recently, however, Martin Ingram has demonstrated a growing use of concepts of civility by the early seventeenth century in describing unlawful sexual relations in religious and popular discourse. Ingram's work, by showing that this language had a hard moral edge and a cultural importance that went well beyond elite courtesy literature, points the study of sex and civility in a welcome direction.[50]

Nevertheless, much more needs to be known about how these concepts shaped understandings of illicit sexuality at a time when social refinement was reaching new heights. This book takes the study of politeness into relatively uncharted territories by looking at how qualities ideally developed in the public sphere of social interaction were applied to more intimate relations between the sexes. In the process, it raises a number of significant issues and questions. Firstly, concepts of civility and politeness have a bearing on the issue of how men and women were socialised against adultery. It suggests changing impulses to virtue at a time when the church's hegemony over moral matters was increasingly open to challenge. Beyond this, one of the significant ideals of civilised polite society was an emphasis on voluntary self-control of the passions rather than externally applied sanctions. How did this impact on the understanding of adultery in the context of weakening judicial mechanisms for the policing of vice? Just what was the connection between the 'small morals' of civility and the bigger moral questions surrounding sex outside marriage? These questions are integral to this survey.

Gender colours indelibly analyses of adultery in this, as in any, period of history. Although historians have long recognised that religious moralists condemned men as well as women for infidelity and that male fornicators, adulterers and fathers of bastards were subject to official punishment, there has been an overwhelming tendency to view early modern perceptions of male and female unchastity in oppositional terms.[51] The notion that in a patriarchal and patrilineal society the adultery of wives, with its damaging effects on property transfer, was more serious than that of husbands forms the basis of Keith Thomas's classic statement of the sexual 'double standard'.[52] Laura Gowing, pointing to the disproportionate importance of chastity to female sexual reputation in early modern England, has argued male and female illicit sex was viewed in 'incommensurable' terms.[53] As such, adultery is seen as a key fault line of gender difference in early modern society.

[50] Martin Ingram, 'Sexual Manners: the Other Face of Civility in Early Modern England', in Burke, Harrison and Slack (eds.), *Civil Histories*, pp. 87–109; see also Isabel V. Hull, *Sexuality, State, and Civil Society in Germany, 1700–1815* (Ithaca, NY, 1996).

[51] Cf. Keith Wrightson, *English Society 1580–1680* (London, 1982), p. 99; Ingram, *Church Courts*, pp. 154, 303.

[52] Thomas, 'The Double Standard'; but cf. Bernard Capp, 'The Double Standard Revisited: Plebeian Women and Male Sexual Reputation in Early Modern England', *PP*, 162 (1999), 70–100.

[53] Laura Gowing, 'Gender and the Language of Insult in Early Modern London', *History Workshop Journal*, 35 (1993), 3.

While this understanding of difference is central to discussing the effects of marital infidelity, important questions remain under-explored. Studies of the gendered nature of adultery have overwhelmingly concentrated on the *consequences* of illicit sexuality rather than its *causes*. We still know relatively little about why people embarked on extra-marital affairs or the emotions and practical or moral dilemmas they raised. Clearly, as historians have noted, motives are closely related to consequences. Shoemaker, pointing to the dangers of venereal infection, pregnancy and the social stigma of being called a 'whore', has suggested that few women would have had an affair for pleasure alone; rather it was more likely that they had 'ulterior motives, such as social or economic advancement'.[54] This may have been true for some women, but it fails to take account of how choices, or perceptions of affairs, may have differed by class and necessarily assumes a distinction between the emotional and the economic, which may not have been so easily distinguishable to contemporaries. The question of what motivated men to have affairs has received even less historical attention. There is no doubt that married men could enjoy affairs with fewer practical risks than their wives could, and that they occupied a far more privileged position in the sexual system. But it is a mistake to assume from this that men's sexuality was necessarily unproblematic. Much more needs to be known about the place of men's sexual behaviour in patriarchal society and the effects of unchastity on male reputation. Adultery, as recent studies have shown, raised critical questions about men's control of women marked by the mockery of ineffectual cuckolded husbands.[55] However, more information is needed about how men's sexuality damaged domestic relations. Moreover, to view cuckoldry purely in terms of men's power relations with women is to ignore the ways in which it brought into focus relations of power and authority between men. Individual emotions and experience are complex, but a close analysis of representations of adultery may provide an insight into how such matters were expressed and conceptualised.

All these matters are complicated by broader changes in thinking about the nature of masculinity and femininity taking place in the late seventeenth and early eighteenth centuries. The representation of women as primary 'domestic dangers' in the sixteenth and early seventeenth centuries had its basis in the scriptures and in humoral medical theories that saw in women's cold and moist constitutions a tendency to deceitfulness and inconstancy. Summarised crudely, women's bodies were believed to be governed more by their uteri than 'masculine' reason, making women more prone to sensual excesses than men. As such they were considered by 'nature' to be the more lustful sex.[56] However, during the later seventeenth century, these traditional perceptions of

---

[54] Shoemaker, *Gender in English Society*, p. 75.

[55] Foyster, *Manhood*, ch. 4; Anthony Fletcher, *Gender, Sex and Subordination in England 1500–1800* (New Haven, CT and London, 1995), ch. 6

[56] Ian Maclean, *The Renaissance Notion of Woman: a Study in the Fortunes of Scholasticism and Medical Science in European Intellectual Life* (Cambridge, 1980); Sara Mendelson and Patricia Crawford, *Women in Early Modern England 1550–1720* (Oxford, 1998), ch. 1.

female nature began to be challenged from a variety of angles, resulting in a reformulation of sexual and gendered identities. Difference between the sexes was increasingly articulated in medical texts around theories of the nervous system rather than the humours. In the new 'culture of sensibility', women were deemed to possess thinner and finer nerves than men which gave them different psychological qualities and greater delicacy.[57] Better appreciation of the different physical characteristics of men and women made for new understandings of gender difference that viewed the sexes as opposites, fundamentally different both physically and in 'nature'.[58] Women were increasingly cast in passive, virtuous roles, considered less likely to effect the ruin of men through a desire to satisfy their sexual urges than as pacifiers of aggressive male desires and reformers of male manners. The ideal, domesticated woman was innately chaste and maternal, desexualised and heroically resistant to men's advances.[59] The triumph of these ideals was represented by the eponymous heroine of Samuel Richardson's novel, *Pamela: or, Virtue Rewarded* (1740), whose stoic defence of her 'natural' feminine chastity against her rapacious employer made her a paradigm of eighteenth-century womanhood.[60]

These changes in understandings of gender difference have been well documented – at least in a literary and medical context – but little is known about how widely they were received or their overall consequences for the meanings of extra-marital sex. This survey explores the impact of these stereotypes on debates about culpability for adultery in literary and legal sources. But it also examines resistance to, or reappropriation of, these ideals on the part of women themselves. Chapter 5, analysing the strategies employed by women defending themselves in marital separation litigation, reveals tensions in these systems of representation, showing how women might either reject these stereotypes entirely or develop them to their own advantage in their stories of infidelity.

Changes in understandings of sexual nature have been imagined chiefly through female bodies, but it is evident that new ideas had an impact on perceptions of male sexuality as well, as they were increasingly cast in the role of the principal instigators of sexual affairs. Masculinity was undergoing important developments of its own which have a crucial bearing on the themes of this book. During the sixteenth and seventeenth centuries, as Foyster's work has shown, a significant means of asserting manhood was through the sexual control of women. A single man might gain respect among his male peers through bragging about his sexual conquests, while it was critically important for married men to control their wives and avoid the stigma of cuckoldry. Sexual honour

---

[57] Barker-Benfield, *The Culture of Sensibility*, ch. 1; Shoemaker, *Gender in English Society*, p. 20.

[58] Thomas Laqueur, *Making Sex: Body and Gender from the Greeks to Freud* (Cambridge, MA and London, 1990).

[59] Ruth Perry, 'Colonizing the Breast: Sexuality and Maternity in Eighteenth-Century England', *Journal of the History of Sexuality*, 2 (1991), 204–34.

[60] Michael McKeon, 'Historicizing Patriarchy: the Emergence of Gender Difference in England, 1660–1760', *Eighteenth-Century Studies*, 28 (1995), 295–322.

played a prominent role, alongside independence, courage, strength, trustworthiness and economic competence, in the theory and practice of manliness.[61] However, as ideas of civility and politeness took hold during the late seventeenth century, it has been argued that there was a re-prioritisation of manly qualities among the middling sort and elite. Carter has argued that the proliferation of guides to polite conduct from the later seventeenth century 'produced important developments in the conceptualisation of idealised manliness from the sexual to the social'. Failed masculinity was measured less in terms of the sexually inadequate husband who could not control his wife, than through the figure of the effeminate fop, whose dress and mannerisms contrasted with the moderation and 'easiness' of the 'man of sense'.[62]

This survey is situated at this transitional moment in the history of masculinity. Historians have neglected the question of how perceptions of cuckoldry changed in this period. The standard assumption is that laughter at deceived husbands, which had been a mainstay of popular humour in the sixteenth and seventeenth centuries, fell foul of rising standards of decorum and new sensibilities that viewed the cuckolded husband more as a figure of sympathy than of derision.[63] But we know little about the processes of this transition or how far cultural meanings of cuckoldry actually changed. Chapter 3 begins to fill this lacuna by exploring debates about cuckoldry as a theme in comic literature and assesses how new genres such as periodicals opened up cultural spaces for the reassessment of the issues surrounding sexual betrayal and failed masculinity. Chapter 6 develops these ideas further by examining the legal issues surrounding cuckoldry as they developed in actions for criminal conversation, whereby a deceived husband sued his wife's lover for damages. Shifting sensibilities concerning cuckold humour are approached afresh by re-examining how and why cuckolding was found funny. It is only by fully appreciating the modes of expression and contexts in which cuckoldry was perceived as a laughing matter (and, conversely, when it was not) that notions of a 'decline' in mockery of the deceived husband can be understood. These chapters form the basis for reappraising the development of masculine anxieties in this period.

How all these changes – in the policing of adultery, in the nature of family life, in print culture, politeness and gender relations – altered the mental

---

[61] Foyster, *Manhood*; cf. Susan Dwyer Amussen, '"The Part of a Christian Man": the Cultural Politics of Manhood in Early Modern England', in Susan D. Amussen and Mark A. Kishlansky (eds.), *Political Culture and Cultural Politics in Early Modern England: Essays Presented to David Underdown* (Manchester, 1995), pp. 213–33; Alexandra Shepard, 'Meanings of Manhood in Early Modern England, With Special Reference to Cambridge, *c*.1560–1640', PhD thesis, University of Cambridge (1998).

[62] Fletcher, *Gender, Sex and Subordination*, p. 323; Carter, *Men and the Emergence of Polite Society*, p. 9.

[63] Keith Thomas, 'The Place of Laughter in Tudor and Stuart England', *Times Literary Supplement*, 21 Jan. 1977, pp. 80–1.

horizons of early modern Englishmen and women regarding extra-marital sex is the substance of this book. Behind these changes lies a still more slippery question concerning the extent to which these developments amounted to a 'secularisation' of moral meanings in this period. 'Secularisation' is a protean concept that cannot be defined simply in terms of a decline of religious belief or power of religious institutions. Recent studies demonstrating the centrality of religion to political life in the late seventeenth century caution us against viewing the Restoration as the beginning of a more 'secular' age.[64] Nevertheless, it is also generally accepted that among the educated classes, religious practice was coming to rely on reasoned understandings of Christian doctrine and was becoming more a matter of personal choice or individual faith.[65] The extension of knowledge of the world through scientific advances and the spread of printed media served to increase scepticism about older theories of causation, such as divine providence.[66] This survey measures 'secularisation' in terms of a process of communication, as a dialogue between ingrained religious modes of explanation and alternative ways of analysing the ways of the world.

APPROACH AND METHODOLOGY

Rather than seeking to uncover an elusive social reality of extra-marital sex, the focus of this book is on the meanings of adultery and the ways in which they were conveyed. Its focus is therefore on *representations* – 'the multiple intellectual configurations by which reality is constructed in contradictory ways by various groups'.[67] Representations are important not simply because they alert us to the ways in which people in the past ordered their world and made sense of social phenomena, but also because they act as a force seeking to delimit human actions and experience.[68] This book's organising principle is the different genres in which marital relations were discussed and experiences of adultery were constituted. Chapters examine the meanings of infidelity in the period's didactic literature, in jokes and comic plays about adulterous wives and cuckolded husbands and in murder pamphlets describing cases of domestic homicide fuelled by lust or jealousy. Recognising that the law had a culture of its own and played a significant role in structuring the mental world of men and women in this period, this survey also explores representations of adultery

---

[64] See (for instance) the contributions to Harris et al. (eds.), *The Politics of Religion in Restoration England*; Claydon, *William III and the Godly Revolution*.

[65] C. John Sommerville, *The Secularisation of Early Modern England: From Religious Culture to Religious Faith* (New York and Oxford, 1992).

[66] Malcolm Gaskill, *Crime and Mentalities in Early Modern England* (Cambridge, 2000), p. 12 and *passim*.

[67] Roger Chartier, *Cultural History: Between Practices and Representations*, trans. Lydia G. Cochrane (Cambridge, 1988), p. 9.

[68] Richard Dyer, *The Matter of Images: Essays on Representations* (London and New York, 1993), p. 3.

in marital separation suits brought before the Court of Arches (the principal conduit of matrimonial litigation in this period) and in pamphlet accounts of trials for criminal conversation.[69] Each category of source material illustrates particular themes which, taken together, reveal the numerous ways in which experiences of adultery were communicated.

Inevitably, choice of source materials has to be selective and there is not space for a truly comprehensive coverage. Sources such as ballads (which have been studied at length elsewhere), newspapers and satirical prints are not neglected, but receive rather less attention.[70] A comprehensive survey of marital discord might indeed pay greater attention to its visual language, but since the domestic print industry was relatively small in scale prior to the mid-eighteenth century, this book focuses primarily on written evidence.[71] The cultural, as opposed to institutional, emphasis of this survey likewise limits the use of legal records – a larger study might incorporate separation litigation from other ecclesiastical jurisdictions and criminal prosecutions of infidelity.[72] These qualifications notwithstanding, the texts explored here give a sense of the rich variety of modes of fashioning adultery and embody significant discourses of extra-marital sex in this period.

The aim of this methodology is to produce a cultural history that not only recognises the existence of cultural pluralities, but places them at the centre of its analysis. If it is recognised that representation never fully captures the complexity of lived experience, it is necessary to understand that different modes of representation establish their relation with reality in diverse ways. Rather than viewing 'representation' and 'reality' in dichotomous terms, this approach argues that each source establishes a different 'point of contact' with the wider social world. This point of contact is established by various means: in subject matter, modes of expression and language, authorial intention and sense of audience, and established forms and textual conventions developed over time. The focus is therefore not just on what was being represented in these sources, but on how the format and conventions of different texts ordered their representation of the wider social world.[73] Set against the backdrop of the explosion of printed materials already described, this approach furthermore allows us not simply to *describe* but to *demonstrate* how the proliferation of

---

[69] The source materials are discussed more fully in later chapters.

[70] On ballads see J. A. Sharpe, 'Plebeian Marriage in Stuart England: Some Evidence from Popular Literature', *TRHS*, 5th ser., 36 (1986), 69–90; Joy Wiltenburg, *Disorderly Women and Female Power in the Street Literature of Early Modern England and Germany* (Charlottesville, VA and London, 1992); Elizabeth A. Foyster, 'A Laughing Matter? Marital Discord and Gender Control in Seventeenth-Century England', *Rural History*, 4 (1993), 5–21.

[71] Timothy Clayton, *The English Print 1688–1802* (New Haven, CT and London, 1992); Sheila O'Connell, *The Popular Print in England 1550–1850* (London, 1999).

[72] Cf. Bailey, 'Breaking the Conjugal Vows'.

[73] For a similar attempt to bring the format of texts to the forefront of analysis see Marion Gibson, *Reading Witchcraft: Stories of Early English Witches* (London and New York, 1999).

genres acted as a motor for cultural change, and how the pace and nature of change might differ across different types of text.

Broadly speaking, the first three chapters of this book are concerned with the development of ideas about adultery through didactic and literary texts while the latter chapters explore the impact of these concepts on the assessment of the behaviour of individuals as evinced by journalistic and legal records. While fully recognising that the latter are more deeply rooted in lived human experience than the former, the notion that the sources used in these chapters constitute the 'reality' against which literary evidence is to be judged is rejected. If the statements of litigants and witnesses in court records, with their compelling social detail, are more obviously grounded in material actuality than, say, the idealised model of domestic relations espoused in a religious conduct book, neither source gives an unproblematic 'reflection' of marital relations or 'attitudes' towards adultery in this period. Infidelity was not a monolithic category of experience, but was fashioned in a variety of ways in different cultural and legal contexts. What we are analysing is a complex and interacting set of codes and meanings from which a cultural reality of infidelity is forged.[74]

It becomes easier to understand the 'shared' elements of a culture if we are more sensitive to the diverse media through which these meanings are constructed. What links these sources together is not so much their subject matter as their recourse to a common language of sexual misconduct. Using a broad set of texts including moral treatises, diaries, novels, periodicals and plays, the opening chapter analyses changes in the words by which adultery and its perpetrators were labelled. Historically, language has played a crucial role in setting boundaries between licit and illicit behaviour. Heavily implicated in structures of power and authority, it both constitutes value systems and positions its speakers in relation to these values. This book takes the words of sources as agents in a process of communication, mediating between texts and their socio-historical context. In this way, as Naomi Tadmor's work has shown, language provides an important means of linking literary texts – traditionally criticised as 'soft' evidence – to broader social structures.[75] It was via a situated use of words, phrases and images that literary and other texts constructed meanings of infidelity in relation to concepts of gender, civility and social differentiation.[76]

---

[74] See also the comments in Tim Harris, 'Problematising Popular Culture', in Harris (ed.), *Popular Culture in England, c.1500–1850* (Basingstoke, 1995), pp. 10–12.

[75] Naomi Tadmor, 'Concepts of the Family in Five Eighteenth-Century Texts', PhD thesis, University of Cambridge (1992), pp. 54–5; Tadmor, '"Family" and "Friend" in *Pamela*: a Case Study in the History of the Family in Eighteenth-Century England', *Social History*, 14 (1989), 289–306; P. J. Corfield, 'Introduction: Historians and Language', in Corfield (ed.), *Language, History and Class* (Oxford, 1991), pp. 1–29. Cf. Peter Laslett, 'The Wrong Way Through the Telescope: a Note on Literary Evidence in Sociology and in Historical Sociology', *British Journal of Sociology*, 27 (1976), 319–42; Keith Thomas, *History and Literature* (Swansea, 1988).

[76] On the 'situated use of language' see Gabrielle M. Spiegel, 'History, Historicism and the Social Logic of the Text in the Middle Ages', *Speculum*, 65 (1990), 59–86.

Any study that relies heavily on cultural artefacts has to confront the problem of reception. The meanings of books and plays are created not simply in the texts themselves, but by a dynamic process of interpretation by those who read, listened to or watched them.[77] Of all the materials used in this survey, the most comprehensively researched in terms of audience is drama, used extensively in the analysis of cuckoldry in chapter 3. Theatre historians have done much to challenge the image of the Restoration theatre as a socially exclusive institution dominated by the court. Performances catering for more socially diverse audiences of merchants, tradesmen and their wives and apprentices were common, while the audience for printed play scripts may have been wider still – opponents of the theatre often cited the reading of plays by servants as evidence of the playhouses' corrupting web.[78] However, for other printed matter the audience is harder to gauge. Prices may give a crude indication of potential audience, though they say little about consumption patterns, while internal evidence, such as advertisements, offers some clues to the readership of periodicals.[79] Where available, this evidence has been incorporated into this survey. But many of the printed sources used here are destined to remain 'texts without contexts', ephemeral publications of shadowy provenance and even more obscure reception.

The majority of readers have left little trace of how they engaged with texts or what message (if any) they derived from them. Nevertheless, there are still possibilities for understanding more about reception within the limits of more readily 'knowable' information about our sources. Closer attention may be paid to the implied reader 'within the text', or communities of readers addressed by authors.[80] One way forward is to analyse the ways in which authors attempted to use representations of adultery to foster group identities based on shared moral visions, in a way suggested by recent work on the London middling sort – a group emerging in this period as major cultural consumers.[81] The intended readership might, of course, be different from the actual or unintended audience, and the messages of texts could be appropriated contrary to the author's intention.[82] It is necessary to recognise the plurality of responses while also acknowledging that

---

[77] Robert D. Hume, 'Texts Within Contexts: Notes Toward a Historical Method', *Philological Quarterly*, 71 (1992), 69–100.

[78] Harold Love, 'Who were the Restoration Audience?', *Yearbook of English Studies*, 10 (1980), 21–44; Allan Botica, 'Audience, Playhouse and Play in Restoration Theatre, 1660–1710', DPhil thesis, University of Oxford (1985).

[79] Raven, 'New Reading Histories'; Jonathan Barry, 'Literacy and Literature in Popular Culture: Reading and Writing in Historical Perspective', in Harris (ed.), *Popular Culture in England*, p. 75.

[80] Roger Chartier, *The Order of Books* (Cambridge, 1994), ch. 1.

[81] For instance, Hunt, *The Middling Sort*, chs. 7, 8. See also Chartier, *Cultural History*, p. 10.

[82] Raven, 'New Reading Histories', 274, 276; Roger Chartier, 'Culture as Appropriation: Popular Cultural Uses in Early Modern France', in Steven L. Kaplan (ed.), *Understanding Popular Culture: Europe from the Middle Ages to the Nineteenth Century* (Berlin, 1984), pp. 229–53.

reception was conditioned by historical circumstances. Readers formed their interpretation of texts within historically specific boundaries, not within a vortex of limitless possibilities.[83] As Raven has observed, the multiplication of texts in this period led to a proliferation of strategies, both implicit and explicit, for guiding readers' responses.[84] Genre had an important role to play in this regard. Functioning like 'a code of behaviour' established between author and reader, the form and layout of texts guided the readers' expectations.[85] Changes in format upset conventional approaches to the subject matter, encouraging readers to consider familiar themes in new and innovative ways. This is not to say that readers necessarily accepted these codes uncritically. However, sensitivity to these strategies gives a better understanding of the cultural and intellectual context of reception. The result is a multi-dimensional approach to the cultural production of meaning in early modern English society.

CHAPTER OUTLINE

The structure of this book, then, takes the form not of a linear sequential argument, but of a series of case studies in which different themes of conjugal infidelity and textual genres are discussed. The book begins with an analysis of the language of marital infidelity. It outlines the importance attached to proper forms of naming vice by religious and social moralists and explores the ways in which the terminology of vice diversified over this period under the impetus of developing ideas of social refinement. The second chapter examines further official meanings of marriage and adultery in this period via an analysis of didactic literature. Evaluating ideals of conduct, it explores shifting strategies of warning against infidelity and methods for inculcating moral standards. Ideals about marriage formed an uneasy symbiosis with comic representations of cuckoldry. Chapter 3 shows how matrimonial comedy drew on prevailing ideas about 'correct' male and female roles within marriage and in turn exposed them to ridicule. This chapter analyses the function, structure and variety of cuckolding humour in the period's comic literature, revealing in the process how adultery could be construed as funny and entertaining and how this changed over time.

In chapter 4 the attention turns from comedy to tragedy through a study of pamphlet accounts of familial murders. The chapter discusses the representation of crimes of passion and how adultery-related homicide raised important questions of provocation and responsibility. Chapter 5 turns its attention away

---

[83] Robert Darnton, *The Forbidden Best-Sellers of Pre-Revolutionary France* (London, 1996), pp. 187–8.
[84] Raven, 'New Reading Histories', 281–2.
[85] Heather Dubrow, *Genre* (London and New York, 1982), p. 2. See also Alistair Fowler, *Kinds of Literature: an Introduction to the Theory of Genres and Modes* (Oxford, 1982).

from printed sources to examine the mass of descriptive material generated by separation suits on the grounds of adultery. Rich in social detail, the statements of litigants and witnesses give an important insight into the social, material and spatial contexts of infidelity. The final chapter examines pamphlet reports of trials for criminal conversation, a new form of legal remedy for adultery developing in this period. It explores in detail the grounds on which these suits were contested, revealing how cases depended not only on establishing whether adultery had taken place, but on the manner in which it had been committed – a key consideration in the assessment of damages. These cases formed a testing ground for new social meanings of adultery and therefore provide a further means for reviewing the ways in which perceptions of adultery were changing by the eighteenth century.

1. *Language, sex and civility*

In 1675 an anonymous author set forth a series of proposals explaining 'why a Law should pass in England to punish Adultery with Death'. Adultery was described as 'a complication of all the wickedness in lust, breach of faith and robbery', breaking the matrimonial vows and robbing a man of his wife's affections. Familiar precedents in Judaic law and the perceived ineffectiveness of judicial separation at the church courts as a remedy for wronged husbands were cited to show the apparent leniency of current laws against vice. Yet it was the moral turpitude of the present times that ultimately justified the reintroduction of this extreme solution. 'The present law being so defective', it was argued, 'the crime grows upon it' and had become 'common'. A key feature of the author's vision of moral depravity was linguistic corruption. 'This Age', he complained, 'gives the soft and gentle French Names of Gallantry and Divertisement' in 'Apology' for adultery.[1]

Language has always been a site of contest in the construction of the social and moral meanings of sexual transgression. The terminology by which infidelity is described acts as a point of identification with a broader system of values. Studies of modern sexual mores have shown that choosing to label extra-marital sex as 'committing adultery', 'playing around', an 'affair' (whether 'casual' or not) or a 'fling', is not just a means of categorising the varying forms such relations can take, but may communicate the speaker's understanding of the relative sinfulness, legitimacy or acceptability of such behaviour.[2] Like other aspects of sexuality, adultery has generated a rich vocabulary, some of it condemnatory, other words more euphemistic, intended to make light of infidelity or to evade its implications by avoiding explicit

---

[1] *A Letter To A Member of Parliament With Two Discourses Enclosed In It. I. The One Shewing the Reason Why a Law Should Pass to Punish Adultery With Death* ([London?], 1675), p. 6. On the death penalty see Keith Thomas, 'The Puritans and Adultery: the Act of 1650 Reconsidered', in Donald Pennington and Keith Thomas (eds.), *Puritans and Revolutionaries: Essays in Seventeenth-Century History Presented to Christopher Hill* (Oxford, 1978), pp. 257–82.

[2] Annette Lawson, *Adultery: an Analysis of Love and Betrayal* (Oxford, 1989), p. 7.

mention of it. Language is a central agency through which sex acquires its meaning in different contexts at each historical moment.[3] To understand social and cultural perceptions of infidelity in the late seventeenth and early eighteenth centuries it is first necessary to decode the vocabularies used to discuss it.

This chapter explores how linguistic forms constituted, conveyed and challenged official teachings on sexuality and assesses how methods of describing adultery and labelling its perpetrators changed over time. Its aim is not to argue that the experience of adultery exists merely as a discourse or has no reality beyond the words used to express it. Rather, it analyses language as a mode of communication, as a means of mediating between cultural texts and the wider social context.[4] Commentators in early modern England were themselves critically aware of the power and significance of language in constituting and expressing social values. The views of the anonymous petitioner of Parliament about the deleterious effects of certain words on the morals of those who used them were consonant with the opinions of many moralists and social commentators in an age when language was considered to be the cornerstone of the social and moral order. A century earlier, the Elizabethan homilies on whoredom had made precisely the same connection between ways of speaking about vice and moral decay, lamenting the apparently popular practice of dismissing unchastity as a 'pastime', a 'dalliance' or a 'touch of youth'.[5] Linguistic propriety, or 'governing the tongue', was deemed by authors of religious conduct literature to be central to the work of ordering families, communities and society at large in England and its colonies.[6] Drawing on the teachings of St Paul in Ephesians iv. 29, that 'Evil words corrupt good manners', moralists regarded the introduction of a 'better sort of converse into the world' as a 'fundamental piece of reformation'.[7]

Yet this project of reformation was only possible if there was a shared set of ideas about the correct naming of vice. If the tone of religious literature appeared to recognise that there was always discrepancy between moral prescription and popular linguistic practice, during the late seventeenth and early eighteenth centuries there emerged more fundamental challenges to theories of labelling of extra-marital sex and its perpetrators. New languages of marital infidelity called into question traditional assumptions about the sinfulness of sexual immorality.

---

[3] Michel Foucault, *The History of Sexuality, Volume I: An Introduction*, trans. Robert Hurley (Harmondsworth, 1978).

[4] For similar methodological approaches see Gabrielle M. Spiegel, 'History, Historicism, and the Social Logic of the Text in the Middle Ages', *Speculum*, 65 (1990), 59–86; Naomi Tadmor, '"Family" and "Friend" in *Pamela*: a Case Study in the History of the Family in Eighteenth-Century England', *Social History* 14 (1989), 289–306.

[5] *Two Books of Homilies Appointed to be Read in Churches*, ed. John Griffiths (Oxford, 1859), p. 118.

[6] Jane Kamensky, *Governing the Tongue: the Politics of Speech in Early New England* (Oxford, 1997).

[7] Richard Allestree, *The Government of the Tongue* (Oxford, 1674), p. 215.

At the same time, a growing impetus towards social refinement raised doubts about the suitability of conventional vocabularies of moral condemnation. The language of politeness increasingly found its way into moral discourse and produced its own distinctive vocabulary for condemning sexual transgression. This chapter traces these linguistic developments and assesses their impact on perceptions of marital infidelity in this period.

CORRUPT COMMUNICATIONS: ADULTERY AND MORAL DISCOURSE

Ordained by God as the 'common tie of society', language was viewed by moralists as the principal medium through which divine will was revealed and through which God was to be praised.[8] Yet the potential for language to corrupt manners was evident from its very inception, as the story of Eve's use of words to tempt Adam powerfully demonstrated. Sermons and books of religious instruction carefully categorised the manifold 'abuses of the tongue' (which applied equally to written and spoken discourse), ranging from blasphemy and licentious speech, to slander and the telling of 'uncharitable' truths.[9] Language manifested directly the health of the soul. To speak 'corruptly' was not only 'an evidence of a corrupt and impure heart' and thus offensive to God, but was also likened to the spreading of a disease, having a potentially 'infectious' effect on the morals of those in earshot.[10] Beguilingly seductive or blatantly 'obscene' and 'filthy' words presented particular dangers to chastity, acting as a 'Pander or Bawd unto Uncleannese'.[11] One Restoration commentator described discourse littered with 'filthy expressions' as 'lip-adulterie'.[12] The progression from words to deeds was a small one. 'Filthy talk and lewd practices seem only to differ in the occasion and opportunity', observed John Tillotson in a sermon on the 'Evil of Corrupt Communication', for 'he that makes no conscience in one will hardly stick at the other when it can be done with secresie and safety'.[13]

---

[8] John Locke, *An Essay Concerning Human Understanding* (1690), ed. Roger Woolhouse (Harmondsworth, 1997), p. 361; Allestree, *Government of the Tongue*, pp. 3–6.

[9] E.g., ibid., p. 204 and *passim*; Isaac Barrow, *Several Sermons Against Evil-Speaking* (London, 1678); Henry Hooton, *A Bridle for the Tongue* (London, 1709), p. 233.

[10] John Tillotson, 'The Evil of Corrupt Communication', in *The Works of the Most Reverend Dr John Tillotson, Late Lord Archbishop of Canterbury*, ed. Ralph Barker (2 vols., London, 1712), II, p. 395. Disease and infection were common metaphors for moral corruption throughout the early modern period: see Martin Ingram, 'Reformation of Manners in Early Modern England', in Paul Griffiths, Adam Fox and Steve Hindle (eds.), *The Experience of Authority in Early Modern England* (Basingstoke, 1996), p. 54; T. C. Curtis and W. A. Speck, 'The Societies for the Reformation of Manners: a Case Study in the Theory and Practice of Moral Reform', *Literature and History*, 3 (1976), 45–64.

[11] George Webbe, *The Arraignment of An Unruly Tongue* (London, 1619), p. 45.

[12] Clement Ellis, *The Gentile Sinner* (London, 1664), p. 37.

[13] Tillotson, 'Evil of Corrupt Communication', p. 395.

The terminology used to name vices and to label their perpetrators was therefore a matter of crucial importance. 'As Good and Evil are different in Themselves, so they ought to be differently marked,' wrote Jeremy Collier at the end of the seventeenth century. 'Ill Qualities ought to have ill Names, to prevent their being Catching.'[14] Yet theologians also recognised that this was problematic, for any words used to discuss sinful things might be appropriated to ill effect. Thus Jeremy Taylor prefaced his discussion of unchastity in his guide to *Holy Living* (1650) with the warning that there were 'some spirits so Atheistical, and some so wholly possessed with the spirit of uncleanness, that they turn the most prudent and chaste discourses into dirt and filthy apprehensions'.[15] Particularly dangerous was the practice of giving vices 'soft' or euphemistic names. Already in the early seventeenth century Lewis Bayly's popular guide to practical theology, *The Practice of Pietie*, had warned that religion and moral instruction were hindered by 'adorning Vices with the names of Vertues', such as referring to 'Whoredome' as 'Loving a Mistresse'. Giving pleasant-sounding euphemistic names to sinful practices enabled the guilty to 'smooth over' the shameful consequences of their actions.[16]

In contrast, it was only by giving acts of sexual immorality proper 'hard names', such as 'adultery', 'whoredom' or 'uncleanness', that potential malefactors would be deterred.[17] Rather like the modern therapeutic technique of making alcoholics starkly declare their addiction as the first step to recovery, moralists believed that it was only by getting sinners to acknowledge their behaviour in the hardest terms, abasing themselves and recognising their weakness to sin, that they could be reformed. The basic principle was succinctly captured in a doggerel verse of the early eighteenth century:

> Adultery, the very Name
> Is hateful to the Guilty
> The Wanton Dame is stabb'd with Shame,
> When e'r she's thought so filthy.[18]

The notion that the language of sexual immorality had the power to shame and strike terror into the minds of sinners was voiced in moral tracts throughout the early modern period. As late as 1749 the author of one such treatise could argue that 'the very Title of a Bawd and a Whore is sufficient to fright a sober Man, not only from their Embraces and Converse, but even of all manner of

---

[14] Jeremy Collier, *A Short View of the Immorality and Profaneness of the English Stage* (London, 1698), sig. A3.

[15] Jeremy Taylor, *Holy Living* (1650), ed. P. G. Stanwood (Oxford, 1989), p. 73.

[16] Lewis Bayly, *The Practice of Pietie: Directing a Christian How to Walke that He May Please God* (London, 1632 edn), p. 199.

[17] [John Dunton], *The Hazard of a Death-Bed Repentance* (London, 1708), pp. 9, 45.

[18] [Edward Ward], *The Forgiving Husband, and Adulteress Wife: Or a Seasonable Present to the Unhappy Pair in Fanchurch Street* (London, n.d. [c.1708]), p. 12.

lustful Thoughts and Inclinations'.[19] The very sound and intonation of these words underscored the heinousness of sexual immorality. Thus the Berkshire gentleman John Verney, relating how his aunt used the term 'whore' to humiliate his cousin, Nancy Nicholas, in a family dispute of 1680, called it an 'ugly name', while to Defoe's Moll Flanders it was an 'unmusical harsh-sounding title'.[20]

'Adultery', 'whoredom' and 'uncleanness' had strong biblical resonance and also expressed the criminality of extra-marital sex, being the terms used in the church's canons of 1604 to categorise the sexual offences falling under the jurisdiction of the ecclesiastical courts.[21] Both moralists and the ecclesiastical authorities used these over-arching categories to cover a multitude of sexual sins, drawing distinctions not so much between individual sexual offences such as adultery, fornication or incest, but more fundamentally between chastity and unchastity.[22] The exhortation against adultery in the Seventh Commandment was understood to have a far-reaching application. Since the sixteenth century the church's official prescriptions on sexual morality had argued that the word adultery, 'although it be properly understood of the unlawful commixtion ... of a married man with any woman beside his wife, or of a wife with any man beside her husband', served as a more general signifier of 'all unlawful use of those parts which be ordained for generation'.[23] Richard Baxter regarded the injunction against adultery in the Seventh Commandment as establishing a duty for all Christians to 'Abhor not only Adultery it self, but all that tendeth to unchastness and the violation of [the] Marriage-Covenant'. Adultery, warned Gabriel Towerson in his guide to the Anglican catechism, was a 'fruitful crime' comprising not only the 'violation of the marriage bed' by the infidelity of a husband or wife but also 'all Deviations from the Institution of Marriage, such as Fornication and Concubinacy'.[24] What might be classified as 'adultery' could thus include anything that stirred up lust, such as songs, ballads, plays,

---

[19] *Satan's Harvest Home: Or, the Present State of Whorecraft, Adultery, Fornication, Procuring, Pimping, Sodomy and the Game at Flatts* (London, 1749), p. 20.

[20] John Verney quoted in Susan E. Whyman, *Sociability and Power in Late-Stuart England: the Cultural World of the Verneys 1660–1720* (Oxford, 1999), p. 97; Daniel Defoe, *The Fortunes and Misfortunes of the Famous Moll Flanders* (1722), ed. G. A. Starr (Oxford, 1971), p. 116.

[21] *Synodalia: A Collection of Articles of Religion, Canons and Proceedings of Convocation in the Province of Canterbury, from the Year 1547 to the Year 1717*, ed. Edward Cardwell (2 vols., Oxford, 1842), I, p. 308; Martin Ingram, 'Law, Litigants and the Construction of "Honour": Slander Suits in Early Modern England', in Peter Coss (ed.), *The Moral World of the Law* (Cambridge, 2000), pp. 134–60, esp. p. 155.

[22] Martin Ingram, *Church Courts, Sex and Marriage in England, 1570–1640* (Cambridge, 1987), p. 239; Faramerz Dabhoiwala, 'Prostitution and Police in London c.1660–c.1760', DPhil thesis, University of Oxford (1995), p. 62.

[23] *Two Books of Homilies*, ed. Griffiths, p. 118.

[24] Richard Baxter, *A Christian Directory: Or, a Sum of Practical Theologie and Cases of Conscience* (London, 1673), p. 521; Gabriel Towerson, *An Explication of the Decalogue of the Ten Commandments, with Reference to the Catechism of the Church of England* (London, 1676), pp. 410, 414. See also Cynthia Herrup, 'Law and Morality in Seventeenth-Century England', *PP*, 106 (1985), 109.

books, dancing and provocative fashions of clothing, especially those adopted by women. Condemning the revealing dresses worn by ladies after the Restoration, the author of *England's Vanity* (1673) warned that 'nakedness of . . . Breasts is Adultery'.[25]

Furthermore, certain practices occurring *within* marriage, which pertained to the 'immoderate use of permitted beds', might also be defined as 'adultery' or 'whoredom'.[26] Although authors of protestant conduct literature regarded regular marital sexual relations as a guard against infidelity, they drew the line at behaviour that tended purely towards the satisfaction of 'lascivious' yearnings rather than procreation.[27] Some Puritans, echoing the views of John Calvin and other continental reformers, had looked upon a husband who used his spouse merely as a sex object as guilty of 'playing the adulterer with his own wife'.[28] Such behaviour, argued Daniel Defoe in the early eighteenth century, was properly defined as 'matrimonial whoredom', and was 'nothing but whoring under the shelter or cover of the Law'.[29]

The language of adultery was thus intended both to mirror and to reinforce the assumptions underlying the perception of unchastity in Christian moral thought and acted as a means of moral policing. It employed a system of labelling that was deliberately inflexible and limited in scope, making no conceptual or linguistic distinction between different types of offence, or between casual sexual encounters and longer-term affairs. Its all-encompassing vocabulary thus communicated the conviction that the same set of words could be applied to all instances of marital infidelity and that all extra-marital sex was sinful. Although adjectives such as 'errant', 'notorious', 'impudent' and 'brasen' might be used to denote more serious offenders, they referred chiefly to the extent to which the perpetrator had deviated from the pathway of Christian conduct, measured through his or her impenitence, rather than to the nature of the transgression *per se*.

As it was noted at the time, the broad-ranging interpretation of adultery employed in religious prescription stood in contrast to other historical discourses on extra-marital sex. In both the Old Testament and Roman civil law, adultery

---

[25] *England's Vanity: Or the Voice of God Against the Monstrous Sin of Pride in Dress and Apparel* (London, 1683), pp. 70, 62. See also Aileen Ribiero, *Dress and Morality* (London, 1986), ch. 5.

[26] Taylor, *Holy Living*, p. 73. For similar sentiments see [Richard Allestree], *The Whole Duty of Man, Necessary for all Families* (London, 1660), p. 169; Baxter, *Christian Directory*, p. 521; N. H., *The Ladies Dictionary* (London, 1694), p. 131.

[27] Anthony Fletcher, 'The Protestant Idea of Marriage in Early Modern England', in Anthony Fletcher and Peter Roberts (eds.), *Religion, Culture and Society in Early Modern Britain: Essays in Honour of Patrick Collinson* (Cambridge, 1994), pp. 174–9.

[28] Charles H. George and Katherine George, *The Protestant Mind of the English Reformation 1570–1640* (Princeton, NJ, 1961), p. 272. See also Elizabeth A. Foyster, *Manhood in Early Modern England: Honour, Sex and Marriage* (London, 1999), p. 75.

[29] Daniel Defoe, *Conjugal Lewdness; Or, Matrimonial Whoredom. A Treatise Concerning the Use and Abuse of the Marriage Bed* (London, 1727), p. 165.

was defined more narrowly according to the marital status of the woman involved. If a single or married man had sex with another man's wife it was legally classified as adultery; if a married man slept with a single woman, the crime was downgraded to fornication. The basis of the law was family honour and inheritance, referring to the possibility that a wife's adultery might result in the begetting of illegitimate children.[30]

While protestant moralists tried to resist such narrow and gender-based definitions of marital infidelity, there is little doubt that the system of labelling used in official discourse was heavily weighted against women. Strictly speaking, there was no direct male equivalent of the term 'whore' used to label adulteresses and other 'lewd' women. Laura Gowing has argued that this absence indicates that contemporaries used a system of labelling which imagined culpability for sexual transgression entirely through women.[31] Yet it was conceded by authors of prescriptive literature that men were equally culpable for 'whoredom', in theory at least, and the terms 'whoremonger' or 'whoremaster', sometimes used in moral treatises and in everyday speech to label adulterous husbands, were intended to reinforce this. In 1696 the author of the *Night-Walker*, a monthly periodical exposing the vices of London, observed that although many men were 'not ashamed to make . . . boasts' of their sexual conquests, they would 'take it as an Affront to be call'd by the Name' of 'Whore-Master', believing that the label had some power to prick men's consciences.[32]

SEXUAL LANGUAGE IN PRACTICE: THE CASE OF SAMUEL PEPYS

How did this system of labelling work in practice? What distinctions did contemporaries make between different varieties of sexual relations, and how consciously did they distinguish between 'hard' and 'soft' terms to label vice and its perpetrators? The diary of Samuel Pepys provides a rich repository of terms used to describe a range of illicit sexual encounters during the 1660s. Although the comments of one elite male cannot be taken as representative of society as a whole, the diary does have a number of advantages for studying the use of sexual language at the start of our period. Aside from Pepys's descriptions of his own physical involvement with numerous partners, his diary records the

---

[30] John Godolphin, *Repertorium Canonicum: Or, An Abridgement of the Ecclesiastical Laws of this Realm Consistent with the Temporal* (London, 1687), p. 472; John Ayliffe, *Parergon Juris Canonici Anglicani: Or a Commentary By Way of Supplement to the Canons and Constitutions of the Church of England* (London, 1726), pp. 49–50; Thomas, 'Puritans and Adultery', p. 261.

[31] Laura Gowing, *Domestic Dangers: Women, Words and Sex in Early Modern London* (Oxford, 1996), pp. 63, 64, 114.

[32] *Night-Walker: Or, Evening Rambles in Search After Lewd Women with the Conferences held with them*, 1, September 1696, sig. A2. See also, Ingram, 'Law, Litigants and the Construction of "Honour" ', pp. 152–7.

extra-marital affairs of men and women of a diverse social background, ranging from the intrigues of the king and his courtiers down to the behaviour of
his more humble neighbours. The diary therefore provides a means of testing,
albeit from the perspective of one particular individual, the extent to which the
labelling of the perpetrators of sexual immorality took account of social background. Pepys was hardly a consistent commentator on extra-marital liaisons –
his sexual double standards are well known.[33] However, the conversational
style of the diary, together with its author's careful attention to reporting the
traits of actual speech, may permit a vivid insight into the verbal usage and
linguistic characteristics of Pepys himself and the diverse men and women who
supplied him with sexual gossip.[34] Beyond this, anomalies and inconsistencies
may themselves reveal tensions in systems of labelling and point to a much more
nuanced and complicated terminology of sexual transgression which could vary
in accordance with context and circumstances.

Samuel Pepys was sexually involved with over a dozen women during the
period 1660–9 covered by the diary.[35] They included familiar sexual acquaintances such as Betty Lane, a haberdasher of Westminster Hall, the daughters of
the proprietors of taverns he frequented, and maids serving in the Pepys household. In his capacity as a senior civil servant in the Naval Office he was solicited
by the wives of naval employees who proffered their sexual services to him,
possibly with their spouses' tacit consent, in the hope of securing the advancement of their husbands' careers. On other occasions he went in search of more
anonymous sexual transactions with 'ladies of pleasure'.[36]

Pepys used a variety of linguistic strategies to record his philandering. Most
striking of all was his frequent, and highly idiosyncratic, recourse to foreign
words and expressions – usually a polyglottal mixture of French and Italian – in
the diary's amorous passages. In a typical example from January 1665, Pepys
described a liaison at an inn with his barber's maid, Jane Welsh, during which
they 'sat an hour or two talking and discoursing and faissant ce que je voudrais
quant a la toucher', but, much to the diarist's frustration, 'she would not laisser
me faire l'autre thing'.[37] At first sight this language appeared to function as
a means of concealing his infidelities from his wife. But this explanation becomes less convincing when it is considered that these phrases were written in
longhand, compared with the shorthand used elsewhere in the diary. Besides,
as an accomplished speaker of French, Elizabeth Pepys would have had little

[33] E.g., Pepys, *Diary*, VI, p. 20, 23 Jan. 1665; VIII, p. 373, 21 Aug. 1667; IX, p. 514, 9 Apr. 1669.

[34] Ibid., I, p. civ.

[35] For a more comprehensive chronological account of Pepys's extra-marital sexual relations see
John Harold Wilson, *The Private Life of Mr Pepys* (London, 1959). Dabhoiwala, 'Prostitution
and Police', pp. 34–6, contains a sensitive discussion of their motives from the point of view of
the women involved.

[36] For the use of this term see Pepys, *Diary*, IV, p. 261, 4 Aug. 1663.

[37] Pepys, *Diary*, VI, p. 22, 27 Jan. 1665.

difficulty in interpreting these passages if ever she had stumbled across them.[38] In contrast, the choice of this mode of expression seems to reflect simultaneous and conflicting impulses, both to reveal and conceal. On the one hand, foreign words and phrases permitted Pepys to take account of his actions while prudishly avoiding the plainer English (and more morally unambiguous) terms for his activities. On the other, the use of polyglot may have worked as a kind of amorous secret code, allowing the diarist to express and savour the secret nature of his sexual adventures.[39]

While Pepys's linguistic traits sometimes expressed the thrill of clandestine correspondence, on other occasions he seems to have felt a keen sense of culpability for his actions. In these instances, he described his temptations, actions and his feelings of remorse through the language of 'folly'. For instance, a visit from the wife of the ship's carpenter William Bagwell on 7 December 1664 is described as putting 'new thoughts of folly' into Pepys's mind which he was 'troubled at', while on 20 March 1667 a liaison with Betty Martin left Pepys feeling 'not pleased with [his] folly'.[40] The language of 'folly' had strong resonances with sexual sin in both biblical and contemporary usage.[41] It also implied loss of reason and self-command. Thus Pepys also described his feelings of jealousy as his 'natural folly'.[42] The language of folly is sometimes used in the diary to denote a lack of self-control caused by lustful desires and its consequences, such as lack of discretion. This is apparent in a number of entries in which Pepys reflected on the rift in his marriage caused by his wife's discovery of him fondling the maidservant Deb Willet in October 1668, in which he felt 'heartily afflicted' for the 'folly' that occasioned it.[43] It is also suggested by a comment on the behaviour of Lord Brouncker, whose public openness in his relationship with his mistress, Abigail Williams, is described by Pepys as 'his folly'.[44] Likewise, Pepys criticised the 'folly' of his patron Lord Sandwich with Betty Becke, the daughter of Sandwich's landlady at Chelsea, on the grounds that his indiscreet and irrational 'private lust' pertained to 'the flinging off of all honour, friends, servants and every thing and person that is good' and consequently becoming a scandal at court.[45]

Pepys rarely used the language of whoredom in describing his own infidelities, but the symbolic and psychological importance of this language is vividly revealed in the entries recording Elizabeth Pepys's verbal reactions to her husband's betrayal following her fateful discovery of him with

---

[38] Edwin Chappell, *The Secrecy of the Diary* ([London?], 1933).

[39] On other occasions Pepys recorded with some relish sexual gossip from court which was an 'infinite' or 'great secret', indicating the particular pleasures of recording illicit affairs: see Pepys, *Diary*, VI, p. 301, 17 Nov. 1665; IX, p. 413, 12 Jan. 1669.

[40] Pepys, *Diary*, V, p. 339, 7 Dec. 1664; VIII, p. 120, 20 Mar. 1667.

[41] For the former see Genesis xxxiv. 7.   [42] Pepys, *Diary*, V, p. 270, 14 Sept. 1664.

[43] Ibid., IX, p. 340, 27 Oct. 1668; IX, p. 343, 31 Oct. 1668.

[44] Ibid., VI, p. 285, 1 Nov. 1665.   [45] Ibid., IV, p. 303, 9 Sept. 1663.

Deb Willet.[46] Pepys records in his diary his wife's anger and resentment and the 'bitter names' and 'hard words' with which she reproached his conduct over the course of the autumn and winter of 1668–9 as he made efforts to appease her.[47] Elizabeth employed the strongest terms available to express her anger at her husband's betrayal of trust, berating him for his 'unkindness and perjury'.[48] The term 'unkindness' had more powerful resonance than it does in modern usage. Being cognate with 'kin', it implied that Pepys's behaviour was not consistent with the intimate companion he was supposed to be to his wife. 'Perjury' was an even stronger expression of betrayal. Moralists sometimes described adultery as an act of 'conjugal perjury', breaking a bond of trust and obligation made between two people in the sight of God and therefore a great affront not only to one's spouse, but to God and to society at large.[49] Beyond this, the word 'perjury' had serious implications for a man of Pepys's position. Perjury was a damaging accusation in a society where so much business credit rested on a man's word.[50] It was also a crime for which a man could be pilloried and lose his ears, and its use in this context played on the threat of public shaming to the reputation of a man of Pepys's status. Indeed, on 19 November Pepys recorded that Elizabeth threatened to leave him, 'and did there demand 3 or 400 l. of me to buy my peace, that she might be gone without making any noise, or else protested that she might make all the world know of it'.[51] On 14 November 1668 she fell into a rage with her husband, calling him 'dog and rogue' and telling him that he had a 'rotten heart', while a few days later she called him 'all the false, rotten-hearted rogues in the world' upon discovering that Pepys had been to see Deb Willet after her dismissal from their household.[52] The word 'rogue' was a generalised term of abuse directed at men sometimes carrying implications of sexual immorality, but in this instance its other associations with falseness and double-dealing made it particularly biting.[53]

On 20 November Elizabeth presented her husband with an ultimatum: if he would write a letter to Willet calling her 'whore' and saying that he 'hated her

[46] Anthony Fletcher, *Gender, Sex and Subordination in England 1500–1800* (New Haven, CT and London, 1995), pp. 170–1, discusses this catastrophic discovery and its aftermath in the broader context of the marital relations of Elizabeth and Samuel Pepys.

[47] Pepys, *Diary*, IX, p. 369, 20 Nov. 1668; IX, p. 413, 12 Jan. 1669.

[48] Ibid., IX, p. 356, 10 Nov. 1668.

[49] For instance, J. S., *A Sermon Against Adultery* (London, 1672), p. 8.

[50] Craig Muldrew, *The Economy of Obligation* (Basingstoke, 1998).

[51] Pepys, *Diary*, IX, p. 367, 19 Nov. 1668. Elizabeth Pepys intended this sum to be a private separation agreement.

[52] Ibid., IX, p. 362, 14 Nov. 1668; IX, p. 367, 19 Nov. 1668.

[53] Ingram, 'Law, Litigants and the Construction of "Honour"', pp. 156–7. For another use of 'rogue' to denote male sexual immorality see Pepys, *Diary*, VIII, p. 588, 23 Dec. 1667, when Pepys is jealous of his wife's attentions to Edward Coleman, reputed 'a very rogue for women as any in the world'.

and would never see her more', she would be prepared to trust him again.[54] To brand Deb Willet in these terms appears at first sight to transfer the moral responsibility of Pepys's infidelity to his maidservant, announcing her greater culpability for the transgression. But Elizabeth's strategy was a good deal subtler than simply assuming a sexual double standard. Firstly, she aimed to force an irretrievable breach between the lovers, making it impossible for her husband to pick up the relationship at a later stage. The diarist knew that if he called Deb a 'whore' he would be faced by two furious women, not just one. Moreover, the strategy of demanding that her spouse write the word 'whore' seems to have been intended by Elizabeth to prick her husband's conscience, acting as a means of making him face up to the guilt of his own transgression by forcing him to refer to it using the language of whoredom. The fact that Elizabeth demanded that her husband *write* the word is also significant. As the seventeenth century progressed, the written word was increasingly invested with the stamp of authority. Edward Reyner in his *Rules for the Government of the Tongue* (1656) had observed that 'a man may do more good or more hurt by writing than by speaking, because what is spoken is transient, and passeth away; but what is written is permanent' and had a deeper impact.[55] The act of informing Deb Willet by writing that she was a whore fixed her character more firmly than if Pepys had merely reproved her verbally.

Pepys was clearly troubled by the word 'whore' and at first tried to write the letter 'sparing that word', only for Elizabeth to tear it up and declare that she 'would not be satisfied till . . . I did write so'. In his second version of the letter Pepys tried to avoid the implications of the word again and, rather than directly calling Willet a whore, wrote somewhat circuitously that he 'did fear she might too probably have been prevailed upon to have been a whore by her carriage'. Eventually a version of the letter was produced that met with Elizabeth's approval, but Pepys secretly instructed his servant Will Hewer, entrusted with conveying the letter, not to show Willet the passage containing the word 'whore'.[56] Pepys's reluctance to use this word may in part have been motivated by a paternalistic desire to protect the reputation and feelings of a young girl for whose misfortunes he bore a large responsibility. Nevertheless, the incident shows in a particularly lucid manner the subtle ways in which the language of whoredom might be used to imply male, as well as female, culpability for sexual sin.

While Pepys was understandably squeamish about using the terminology of whoredom in relation to his own circumstances, he used it more freely of other

[54] Pepys, *Diary*, IX, p. 370, 20 Nov. 1668.

[55] Edward Reyner, *Rules for the Government of the Tongue* (London, 1656), Dedication, cited in Robert B. Shoemaker, 'The Decline of Public Insult in London 1660–1800', *PP*, 169 (2000), 122. See also Adam Fox, 'Custom, Memory and the Authority of Writing', in Griffiths et al. (eds.), *The Experience of Authority*, pp. 89–116.

[56] Pepys, *Diary*, IX, p. 370, 20 Nov. 1668; IX, p. 371, 21 Nov. 1668.

people. The label 'whore' was used to denote offenders of all social ranks, both to describe women of lowly social background, like Betty Becke whom Pepys refers to as a 'common whore', and to label aristocratic adulteresses like Lady Castlemaine and Anna Maria Talbot, Countess of Shrewsbury, 'a whore to the Duke of Buckingham'.[57] However, it is also evident from the ways in which Pepys recorded gossip in the diary that older distinctions between 'hard' and 'soft' terms to label the perpetrators of sexual immorality were becoming less clear cut by the Restoration. Jacobean works of popular devotion such as *The Practice of Pietie* had placed 'whoredom' and 'loving a mistress' at opposite poles of morality on the grounds that the term 'mistress' still bore its more virtuous meaning as the object of unconsummated courtly love. But by the 1660s the terms 'whore' and 'mistress', now used more commonly to mean a courtesan or 'private whore', and many other words, could in practice be used more or less interchangeably to label the same person. Hence on different occasions between 3 September and 3 October 1665 Pepys referred to Abigail Williams as 'my Lord Brounker's lady of pleasure', his 'doxy' (a slang term for a prostitute), his 'mistress', his 'whore' and 'my lord Bruncker's ugly mistress whom he calls cosen'.[58] The implication of more reproachful labels could also be altered by the register in which they were used, for instance if spoken in jest. On a visit to Brounker's house on 22 December 1665 Pepys spoke 'a free word to [Abigail Williams] in mirth, calling her a mad Jade' to which she returned the 'snappish answer' that 'we were not so well acquainted yet'.[59]

Other words, by their usage in different contexts, resisted any straightforward classification as 'hard' or 'soft' terms. The word 'amour' was occasionally used by Pepys to romanticise or fantasise his own extra-marital relations. Meeting the newly married innkeeper's daughter Sarah Udall on a visit to the Swan tavern in Westminster on 30 November 1666, for instance, he 'did lay the beginnings of a future amor con ella'.[60] Yet on other occasions 'amours' took on more negative connotations. In November 1665 Pepys recorded how the court was 'in an uproare' about the 'loose amours' between the Duke of York and Lady Frances Stuart. Similarly, the term 'pleasure' was used in strikingly different ways to describe illicit sexual relations. Pepys frequently described his own physical encounters using the language of pleasure, referring to the sexual act as 'having pleasure' of his partner or as 'being pleased' with her.[61] However, the word

---

[57] Ibid., IV, p. 303, 9 Sept. 1663; III, p. 139, 16 July 1662; IX, p. 27, 17 Jan. 1668; IX, p. 558, 19 May 1669.

[58] Ibid., VI, p. 212, 3 Sept. 1665; VI, p. 213, 5 Sept. 1665; VI, p. 217, 8 Sept. 1665; VI, p. 234, 20 Sept. 1665; VI, p. 251, 3 Oct. 1665.

[59] Ibid., VI, p. 337, 22 Dec. 1665. Although the term 'jade' was sometimes associated with whoredom, its moral implications were more ambiguous than the term 'whore'.

[60] Ibid., VII, p. 392, 30 Nov. 1666.

[61] E.g., ibid., V, p. 219, 23 July 1664; V, p. 242, 15 Aug. 1664; V, p. 322, 15 Nov. 1664; VII, p. 81, 23 Mar. 1666.

could be contrasted with 'business' to denote more specifically the idleness associated with whoring. On 15 May 1663 Pepys recorded a conversation with Sir Thomas Carew in which they lamented the 'unhappy posture' of affairs of state occasioned by the king minding 'nothing but pleasures'. Similarly, on 13 October 1666 Pepys noted that the Duke of York had 'gone over to his pleasures again, and leaves off care of business', spending too much time with 'his woman, my Lady Denham'.[62] In practice, therefore, the labelling of vice was complicated by many factors: by popular linguistic traits which defied straightforward categorisation; by the variable signification of certain words in different social, political or cultural contexts; and by the dictates of individual conscience. Such factors acted as a persistent drag on moralists' efforts to prescribe proper and improper modes of discussing adultery.

EXPANDING THE LANGUAGE OF MARITAL INFIDELITY

If there had always been a degree of discrepancy between prescription and practice, by the later seventeenth century more pronounced fears were emerging that the labelling of illicit sexuality and its perpetrators was becoming increasingly diverse and fragmented. The instability of language was a much-debated topic in contemporary social commentaries. In the first place, the basic premise that language bonded society together was undermined by the civil strife of the 1640s and '50s, the effects of which were sometimes imagined in terms of Babel-like confusion.[63] Commentators feared that the English language had become sullied by 'fantastical terms' and 'outlandish phrases' which confused traditional meanings and bred misunderstandings and divisions among the populace. Such anxieties underpinned projects proposed by a range of authors – most famously Jonathan Swift and Daniel Defoe – for a 'reformation of language'.[64] At the same time, the gathering momentum towards social refinement, stimulated by the burgeoning publication of guides to civilised conduct from the later seventeenth century, forced a more general reassessment of verbal communication.

---

[62] Ibid., IV, p. 136, 15 May 1663; VII, p. 320, 13 Oct. 1666.

[63] Thomas Hobbes, *Leviathan: Or the Matter, Forme, and Power of a Commonwealth Ecclesiastical and Civil* (1651), ed. C. B. Macpherson (Harmondsworth, 1968), p. 101.

[64] Richard Bailey, *Images of English: a Cultural History of the Language* (Cambridge, 1992), p. 57; Ann Cline Kelly, *Swift and the English Language* (Philadelphia, 1988), pp. 89–96; Barbara Shapiro, *Probability and Certainty in Seventeenth-Century England: a Study of the Relationships Between Natural Science, History, Law, and Literature* (Princeton, NJ, 1983), ch. 7; Michele Cohen, *Fashioning Masculinity: National Identity and Language in the Eighteenth Century* (London and New York, 1996), p. 28; Fenela Childs, 'Prescriptions for Manners in English Courtesy Literature 1690–1760, and their Social Implications', DPhil thesis, University of Oxford (1984), p. 192. For examples see Jonathan Swift, *A Proposal for Correcting, Improving and Ascertaining the English Tongue* (London, 1712); [Daniel Defoe], *An Essay Upon Projects* (London, 1697), esp. pp. 227–49.

Language use, just like clothing, etiquette and general demeanour, had long been an important way of communicating status, manners and good breeding. An increasingly 'literate' culture placed a premium on verbal dexterity and polite and fluent discourse. In the process, language use became even more sharply associated with social differentiation.[65] The widening gulf between 'genteel' and 'vulgar' modes of expression involved new criteria for assessing the propriety of the language of extra-marital sex and, as we shall see, would pose a more serious threat to the ideal of linguistic unity upon which prescriptions for the naming of vice had rested.

The most controversial linguistic development in this respect was the growing currency of a set of polite or 'civilised' words to describe extra-marital sex and its perpetrators. The linguistic restyling of adultery is described in Edward Ravenscroft's play *The London Cuckolds* (1682), by a serving maid sent on an errand to arrange an assignation for her adulterous mistress:

> This employment was formerly styled bawding and pimping – but our age is more civilized – and our language more refined – it is now a modish piece of service only, and said, being complaisant, or doing a friend a kind office. Whore – (O filthy broad word!) is now prettily called mistress; – pimp, friend; – cuckold-maker, gallant: thus the terms being civilised the thing becomes more practicable, – what clowns they were in former ages![66]

Concerns about the development of such discourses and their effects on public morals were first raised during the 1670s. This was in part a consequence of the popularity on the stage of sex comedies which used new languages of adultery to distinguish modern sexual mores from the restraints of the puritan past. At the same time, to critics of the francophilia and crypto-Catholicism of the king and his courtiers, these new terms (believed to originate in France) became powerful symbols of morally enervating foreign influences on the polity. The pamphlet that cited the growing use of the 'soft and gentle French Names of Gallantry and Divertisement' as grounds for reintroducing the death penalty for adultery in 1675, with which we began this chapter, seemed to have exactly these concerns in mind.

The issues raised by the introduction of new 'refined' languages of extra-marital sex interfaced with a wide range of contemporary concerns, principally with the effects of French models of civility on prescriptions for English manners. While Italian models of courtesy had dominated the literature of

---

[65] Peter Burke, 'A Civil Tongue: Language and Politeness in Early Modern Europe', in Peter Burke, Brian Harrison and Paul Slack (eds.), *Civil Histories: Essays Presented to Sir Keith Thomas* (Oxford, 2000), pp. 31–48; Adam Fox, *Oral and Literate Culture in England 1500–1700* (Oxford, 2000), ch. 1; Childs, 'Prescriptions for Manners', pp. 186–92, 210–25; Cohen, *Fashioning Masculinity*; James Raven, *Judging New Wealth: Popular Publishing and Responses to Commerce in England, 1750–1800* (Oxford, 1992), ch. 7.

[66] Ravenscroft, *London Cuckolds*, III. i. p. 483. See also *The Character of a Towne-Misse* (London, 1675), p. 3.

civility published in sixteenth- and early seventeenth-century England, the influence of French ideas of 'politesse' increased greatly during later decades of the seventeenth century. This shift owed something to French influence on the culture of the exiled Royalists during the Interregnum, to an explosion of courtesy literature in France during the latter part of the century and its subsequent translation into English, and to the growing popularity of France as a destination on the gentleman's grand tour after the Restoration.[67] One important aspect of the influence of French models of polished expression was the translation and publication of a growing number of romances and books of compliments which promoted a more general refinement of the language of love. From the middle decades of the seventeenth century a range of publications offered advice, principally to young ladies and gentlemen but also to the 'meaner sort', on how to express their amorous passions in 'Eloquent Expressions, Complemental Ceremonies' and 'lofty language suitable for all occasions'.[68]

Yet as Michele Cohen has shown, attitudes towards French culture and language in this period were deeply ambivalent. While the French language was admired for its sophisticated and fluent modes of expression, it was also feared that the infiltration of 'Frenchified' words would emasculate and enervate the English tongue.[69] As popular anti-French sentiment grew from the 1670s, the English language became elevated in patriotic literature as a powerful symbol of national strength. Thus one commentator writing in 1673 criticised the habit of fashionable folk to 'lard' their 'discourses with ends of French', contrasting it with the speech of their noble forefathers who, 'careful to the true glory of English men', were apt to 'justifie the Dominion of their Language, equal to the Dominion of the Seas'.[70] Significantly, the spoiling of the English language by foreign incursions was frequently expressed through metaphors of illicit seduction, for instance as English's scandalous intimacy with French's 'adulterous Charms'.[71] Therefore, as adultery was a powerful metaphor for linguistic corruption, so the use of modish foreign words to denote illicit sexuality became a particular focus of attention in moral polemic and social commentary.

---

[67] The dimensions of this cultural shift have yet to be fully explained. Various aspects are explored in Anna Bryson, *From Courtesy to Civility: Changing Codes of Conduct in Early Modern England* (Oxford, 1998); Peter Burke, *The Art of Conversation* (Cambridge, 1993), ch. 4; Cohen, *Fashioning Masculinity*; Childs, 'Prescriptions for Manners'.

[68] B. D., *The Art of Courtship* (London, 1662), Title page.

[69] Cohen, *Fashioning Masculinity*, p. 39 and *passim*.

[70] *Remarques on the Humours and Conversations of the Gallants of the Town* (London, 1673), p. 96. See also *The Character of a Town-Gallant; Exposing the Extravagant Fopperies of Some Vain Self-Conceited Pretenders to Gentility and Good Breeding* (London, 1675), p. 4; Steven C. A. Pincus, 'From Butterboxes to Wooden Shoes: the Shift in English Popular Sentiment from Anti-Dutch to Anti-French in the 1670s', *Historical Journal*, 38 (1995), 359.

[71] Charles Gildon and John Brightland, *A Grammar of the English Tongue* (London, 1711), Preface, cited in Cohen, *Fashioning Masculinity*, p. 39.

Chief among the concerns raised by the new language of adultery was the belief that it made immorality reputable and consistent with good breeding, thus confusing customary distinctions between vice and virtue. This ambiguity was especially apparent in the depiction of extra-marital relations as acts of 'gallantry'. In its traditional usage 'gallantry' comprised an amalgam of chivalrous values, including military valour and bravery, loyalty and service, and courteous attention to the female sex manifested through the conventions of honourable courtship and platonic love.[72] These uses persisted throughout the early modern period, but by the early seventeenth century, the terms 'gallant' and 'gallantry' were also used to denote varieties of rakish behaviour conducted under a veil of spurious respectability. The Jacobean 'gul' or 'gallant' combined an exterior appearance of gentility through his fashionable dress with insolent and boorish manners and a lewd and profligate lifestyle.[73] This image of the gallant as a licentious youth, addicted to showy self-display and worldly pleasures, fed into Restoration satires of 'town gallants'.[74]

By the Restoration, 'gallantry' was used in a more explicitly pejorative sense, as a catch-all under which critics of modern manners could subsume a variety of 'modish' behavioural traits, ranging from rakish violence and inveterate whoring and drinking, to affectation, superficiality and foppery.[75] However, on the later seventeenth-century stage, and in the literature of cuckoldry more generally, the terms 'gallantry' and 'gallant' were coming to have more specific associations with conjugal infidelity. This usage had become standardized by the eighteenth century as dictionaries defined the 'gallant' as 'A Lover, Beau, or Spark, particularly spoken of one that is kept by or criminally converses with another Man's wife'.[76] Although there were attempts through the eighteenth century to reclaim the term to denote a refined state of sensitivity, courtesy and bearing, by this time the association of 'gallantry' with sexual immorality had been fixed. Thus an *Essay Upon Modern Gallantry* of 1726 stated that gallantry 'in the modern sense of that Word' should be understood as 'a constant Application to the good works of Adultery and Fornication; of the prevailing Art of debauching by any methods, the wives and daughters of

---

[72] *OED*, s.v. 'Gallantry'.

[73] Thomas Dekker, *The Gul's Horn-Book* (1609), ed. R. B. McKerrow (New York, 1971); Bryson, *From Courtesy to Civility*, pp. 245–7 and ch. 7 *passim*; Philip Carter, *Men and the Emergence of Polite Society, Britain 1600–1800* (London, 2001); Tamsyn Williams, '"Magnetic Figures": Polemical Prints of the English Revolution', in Lucy Gent and Nigel Llewellyn (eds.), *Renaissance Bodies: the Human Figure in English Culture, c.1540–1660* (London, 1990), p. 93.

[74] For instance, *Remarques on the Humours and Conversations of the Gallants of the Town*; *Character of a Town-Gallant*; and *News from Covent-Garden: Or, the Town-Gallants Vindication* (London, 1695).

[75] Etherege, *Man of Mode*, I. i. 392–4. On the relationship between 'foppery' and 'gallantry' see Carter, *Men and the Emergence of Polite Society*, p. 140.

[76] Thomas Dyche, *A New General English Dictionary* (London, 1735), s.v. 'Gallant'.

any men whatsoever, especially those of our dearest Friends and most intimate Acquaintance'.[77]

Yet, as its critics recognised, given its virtuous antecedents 'gallantry' was a term which could be appropriated to glorify licentiousness. To describe an adulterer or cuckold-maker as a 'gallant' was, as one commentator observed, to 'civilize the title'.[78] Some commentators were at pains to distinguish 'modern' gallantry from the virtuous 'true gallantry' possessed by Englishmen of old.[79] While the terminology of 'adultery' or 'whoredom' was intended to express the aberrance of conjugal infidelity, the language of gallantry threatened to normalise the act and even made it consistent with virtue or valour. The term 'gallantry' was sometimes specifically used to denote a love affair which required the exercise of a degree of ingenuity or skill to bring off successfully. To have a 'gallantry' with a 'lady', noted the libertine Dorimant in Sir George Etherege's play *The Man of Mode* (1676), was a necessary means of confirming a fashionable man's 'wit', just as a duel was to prove a man's 'courage'.[80] Likewise, the term 'intrigue', another fashionable term for a love affair, implied the exercise of amorous skill in its execution. Dyche's *Dictionary* of 1735 defined 'intrigue' as a 'private Affair that has Difficulty in the management' and was therefore a particularly apt term for a relationship 'carried on by Parties who are otherwise engaged, as between the Wife of one Man, and the Husband of another Woman'.[81] The languages of gallantry and intrigue, complained Arthur Bedford in 1706, referring to their use in stage plays, turned illicit affairs 'even into a science'.[82] In some texts the term 'gallant' was used interchangeably with other labels such as 'amorist' or 'love-merchant' to denote a particular masculine status achieved through adultery or the skill of cuckold-making.[83]

The language of gallantry thus celebrated a culture of male sexual prowess and constructed adultery as something brave and exciting. With the term's older associations of valour earned on the battlefield, the language of 'gallantry' was part of a set of military metaphors, such as 'laying siege to', 'attacking' or 'storming' a woman's 'fortifications' popular throughout the early modern period, but especially common in the later seventeenth century, to describe illicit seduction.[84] The languages of 'intrigue' and 'gallantry' also paved the way for

---

[77] *An Essay Upon Modern Gallantry* (London, 1726), p. 10. Cf. Carter, *Men and the Emergence of Polite Society*, p. 68.

[78] Ellis, *Gentile Sinner*, p. 10.   [79] *Character of a Town-Gallant*, p. 2.

[80] Etherege, *Man of Mode*, II. iii. 236–8.

[81] Dyche, *New General English Dictionary*, s.v. 'Intrigue'.

[82] Arthur Bedford, *The Evil and Danger of Stage Plays: Shewing their Natural Tendency to Destroy Religion, and Introduce a General Corruption of Manners* (London, 1706), p. 130.

[83] E.g., *Poor Robin's Intelligence*, 6 June 1676, 7 Aug. 1676.

[84] For examples see David M. Turner, 'Rakes, Libertines and Sexual Honour in Restoration England, 1660–1700', MA thesis, University of Durham (1994), pp. 14–16.

what might be seen as a 'glamorisation' of extra-marital sex. By the early eighteenth century titles of popular works of scandalous prose fiction advertised 'extraordinary pieces of British gallantry', 'luscious' and 'ingenious' intrigues and cunning 'stratagems' of love acted out by 'celebrated' practitioners frequently given pseudonyms to excite the reader's curiosity.[85] Such publications presented tales of illicit seduction in romantic prose. Thus Captain Alexander Smith's compilation of *Court Intrigues* (1730), while dubiously claiming to 'declare the ill Effects of Adultery and Fornication', at the same time glamorised the proclivities of 'the most celebrated Beauties and most Famous Jilts, from the Restoration to the present Time'.[86] King Charles II's adulterous passion for the Duchess of Castlemaine is described as his becoming 'fast fetter'd in the golden Chains of Love', and their lust is expressed 'with amorous Glances and melancholy Sighs, the Dumb but powerful Rhetorick of ardent Lovers'.[87] Peter Wagner has suggested that such publications, with their polished vocabulary and their romanticised portrayal of extra-marital sex, may have reflected a more general shift in sensibilities whereby adultery effectively lost its former association with sin and became an outlet for passionate love normally denied by the mercenary marriages of the social elite.[88] This is an exaggeration, but there can be no doubt that these vocabularies presented adultery in an attractive, genteel way. The eighteenth-century literature of gallantry is best seen as part of a much wider 'glamorisation' of love in contemporary print culture visible elsewhere in conduct literature and the periodical press.[89]

However, the refinement of the language of illicit sex also raised more sinister fears of dissimulation. The use of more 'civilised' terms for adultery, together with the refinement of the language of love more generally, renewed anxieties that 'soft' language might be used as a tool for seduction. It was feared especially that rapacious men would use the newly polished languages of courtship to dress

---

[85] E.g., *The Adventuress; Or the Lady's Flight From Scotland Yard . . . To Which is Added, Several Entertaining Intrigues, and Extraordinary Pieces of British Gallantry* (London, n.d. [c.1725?]); *Twelve Delightful Novels, Displaying the Stratagems of Love and Gallantry* (London, 1719); *Dirty Dogs For Dirty Puddings. Or, Memoirs of the Luscious Amours of . . . Several Persons of Both Sexes of Quality and Distinction* (London, 1732). See also J. J. Richetti, *Popular Fiction Before Richardson: Narrative Patterns 1700–1739* (Oxford, 1969), chs. 2–4; Donna T. Andrew, '"Adultery A-La-Mode": Privilege, the Law and Attitudes to Adultery 1770–1809', *History*, 82 (1997), 13.

[86] Alexander Smith, *Court Intrigues: Or, an Account of the Secret Amours of Our British Nobility and Others* (London, 1730), Title page and Preface [no pagination].

[87] Ibid., p. 14.

[88] Peter Wagner, 'The Pornographer in the Courtroom: Trial Reports About Cases of Sexual Crimes and Delinquencies as a Genre of Eighteenth Century Erotica', in P. G. Boucé (ed.), *Sexuality in Eighteenth Century Britain* (Manchester, 1982), pp. 134–5.

[89] This trend is described in Vivien Jones, 'The Seductions of Conduct: Pleasure and Conduct Literature', in Roy Porter and Marie Mulvey Roberts (eds.), *Pleasure in the Eighteenth Century* (Basingstoke, 1996), pp. 108–32; Amanda Vickery, *The Gentleman's Daughter: Women's Lives in Georgian England* (New Haven, CT and London, 1998), p. 41 and ch. 2 *passim*.

up and conceal their base and lustful intentions. 'Solomon says, a soft word breaks the bone', warned Francis Boyle, Viscount Shannon, in 1696: 'therefore no wonder if smooth praises and complements should charm a young Ladies tender heart; for sure 'tis no wonderful operation in our times, for small freedoms like little Thieves to open the Doors to great Liberties, and venial wantonness, to turn to modish wickedness.' By this means a 'Gallant' ensnares his 'mistress' and 'uses' her as a 'conquer'd Captive'.[90] The use of refined terms as a tool for dissimulation and seduction formed a mainstay of the attack on the stage's representations of adultery around the turn of the eighteenth century. Defoe criticised the stage's 'Representations of Lewdness, under the Foppish Disguises of Love and Gallantry', while Bedford singled out the songs included in some plays for their seductive 'soft Chromatick notes' which 'strike gently upon the passions' and for their words which 'stir up Lust, under the Name of Love'.[91] William Law, leading a renewed attack on the stage in 1726, also pointed to the 'Genteelity and Politeness' of the expressions in which adultery was represented and warned that such language was liable to fill the audience 'with such Passions and Pleasures, as quite extinguish the gentle Light of Reason and Religion'.[92]

If 'gallantry' and other terms appeared to exalt adultery, making it consistent with virtue and good breeding, or to legitimise 'base' and 'unlawful' passions, there was also a strong sense that this language trivialised extra-marital sex and diminished its consequences. The rapid turnover of 'modish' words for illicit sexuality was an important feature of Restoration social satire and portrayed a world in which moral values had become commodified. John Dryden's play *Marriage A-La-Mode* (1671) mocked the affected Frenchified vocabulary used by the fashionable lady Melantha to describe her love affairs, sending her maid on a daily search for new words she might use in conversation. When the maid, Philotis, describes her mistress's designs on Rhodophil, a married man, as an 'intrigue', Melantha replies, 'Intrigue, Philotis! That's an old phrase; I have laid that word by. Amour sounds better. But thou art heir to all my cast words, as thou art to my old wardrobe.'[93] To its critics, nothing epitomised the superficiality or the throwaway morals of later seventeenth-century fashionable society more than its constant 'round of words'.[94]

By the eighteenth century, the trivialisation of adultery through the language of gallantry and other terms was intimately bound up with the perception that attitudes towards adultery were increasingly becoming socially distinct. In the

---

[90] Francis Boyle, *Discourses Useful For the Vain Modish Ladies and Their Gallants* (London, 1696), Third Discourse, p. 7.

[91] *Review*, VI, 64, 30 Aug. 1709, p. 254; Arthur Bedford, *Serious Reflections on the Scandalous Abuse and Effects of the Stage* (Bristol, 1705), p. 28.

[92] William Law, *The Absolute Unlawfulness of the Stage-Entertainment Fully Demonstrated* (London, 1726), p. 45.

[93] John Dryden, *Marriage A-La-Mode* (1671), ed. David Crane (London, 1991), II. i. 15–17.

[94] *Remarques on the Humours and Conversations of the Gallants of the Town*, p. 37.

Restoration the term 'gallant' could still be used as a general term for a lover irrespective of his rank. In a popular literature such as the humorous journal *Poor Robin's Intelligence*, which presented stories of cuckolding in the convention of news, the term was used to denote the journeyman who cuckolded his master as well as the upper-class rake.[95] But increasingly the language of gallantry was used to delineate certain spaces and particular social groups where and for whom conventional rules of morality apparently did not apply. Defoe's *Moll Flanders* describes Bath as a 'Place of Gallantry', echoing the much-stated opinion of the fashionable resort as a nursery of adulterous intrigue.[96] Moreover, the author of the tract *Hell Upon Earth* (1729) criticised the practice of 'Folks of Fashion' or 'Persons of Figure' to style the 'Breaches of their Marriage Vow' in their own language which 'In the Man it is but taking a Wench, and in the Married Ladies 'tis only a Piece of Gallantry'.[97] The *Grub Street Journal* remarked in 1730 that 'all well-bred persons esteem' adultery as 'a piece of gallantry, and not a crime', while George Berkeley noted that in the 'dialect' of the high-born, 'a vicious Man is a Man of Pleasure ... A Lady is said to have an Affair: A Gentleman to be Gallant'.[98]

The demarcation of 'gallantry' as a 'dialect' of morally lax 'folks of fashion' dealt a serious blow to the notion that language held together the fabric of society. Although such sentiments are undoubtedly more revealing about the prejudices of middling sort writers against their social superiors, the regularity with which they were voiced is suggestive of a more fundamental shift in the perception of sexual vice.[99] Through this language adultery is being judged not by absolute moral standards but by the mores of different social groups. In the process, some of the most fundamental assumptions about the labelling of vice were called into question.

RETHINKING THE LANGUAGE OF ADULTERY AND WHOREDOM

As the language of extra-marital sex diversified in this period, so questions were raised about the propriety of traditional 'hard' terms to label marital infidelity and its perpetrators. By the beginning of the eighteenth century more and more doubts were raised about whether such terms were consistent with concepts of civility and polite discourse. Such questions were not without precedent. Although many Christian conduct writers into the eighteenth century regarded

---

[95] E.g., *Poor Robin's Intelligence*, 11 Sept. 1676.   [96] Defoe, *Moll Flanders*, p. 106.

[97] *Hell Upon Earth: Or, the Town in an Uproar* (London, 1729), p. 14.

[98] *Memoirs of the Society of Grub Street* (2 vols., London, 1737), I, p. 61; George Berkeley, *Alciphron: Or, the Minute Philosopher* (2 vols., London, 1732), II, p. 75.

[99] Margaret R. Hunt, *The Middling Sort: Commerce, Gender and the Family in England 1680–1780* (Berkeley and Los Angeles, CA, 1996), pp. 198–202.

'soft' language in the naming of vice as pernicious, there was also a tradition of thought in the early modern period which argued to the contrary that vice was more safely represented using euphemistic terms. The most articulate exponent of this position was the sixteenth-century Italian bishop Giovanni della Casa whose guide to civility in conversation, *Galateo*, had been translated into English in 1576. *Galateo* cautioned against all forms of 'unhonest and filthie talke' which necessitated the avoidance of 'broad' terms for immoral actions and persons. Thus the 1576 version argued that 'it better becomes a ma[n]s and a womans mouth, to call Harlots, women of the worlde'.[100] A new translation of *Galateo* was published in 1703, which extended the discussion of unseemly forms of labelling vice. Arguing that the decency of words 'consists either in sound or signification', it was important in discourse to 'reject such words as are really immodest, but such also as may easily be drawn to any impure construction'.[101] In cases where 'two or more words may signifie the same thing', it was important to choose the least harsh or offensive sounding one:

> For instance, we may say decently enough, that such a one is naught with such a Woman, whereas to express the same meaning by a more proper Word, might justly offend a modest Ear. And thus it becomes persons of breeding to call a Whore a Miss, or a Woman of ill fame, and so of like Words.[102]

Underlying *Galateo*'s arguments was the familiar desire to avoid 'corrupt communication'. By the end of the seventeenth century, some commentators argued that a special kind of 'complaisance' or courtesy should be used when addressing women. The increasingly popular tendency for writers to refer to women in patronising terms as the 'soft' or 'fair' sex, possessing a greater delicacy and sensitivity than men, raised problems about whether it was proper to use blunter terminology when discussing vice. For instance, the *Secret Mercury*, a weekly publication of 1702 which set out to expose the 'secret Lewdness of the Town', felt the need to defend its condemnation of adulterous women of all ranks through the language of whoredom, arguing that 'the Ladies' should not 'escape on account of their Sex' for if they 'discard Modesty and Morality' they must 'expect Complaisance agreeable to Character and Aggravation'. But the implication was that women, in particular upper-class 'Ladies', might indeed expect to escape the labelling of whoredom 'on account of their Sex'.[103] The point was made more explicitly in a letter from 'Francis Courtly' to the *Spectator* in 1712, which argued for a more polite language to be employed when speaking to 'Ladies' to protect their natural modesty, for 'A Man of Breeding speaks of even Misfortune among Ladies, without giving it the most

---

[100] [Giovanni della Casa], *Galateo, Or Rather, a Treatise of the Manners and Behaviours it Behoveth a Man to Use and Eschewe, in His Familiar Conversation*, trans. Robert Peterson (London, 1576 edn), p. 82.

[101] [Giovanni della Casa], *Galateo of Manners: Or, Instructions to a Young Gentleman How to Behave Himself in Conversation* (London, 1703 edn), p. 100.

[102] Ibid., p. 101.   [103] *The Secret Mercury, Or, the Adventure of Seven Days*, 1, 9 Sept. 1702.

terrible Aspect it can bear; and this Tenderness towards them, is much more to be preserved when you speak of Vices.'[104] The correspondent justified the differentiation of language on the basic premise of politeness, that a person's mode of discourse should take account of the people in his or her company and should adapt its expressions and vocabulary accordingly.

This view was sharply criticised in a later issue of the *Spectator* by a correspondent who argued, in significant contrast to the position outlined in *Galateo*, that 'the Difference between obscene and modest Words expressing the same Action, consists only in the accessary Idea, for there is nothing immodest in Letters and Syllables'. Therefore, 'Fornication and Adultery are modest Words, because they express an evil Action as criminal . . . Whereas Words representing the Pleasure rather than the Sin, are for this Reason indecent and dishonest.' Nevertheless, the correspondent's view that the same terminology should apply to 'pamper'd Vice in the Habitations of the Wealthy' as it did to 'the Harbours of the Brothel' implicitly recognised that patterns of labelling were shifting and becoming socially reoriented.[105] As Martin Ingram has recently observed, the use of the language of whoredom in religious polemic and official moral discourse essentially upgraded what had been since medieval times a discourse of vulgar abuse.[106] The emergence of supposedly more refined ways of speaking about illicit sexuality paved the way for a re-vulgarisation of this terminology. A correspondent to *Mist's Weekly Journal* in the early 1720s sardonically observed that among women of the upper ranks the terms 'whore and bawd', whatever their truth, are 'Scurrilities, Indecencies, something worse than the Vices they imply'.[107] Several years later, when the theologian William Law attacked the immorality of the stage and its genteel patrons, his plain means of expression was criticised as 'Billingsgate Language', with its connotations of fishmarket vulgarity and slanderous abuse.[108] Changes in patterns of litigation for sexual slander illustrate this point further. Over the course of the eighteenth century, there was a marked decline in defamation suits brought by married women from the substantial middling sort based on the insult 'whore', suggesting that such language was an improper term to use in polite society.[109]

Just as some commentators viewed it as impolite to use the language of whoredom to discuss the vices of the wealthy and well-bred, so traditional terms for sexual offenders became more socially specific. While Samuel Pepys had used the term 'whore' to label immoral women irrespective of their social

---

[104] *Spectator*, II, p. 574.   [105] Ibid., III, p. 15.

[106] Ingram, 'Law, Litigants and the Construction of "Honour" ', p. 155.

[107] *A Collection of Miscellany Letters, Selected out of Mist's Weekly Journal* (4 vols., London, 1722–7), II, p. 274.

[108] John Dennis, *The Critical Works of John Dennis*, ed. E. Niles Hooker (2 vols., Baltimore, 1939), II, p. 321.

[109] Shoemaker, 'Decline of Public Insult'; S. D. Waddams, *Sexual Slander in Nineteenth-Century England: Defamation in the Ecclesiastical Courts, 1815–1855* (Toronto and London, 2000).

background, later diarists increasingly used the word more narrowly to refer to streetwalking prostitutes. In 1715 the young Dudley Ryder referred to 'the whores' as inhabitants of a dark sexual underworld lurking around the playhouses and alley-ways of Hanoverian London.[110] Writing a century after Pepys, James Boswell also used the term 'whore' in this way, to denote a street-walker who carried the risk of venereal disease. To Boswell and other men of his generation, the term 'whore' denoted 'a grovelling-minded, ill-bred worthless creature' with whom sex was merely commercial and qualitatively inferior to the more emotionally and sensually fulfilling 'intrigue' to be had with a more genteel woman of 'gallantry'.[111] Tinged with such class and gender prejudices, the label 'whore' perhaps became even more contemptuous than it had been in the seventeenth century.

The effect of these linguistic developments was thus to strengthen the languages of adultery and whoredom as powerful expressions of sexual sin. In *Moll Flanders*, for example, Defoe reserved the older terms for immorality for moments of truth when characters are brought to full, horrific realisation of their culpability for sexual sin. In this context, the words appear shockingly frank. When Moll's lover in Bath, lying on his death bed, reflects upon his past life of debauchery, he realises that 'his past life of Gallantry and Levity' was 'neither more or less, than a long continu'd Life of Adultery ... and he look'd upon it now with a just, and religious Abhorrence'.[112] But by the eighteenth century another discourse was becoming increasingly prominent as a means of expressing the heinousness of extra-marital sex – a set of words that would not only satisfy the demand for euphemism, but constitute a significant re-mapping of the meanings of illicit sex.

CRIMINAL CONVERSATIONS: INCIVILITY AND IMMORALITY

Concepts of civility and politeness increasingly influenced the labelling of sexual immorality and its perpetrators in the later seventeenth and early eighteenth centuries. The hallmark of civility, as it had developed in the seventeenth century, was the principle of accommodating one's words and behaviour to others. It was this notion, powerfully established in guides to civilised conduct, that raised doubts about the suitability of using traditional 'hard names' for immorality, especially when in polite, mixed company. Conversely, by referring

---

[110] E.g., Dudley Ryder, *The Diary of Dudley Ryder 1715–1716*, ed. William Matthews (London, 1939), pp. 49, 57, 67. See also William Byrd, *The London Diary (1717–1721) and Other Writings*, ed. Louis B. Wright and Marion Tinling (New York, 1958), pp. 138, 161, 204.

[111] James Boswell, *Boswell's London Journal 1762–1763*, ed. Frederick A. Pottle (London, 1950), pp. 84, 97, 240–1, 264.

[112] Defoe, *Moll Flanders*, p. 123.

to illicit behaviour and its perpetrators using the 'soft words of civility', such as 'intrigue' or 'gallantry', it was also feared that acts which might have been viewed in a more austere age as disreputable and demeaning might now appear respectable, even as essential to the fashioning of an urbane and genteel person.[113] But aside from establishing models of behaviour that might be at odds with conventional morality or act as a cloak for sin, concepts of civility were also invoked to emphasise the heinousness of illicit sexuality and set up alternative indices against which adultery might be judged. These words emphasised that adultery was not only morally wrong, but also wholly inconsistent with good breeding, manners and, especially, the virtuous sociability between the sexes that was so essential to refinement.

The foundations of this language had been laid in the early seventeenth century. The lists of offences brought against adulterers and fornicators in the church courts, which we will explore in greater depth in a later chapter, often alleged that the accused had 'kept company' in a suspicious manner with persons of the opposite sex – not necessarily indulging in sexual relations *per se*, but certainly behaving in a manner that was suggestive of improper intimacy that was contrary to normal social codes.[114] Unlawful sexual relations were cast as excessive forms of social freedom and familiarity. The use of this language increased exponentially as the period progressed, thanks to a proliferation of new media such as periodicals, conduct books and novels. Richardson's Pamela described the sexual advances of her rapacious master as his 'offering freedoms'.[115] Similarly, adulterous behaviour was characterised as behaving 'very familiarly' or as taking a 'criminal familiarity', or described as a 'farther familiarity'.[116] This usage was enshrined in Dyche's *New General English Dictionary* of 1735 which recognised that while familiarity referred ideally to 'the great Freedom, Openness and Friendship that one intimate Friend or Acquaintance uses or expresses towards another', it might also denote 'an illegal Conversation between the two Sexes'.[117]

Another set of words expressed adultery as a breach of 'decency' in personal deportment or sociability. 'Decency', and its opposite 'indecency' or 'indecent', had a variety of applications, but held a particular resonance with

---

[113] Bryson, *From Courtesy to Civility*, pp. 161–3 and ch. 5 *passim*; Martin Ingram, 'Sexual Manners: the Other Face of Civility in Early Modern England', in Burke, Harrison and Slack (eds.), *Civil Histories*, pp. 93–4.

[114] Ingram, 'Sexual Manners', pp. 97–108, gives many examples.

[115] Samuel Richardson, *Pamela: Or, Virtue Rewarded* (1740) (2 vols., London, 1962), I, p. 10. See also *The Female Tatler*, ed. Fidelis Morgan (London, 1992 edn), p. 125; Defoe, *Moll Flanders*, p. 119.

[116] *Female Tatler*, p. 125; *The Universal Spectator*, ed. Henry Stonecastle (2 vols., London, 1736), II, p. 58; Daniel Defoe, *The History and Remarkable Life of the Truly Honourable Col. Jacque Commonly Call'd Colonel Jack* (1722), ed. Samuel Holt Monk (London, 1965), p. 227.

[117] Dyche, *New General English Dictionary*, s.v. 'Familiarity'.

regard to sexual behaviour.[118] The importance of marriage to the social order was frequently conceptualised in terms of its role in upholding 'decency' and 'decorum' in wider social relations. These concepts connoted more than 'acceptable' or 'proper' behaviour; they were, in the words of Defoe, necessary for 'all People who pretend to live and Act as Christians do'.[119] Defoe's novels and a range of other contemporary sources frequently described illicit sexual intercourse as an act of 'indecency'. The courtship offered to Moll Flanders by a bank clerk in London is described as honourable by his not giving 'the least offer of any Undecency'.[120] Sexual transgression was also characterised as 'rude' behaviour or as an act of 'rudeness', the antithesis of polite deportment. It was used in particular to describe the breach of civilised relations between the sexes brought about by men's sexual advances to women – Defoe's Roxana describes giving up her virtue as 'suffering' her lover's 'rudeness'.[121] Similarly in *Bath Intrigues*, a scandalous novella of 1725, a married lady resists her lover's advances, bidding him to 'cease [his] rudeness', while Pamela, explaining her decision to leave her master's house after his unsuccessful sexual advances, describes his conduct as being 'very rude'.[122] Such behaviour was considered vulgar, beneath the conduct of a civilised person.

The terminology which captured the convergence of notions of incivility and immorality most strikingly was the language of 'criminal conversation'. The word 'conversation' had long been used in a bawdy sense to denote illicit sexual intimacy.[123] Moreover, as we shall see in chapter 6, from the late seventeenth century the term 'criminal conversation' had specific legal connotations in its emerging use as the name for the civil action whereby a cuckolded husband sued his wife's lover for damages. But by the eighteenth century the term 'criminal conversation', and its variants 'criminal correspondence' or 'criminal commerce', had also become the pre-eminent means of representing vice in periodicals and other literature. 'Criminal conversation' and 'criminal commerce' were used both in general terms to refer to illicit intimacy between the sexes and more specifically to denote adultery.[124] 'Criminal' or 'wicked' correspondence likewise denoted adulterous sexual relations. Moll Flanders, for instance, stated that a life of 'criminal correspondence' was synonymous with 'a long continued life of adultery' while the cleric John Thomlinson of Rothbury in Northumberland recorded in his diary in 1718 how one Metcalf, a minister in

[118] Ingram, 'Sexual Manners', p. 90.   [119] Defoe, *Conjugal Lewdness*, p. 370.

[120] Defoe, *Moll Flanders*, p. 181.

[121] Daniel Defoe, *Roxana: the Fortunate Mistress* (1724), ed. John Mullan (Oxford, 1996), p. 151.

[122] [Eliza Haywood?], *Bath Intrigues: In Four Letters to a Friend in London* (London, 1725), p. 36; Richardson, *Pamela*, I, p. 48.

[123] Eric Partridge, *Shakespeare's Bawdy* (London and New York, 1990), p. 85.

[124] E.g., *Collection of Miscellany Letters, Selected out of Mist's Weekly Journal*, IV, p. 235; Defoe, *Conjugal Lewdness*, pp. 163, 353; *Spectator*, II, p. 534 (4 Jan. 1712).

Morpeth, was 'descarded and hooted out of Town – for some criminal correspondence or however some attempt [tha]t way upon a woman'.[125]

The significance of this language lay in its expression of traditional ideas about the unlawfulness of adultery while locating its transgression firmly in the arena of social interaction. 'Conversation' bore a number of inter-related meanings in this period and could refer to company or 'society', behaviour and deportment or to verbal interaction.[126] More than the ability to speak well, good 'conversation' was the ability to engage with others in a respectful, 'easy' and accommodating manner and was regarded by many commentators to be 'central to the polite ideal and a key requirement of the modern gentleman'.[127] 'Commerce' similarly referred not only to trade or dealing (in its modern usage) but also to social interaction, while 'correspondence' was defined by Nathan Bailey as 'holding [a] mutual intelligence, commerce and familiarity'.[128] All three terms were crucial metaphors in early eighteenth-century social thought for the virtuous social interaction between the sexes central to the inculcation of politeness.[129] Therefore, since polite and civilised manners were believed to be perfected by social contact in mixed company, 'criminal conversation' became a strong term for the danger posed by illicit sexuality to the rules of interaction upon which civilised society was founded. Furthermore, by emphasising the 'criminality' of adultery, this terminology provided a powerful contrast with the language of 'gallantry', which appeared to play down responsibility and culpability for extra-marital sex. In this way adultery was constituted as something which was as socially repugnant as it was morally wrong.

Through language, the raw material from which adultery was fashioned, it is possible to chart important shifts in the understanding of the social and moral meanings of infidelity. It is clear that language was heavily implicated in

[125] Defoe, *Moll Flanders*, p. 123; British Library Add. MS. 22560 (Diary of the Rev. J. Thomlinson), fo. 90.

[126] For examples of these respective uses in contemporary novels see Alexander Oldys, *The Female Gallant Or, the Wife's the Cuckold. A Novel* (London, 1692), p. 48; Defoe, *Roxana*, p. 301; Defoe, *Moll Flanders*, p. 151. See also the varying definitions of 'conversation' in Elisha Coles, *An English Dictionary* (London, 1685); Dyche, *New General English Dictionary*. More generally, Burke, *Art of Conversation*, ch. 4; Childs, 'Prescriptions for Manners', pp. 210–16. Cf. Laura Hanft Korobkin, *Criminal Conversations: Sentimentality and Nineteenth-Century Legal Stories of Adultery* (New York, 1998), p. 21.

[127] Carter, *Men and the Emergence of Polite Society*, p. 62.

[128] Stephen Copley, 'Commerce, Conversation and Politeness in the Early Eighteenth-Century Periodical', *British Journal for Eighteenth-Century Studies*, 18 (1995), 63–77; Nathan Bailey, *An Universal Etymological English Dictionary* (London, 1724), s.v. 'Correspondence'.

[129] Lawrence E. Klein, *Shaftesbury and the Culture of Politeness: Moral Discourse and Cultural Politics in Early Eighteenth-Century England* (Cambridge, 1994), p. 4 and *passim*; Lawrence E. Klein, 'Gender, Conversation and the Public Sphere in Early Eighteenth-Century England', in Judith Still and Michael Worton (eds.), *Textuality and Sexuality: Reading Theories and Practices* (Manchester, 1993), pp. 100–15; Copeley, 'Commerce, Conversation and Politeness'; Cohen, *Fashioning Masculinity*, pp. 2, 13–25.

structures of power in early modern England. The theologians and others spent a good deal of time attempting to regulate communication and establish a proper language for discussing adultery and casting its protagonists as sexual deviants. The project of 'governing the tongue' supported the efforts of the church courts in the public regulation of sexuality. Its aim was not so much to *repress* discussion of extra-marital sex, as to express essential distinctions between licit and illicit behaviour and categorise legitimate and illegitimate ways of labelling vice – the distinction between 'hard' and 'soft' words.

As the period progressed, there was a palpable sense that these traditional values were under threat from quite different modes of expressing adulterous passions. The key agents of change were the development of polite society and gathering notions of social refinement, sharpening social differentiation interwoven with considerations of gender, and a multiplication of genres which opened up spaces for the exploration of familiar themes in new and challenging ways. The ideals of complaisance and accommodation emphasised that modes of discourse should vary according to company and social setting. In the process, the frank vocabulary used by religious moralists was increasingly seen as too harsh for the delicate sensibilities of the polite and, in particular, too crude for use by or before ladies. By the eighteenth century it was recognised that moral discourse had to follow the principles of politeness and adapt itself to its audience. For those supposedly influenced by new languages of polite seduction, of 'gallantry' and 'intrigue', subtler strategies were required to warn them of the wrongfulness of adultery. The author of *An Essay Upon Modern Gallantry* (1726) argued that 'because most of those pretty gentlemen' at whom his tract was directed 'have Stomachs too nice to digest any Arguments drawn from Religion, I shall throw Divinity out of the Question' and address them in language more appropriate to 'Men of Pleasure and Men of Sense'.[130]

Did the diversification of the language of marital infidelity really cast out divinity from moral discourse and constitute a 'secularisation' of understandings of sexual immorality? There is no doubt that the result of these changes was a language of adultery which expressed sexual transgression principally in terms of its violation of codes of civilised social interaction rather than its offence to God or religion. However, it is better to view this shift in terms of a change of emphasis rather than the wholesale replacement of one set of ideas with another. The principles that underlay the keywords of sexual misconduct in the novels and periodicals of the eighteenth century had a longer history of involvement in discourses of sexual immorality, as we will see in the next chapter. The premium of such words rose in response to forms of expression which attempted to portray adultery as compatible with civilised conduct, a practice which Defoe regarded as not only a sin against God, but also 'unmannerly, a Sin against

---

[130] *Essay Upon Modern Gallantry*, p. 10.

Breeding, and Society, a Breach of Behaviour, and a saucy affront to all Company'.[131] Nevertheless, there can be little doubt that the traditional assumptions which underpinned the naming of vice and its perpetrators in Christian moral thought were increasingly open to challenge as the period progressed. Implicit in much of this material was the growing conviction that virtue had a number of impulses and that religious teaching was not the only source of morality. This would become an important, and hotly debated, theme in the proliferation of texts offering advice on social conduct and marital relations.

[131] [Daniel Defoe], *Serious Reflections During the Life and Surprising Adventures of Robinson Crusoe* (London, 1720), p. 105.

2. *Marital advice and moral prescription*

Marriage, the family and household order were matters of central social concern in early modern England. For people of all ranks marriage was the principal means of transferring property of all kinds, connections and expertise across generations and social groups, while the household-family was a primary unit of production and consumption. Getting married was likened to a form of civilising process in which 'brutish lusts' were tamed and transformed into lawful, procreative sexuality.[1] It marked the transition from youth to adulthood and conferred special roles and responsibilities on both men and women. As an important unit for the education and socialisation of children, the family had wider social and political importance. More than a 'private' institution, the family was regarded in the sixteenth and seventeenth centuries as the foundation upon which the strength, prosperity and well-being of the whole nation depended. Moralists and social commentators acclaimed well-ordered familial relations as the hallmark of great civilisations, the matrimonial bond fortifying the body politic against the corrupting influences of 'luxuries and effeminacies'.[2] The marriage covenant was analogous to the 'love and union between Christ and his Church', while the patriarchal family was idealised as the mirror of 'discipline and a happy government' in the commonwealth, the basis of 'peace and quiet' in the kingdom.[3] Though the analogy between the family and the state arguably carried less symbolic freight after 1688, there is no doubt that marriage remained important to notions of respectability in civil society.[4]

[1] *Remarques on the Humours and Conversations of the Gallants of the Town* (London, 1673), Part II, p. 39.

[2] Ibid., p. 54.

[3] J. S., *A Sermon Against Adultery* (London, 1672), p. 7; J. H., *Essays of Love and Marriage* (London, 1673), p. 40. See also A. N., *An Account of Marriage, or, the Interests of Marriage Considered and Defended against the Unjust Attacques of the Age* (London, 1672), p. 20.

[4] Richard B. Schlatter,*The Social Ideas of Religious Leaders 1660–1688* (London, 1940), pp. 1–30; Susan Dwyer Amussen, *An Ordered Society: Gender and Class in Early Modern England* (Oxford, 1988), ch. 2.

This chapter explores the meanings of marriage and adultery in didactic publications and guides to marital advice. Conduct literature of various kinds was a significant feature of the cultural landscape of late seventeenth- and early eighteenth-century England and provides the primary means of exploring rules and ideals about the conduct of matrimonial relations and for analysing the consequences of adultery within the framework of official morality. This chapter reveals what these writers thought to be the principal threats to domestic stability, and how these changed over time. It also explores the ways in which they tried to persuade people to value marriage and remain faithful to their partners. It goes on to explore ways in which the prescriptions of moralists were challenged and modified as the literature of advice expanded and ordinary people were given greater scope to discuss their marital problems and affairs in print. In the process, it demonstrates important changes in the context and idiom of marital advice, which was becoming both more questioning of established moral thinking and increasingly oriented around notions of civility and politeness.

Marriage was a popular topic of discussion in early modern England. As an eligible bachelor at an age ripe for marrying, Dudley Ryder, the 24-year-old son of a wealthy Hackney tradesman, frequently found himself discussing matrimonial matters with his family, friends and social acquaintances. His conversations on these issues were carefully detailed in his diary, possibly as a memorandum of his increasing education in these matters. The birth of a child to his married cousin Joseph Billio on 4 July 1715 occasioned a conversation with his male cousins 'upon matrimony and the pleasures and delights of that state'. At dinner at the house of his cousin Watkins on 24 June 1716 the conversation fell 'chiefly upon the subject of matrimony and my good disposition and inclination towards it' and Ryder recorded that he was 'very free with Cousin Watkins' wife upon that subject in asking her questions about it and her courtship'. Even complete strangers might offer their opinions on the best way to achieve marital bliss. Travelling to the City of London later that year, Ryder happened to share the coach with an 'old woman' who 'talked very much, gave advice about matrimony [and] how to behave in that state and the necessity of mutual forbearance between man and wife'. The diarist noted that she 'talked really well on that subject', making her fellow travellers 'pretty merry and gave me an opportunity of talking much more than I should have done else'.[5]

These everyday discussions of marriage were complemented and encouraged by a wide range of conduct literature devoted to the discussion of domestic relations. Ryder, an avid consumer of printed matter, sometimes made connections between his conversations about marriage with his family and social acquaintances and the descriptions of ideal unions he had read about in the didactic

---

[5] Dudley Ryder, *The Diary of Dudley Ryder 1715–1716*, ed. William Matthews (London, 1939), pp. 47, 262, 345.

press. On a number of occasions he likened the happy marital relations of his neighbours Mr and Mrs Barrett to 'the best example . . . of that happy state of matrimony that is described in the *Spectators, Tatlers, Guardians*, and their life together seems almost to be regulated from those rules that are there laid down'.[6] Since the Reformation theologians and moralists had set out prescriptions for the formation of marriage, laid down rules for the ordering of domestic relations based around a set of 'duties' for each member of the family, and warned of the causes and consequences of adultery and marital discord. Prescriptions for marriage and morality appeared in a number of textual forms ranging from printed sermons, conduct books and letters of advice aimed principally at a gentry readership, down to the 'penny godlinesses' and religious broadsides apparently directed towards a humbler audience. Ideals were also expounded at length from the pulpit in church services and to the young through catechism.[7] The period from the Restoration to the mid-eighteenth century witnessed an outpouring of didactic literature on an unprecedented scale. Religious works dominated the market, led by the best-selling *Whole Duty of Man* by Richard Allestree, first published in 1657.[8] To the traditional sources of religious instruction was added advice on courtship and family life served up by new genres such as 'companions', 'vade mecums', 'manuals', dictionaries and 'family books'.[9] By the eighteenth century, the periodical press provided regular updates on manners and morals. The most successful of these ventures, such as the *Spectator* papers of Joseph Addison and Richard Steele, typically had a circulation of 3,000 or 4,000 per issue.[10]

The ability of writers to prescribe advice on marriage rested on the broad acceptance of a set of universal principles through which the myriad of conjugal relations could be channelled. Nevertheless, throughout the seventeenth century the topics of marriage and sexual morality were areas of debate, uncertainty

---

[6] Ibid., p. 76; see also p. 123.

[7] Kathleen M. Davies, 'Continuity and Change in Literary Advice on Marriage', in R. B. Outhwaite (ed.), *Marriage and Society: Studies in the Social History of Marriage* (London, 1981), pp. 58–80; Anthony Fletcher, 'The Protestant Idea of Marriage in Early Modern England', in Anthony Fletcher and Peter Roberts (eds.), *Religion, Culture and Society in Early Modern Britain: Essays in Honour of Patrick Collinson* (Cambridge, 1994), pp. 161–81; Keith Thomas, 'Cases of Conscience in Seventeenth-Century England', in John Morrill, Paul Slack and Daniel Woolf (eds.), *Public Duty and Private Conscience in Seventeenth-Century England: Essays Presented to G. E. Aylmer* (Oxford, 1993), pp. 27–56; Tessa Watt, *Cheap Print and Popular Piety, 1550–1640* (Cambridge, 1991); Amussen, *An Ordered Society*, p. 35.

[8] C. John Sommerville, *Popular Religion in Restoration England* (Gainesville, FL, 1977), p. 38.

[9] Lawrence E. Klein, 'Politeness for Plebes: Consumption and Social Identity in Early Eighteenth Century England', in Ann Bermingham and John Brewer (eds.), *The Consumption of Culture 1600–1800: Image, Object, Text* (London and New York, 1995), pp. 362–82; Fenela Childs, 'Prescriptions for Manners in English Courtesy Literature 1690–1760, and their Social Implications', DPhil thesis, University of Oxford (1984).

[10] Philip Carter, *Men and the Emergence of Polite Society: Britain 1660–1800* (London, 2001), p. 34.

and conflicting opinion, and writers of didactic literature were aware that their prescriptions could not be taken for granted, for, in spite of the widely acknowledged social and political importance of marriage and the family, prescriptions for marriage were often accompanied by the anxiety that adultery was rampant and condoned by popular standards.[11] The proliferation of genres provoked public debate about the reliability of customary sources of advice. Once the new periodical press allowed correspondents to exemplify marital problems with (often painful) personal circumstances, generalised precepts became more difficult to apply. Much of the new literature of advice produced during the later seventeenth and early eighteenth centuries had an urban, metropolitan audience in mind. In part, this reflected the fact that most of the nation's printing presses were located in the capital, together with the desire of publishers to profit from the higher rates of literacy among Londoners. But it was also felt that in this complex, urbanising society, with its new opportunities for mobility, sociability and consumption, rules for behaviour were less certain than in the countryside where they had been established over generations, and social codes had to be written afresh.[12] Such factors generated a hunger for didactic literature, but also made for an atmosphere of uncertainty. 'The commerce in the conjugal state is so delicate', admitted the *Tatler* in 1710, 'that it is impossible to observe rules for the conduct of it, so as to fit ten thousand nameless pleasures and disquietudes which arise to people in that condition.'[13] Before we chart this pathway to uncertainty, let us begin by exploring the traditional assumptions concerning marriage and infidelity in Christian conduct literature.

TRADITIONAL MEANINGS OF MARRIAGE AND ADULTERY

Theological discourse located monogamous marriage in the commands of God and the laws of reason and nature. Sermons, conduct books, expositions upon the catechism and the Ten Commandments and other didactic texts stressed that marriage was ordained by God for specific purposes: for the procreation and education of children, as a remedy against sin and bulwark against fornication, and for mutual society, help and comfort.[14] Matrimony was an institution 'to which God hath affixed especial marks of respect and sanctity' and as 'the most solemn and tremendous vow and promise' the marital bond was invested with

---

[11] Thomas, 'Cases of Conscience', p. 47; Martin Ingram, *Church Courts, Sex and Marriage in England, 1570–1640* (Cambridge, 1987), p. 154.

[12] Susan E. Whyman, *Sociability and Power in Late-Stuart England: the Cultural Worlds of the Verneys 1660–1720* (Oxford, 1999), p. 93; John Brewer, '"The Most Polite Age and the Most Vicious": Attitudes towards Culture as a Commodity, 1660–1800', in Bermingham and Brewer (eds.), *The Consumption of Culture 1600–1800*, pp. 341–61.

[13] *Tatler*, II, p. 339.   [14] Schlatter, *Social Ideas of Religious Leaders*, p. 7.

a special status.[15] Marriage was viewed as a process whereby men and women became united in 'one flesh' and also united with God. These ideas, which had a long tradition in classical thought and Christian theology, were given renewed emphasis in the outpouring of conduct literature on domestic relations published in Elizabethan and Jacobean England, and remained an important point of reference well into the eighteenth century.[16] According to William Gouge, marriage was a process by which men and women became 'glued' together, forming 'parts of the same body, and the same flesh', and creating an 'inviolable bond'.[17] In marriage men and women were imagined as comprising a single corporeal entity, with the husband as its head and the wife as the body. In this process, the wife became an extension of her husband's being. Only in marriage could a man achieve the completeness and independence deemed necessary to take up his place in patriarchal society – a bachelor was sometimes described as an 'unbuilt' man, or 'but half a man', his masculinity not yet fully achieved.[18]

This notion was used to stress that husband and wife had mutual obligations. 'The wife of your Bosom is your second self', counselled the *British Apollo* periodical in July 1709, drawing on a familiar image of perfect friendship, 'whence it is deserving of your best endeavours to Establish an Entire Agreement, to Cultivate a Perfect Harmony between your self and so dear a Relative.'[19] First and foremost they had to care for each other's soul and body. If the image of the husband as the head, the seat of reason, was a means of inscribing male hegemony in marriage, it was also emphasised that the head could not survive without the body and vice versa. The 'one flesh' model of marital relations demanded that a husband treat his wife's body with respect and that he should not use excessive force to correct her. In marriage, argued the editor of the *Post Angel* periodical in March 1701, a woman became 'naturaliz'd into, and part of her Husband'. It was 'ridiculous' for a man to use severe force against his spouse since it went against reason for a man to beat part of himself and be 'an Accessory to his own Torture'.[20] Husbands and wives also had a special duty to protect each other's reputation. 'So nearly are husbands and wives joined together', wrote Gouge, that 'the good name of one cannot but tend to the honour and credit of the other.'[21]

---

[15] Isaac Barrow, *The Theological Works of Isaac Barrow*, ed. Alexander Napier (9 vols., Cambridge, 1859), VII, p. 491; William Fleetwood, *The Relative Duties of Parents and Children, Husbands and Wives, Masters and Servants Consider'd in Sixteen Sermons* (London, 1705), p. 179.

[16] Carolyn D. Williams, '"Another Self in the Case": Gender, Marriage and the Individual in Augustan Literature', in Roy Porter (ed.), *Rewriting the Self: Histories from the Renaissance to the Present* (London, 1997), pp. 91–118.

[17] William Gouge, *Of Domesticall Duties* (London, 1622), p. 112.

[18] Elizabeth A. Foyster, *Manhood in Early Modern England: Honour, Sex and Marriage* (London, 1999), p. 48.

[19] *British Apollo*, ii, 28, 1 July 1709; cf. F[rancis] L[enton], *Characterisimi: Or, Lenton's Leasures Expressed in Essays and Characters* (London, 1631), sig. H, 'A True Friend'.

[20] *Post Angel*, March 1701, 200.   [21] Gouge, *Of Domesticall Duties*, pp. 247–8.

To break apart this physical and spiritual union invited catastrophe. The breach of wedlock, moralists asserted, 'whether it be by the man or by the woman', was a 'great sin' both 'in respect of God' and 'in respect of man'.[22] To commit adultery was to 'take the members of Christ and make them the members of a harlot', for which its perpetrators were liable to feel the wrath of divine judgement.[23] Cautionary tales warning of the strange, agonising or sudden deaths awaiting adulterers were a stock-in-trade for seventeenth-century moralists as they had been for their medieval forebears. One popular tale concerned a nobleman of Thuringia who, being caught *in flagrante delicto* by his lover's husband, was bound hand and foot and cast into prison. There he was 'kept fasting', while each day 'hot dishes of meat' were set before him to 'tantalize him with the smell'. Ultimately the torture proved too much for the 'letcher' who 'gnawed off the flesh from his own Shoulders, and on the 11th Day he died'.[24] Providential stories also conveyed the message that any toleration of adultery invited divine retribution on the nation as a whole. More than a 'private' matter of personal morality, the effects of infidelity rippled outwards threatening to engulf the whole of society. In adultery, stated the *British Apollo* in 1709, repeating a standard line from Christian conduct literature, not only do 'we Pollute our selves' and 'Debase our Dignity', but also 'we are Instrumental to the Iniquity of our Neighbour; we Double our own Guilt, and become Partakers of Another's Sin'.[25] As the theologian Isaac Barrow warned, a person's adultery was 'a great evil against God, against his neighbour, against himself, against the common society of men'.[26]

As a corollary to this argument, moralists highlighted the severe punishments meted out on adulterers and fornicators in 'heathen' societies. Their aim was to castigate the laxity of English moral standards by demonstrating that even non-Christians recognised the seriousness of extra-marital sex.[27] Originally, this was done by giving historical examples of the punishment of offenders in ancient

---

[22] Mordecai Moxon, *The Character, Praise and Commendation of a Chaste and Virtuous Woman: in a Learned and Pious Discourse against Adultery* (London, 1708), p. 3.

[23] J. S., *Sermon Against Adultery*, p. 21. See also Davies, 'Continuity and Change', p. 73; Roderick Phillips, *Putting Asunder: a History of Divorce in Western Society* (Cambridge, 1988), p. 347.

[24] William Turner, *A Compleat History of the Most Remarkable Providences, Both of Judgement and Mercy, Which have happened in the Present Age* (London, 1697), pp. 46–7. See also George Meriton, *Immorality, Debauchery and Profaneness Exposed to the Reproof of Scripture and the Censure of the Law* (London, 1698), p. 114; Keith Thomas, *Religion and the Decline of Magic: Studies in Popular Beliefs in Sixteenth and Seventeenth Century England* (Harmondsworth, 1973), pp. 100–1; Alexandra Walsham, *Providence in Early Modern England* (Oxford, 1999), ch. 2.

[25] *British Apollo*, ii, 21, 8 June 1709.   [26] Barrow, *Theological Works*, VII, p. 491.

[27] Keith Thomas, 'The Puritans and Adultery: the Act of 1650 Reconsidered', in Donald Pennington and Keith Thomas (eds.), *Puritans and Revolutionaries: Essays in Seventeenth-Century History Presented to Christopher Hill* (Oxford, 1978), p. 268; Martin Ingram, 'Sexual Manners: the Other Face of Civility in Early Modern England', in Peter Burke, Brian Harrison and Paul Slack (eds.), *Civil Histories: Essays Presented to Sir Keith Thomas* (Oxford, 2000), p. 95.

civilisations mixed with a collection of lurid examples from other European societies. The Elizabethan homily on whoredom listed biblical precedents for the punishment of adulterers such as the flood, the destruction of Sodom and Gomorrah and the Egyptian plagues alongside various gruesome punishments meted out against sexual offenders in ancient Greece, Rome and Egypt. Other examples of retribution were included, such as those of the Turks, Arabians and 'the barbarous Tartarians', all of whom favoured the death penalty. Even these 'heathens' were 'so influenced with the love of honesty and pureness of life, that, for the maintenance ... of that, they made godly statutes suffering neither fornication nor adultery to reign in their realms unpunished'.[28] Similarly, a later seventeenth-century moral tract described how in Brazil 'the crime seemed of so black a dye that the inraged Husband had Power and Authority at Will both to be the Judge, Jury and Executioner of his own Adulterous Wife'. In Ethiopia, by contrast, 'the Penalty was more moderate' for the 'Offender only lost his Nose' by means of punishment.[29]

Over the course of the early modern period, the expanding colonisation of the New World, Asia and Africa stimulated cross-cultural comparison and an out-pouring of publications describing the manners and customs of the indigenous inhabitants.[30] Travellers' accounts, stories of sailors captured by Moors or other 'barbarous' peoples, even dictionaries, frequently contained a discussion of the native people's marriage customs and laws against sexual immorality. Roger Williams of Providence, Rhode Island, wrote in his guide to native American language and culture of the 'High and Honourable esteeme of the Marriage bed' held by the tribes of New England and praised the fact that they viewed 'the Violation of that Bed' as 'Abominable'. Such natural decency exhibited even by the 'Wildest of the sonnes of Men' was contrasted with the 'thousand Whoredoms' practised in European society by 'Papists', about whom the 'Indians' supposedly asked:

> ... if such doe goe in Cloaths
> And whether God they know[?]
> And when they heare they're richly clad,
> Know God, yet practice so.

---

[28] *Two Books of Homilies Appointed to be Read in Churches*, ed. John Griffiths (Oxford, 1859), pp. 127–30, quoting from p. 130.

[29] A. M., *The Reformed Gentleman: Or, The Old English Morals Rescued from the Immoralities of the Present Age* (London, 1693), p. 68. See also Meriton, *Immorality, Debauchery and Profaneness*, pp. 113–15; *An Essay Towards a General History of Whoring* (London, 1697).

[30] The origins of early modern anthropology are discussed in Anthony Pagden, *The Fall of Natural Man: the American Indian and the Origins of Comparative Ethnology* (Cambridge, 1982); see also Linda Colley, 'Going Native, Telling Tales: Captivity, Collaboration and Empire', *PP*, 168 (2000), 170–93.

No sure they're Beasts not men (say they,)
Mens shame and soule disgrace
Of men have mixt with Beasts and so,
Brought forth that monstrous Race.[31]

Dudley Ryder, making notes on George Psalmanazar's *Historical and Geographical Description of Formosa* (1704) in November 1715, recorded that the Formosans' laws were 'exceeding Strict. Adulteries for the second offence were punished with death, but a man was allowed to have as many wives as he could maintain which was to be judged of by an officer for that purpose.'[32] Some of this material seemed morally ambiguous – in this case the harshness of laws against adultery was intermixed with orientalist fantasies of polygamy. Undoubtedly another pamphlet's description of the punishment of adulterous wives in Moorish society, where they were apparently 'almost stung to death' by ants, was prurient and sadistic, serving more to titillate an English audience and confirm their prejudices about the 'barbarity' of Africans.[33] However, moralists continued to believe that such examples held up a mirror to Christian society, so that, as another tract put it, they should 'sufficiently let us see what Construction [other societies] made upon the odious and detestable sin of Adultery; and . . . shame us into a better Consideration of the nature of such a Beastiality'.[34]

Closer to home, moralists paid close attention to the manifold snares that threatened to trap the unwary into a life of unchastity. Taking a fundamentally pessimistic view of human nature derived from the story of the Fall of Man in the book of Genesis, authors of religious conduct literature depicted a world in which matrimonial fidelity was under sustained assault from worldly pleasures and lascivious desires. 'Loose books', 'impure songs' and 'offensive plays' constantly threatened to tempt the vulnerable into sensory abandon,[35] while strict vigilance was required to avoid falling into the company of people of 'loose and immodest behaviour'.[36] By far the surest safeguard against debauchery was to 'marry prudently' in the first place.[37] The future stability of a

---

[31] Roger Williams, *A Key Into the Language of America: Or, An Help to the Language of the Natives in that part of America called New England* (London, 1643), p. 151.

[32] Ryder, *Diary*, p. 133.

[33] *A True Relation of the Inhumane and Unparallel'd Actions and Barbarous Murders of Negroes or Moors: Committed on three Englishmen in Old Calabar in Guinney* (London, 1672), p. 17.

[34] A. M., *Reformed Gentleman*, p. 68. For other examples see Nathaniel Wanley, *The Wonders of the Little World: Or, A General History of Men* (London, 1678), Book IV, ch. 50. See also Anthony Pagden, 'The Savage Critic: Some European Images of the Primitive', *Yearbook of English Studies*, 13 (1983), 32–45; Bernard W. Sheehan, *Savagism and Civility: Indians and Englishmen in Colonial Virginia* (Cambridge, 1980), chs. 1–3.

[35] Gabriel Towerson, *An Explication of the Decalogue of the Ten Commandments, With Reference to the Catechism of the Church of England* (London, 1676), p. 416.

[36] Jean Frederic Ostervald, *The Nature of Uncleanness Consider'd* (London, 1708), pp. 118, 124.

[37] A. B., *A Letter of Advice Concerning Marriage* (London, 1676), p. 2. See also N. H., *The Ladies Dictionary* (London, 1694), p. 195.

marriage crucially rested on the initial choice of spouse and moralists believed that this was best achieved through the ideal of parity or at least comparability between partners, particularly in respect of religious persuasion, rank and breeding, wealth and age. The ideal marriage was a harmonious union based on the 'multilateral consent' of the couple themselves and their parents, and was expected to be broadly acceptable to the wider community.[38] As puritan moralists had frequently stressed, love was expected to play an important part in this matrix. 'Forced' or 'mercenary' marriages, based purely on financial considerations, were bitterly denounced. The development of the London 'season' had created a gentry marriage market in the capital, increasing the choice of partners for the children of the elite, but also prompting cynicism about the commercial motives of match-making.[39] A loveless match, opined one Restoration commentator, was 'but a shadow, a carcass of marriage', liable to breed the distrust upon which unions so often foundered. Defoe regarded those who married with only superficial affection and principally for profit as little more than 'legal prostitutes', 'whores' and 'knaves'. Even worse, to marry someone for their riches while remaining in love with another was considered a 'kind of civil, legal adultery', for it 'makes the man or woman be committing adultery in their hearts every day of their lives'.[40] Love was the glue that held together the marital bond and represented 'the surest and most likely way' of preventing husbands and wives from 'falling into ... adulterous and abominable snares'.[41]

Some commentators argued that marital fidelity was strengthened by having children. Defoe's *Review* periodical counselled that the presence of children in a marriage was an important means of encouraging men in particular to value conjugal love. Fatherhood was supposed to bestow a sense of paternal responsibility and remind men of their other domestic duties, for 'he that loves his Children very tenderly, may be the better suppos'd to love a wife; as he that discharges one Relative Duty well, may be thought the most likely to discharge another'.[42] Parents had a responsibility to provide for their offspring and references to neglected, hungry children were used to castigate profligate husbands who frittered away the household resources on drinking, gaming and whoring.[43] Mothers and fathers were enjoined to set a good example of Christian conduct to their children and were warned that vices such as lust were liable to distract them from their parental duties.[44] Stories of legitimate

---

[38] Ingram, *Church Courts*, p. 136.

[39] Lawrence Stone, *The Family, Sex and Marriage in England 1500–1800* (London, 1977), chs. 7 and 8; Whyman, *Sociability and Power*, ch. 5.

[40] Daniel Defoe, *Conjugal Lewdness; Or, Matrimonial Whoredom. A Treatise Concerning the Use and Abuse of the Marriage Bed* (London, 1727), pp. 102–3, 181, 199.

[41] [Richard Allestree], *The Ladies Calling* (Oxford, 1673), p. 166; Fleetwood, *Relative Duties*, p. 323.

[42] *Review*, Supplementary paper, September 1704, p. 8.

[43] Fleetwood, *Relative Duties*, p. 111.

[44] E.g. Gouge, *Of Domesticall Duties*, p. 499; Fleetwood, *Relative Duties*, p. 104.

children being disinherited by their bastard siblings were also used to offer stark warning of the practical consequences of adultery.[45] However, moralists did not point to any psychological damage caused to children by the breakdown of their parents' marriage in their arguments against infidelity. The view from conduct literature of various kinds was of a culture which took the welfare of children seriously, at least as a social ideal, but had not yet arrived at a sentimental view of childhood which recognised that children had emotional lives of their own. Authors advised both men and women to forgive a penitent unfaithful partner and discouraged separation, but there was no seventeenth-century equivalent of the modern opinion that a dysfunctional couple should try to patch up their differences and hold together a failing marriage for the sake of their children.[46]

THE POLITICS OF BLAME AND RESPONSIBILITY

Once marriage was established, moralists considered sexual continence and fidelity to be matters of the first importance to both husbands and wives. Religious conduct books repeatedly asserted that whoredom was equally sinful in both men and women and emphasised that avoidance of sin was for everyone a matter of personal responsibility. However, moralists drew an important distinction between the absolute sinfulness and criminality of adultery on the one hand, and the question of blame which could be determined by more subjective criteria. First and foremost, the gravity of any act of marital infidelity was judged by the extent of its deviation from the principles of Christian morality. Thus adultery committed openly, with malice or with 'delight', served to exacerbate its injury and made penitence more difficult to achieve, thus plunging the perpetrator's soul deeper into jeopardy.[47] Likewise, 'double' adultery, in which both protagonists were married, was regarded as an especially 'aggravated' form of the crime.[48] The degree of offence was also determined by 'the dignity of the person in the honour and severity of being a Christian'.[49] The immorality of clergymen, whose role as the 'people's looking-glass' required a 'more stricte kind of conversation', generated particular revulsion.[50] Some

[45] Thomas, 'Puritans and Adultery', p. 260.

[46] See also Elizabeth A. Foyster, 'Silent Witnesses? Children and the Breakdown of Domestic and Social Order in Early Modern England', in Anthony Fletcher and Stephen Hussey (eds.), *Childhood in Question: Children, Parents and the State* (Manchester, 1999), pp. 57–73.

[47] G. A. Starr, *Defoe and Casuistry* (Princeton, NJ, 1971), p. 112; Faramerz Dabhoiwala, 'Prostitution and Police in London, c.1660–c.1760', DPhil thesis, University of Oxford (1995), p. 63.

[48] Ingram, *Church Courts*, p. 239.

[49] Jeremy Taylor, *Holy Living* (1650), ed. P. G. Stanwood (Oxford, 1989), p. 73.

[50] Robert Foulkes, *An Alarme for Sinners* (London, 1679), p. 16. See also Thomas Beard, *The Theatre of God's Judgements* (London, 1648), p. 270; John Ayliffe, *Parergon Juris Canonici: Or a Commentary By Way of Supplement to the Canons and Constitutions of the Church of England* (London, 1726), p. 51; John Spurr, *The Restoration Church of England, 1646–1689* (New Haven, CT and London, 1991), p. 197.

moralists placed special emphasis on the heinousness of the sins of 'great' persons, who, because of their superior breeding and education, were expected to know better and show a good example to others. Thus one popular guide to Christian piety complained that the 'evill example' of members of the nobility and gentry as 'swearers, adulterers, carowsers, oppressors etc.' encouraged their social inferiors to follow suit, giving the impression that 'holy ordinances' were 'not matters of so great moment'.[51]

Within this framework the weighting of prescriptions for marital chastity, together with the measure of blame borne respectively by men and women, could be expressed in quite different ways. Although sin itself was not 'inherently gendered', blame was often discussed in gender-specific terms.[52] Manuals of marital advice aimed at house-holding, propertied groups in society often stressed that in terms of its material consequences, a wife's adultery was the more 'blameable' since it risked the issue of illegitimate children. A woman's adultery, warned Richard Allestree, had very serious repercussions for patriarchy, property and her spouse's reputation, 'robbing her husband of his posterity; obtruding a base and adulterous issue, and so stealing away his estate and inheritance by giving it to a stranger'.[53] The biblical precedent, that 'whatever springs from an adulterous bed is rarely of a long continuance', served to heighten the seriousness of female adultery amidst pervasive concerns in later seventeenth-century England about declining rates of fertility.[54] The story of Eve's deceit, together with humoral physiology that saw in women's weaker, cold and moist constitutions a propensity for sensuality and inherent lustfulness, provided further proof of the dangers, and ever-present risk, of female sexual excess.[55]

The duty of chastity fell particularly onerously upon women. Wives were required to maintain a 'chaste conversation' at all times, not simply 'refraining from adulterous practice' but also constantly deporting themselves in an 'honest and inoffensive' manner that would communicate 'inward purity'.[56] Chastity was a burden women were supposed to bear with pride. As Sir George Savile told his daughter, whatever 'disadvantage' women suffered by this double standard

---

[51] Lewis Bayly, *The Practice of Pietie: Directing a Christian How to Walke that He May Please God* (London, 1632), pp. 200–1.

[52] Anthony Fletcher, *Gender, Sex and Subordination in England 1500–1800* (New Haven, CT and London, 1995), p. 101.

[53] [Richard Allestree], *The Government of the Thoughts: a Prefatory Discourse to the Government of the Tongue* (London, 1694), p. 107.

[54] 'Castamore', *Conjugium Languens: or, the Natural, Civil and Religious Mischiefs Arising from Conjugal Infidelity and Impunity* (London, 1700), p. 9; Rachel Weil, 'Sexual Ideology and Political Propaganda in England, 1680–1714', PhD thesis, Princeton University (1991), p. 118.

[55] These stereotypes have been well rehearsed: see Ian Maclean, *The Renaissance Notion of Woman: a Study in the Fortunes of Scholasticism and Medical Science in European Intellectual Life* (Cambridge, 1980); Fletcher, *Gender, Sex and Subordination*, chs. 2–4.

[56] Fleetwood, *Relative Duties*, pp. 178, 188.

was 'more than recompenced, by haveing the honour of Families in [their] keeping'. Such rhetoric may have been designed to instil a particular sense of moral responsibility in wives by which they might shame an adulterous spouse. Some moralists explicitly asserted the right of a deceived wife 'by the reason of Gods law' to forbear sexual relations with her husband. Nevertheless, most placed a premium on a wife's patient bearing of her husband's faults in order, eventually, to reclaim him by her virtuous example.[57]

Pervasive as it was, however, this model of unchastity was not the only way in which authors of conduct literature gendered adultery. When writers approached the question of blame from the perspective of personal responsibility, rather than material consequences, they argued that men's adultery was the more serious. The privileged position of authority occupied by the husband in marriage necessitated that he set a virtuous example, and since it was believed that 'the husband hath generally more reason to restrain his exorbitant passions by', some commentators asserted that his adultery was logically the more blameworthy.[58] But a persistent theme in conduct literature was that men constantly needed to be persuaded of their responsibilities. When Richard Baxter listed ten 'Special Motives to perswade Men to the Holy Governing of their Families' in his *Christian Directory* (1673), he was implicitly acknowledging that men might need some encouragement to behave like patriarchs.[59] Although plays such as *King Lear* and *Much Ado About Nothing* had warned that problems such as bastardy might come back to haunt adulterous men, there was a feeling among authors of conduct literature that men were too apt to believe that their infidelities bore few tangible risks to their families. Consequently, moralists had to draw on different, more creative, strategies to persuade men of the necessity to remain faithful.

According to religious conduct literature, men as well as women posed 'domestic dangers' to the patriarchal family. The power traditionally conferred on men through marriage and becoming head of the household could present its own problems if it was not exercised carefully or accorded proper respect by husbands themselves. Patriarchal authority could breed arrogance or complacency in men with regard to their moral duties. For instance, Gabriel Towerson warned that husbands 'may arrogate to themselves a greater authority than ever God intended' which might be put to vicious ends. Similarly, William Fleetwood believed that men were 'not so much masters of themselves as they imagine', and 'they do not understand their power and strength sufficiently,

---

[57] George Savile, *The Works of George Savile, Marquis of Halifax*, ed. Mark N. Brown (3 vols., Oxford, 1989), II, p. 372; Fleetwood, *Relative Duties*, pp. 280, 289; cf. [Allestree], *The Ladies Calling*, pp. 168–9; William Thomas, *Christian and Conjugall Counsell, Applyed Unto the Marriage State* (London, 1661), p. 69.

[58] Gouge, *Of Domesticall Duties*, p. 219; Towerson, *Explication of the Decalogue*, p. 406.

[59] Richard Baxter, *A Christian Directory: Or, a Sum of Practical Theologie and Cases of Conscience* (London, 1673), pp. 512–15.

when they intend to be good husbands, and yet frequent the company of wicked women'.[60] Anxious to distance themselves from any semblance of a sexual double standard, moralists felt that the heinousness of male adultery had to be specially reiterated. Men were sometimes encouraged to try to empathise with the less powerful female members of the household to understand better their own responsibilities. In order to imagine both the personal injury caused by male adultery and its threats to patriarchal order, Fleetwood urged a husband to step back for a moment from the case of his own infidelity and

> consider it in the case of his mother or his own daughter, whether he would not think them injur'd in the highest manner, if either of their husbands should prove false and wander from their beds, in pursuit of unhallow'd pleasures; and just as he imagines they would take the falsehood and injustice of their husbands, let him imagine that his own wife takes his, and bears it with the same concern and heaviness.

If such thoughts moved him 'either to rage or pity' they might instruct him 'what deep wounds his own vile perjuries are dealing daily to his partner'.[61] Fleetwood's arguments appear to have been designed to appeal not only to men's feelings of protectiveness towards their female relatives, reminding them of their sense of duty, but also to a more submissive side, encouraging them to identify with those in a position of vulnerability, pain and powerlessness.

Concepts of civility bore especially heavily on moralists' discussions of male sexuality. Advice literature represented the male body as unruly and in need of taming. If, in theory at least, men were supposed to possess a greater capacity for reason than women, it was still a rationality that had to be learned and, once attained, guarded closely to prevent reversion into an uncivilised state.[62] The idea already explored that adultery threatened a person's 'dignity' had particular resonance in moralists' appeal to men of genteel status and reasserted the connection between matrimonial fidelity and social respectability.[63] There emerged in the period following the Restoration a particular genre of conduct literature aimed at gentlemen, in which civility became particularly prominent in fashioning both social and gender identity.[64] This literature had a hard moral edge. Sir George Mackenzie in his tract *Moral Gallantry* (1685) set out to prove that sexual immorality was not only sinful, but also unbecoming the civilised and well-bred 'man of honour'. Mackenzie drew on the writings of Seneca to

---

[60] Towerson, *Explication of the Decalogue*, p. 396; Fleetwood, *Relative Duties*, p. 323.

[61] Fleetwood, *Relative Duties*, pp. 320–1.

[62] Alexandra Shepard, 'Meanings of Manhood in Early Modern England, with Special Reference to Cambridge, *c*.1560–1640', PhD thesis, University of Cambridge (1998), ch. 1.

[63] Jonathan Barry, 'Bourgeois Collectivism? Urban Association and the Middling Sort', in Jonathan Barry and Christopher Brooks (eds.), *The Middling Sort of People: Culture, Society and Politics in England 1550–1800* (Basingstoke, 1994), pp. 84–112.

[64] Fletcher, *Gender, Sex and Subordination*, p. 323; Carter, *Men and the Emergence of Polite Society*, p. 32.

the effect that sin was a 'mean' thing and 'unworthy a Gentleman'. Whoredom was inconsistent with decorum, leading a man of honour to behave in a manner beneath himself. 'Doth not this Vice perswade men to lie in Cottages with Sluts, or (which is worse) Strumpets?' asked Mackenzie, '. . . to lurk in corners; to fear the encounter of such as know them, and to bribe and fear those servants, who by serving them at such occasions, have by knowing their secrets, attained to such a servile mastery over them; that I have been ashamed to hear Gentlemen upbraided by these Slaves'.[65]

As the period progressed, moralists began to supplement these warnings with more positive arguments against adultery, which appealed to men's humanity, fellow feeling and sense of justice. The central argument of the *Reformed Gentleman* (1693) was that vices such as swearing, drinking, whoring and sabbath-breaking were incompatible with the 'True Generosity of an English Man'.[66] Generosity was central to the principle of benevolent sociability that was at the core of emerging notions of politeness. It comprised a complex amalgam of virtues including 'a masculine Firmness and Constancy, Presence of Mind and Sweetness of Temper'.[67] Above all it involved taking 'all opportunities of doing what is Fit and Right, Good and Reputable, and of promoting the happiness of others'.[68] There was no true nobility or gentility without virtue, and refraining from vice was a means of increasing a man's self-esteem. The generous man would be respected for his 'kindness and beneficence to others' and his willingness to 'do right, both to himself, and likewise to everybody else'. It was therefore imperative to avoid all vices contrary to justice, including adultery, which injured another man by robbing him of his wife's affections.[69] By representing adultery as contrary to 'generosity', moralists highlighted the dangers of extra-marital sex both to homosocial relations of friendship and respect between men, and to a man's own feelings of worth and self-esteem. The message was that adultery was not just morally wrong, but beyond the pale of polite society.

MORAL AMBIGUITY AND THE LIMITS OF PRESCRIPTION

By the 1690s, the style, format and idiom of matrimonial advice were changing significantly. The most exciting and innovative of the new advice literature was John Dunton's hugely successful bi-weekly question-and-answer periodical, the *Athenian Mercury* (1691–7). Following a simple, yet original, format of answering questions submitted by its readers, the *Athenian Mercury* established a new trajectory in English publishing, setting a precedent that encouraged many

---

[65] George Mackenzie, *Moral Gallantry* (London, 1685), pp. 9, 51.
[66] A. M., *The Reformed Gentleman*, title page and pp. 55–92 *passim*.
[67] [John Somers], *A Discourse Concerning Generosity* (London, 1695), p. 14.
[68] *Gentleman's Magazine*, viii (1738), 62.
[69] [Somers], *Discourse Concerning Generosity*, pp. 66, 81.

imitators, most famously Daniel Defoe's *Review*, the *British Apollo* and the *Spectator* and *Tatler*. Letters were sent by penny post to Smith's coffee house in Stock's market where they were answered by a team of editors consisting chiefly of Dunton himself and his two brothers-in-law, the minister Samuel Wesley and the mathematician Richard Sault.[70]

With each copy retailing for a penny, the *Athenian Mercury* seems to have been aimed at a broad and inclusive readership. Though its circulation was largest in the capital, there is evidence that the paper was read beyond the metropolis, such as by the Sussex astrologer Samuel Jeake who records in his diary sending a letter to the journal on a scientific matter.[71] Although correspondence was printed anonymously, internal evidence from advertisements and the letters themselves suggests that correspondents, where identifiable, were drawn from a range of social groups from apprentices and household servants up to gentlemen, and also, crucially, included many women from an equally varied background. Of course, given the anonymity of correspondents and the paucity of general data about readership, it is impossible to verify the authenticity of the queries, whether they were the products of the editors' imagination or genuinely sent in by readers. It seems likely that Dunton and his colleagues may have at least edited letters for publication, but the sheer volume of correspondence dealt with by the *Mercury* would suggest that the majority of the letters were genuine.[72]

Questions were submitted on a wide range of intellectual, scientific, religious and practical topics. However, with its large number of queries relating to love and marriage the periodical predominantly served as a public forum for debating matters relating to domestic conduct and sexual morality. To cater for the popularity of these topics, the editors announced on 3 June 1691 that the issue of the first Tuesday of each month would be set aside to 'answer all the Reasonable Questions sent us by the Fair Sex, as also any others relating to love and marriage' and in February 1693 Dunton launched a short-lived spin-off publication, the *Ladies Mercury*, to answer similar queries.[73] It is evident that Dunton

---

[70] On the background, sale and distribution of the *Athenian Mercury* see Stephen Parks, *John Dunton and the English Book Trade: a Study of his Career with a Checklist of his Publications* (New York and London, 1976), ch. 3; Gilbert D. McEwen, *The Oracle of the Coffee House: John Dunton's Athenian Mercury* (San Marino, CA, 1972); Kathryn Shevelow, *Women and Print Culture: the Construction of Femininity in the Early Periodical* (London and New York, 1989), chs. 2 and 3; Helen Berry, '"Nice and Curious Questions": Coffee Houses and the Representations of Women in John Dunton's *Athenian Mercury*', *The Seventeenth Century*, 12 (1997), 257–76; Berry, 'Gender, Society and Print Culture in Late Seventeenth-Century England, with Special Reference to the *Athenian Mercury* (1691–97)', PhD thesis, Cambridge University (1998); Dabhoiwala, 'Prostitution and Police', pp. 248–53.

[71] Berry, 'Gender, Society and Print Culture', p. 40.

[72] Ibid., esp. chs. 1–2; Shevelow, *Women and Print Culture*, pp. 37–41.

[73] *AM* II/3, 3 June 1691. References to the *Athenian Mercury* are given in the form volume number/ issue number, question number (if applicable), date. The *Ladies Mercury* was published weekly, 28 February–17 March 1693.

intended his periodical to give women a unique forum for asking for advice on matters of courtship and marriage. Dunton and his fellow editors showed considerable sympathy for women stuck with profligate husbands and provided a public space for wronged wives to air their grievances. Yet matters of 'love and marriage' also attracted a great deal of correspondence from men, seeking help on such topics as cuckoldry, the legality of certain relationships with the opposite sex, and guidance on interpreting the mysteries of women's behaviour. Their letters reveal a popular sexual culture significantly removed from the world of street insult and tavern talk that historians have reconstructed using the records of defamation litigation, in which men appear as confident braggarts, secure of their place in the sexual system.[74] As we shall see, male correspondents, as well as their female counterparts, approached sexual relations tentatively, their letters conveying worries about the health of their souls, how their behaviour would be perceived by others and potentially damage their reputation and, in some cases, concerns about the consequences of their behaviour for the women involved.

The avowed aims of Dunton's 'question project' were didactic, 'to open the avenues, raise the Soul, as it were into Daylight, and restore the knowledge of Truth and Happiness, that had wandred so long unknown, and found out by few'.[75] In this respect, Dunton situated his publication at the vanguard of the campaign for moral reformation that emerged in the wake of the Glorious Revolution.[76] Indeed, Dunton gave a good deal of free publicity to the Societies for the Reformation of Manners that emerged in London during the decade and supported their efforts to suppress bawdy houses, swearing and drunkenness.[77] His career had been founded on the sale of sermons and religious tracts and much of the *Athenian Mercury*'s advice followed the conventional routes set out in standard manuals of practical devotion such as *The Whole Duty of Man*.[78] However, by virtue of its periodicity, Dunton envisaged the *Athenian Mercury* as playing a much more direct role in the lives of its audience than conduct books had done. More than a passive resource of advice, the periodical could perform a proactive role as an agent of moral regulation. From an early stage, Dunton championed the use of publicity and the printing press as a means of identifying and shaming offenders. In the issue of Saturday 8 August 1691, a female correspondent, 'plagued with an ill husband', was advised to show her spouse 'this *Mercury* and tell him if he don't amend his name shall be printed in't at length the first Tuesday of the next month'.[79] Although the fear of initiating libel actions probably accounted for the fact that no suspected malefactors were

---

[74] Cf. Laura Gowing, *Domestic Dangers: Women, Words and Sex in Early Modern London* (Oxford, 1996), ch. 3; Tim Meldrum, 'A Women's Court in London: Defamation at the Bishop of London's Consistory Court, 1700–1745', *London Journal*, 19 (1994), 10–11.

[75] John Dunton, *The Life and Errors of John Dunton, Citizen of London*, ed. J. B. Nichols (2 vols., London, 1818), I, p. 188.

[76] Dabhoiwala, 'Prostitution and Police', pp. 248–53.   [77] E.g., *AM* III/3, 4 Aug. 1691.

[78] *AM* VIII/5, q. 1, 26 Jul. 1692; IV/16, q. 2, 21 Nov. 1691.   [79] *AM* III/4, q. 2, 9 Aug. 1691.

ever actually named in this way, the threat of exposure was intended to be taken seriously. It was certainly consistent with the developing role of the press as an agent in law enforcement, with advertisements being placed in the London *Gazette* and other titles for the apprehension of malefactors or return of stolen goods.[80]

However, the intent of the periodical's editors was not shared by all its correspondents. Rather than simply seeking advice rooted in the platitudes of religious teaching, some correspondents demanded more pragmatic guidance. One writer, asking for help on how to disengage himself from 'an unlawful, tho' successful amour' with a married woman, told the editors that he knew full well 'the Sin I commit, as well as the Injury I do to the Husband', so instead demanded practical counsels, 'besides those prescrib'd by Religion'.[81] The *Athenian Mercury*'s avowed aim as an agent of moral reform and supporter of the Societies for the Reformation of Manners could be at odds with its policy of allowing readers to present their own versions of their problems which might include implicit or explicit questioning of the same moral standards the periodical was at such pains to uphold. For as well as being a decade of campaigns for moral renewal, the 1690s witnessed a greater questioning of religious and moral issues. The official sanctioning of a limited freedom of religious association by the Toleration Act of 1689, by removing the coercive powers of the Anglican church to regulate attendance at public worship, symbolically dealt a blow to claims to a unitary approach to religious and moral instruction. Although the granting of toleration was never intended as licensing a moral free-for-all, as some conservative Anglicans feared, it may have acted as a catalyst to encourage a more personal approach to matters of religion and morality, more conducive to individual conscience, needs and values rather than universal laws.[82] The *Athenian Mercury* functioned as a forum for setting the dictates of individual conscience against the time-worn prescriptions of religious teaching. Its letters highlighted vividly the tensions between human sympathies and moral judgement. In the process a more rounded picture of the problems surrounding adultery emerged, the limits of moral prescription were exposed, and the very meaning of extra-marital sex was interrogated.

This was especially apparent in cases of infidelity where the initial marriage contract was uncertain. The heinousness of adultery, as we have seen, was predicated on its dissolution of a covenant whose inviolability was rooted in

---

[80] Michael Harris, 'Timely Notices: the Uses of Advertising and its Relationship to News during the Late Seventeenth Century', in Joad Raymond (ed.), *News, Newspapers and Society in Early Modern Britain* (London, 1999), pp. 147–8.

[81] *AM* V/13, q. 1, 12 Jan. 1692.

[82] John Dunn, 'The Claim to Freedom of Conscience: Freedom of Speech, Freedom of Thought, Freedom of Worship?', in Ole Peter Grell, Jonathan I. Israel and Nicholas Tyacke (eds.), *From Persecution to Toleration: the Glorious Revolution and Religion in England* (Oxford, 1991), pp. 171–93; Dabhoiwala, 'Prostitution and Police', pp. 65–6.

human laws and divine commands. Could there be such a thing as 'conjugal perjury' if the legal status of the marital contract was in doubt? Queries relating to the validity of different varieties of conjugal union were a standard feature of seventeenth-century casuistical writing and the *Athenian Mercury* treated many cases of this kind.[83] In spite of the crucial social and symbolic importance of marriage, there was a good deal of legal ambiguity about what actually constituted a valid marital union.[84] A binding union could be created simply by verbal agreement in which an eligible man and woman took each other as man and wife using the words of the present tense. Although ecclesiastical law stipulated that contracts should be publicised by the calling of banns and solemnised by a priest in church before the congregation, an unsolemnised or 'clandestine' union, while considered irregular, might still be fully binding.[85]

Irregular marriages were becoming an important matter of public debate in the later seventeenth century. Common lawyers, spurred by statutory measures to tighten rules of evidence, increasingly insisted upon substantial (written) proofs that marriage contracts had been agreed. Bills to prevent unsolemnised marriages were proposed in Parliament on a regular basis throughout the later seventeenth century, albeit without legislative success.[86] By this time, however, the main concern was with an increasing number of marriages solemnised in private without the reading of banns, especially in London. Certain 'lawless' churches, falling outside the jurisdiction of the Bishop of London, such as St James's, Duke's Place and Holy Trinity in the Minories, became notorious after the Restoration for performing private marriage ceremonies. From the final decade of the century they were superseded by the marriage trade centred on the chapels of London's prisons, most notoriously the Fleet. By 1700 it is possible that up to 2,000 couples a year were availing themselves of the prison's marriage services. A brisk trade in blank marriage licences grew up in the capital – for ten shillings citizens could purchase a licence to solemnise matrimony without the reading of banns.[87] 'Private' marriages by licence had been unusually high in London throughout the seventeenth century and by the

---

[83] Thomas, 'Cases of Conscience', p. 46.

[84] For litigation arising out of disputed contracts see Ingram, *Church Courts*, ch. 6; Lawrence Stone, *Road to Divorce: England 1530–1987* (Oxford, 1990) pp. 67–81.

[85] Ingram, *Church Courts*, p. 190; R. B. Outhwaite, *Clandestine Marriage in England, 1500–1800* (London and Rio Grande, OH, 1995), pp. 1–17.

[86] Outhwaite, *Clandestine Marriage*, pp. 2, 13; Julian Hoppit (ed.), *Failed Legislation, 1660–1800: Extracted from the Commons and Lords Journals* (London and Rio Grande, OH, 1997), s.v. 'Law and order: marriages'.

[87] Outhwaite, *Clandestine Marriage*, pp. 19–49; Roger Lee Brown, 'The Rise and Fall of the Fleet Marriages', in Outhwaite (ed.), *Marriage and Society: Studies in the Social History of Marriage* (London, 1981) pp. 117–36; Jeremy Boulton, 'Clandestine Marriages in London: an Examination of a Neglected Urban Variable', *Urban History*, 20 (1993), 191–210; Boulton, 'Itching After Private Marryings? Marriage Customs in Seventeenth-Century London', *London Journal*, 16 (1991), 15–34.

Restoration had become 'a social custom of huge popularity' in the capital.[88] In the eighteenth century it was becoming apparent that things were getting 'out of control', finally prompting legislative action in the form of Hardwicke's Marriage Act of 1753.[89]

A number of reasons have been suggested for the spectacular growth of irregular marriages in this period, among them a wish to circumvent parental or official opposition to an intended union, attempts to protect the modesty of a pregnant bride, a desire to marry quickly or avoid gossip about an apparently mismatched union, and an increasing desire for privacy among the urban middling sort.[90] What is of more concern here are the implications of irregularity upon the social, cultural and legal assessment of sexual immorality and marital infidelity. Since the publicity of marriage was intended to prevent sinful or undesirable choices, irregular marriages were morally, as well as legally, contested territories.[91]

The *Athenian Mercury* devoted a whole issue on Tuesday 23 May 1693 to the practical, legal and moral ambiguities posed by a single case of clandestine marriage. It is especially revealing of the ways in which an irregular union blurred the boundaries between licit and illicit sexual relations. The correspondent described how he 'came in a very mean condition to a small Garrison in Their Majesties Dominions' where he became a servant to the Lieutenant, 'a person of good influence and power in that Place'. At length, he married a fellow servant with his master's 'encouragement and consent', but 'the ceremony was perform'd, tho by a Minister, yet very indecently, not in the Church, but in a mean Room in my Masters house'. Not long after the wedding he discovered that his wife was pregnant by his master but nevertheless 'for [his Master's] Honour and my Reputation, I conceal'd and own'd the child, and liv'd with the woman at least 7 or 8 years, in which time I had 3 children by her'. Despite the unfortunate revelation of his wife's pre-marital affair, the correspondent admitted that she was, after their marriage, never 'false to my Bed or Interest, but very Loving, obsequious and industrious'. In fact the union proved highly lucrative to him, for his master 'in order to make me amends for taking such crack'd ware off of [*sic*] his hands, kept me into some posts of good Advantage to me, whereby I was enabled to live handsomely, and sav'd money'.

---

[88] Boulton, 'Clandestine Marriages in London', p. 197. See also Peter Earle, *The Making of the English Middle Class: Business, Society and Family Life in London, 1660–1730* (London, 1989), pp. 178–80; Earle, *A City Full of People: Men and Women of London 1650–1750* (London, 1994), pp. 158–9.

[89] David Lemmings, 'Marriage and the Law in the Eighteenth Century: Hardwicke's Marriage Act of 1753', *Historical Journal*, 39 (1996), 345.

[90] Outhwaite, *Clandestine Marriage*, pp. 51–73; Boulton, 'Clandestine Marriages in London', pp. 202–10; John Gillis, 'Conjugal Settlements: Resort to Clandestine and Common Law Marriage in England and Wales 1650–1850', in John Bossy (ed.), *Disputes and Settlements: Law and Human Relations in the West* (Cambridge, 1983), pp. 261–84.

[91] Outhwaite, *Clandestine Marriage*, p. 4.

Following his master's death, however, the correspondent fell 'deeply in Love with a Man's daughter of the place', herself having a 'base child before I became acquainted with her, but she is now very constant to me'. Leaving his wife, he had made a verbal contract with this woman, laying himself under 'the sacred obligation of a solemn oath, to be true and constant to her, as she has likewise reciprocally done to me'. Since the correspondent was now 'censur'd for these my actions by some People', he turned to the *Athenian Mercury* for guidance on whether his marriage, by virtue of its clandestinity and the fact of his wife's ante-nuptial fornication, was technically illegal and thus offering sufficient grounds to marry his new lover. At the very least, he wondered whether it would allow him to leave his first wife and live with his new partner 'as my real wife in the sight of God'.

The case centred upon the common casuistical question of whether the adultery of one spouse released the other from conjugal vows. However, the two irregular marriage contracts which bookended the narrative problematised the question of how adultery itself was to be defined. For, as the editors put it in their reply (following the letter of ecclesiastical law), 'adultery being a breach of a marriage contract, does presuppose a contract, for there can be no breach of what is not'. The presentation of the case highlights particularly vividly how ambiguities in the law of marriage might create areas of moral ambivalence in which traditional codes could be adjusted to fit aberrant situations, needs and values. By setting one quasi-marital contract against another, the case raised questions about just where the transgression takes place: was it in the first marriage, told in a story of poverty, vulnerability and master–servant exploitation – yet solemnised by a priest and ultimately profitable – or in the second contract, undoubtedly irregular yet couched in the ennobling language of 'sacred obligation', 'solemn oath' and ardent and sincere love? In a lengthy and reflective reply, the editors stressed that though the first marriage was 'contrary to the Advice and Custom of the Church', it was none the less legally binding and, since it was solemnised by a priest, had been witnessed by God. The fidelity of his wife, combined with the fact that the correspondent had had three children by her, made amends for her original actions. Although conceding that he was 'unhandsomely dealt with at first', the editors told the correspondent that 'the Trick that was put upon you was owing to your own Indiscretion and Folly, that could not see through the Disguise and pretences'. They therefore urged him to 'go home, beg your wife's pardon, admonish the other woman of her sin, and by a better Life shew the Evidence of your Repentance towards God and the World, which you have injur'd by your example'.[92]

A significant number of matrimonial cases presented to the *Athenian Mercury* were concerned with the validity of different varieties of bigamous

---

[92] *AM* X/17, 23 May 1693. See also Ayliffe, *Parergon*, p. 50.

or quasi-bigamous union. These cases dovetailed with a broader set of questions concerning the extent to which adultery could ever be 'innocent' or even justifiable. Bigamy had long been associated with the ill effects of clandestine marriage and opponents of the practice argued that the uncertainty of wedlock facilitated secret remarriage, whether intentionally or not.[93] The Bigamy Act of 1604 had made it a felony to remarry during the lifetime of the first spouse, except where the husband or wife had been absent for seven years, the original marriage had taken place before one or both spouses had reached puberty, or the couple had been officially 'divorced' in an ecclesiastical court.[94] Prosecutions were regular but infrequent, and had an exemplary function.[95] However, high levels of migration and relatively poor communications throughout the seventeenth century made it relatively easy to contract multiple marriages, especially in the more anonymous environment of the metropolis.[96] At the same time information about an errant spouse was often unreliable, thus making it possible to contract a bigamous partnership unwittingly on the false assumption that one's spouse was dead, or to be duped into marrying someone not knowing that his or her spouse was still alive. Even as draconian a statute as the Adultery Act of 1650 had been forced to take cognisance of such potential areas of uncertainty and had contained clauses which absolved cases where the perpetrator did not know that his or her spouse was already married.[97]

Generally speaking, the editors of the *Athenian Mercury* treated sympathetically cases where ignorance of an absent spouse's whereabouts seemed genuine. A letter appearing on Saturday 18 June 1692 described a case in which a man who 'after one months cohabitation' with his wife 'resolved to forsake' her and in order that she 'might be married to another husband' sent her several counterfeit letters giving news of his death. Believing the letters to be genuine, 'and hearing nothing contrary for 4 years', his wife at length married another man, at which point he returned 'rejoycing that she hath another husband, that he may marry another wife'. The query was whether 'the woman continuing with the second husband, lives in Adultery'. The editors replied that 'the woman being right in her intention in marrying her second husband, because it was grounded upon the death of her first, therefore she being innocent there is no appearance of Adultery'. As for her first husband, 'his Fraud deserves not a new wife as a Reward, but a Celibacy during her life, which is the Punishment

---

[93] Ingram, *Church Courts*, p. 149. Similar arguments were made in support of Hardwicke's Marriage Bill in the 1750s: Lemmings, 'Marriage and the Law', p. 354.

[94] Ingram, *Church Courts*, p. 150; Phillips, *Putting Asunder*, p. 296. The use of the term 'divorce' in the Bigamy Act was ambiguous. It may have been intended to mean 'annulment' but was interpreted by the courts to include separation from bed and board.

[95] Phillips, *Putting Asunder*, pp. 296–300; Ingram, *Church Courts*, pp. 179–80; J. A. Sharpe, *Crime in Early Modern England 1550–1750* (London and New York, 1984), pp. 54, 66.

[96] Gowing, *Domestic Dangers*, p. 182; cf. Ingram, *Church Courts*, pp. 178–80.

[97] Thomas, 'Puritans and Adultery', p. 278.

of his own preparing'.[98] In this case, it was not only the husband's deception that absolved the wife's 'adultery', but also her general moderation and caution, doing everything possible to ascertain that the stories of her husband's death were true.

More contentious was the question of the extent to which bigamy or adultery might actually be justified by appealing to practical difficulties of obtaining a divorce which would legally permit remarriage. Bigamy had long been associated with problems of interpreting the letter of the law in cases of separation and divorce. Ingram has noted that confusion about the meaning of 'divorces' from bed and board (*a mensa et thoro*) pronounced in the church courts, which legally did not allow remarriage while both separated spouses were still living, might have underpinned some cases of bigamy in the late sixteenth and early seventeenth centuries.[99] In the *Athenian Mercury* and other publications of the 1690s and early 1700s, however, the main concern was with the ways in which the expense and practical difficulties of obtaining a divorce might act as an incentive to adultery, or might actually force people to take the law into their own hands and contract bigamous marriages or commence other unorthodox relationships. One of the queries posed by the servant who sought to dissolve his clandestine marriage, discussed earlier, was whether in view of the 'tedious and chargeable' and 'dilatory way' of the church courts he might by 'the law of conscience' live with the new object of his affections 'as my real wife in the eyes of God'.[100] Another letter described the case of a married man who, frustrated with the difficulties of securing adequate proofs of his wife's adultery necessary to get a divorce, wished to circumvent the law altogether and marry another woman, if necessary by removing his lover by 'force' to a 'remote place'.[101]

The backdrop of such issues was a much wider debate in the final decade of the seventeenth century about the nature, practicalities and legality of breaking the matrimonial contract. The legal arguments surrounding the forced abdication of James II, together with the long drawn out and heavily publicised attempts of the Duke of Norfolk to obtain a parliamentary divorce between 1692 and 1700, generated questions about whether all contracts, including the supposedly inviolable marriage contract, might be lawfully dissolved if one party breached the conditions.[102] The *Athenian Mercury* provided an outlet for this controversy. On the one hand, the editors upheld the ideal of the inviolable marriage contract and stressed that the proper tribunal for the hearing of matrimonial transgressions lay beyond death in 'the other world'. But on the other, they were prepared to concede that the present divorce laws offered little in the

---

[98] *AM* VII/24, q. 1, 18 June 1692.   [99] Ingram, *Church Courts*, p. 179.
[100] *AM* X/17, 23 May 1693.   [101] *AM* XVII/25, q. 7, 26 June 1695.
[102] Weil, 'Sexual Ideology', pp. 177–83; Stone, *Road to Divorce*, pp. 313–17.

way of practical remedy for injured parties and, being difficult to execute, might actually be 'kind' to adulterers and act as an 'encouragement to offenders'.[103]

The most interesting treatment of these matters occurred in a case presented to the *Athenian Mercury*'s spin-off publication, the *Ladies Mercury*, on Friday 10 March 1693. A writer describing himself as a 'man of honour' and the 'most faithful and fondest of Husbands' related how, after less than half a year of marriage, he happened to catch his wife 'in the very act of Adultery'. He responded to this awful discovery by turning his wife away from his bed, 'being neither obliged as a Gentleman or a Christian to take Infamy and Pollution into my Embraces'. However, by reason of the urgency of his sexual desire, being, as he put it, 'not able to live without a woman', he had taken a mistress. The correspondent declared his willingness to marry his lover, she being a 'companion so dear' to him, and live honestly, but he complained that, 'as the highest Favour the strait-laced Drs Commons will give me is a Divorce only *a mensa et thoro*, from my first hard bargain, that performance is above my power'. Given these circumstances he therefore questioned whether his affair was 'Adultery or not' (seeing that his wife's infidelity had theoretically dissolved the marriage contract), and sought the editors' opinion 'of our present Law that in cases of Adultery will no farther unty the Marriage-knot than by a separation only from bed and board'.

Although the editors reiterated that the correspondent's keeping of a mistress was immoral and liable to divine punishment, they conceded that his actions were a product of the failings of the law and showed considerable sympathy towards him. Agreeing with him that the present laws were but a 'weak piece of justice', they recognised that the granting of separation would simply allow his adulterous partner 'a licence to riot and revel in the full luxury of her sin, which possibly, under the roof of her husband, she could only snatch by starts and stealth'. The editors went even further by drawing attention to an apparent contradiction between divine law and human laws, arguing that 'as our Saviour admitted of a full Divorce for a Man to put away his wife, loosed from the Bond of Wedlock it self for Adultery', it was a 'very hard case' that 'Christ should grant that Dispensation, which a Christian Government and Christian Law condemns and denies us'.[104]

Correspondents also raised the question of how far bigamy or adultery might be justified by a sense of injury or by appealing to 'necessity'. The accent of these letters was on inversion, juxtaposing the overt cruelty or immoral

---

[103] E.g., *AM* IV/2, qs. 6 and 7, 3 Oct. 1691; III/13, q. 5, 8 Sept. 1691; VIII/25, q. 8, 22 Nov. 1692; XVIII/11, q. 3, 20 Aug. 1695.

[104] *Ladies Mercury* I/3, q. 2, 10 Mar. 1693. For a similar line of argument used in a later question and answer periodical see *British Apollo*, Supplementary paper no. 6, Sept. 1708. This controversy was reminiscent of the late sixteenth- and early seventeenth-century debate about remarriage after divorce for adultery: see Ingram, *Church Courts*, pp. 146–7.

behaviour of spouses with the apparent virtue and kindness of lovers. One correspondent described the predicament of a gentlewoman whose husband not only 'used her barbarously' and made her 'go in danger of her life' but also 'keeps a whore, refusing to live with her, but making her work for her bread'. Lately, however, she had received 'the offer of a single Gentleman that will maintain her very well' and therefore wondered whether 'it be any sin to accept of his kindness'. The injury of the husband's adultery and cruelty was heightened by the gentlewoman's economic misfortune and decline in social standing occasioned by her spouse's neglect. The attentions of her 'gentleman', in contrast, are presented as a means of restoring her to her proper status. As the editors pointed out in their response, the letter deliberately employed 'several ambiguous words' and 'fine clean language' to deflect the sense of sin, such as 'maintain' (normally used in the context of a husband's duty to look after his wife) instead of the more pejorative 'keeping' (as a mistress) and 'kindness' which might also be read as a sexual euphemism. They concluded that even if such an arrangement were innocently intended, it would at best be a 'dangerous experiment'.[105]

Other female correspondents used similar strategies to weight opinion in their favour. On Tuesday 26 July 1692 a 'young woman' described her predicament, having an 'intollerable Jealous Husband (without provocation I protest)' whom she had recently 'surpriz[ed] with a woman' and now 'being strongly solicited by a Gentleman much above my Quality, and extreamly obliging' sought advice whether she might 'lawfully yield him those Favours not fit to be mention'd here, and whether it wou'd be a crime, considering [her] Husband's provocation by Jealousie, as also his falseness'.[106] Another writer sought advice on behalf of a neighbour whose husband had 'abandoned her company' seventeen years previously to set up as a procurer for 'the lewd women of the town' and 'as she is informed, marry'd to one, (if not two since)'. Since she had now received 'the proffer of a good husband and fortune both' she asked whether it would be lawful to marry this man.[107] It was not just women who sought advice on these issues. Men who took in deserted wives and their children also displayed scruples of conscience. The *British Apollo* printed a letter from a man who cohabited with a woman 'in all respects a wife' and treated her and her children 'with the Affection of a Husband and Father', but was concerned whether he sinned against God 'by omitting the Ceremony of Matrimony'. In response, the paper's editors remarked that 'in a State of Nature' it would 'pass for a Marriage, since it Answers the ends of it', but by the letter of the Scriptures and the 'Laws and Restrictions of Civil Society', it was still 'fornication'.[108] Elsewhere in the same periodical, a gentleman forced to leave his wife by reason of her 'loose and Extravagant life' had formed an affectionate relationship with a 'very Good

---

[105] *AM* V/13, q. 2, 12 Jan. 1692.   [106] *AM* VIII/5, q. 1, 26 Feb. 1692.
[107] *AM* XIII/5, q. 4, 20 Feb. 1694.   [108] *British Apollo*, ii, no. 108, 3 Mar. 1710.

Gentlewoman who has got as bad a Husband as he has a [bad] Wife', and wished to cohabit with her. The query, whether this was 'no farther a Crime than the breach of the Law of the Land', implied a distinction between relationships that were thought to be morally right and those sanctioned by law alone.[109]

The plainest statement of this tension between official morality and moral sympathy was made in a letter printed in the *Athenian Mercury* on Tuesday 23 October 1693. The author, a 'gentlewoman of a small fortune', described how her husband had forsaken her and gone abroad, leaving her to fend for herself and her children. Being neglected by her husband's 'friends' and 'very chargeable and troublesome' to her own relatives, in the process losing their goodwill, she found herself in the position where 'a gentleman now Importunes me very much to be his Mistress' – a man whom she knew to love her 'passionately' and who would provide for her family. The choice, she wrote, was stark: 'either to yield to this Temptation, or see my Children starve?', adding that 'I know I ought not to do the least Evil that Good may come of it, but yet of two evils we must choose the least'.

While acknowledging that this was indeed a 'sad story' and wishing that 'it mayn't be true', the editors in answer to this and similar cases reiterated the over-riding authority of the Seventh Commandment, asserting that God's law allowed no 'proviso', 'restriction' or 'necessity' to sanction sinful actions.[110] Yet the construction of the subjects of these and other cases as passive victims of evil, 'forsaken' by their husbands, 'importun'd' by lovers, presented a challenge to ingrained assumptions concerning culpability and moral responsibility. As these publications began to explore more closely the actual circumstances of sexual immorality, so it became increasingly clear that older stereotypes of female lubricity failed to explain the complexity of extra-marital sex. Moreover, by appealing to extenuating social factors these cases questioned the extent to which people were personally responsible for their actions – adultery is presented more as a social problem than as a matter of personal sinfulness and moral depravity.[111]

Aside from questions relating to the practicality and lawfulness of certain unions, writers to the early periodical press sought advice on other matters that problematised meanings of adultery. One prominent theme focused on what theologians referred to as 'adultery of the heart' – lustful thoughts for another, albeit unconsummated. Thinking about someone else during lovemaking was traditionally seen as a dangerous activity for women due to concerns about the powers of maternal imagination. Popular works of medical folklore such as *Aristotle's Masterpiece*, first published in 1690, held that the features of children were believed to resemble whomever (or whatever) the woman imagined

---

[109] *British Apollo*, i, Supplementary paper no. 6, Sept. 1708.
[110] *AM* XI/25, q. 4, 23 Oct. 1693.   [111] Cf. Dabhoiwala, 'Prostitution and Police', pp. 174–89.

during conception.[112] For men, an active sexual imagination raised a different set of dilemmas concerning the point at which adultery was believed to begin. The issue was raised in Dunton's *Athenae Redivivae* in 1704, in a letter from a man who found his imagination wandering during conjugal sex from his 'dear consort' to his 'wife deceased, or . . . some other'. This was met with the standard moralists' response that adultery began at the point of intent rather than actual consummation 'for he that Lusts after a Woman, wants nothing to the Consummation of the Act, but some Convenient Circumstances'.[113]

More complicated (and rather far-fetched) was a case described in the *Athenian Mercury* for 14 July 1691, which related how a man had fallen in love with his wife's maid and arranged an assignation with her in a 'dark Cellar'. However, the 'honest maid' acquainted her mistress with the man's design, and the wife decided to take the maid's place in the cellar. Doing so 'with that cunning, that her Husband perceived not his mistake', the wife allowed her spouse to make love to her, whereupon he 'being more vigorous than ordinarily, by the strength of Fancy, he got his Wife with Child of two Boys'. Was it adultery and were these children bastards? The editors replied that without doubt the man had 'committed Adultery with his own Wife', but it was much harder to determine the legitimacy of the children since his wife's intentions were 'honest'. The children were bastards only in respect of their father's 'intentionality'.[114]

The new periodical press probed a series of ancillary ethical dilemmas raised by adultery. The ubiquity of servants and apprentices in households even relatively low down the social scale meant that adultery affected the lives of many innocent bystanders. Servants who witnessed their master's or mistress's adultery were placed in a difficult position, often involving a conflict of loyalty. Revelation of the affair might result in the break-up of the household that was both their home and source of livelihood.[115] In July 1692 an apprentice told the *Athenian Mercury* that he had accidentally surprised his mistress in bed with a gentleman lodger, who had offered him a guinea not to divulge the affair. Having scruples of conscience about whether he should have accepted the bribe, or should now reveal the affair, he sought the opinion of the paper's editors. They

---

[112] Paul-Gabriel Boucé, 'Imagination, Pregnant Women and Monsters in Eighteenth-Century Britain and France', in G. S. Rousseau and Roy Porter (eds.), *Sexual Underworlds of the Enlightenment* (Manchester, 1987), p. 94; Roy Porter and Lesley Hall, *The Facts of Life: The Creation of Sexual Knowledge in Britain, 1650–1950* (New Haven, CT and London, 1995), chs. 1–3.

[113] *Athenae Redivivae: Or the New Athenian Oracle* (London, 1704), pp. 113–14. See also *AM* XIII/9, q. 8, 6 Mar. 1694.

[114] *AM* II/15, q. 7, 14 July 1691. For variations of this story see the *Secret Mercury*, no. 3, 23 Sept. 1702; *The Honest London Spy, Discovering the Base and Subtle Intreagues of the Town* (London, 1706), pp. 83–114.

[115] Tim Meldrum, *Domestic Service and Gender 1660–1750: Life and Work in the London Household* (London, 2000), ch. 4. Some of these issues are examined further in chapters 3 and 5 below.

told him in no uncertain terms that he ought to try to urge the guilty couple
to reform their ways or else discover them to the authorities. By accepting the
money he was nothing but a 'partner in their wickedness, by keeping it conceal'd to others'.[116] Elsewhere, however, periodicals urged a more pragmatic
approach to disclosure. The more moderate *British Apollo* advised that servants
should never reveal a master's or mistress's affair to 'the Party injur'd' without
'Mature Deliberation' or the 'Advice of a Faithful Friend', and urged caution,
for 'in many Circumstances the Injur'd Party may be more happy in the suppos'd
Innocence of their Adulterous Mate, than under the torture of so Ungrateful a
Disclosure'. It was only if the deceived spouse faced 'ruin' as a result of the
affair that it should be revealed.[117]

An intriguing variation of this dilemma was revealed in a letter sent to the
Athenian Mercury in October 1694 by a man who confessed to 'Deluding a
married woman', but now aimed to repent his sins. Desiring to receive Holy
Communion, which he could only do if he were at peace with his neighbours, he
asked whether he should first reconcile himself to the cuckolded husband, who
remained ignorant of the affair. Such an exposure, he admitted, was likely to
'make a difference between [husband and wife], which instead of extenuating,
may add to the Enormity'. Perhaps feeling that the correspondent's story about
taking communion was somewhat disingenuous, the *Athenian Mercury*'s editors
answered in more general terms about the need for repentance and the ethics
of revelation. To inform the husband of the affair, albeit in order to beg his
pardon, would undoubtedly 'encrease' the injury done to him, 'for it wou'd
give him continual disquiets, and the Trespass being of such a Nature as you
can never repair, or make any Satisfaction for, 'tis much better concealed than
discovered'. The best he could do, therefore, was to be 'silent in [his] repentence'
and encourage his partner to make a 'thorough reformation'.[118] Adultery could
thus expose tensions between religious concerns and more pragmatic matters
of neighbourliness, charity and care for another's emotional well-being. Also
at stake was the bigger question of whether or not adultery should be made
public – and therefore invite punishment by the courts – or kept as a private
matter for personal repentance. The message conveyed here was that adultery
was more a matter for personal conscience than for official regulation.

SOCIABILITY AND ADULTERY IN THE EIGHTEENTH CENTURY

The emergence of question-and-answer periodicals in the last decade of the
seventeenth century marked a watershed in the literature of advice. Although

---

[116] *AM* VIII/5, q. 5, 26 July 1692. [117] *British Apollo*, Supplementary paper no. 5, Aug. 1708.
[118] *AM* XV/14, q. 2, 20 Oct. 1694.

sermons and religious conduct books continued to warn against adultery with time-worn admonitions, new genres of advice literature permitted a greater questioning of these rules by a literate and increasingly diverse audience that was becoming more independent in its approach to moral issues. It is true that works such as the *Athenian Mercury*, Defoe's *Review* and the *British Apollo* arose from a long-established casuistical tradition in which divines were called upon to probe the grey areas of personal morality or 'cases of conscience'.[119] But while the editors of the new periodicals frequently drew upon scriptural teach-ings and popular theology to answer readers' questions, the context was increas-ingly secular, or at least religiously pluralistic. Question-and-answer periodicals were not just remnants of an older tradition, but products of a changing cultural atmosphere in the late seventeenth and early eighteenth centuries generated by changes in the social milieu which demanded a broader reassessment of sexual and social mores.

The ongoing development of arenas of polite sociability, such as the pleasure gardens, theatres and assemblies of London and provincial resorts, together with the round of visiting that glued together polite social relations, called for a renewed definition of virtuous relations between the sexes congruent with refined social ideals. All forms of social contact and gestures were dissected in the context of polite sociability. A central assumption of the advice literature that burgeoned in England between the 1690s and the mid-eighteenth century was the notion that the behaviour of individuals should vary according to their place in society and should be conformable to their immediate social milieu.[120] John Brewer has recently suggested that, as a result, conduct came to be judged not by its conformity to universal moral laws but on the more subjective basis of how it affected others.[121] 'By manners I do not mean morals', wrote Joseph Addison in the *Spectator*, but 'Behaviour and Good Breeding, as they show themselves in the Town and the Country'.[122]

This should not be interpreted as an abandonment of moral absolutes in favour of unrestrained relativism. As we have seen, moralists could appeal to 'polite' notions of accommodation and benevolence to others to buttress their attempts to reform male manners. However, the line between vice and virtue became increasingly debated as authors accepted that it could be determined by social context and relations between the parties involved. Few examples illustrate this better than a case considered in the *Review* periodical in its supplementary issue for November 1704. The correspondent, 'C. D.', urged the paper's editors

---

[119] Thomas, 'Cases of Conscience', p. 55; Starr, *Defoe and Casuistry*, pp. 1–50.

[120] Childs, 'Prescriptions for Manners', p. 95.

[121] John Brewer, *The Pleasures of the Imagination: English Culture in the Eighteenth Century* (London, 1997), p. 106.

[122] *Spectator*, I, p. 486; cf. Martin Ingram, 'Reformation of Manners in Early Modern England' in Paul Griffiths, Adam Fox and Steve Hindle (eds.), *The Experience of Authority in Early Modern England* (Basingstoke, 1996), pp. 52–4.

to settle a wager of whether a 'woman that would permit a Man to sit upon her Bed, after she is in it, and the whole Family before that time being gone to rest, would not, in all likelihood, admit him in some time to the same'. In response, the *Review* began by rebuking the correspondent and his friends for their implicitly negative view of female virtue, which, it argued, was quite unjustified as men were frequently the 'aggressors' in matters of illicit sex. But returning to the matter in question, it argued that no straightforward answer was possible. The act itself might be unorthodox or imprudent, but the 'character' of those involved had to be considered, for 'if he was a Man of known Vertue and Modest Character, the Freedom, tho' unusual, might have no more Scandal, than if the Person had not been in Bed; for what signifies the Accidents of Place and Posture?' In fact, the paper argued, 'the exact Rules, the stated Bounds or Preliminaries of Vice and Virtue, have never yet been settled', and while some might style such 'common undesigning freedoms' as 'vitious Excursions' their interpretation depended much on circumstances.[123]

The growing social imperative to behave with decorum was represented as making people more self-conscious about their behaviour. This is illustrated by, among other examples, the rash of letters sent to periodicals about the propriety of kissing as a form of greeting between men and women who were not blood relatives. Kissing was a common form of salutation in early modern England and foreign visitors to the country in the sixteenth and seventeenth centuries frequently remarked on the lack of inhibition displayed by its inhabitants.[124] Yet letters to the periodical press from the 1690s onwards present a growing anxiety with the interpretation of this gesture. In April 1695 a correspondent described in the *Athenian Mercury* how the wife of 'a very intimate aquaintance' would insist on being very 'familiar' in her behaviour towards him, 'insomuch that if I don't kiss her, she'll kiss me, and other great familiarities'. Her husband, 'an infirm man', seemed 'very well pleas'd with our conversation', but the correspondent felt uncomfortable, for he was a 'single man, and wou'd not be rude'. Here, 'rude' has a double meaning: to discourage her kisses might be interpreted as a social rebuff, yet the correspondent was anxious to avoid imputations that their kissing implied 'rude' behaviour of another kind, the cuckolding of a man by all accounts incapable of satisfying his wife sexually. Although such kisses were not 'directly criminal', the editors responded, 'yet the consequences of 'em are so dangerous, and so plain in view' that the correspondent should try 'by all means to change such a course of life' for the sake of his 'own Honour or Happiness'.[125]

---

[123] *Review*, I, Supplement 3, Nov. 1704, pp. 20–1.
[124] William Brenchley Rye (ed.), *England as seen by Foreigners in the Days of Elizabeth and James the First* (London, 1865), pp. 90, 260–2; cf. Paul Langford, *Englishness Identified: Manners and Character 1650–1850* (Oxford, 2000), p. 163.
[125] *AM* XVII/7, q. 5, 23 April 1695. See also VI/7, q. 5, 23 Feb. 1692.

Politeness involved a good deal of watchfulness over oneself and others. Without proper care every social familiarity was apt to be distorted by jealous spouses and by the 'nice and censorious' who were apt to turn 'a visit into an Intrigue, and a distant salute into an Assignation'.[126] In November 1712 a correspondent writing to the *Spectator* periodical under the pseudonym 'Philagnotes' related the unfortunate consequences of a visit to see his female cousin in town. During the visit he had spent three hours alone with her, which, as he later discovered, had sent her husband into a jealous rage. While they were together the suspicious spouse had listened at the door to their conversation, and in his fit of jealousy had imagined that his wife was conversing not with her cousin, a 'beardless stripling', but with a 'rakish gay Gentleman of the Temple'. Finally, his suspicions seemed to be confirmed by the cousins' 'parting kiss' which, the correspondent believed, 'mightily nettles him and confirms him in all his Errors'. The correspondent learned that ever since that 'fateful afternoon', his cousin had been 'most inhumanly treated' by her husband, who had 'publickly storm'd' that he had been made a cuckold. 'Philagnotes' protested that his behaviour was consistent with the tradition of kissing as a common and broadly accepted mode of salutation and was concerned that 'this Accident may cause a virtuous Lady to lead a miserable life with a Husband, who has no grounds for his Jealousy'. Yet the fact that his behaviour could be perceived as causing a scandal led the correspondent to seek the advice of the paper's editors as to whether 'the general Custom of Salutation should excuse the Favour done me' or else they should 'lay down Rules when such Distinctions are to be given or omitted'.[127]

Authors of didactic literature of the eighteenth century utilised this concern with discretion and social propriety in their advice to married couples. Guides to marital relations in the early eighteenth century placed considerable emphasis on the usefulness of qualities developed in the realm of social interaction to the conduct of relations between husbands and wives. Although many writers viewed the domestic sphere as affording greater scope for intimacy and the expression of feelings, the qualities that were learned and cultivated in social life, in particular an awareness of the sensitivities of others, good-natured 'easiness', modest respectfulness and moderation, were acclaimed by conduct writers as important for the protection of mutual affection and the stability of marital relations.[128] Eustace Budgell wrote in the *Spectator* that love was

---

[126] N. H., *Ladies Dictionary*, p. 169; *Spectator*, IV, p. 113.

[127] *Spectator*, IV, pp. 378–9. On these issues more generally see David M. Turner, 'Adulterous Kisses and the Meanings of Familiarity in Early Modern Britain', in Karen Harvey (ed.), *The Kiss in History* (Manchester, forthcoming).

[128] Edmund Leites, 'Good Humor at Home, Good Humor Abroad: the Intimacies of Marriage and the Civilities of Social Life in the Ethic of Richard Steele', in Edward A. and Lillian D. Bloom (eds.), *Educating the Audience: Addison, Steele and Eighteenth-Century Culture* (Los Angeles, CA, 1984), pp. 51–89, esp. p. 59. See also Amanda Vickery, *The Gentleman's Daughter: Women's Lives in Georgian England* (New Haven, CT and London, 1998), p. 202.

'banished' from the marriage state by husbands and wives observing 'too great a familiarity, and laying aside the common rules of Decency'.[129] In 1739 an essay outlining the principles of 'Matrimonial Decency and Civility', published in the weekly essay periodical the *Universal Spy*, argued that though 'the Matrimonial intimacies between a Man and his Wife may discharge them of much of the bondage of ceremony in the circumstances', this was not a licence to privately treat each other with 'rudeness and indecency' or 'want of manners'. The key to successful marital relations was not the kind of familiarity which bred contempt, but an 'Abundance of Discretion, as well as Affection' to 'preserve the rules of Decency, and to keep up the Bounds of Modesty in their Family Conversation'.[130]

Husbands and wives were also encouraged to exercise discretion in their behaviour in company and in particular to regulate their 'familiarities' so they would not prove offensive to others or even encourage vice. On the one hand, excessive displays of affection in public were considered a 'great offence'. The *Ladies Dictionary* argued that 'a Man ought not to embrace his Wife without a flattening kind of severity: For this publick Billing sheweth the way to unexperienc'd youth to commit Riot in private'. Public displays of affection not only showed a disregard for the sensibilities or moral health of others, but also lowered the threshold of shame with the result that 'little by little, [matrimonial] chastity is abolish'd'.[131] On the other hand, conduct writers complained of the apparent tendency of some married people who, in order to 'avoid the Appearance of being over-fond', treated each other with reserve, indifference, or even 'exasperating Language' or outright contempt.[132] Such behaviour was considered a breach of decency and modesty and liable to endanger matrimonial harmony and encourage adultery.[133]

When it came to fundamentals, the marital advice available in the early eighteenth century was not radically removed in substance from that supplied by Puritans in the first wave of conduct literature produced a century earlier. Authors did not abandon the principle that adultery was morally and socially wrong, and that all due care should be taken that relations between the sexes remained free from the taint of vice and lure of temptation. Yet the tone of this literature, and the media of expression, were changing. Traditional religious sources of marital advice saw adultery as both personally and socially destructive, its effects rippling outwards to destroy the love between man and

---

[129] *Spectator*, IV, p. 295. See also *Universal Spectator*, ed. Henry Stonecastle (2 vols., London, 1736), II, p. 83.
[130] *Universal Spy; Or, The London Weekly Magazine*, 26, 5 Oct. 1739, 252–4, quoting at 253, 254.
[131] N. H., *Ladies Dictionary*, p. 155; see also *Spectator*, III, p. 72.
[132] *Tatler*, II, p. 333.
[133] *Universal Spy*, 26, 5 Oct. 1739, 252–4; Defoe, *Conjugal Lewdness*, p. 73.

wife, and the stability of neighbourhoods, communities and the polity at large. In an attempt to persuade people to chastity, sermons and books of religious devotion emphasised both the importance of love and fidelity to one's spouse, while simultaneously warning in providential terms of the social catastrophe of extra-marital sex. Over the course of the period, however, the emphasis of marital advice literature gradually began to shift. Concepts of civility played an increasingly prominent role in persuasions against adultery. In pulpit rhetoric, adulterous sex had long been associated with the bestial, and since the Elizabethan homilies moralists had associated a firm policy against vice with the values of civilised society. But as the period progressed, civility began to be used more subtly, and apparently more socially exclusively, in moral prescription. In a new genre of conduct literature emerging after 1660, aimed at fashioning the polite gentleman, writers counselled against adultery by appealing to men's generosity, humanity and fellow feeling. The impulse to virtue should come from within, from a social desire to be accommodating to others and do right by one's fellow man, rather than through fear of providential discovery or punishment by judicial authorities. This adds further support to the notion explored in chapter 1 that the elite increasingly needed to be addressed in a different moral language from the rest of society. Beyond this, the periodical press of the eighteenth century increasingly stressed the importance to relations between husbands and wives of qualities developed in the public sphere of social interaction. Respect towards one's spouse, a key dissuasive against adultery, was re-cast in terms of ideals of decorum and politeness.

At the same time, publications such as the *Athenian Mercury* enabled increasing levels of popular involvement in moral debate. Letters to periodicals reveal a willingness of ordinary men and women to question customary moral precepts and raise tensions between official morality and moral sympathy. The frankness of their letters shows that beneath the elite, men and women were less bound by polite ideals of restraint and decorum in discussing intimate matters. Their correspondence began to reveal the full complexity of extra-marital sex, showing that people might have an affair for reasons as varied as economic necessity, emotional fulfilment, even as result of confusion about what adultery actually meant. They demonstrate an increasingly complex social world in which traditional rules of conduct did not easily fit individual circumstances. But elsewhere in popular culture there was a tradition of inverting official values and testing the limits of moral teaching. Adultery was not just a topic for solemn pronouncement, but also a regular source of entertainment and laughter in early modern England. It is to the inverted, comic world of cuckolding humour that we now turn.

3. Cultures of cuckoldry

On a trip to London in August 1661 the Dutch artist and traveller William Schellinks paid a visit to 'Cuckold's Haven', a point on the Thames near Deptford. The promontory had a special significance in the popular culture of seventeenth-century England, being the place where, as legend had it, since the time of King John the cuckolded husbands of London had gathered early in the morning of 18 October to parade to the 'horn fair' at Charlton. As accounts of the fair reported, the men were instructed to come 'well fitted with a Basket, Pick-Axe and shovel' and then march to nearby gravel pits to 'dig sand and gravel for repairing the foot-ways' so that their wives and their wives' gallants 'may have pleasure and delight in walking to horn fair'. This task completed, the crowd of husbands, wives and lovers passed through Deptford and Greenwich Heath, where skirmishes were apt to break out between the women, wielding ladles, and their hapless spouses.[1] Although such accounts seem to have had little basis in fact, an annual fair did indeed take place at Charlton which acquired a reputation for boisterous debauchery. It is not known whether descriptions of such events had led Schellinks to include Cuckold's Haven on his itinerary, but he appears to have been impressed and bemused by the curious sight he witnessed on arrival. 'A tall flagpole stands there', he recorded in his journal, 'to which horns of all kinds and descriptions are fixed, in honour of all the English cuckolds or horn carriers (of whom there are quite a few in London!), and the English have much fun and amusement with each other, as they pass by and doff their hats to all around'.[2]

'Cuckoldry' was conceptually different to 'adultery' in that it deflected the sinfulness of marital infidelity by mocking the follies or inadequacies of the adulteress's husband. The horn-laden pole at Cuckold's Haven was but one

---

[1] *A General Summons for those Belonging to the Hen-Peckt Frigat, to Appear at Cuckold's Point on the 18th of this Instant October* (London, n.d. [*c*.1680]); see also Elizabeth A. Foyster, *Manhood in Early Modern England: Honour, Sex and Marriage* (London, 1999), pp. 110–11.

[2] William Schellinks, *The Journal of William Schellinks' Travels in England, 1661–1663*, trans. and ed. Maurice Exwood and H. L. Lehmann, Camden Society, 5th ser., 1 (London, 1993), p. 47.

aspect of a shared culture of insults, jokes, ballads, plays and proverbs that poked fun at deceived husbands and their faithless wives which flourished in early modern England.[3] Cuckolding jokes appear to have been popular at all social levels, judging from the numerous jests recorded on the topic in gentry commonplace books, the 'prodigious crowds' of metropolitan citizens and apprentices who flocked to see Edward Ravenscroft's bawdy farce *The London Cuckolds* each Lord Mayor's Day from its debut in 1682 until 1751, and the mocking ballads and libels of plebeian composition which circulated in the taverns and streets of early modern England.[4]

But in spite of its ubiquity, cuckoldry remains an elusive phenomenon. While mocking a man for his wife's supposed infidelity remains a powerful mode of insult in modern southern European societies such as Italy, Spain and Portugal, in Britain the cuckold's horns have virtually disappeared as a gesture of abuse or source of 'fun and amusement'.[5] How, then, is the seventeenth-century fixation with cuckoldry to be explained? Why did people find it so funny? What meanings did cuckoldry hold in the minds of contemporaries and how did these change over time? Such questions lie at the heart of this chapter.

As with marital advice, thinking about cuckoldry in the later seventeenth and early eighteenth centuries was influenced by a proliferation of genres deliberating on the fate of the wronged husband. The later seventeenth century is regarded as marking the apogee of cultural interest in cuckoldry. Alongside the ubiquitous cuckolding comedies on stage, jestbooks and ballads, appeared pseudo-scientific tracts about the properties of horns and proto-anthropological discussions of the varieties of cuckoldry in European and more 'exotic' societies. These texts debated the nature of cuckoldry and its bearing on male sexual honour. At the same time, comic literature and social documentaries used cuckold humour to explore a range of social tensions. By the end of the seventeenth century the new periodical press began to allow deceived husbands to present alternative stories of infidelity which challenged the clichés of cuckoldom and elicited sympathy for their circumstances. As well as explaining the popularity

---

[3] For examples see John Wardroper (ed.), *Jest Upon Jest: a Selection from the Jestbooks and Collections of Merry Tales published from the Reign of Richard III to George III* (London, 1970), pp. 28–61; Morris Palmer Tilley (ed.), *A Dictionary of the Proverbs in England in the Sixteenth and Seventeenth Centuries* (Ann Arbor, MI, 1950), nos. C876–C889.

[4] Nicholas L'Estrange, *'Merry Passages and Jeasts': a Manuscript Jestbook of Sir Nicholas L'Estrange (1603–1655)*, ed. H. F. Lippincott (Salzburg, 1974), *passim*; Harold Love, 'Who were the Restoration Audience?', *Yearbook of English Studies*, 10 (1980), 28; Allan Botica, 'Audience, Playhouse and Play in Restoration Theatre, 1660–1710', DPhil thesis, University of Oxford (1985), p. 119; *Tatler*, I, p. 72 (28 Apr. 1709); *London in 1710, From the Travels of Zacharius Conrad von Uffenbach*, trans. and ed. W. H. Quarrell and Margaret Mare (London, 1934), p. 38; Adam Fox, 'Ballads, Libels and Popular Ridicule in Jacobean England', *PP*, 145 (1994), 47–83.

[5] Desmond Morris, Peter Collett, Peter Marsh and Marie O'Shaughnessy, *Gestures: Their Origins and Distribution* (London, 1979), p. 131.

of concepts concerning cuckoldry, therefore, this chapter examines the forces that would challenge its status as a source of 'fun and amusement'.

THE NATURE OF CUCKOLDRY

The common image of the cuckolded husband was one of humiliation and degradation. Such was the discomfort associated with the condition that some writers made the word 'cuckold' literally unspeakable. Thus when Mr Modern, the central figure in Henry Fielding's play *The Modern Husband* (1731), considers prostituting his wife to a rich suitor as a means of paying his gambling debts, he 'cannot name the title' that other people would call him for his despicable conduct. Elsewhere in literature, more innocent victims of adultery also found the word painful to utter. When one of Moll Flanders's lovers relates the story of his wife's infidelity that led to the collapse of his marriage, Defoe's heroine observes that when he described himself as a 'cuckold' he did so 'in a kind of Jest, but it was with such an awkward smile, that I perceiv'd it was what stuck very close to him, and he look'd dismally when he said it'.[6]

The starting point for understanding the shame associated with the cuckolded husband, who was, after all, the apparent victim in the adulterous triangle, was the familiar notion that marriage was a process in which men and women metaphorically became 'parts of the same body and the same flesh'. As we saw in the previous chapter, for a bachelor getting married and setting up a household provided the gateway to patriarchal society, central to the very process of becoming a man. Yet a married man's public standing and, by the logic of the 'one flesh' model, the very integrity of his sense of self, was constantly at risk from his relationship with his wife. There was a strong connection between male honour and the body. The anxiety of cuckoldry was expressed first and foremost in terms of dehumanisation. The humiliation suffered by a man through his wife's adultery was imagined in terms of a physical loss, in which part of his body was metaphorically surrendered to another man. 'I cannot but pity and lament', wrote the editor of the *Post Angel* periodical in June 1701, addressing one 'Mr S.', married to an unfaithful partner, 'that your own Bosom is false to you; that your self, with shame and with Sin, was pull'd from your self, and giv'n to whom you wou'd not; an Injury that cannot be parallell'd upon Earth.'[7] Cuckoldry exposed the limits of men's control over their wives' bodies, and with it the fragile basis of their selfhood. Cuckolds were described in satirical literature as incomplete men, for instance as 'eight times less than another man'.[8]

---

[6] Henry Fielding, *The Modern Husband* (1731), in *The Works of Henry Fielding Esq.*, ed. Leslie Stephen (10 vols., London, 1882), II, p. 149; Daniel Defoe, *The Fortunes and Misfortunes of the Famous Moll Flanders* (1722), ed. G. A. Starr (Oxford, 1971), p. 135.

[7] *Post Angel*, June 1701, 410.   [8] *Poor Robin's Intelligence*, 22 May 1676.

Given that protestant prescriptions for marriage placed a high premium on reciprocity, it was considered possible, at least technically, for a woman's reputation and self-esteem to be damaged by her husband's infidelity. For some writers the idea that women might be mocked as 'cuckqueanes' – the female equivalent of the cuckold – and wear the horns for their husbands' infidelity was an intriguing possibility. In Shakespeare's *Much Ado About Nothing*, for instance, Beatrice responds to the accusation that she will not attract a husband for being 'too curst' and 'shrewed' of tongue with the punning riposte that 'God sends a curst cow short horns – but to a cow too curst he sends none'. For Beatrice, being 'too curst' (shrewish and domineering) was a strategy for avoiding marriage and with it the potential 'curse' of being made a cuckold by her husband.[9] The topic was treated at greater length in William Percy's 1601 play, *The Cuckqueanes and Cuckolds Errants*, in which the audience is invited to laugh at the parallel deception exercised by husbands and wives in two married couples.[10]

Admittedly, however, such dubious displays of sexual equality were extremely rare and the phenomenon of women being mocked as 'cuckqueanes' was very seldom considered in popular literature.[11] By the inverse logic of the sexual double standard, horns had sometimes been depicted as growing from women's heads to signify their own infidelity. It was suspected that the 'myraculous and monstrous' phenomenon of a crooked horn that grew from the forehead of a sixteenth-century Montgomeryshire woman, Margaret Griffiths, was divine punishment for her 'light behaviour' that made her husband believe she had 'given him the horn[s]'. But these images were also comparatively rare and seldom found in the later seventeenth century.[12] When in 1676 a 'Strange and Wonderful Old Woman', apparently living at the Swan Inn in Charing Cross, was discovered with what seemed to be a pair of horns growing out of her head, the popular pamphlet recording the phenomenon made no reference at all to cuckoldry or infidelity as a possible explanation. Had a horned old *man* been found there instead, it seems inconceivable that such references could have

---

[9] Anne Parten, 'Beatrice's Horns: a Note on *Much Ado About Nothing*, II.i. 25–27', *Shakespeare Quarterly*, 35:2 (1984), 201–2.

[10] William Percy, *The Cuckqueanes and Cuckolds Errants, or the Bearing Down the Inne*, ed. John Arthur Lloyd (London, 1824).

[11] For later examples see *The Horn Exalted, Or Roome for Cuckolds. Being a Treatise Concerning the Reason and Original of the Word Cuckold and Why Such are said to wear Horns* (London, 1661), Preface (unpaginated); Alexander Oldys, *The Female Gallant: Or, the Wife's the Cuckold. A Novel* (London, 1692). Cf. Laura Gowing, *Domestic Dangers: Women, Words and Sex in Early Modern London* (Oxford, 1996), p. 63.

[12] *A Myraculous and Monstrous but yet most True and Certayne Discourse of a Woman . . . in the midst of whose Forehead (by the wonderful work of God) there groweth out a Crooked Horne of Four Inches Long* (London, 1588), sig. A2v. See also Alexandra Walsham, *Providence in Early Modern England* (Oxford, 1999), pp. 199–200. For a later depiction of horned adulteresses see the illustrations to *A General Summons to all the Hornified Fumblers, To assemble at Horn Fair October 18* (London, n.d. [*c*.1830]).

been avoided.[13] Just as the consequences of men's and women's adultery were fundamentally different, so it was difficult to equate male and female cuckoldry or speak of it in the same terms. This is surely a reflection of the ways in which honour and reputation could be gendered in early modern England, with an overwhelming emphasis in discussions of female dishonour on the effects of a woman's unchastity. In the body paradigm a wife's adultery corrupted the flesh, while the husband, as the head, was held in contempt for being unable to prevent it. Cuckoldry exposed the failure of manly reason to subordinate the (feminine) sensual parts. In answer to a reader's query 'Why Cuckolds are said to wear Horns, and not their wives?', the *British Apollo* explained that 'tho' a Man and his Wife are but one Flesh, yet the Husband is the Head, and must consequently wear the Horns, by the Law of Nature'.[14] Thus it was the husband, owing to his privileged position in patriarchal marriage, who was most liable to be ridiculed for cuckoldry.

The depiction of cuckolded husbands wearing horns was central to the image of cuckoldry as a dehumanising condition. Records of defamation and marital litigation in the church courts reveal that in the towns and villages of early modern England a deceived husband might find himself stigmatised by the hanging of animal horns or antlers on his house – a practice that continued well into the eighteenth century.[15] Since cuckoldry was frequently linked to a husband's poor sexual performance, it makes sense to explain cuckold's horns as 'phallic symbols which made a man a fool because of their lack of potency'.[16] Lacking the insights of Freudian psychology, however, contemporaries turned to other explanations. Several publications devoted themselves to exploring the origins and meanings of this symbol. *The Horn Exalted*, an 84-page treatise on this subject published in 1661, explained that horns might signify the infamy of cuckoldry by resembling a device by which a man's predicament might be 'trumpeted' to the world.[17] Moreover, in classical mythology horns were dedicated to Diana, the moon goddess, who punished men who fell into her disfavour by turning them into horned beasts. Most famous of these was Actaeon, turned into a stag and torn apart by his own dogs after the goddess caught him gazing on her while bathing. Descriptions of cuckolds as 'Actaeons' implied that cuckoldry was a natural punishment for men's lusts. The story also conveyed women's powers to effect men's destruction. In keeping with his gloomy advice to his son

---

[13] *A Brief Narrative of a Strange and Wonderful Old Woman that hath a Pair of Horns Growing Upon her Head* (London, 1676).

[14] *British Apollo*, i, no. 2 (18 Feb. 1708).

[15] Martin Ingram, 'Ridings, Rough Music and the "Reform of Popular Culture" in Early Modern England', *PP*, 105 (1984), 79–113; Foyster, *Manhood*, pp. 107–15; David Underdown, *Revel, Riot and Rebellion: Popular Politics and Culture in England 1603–1660* (Oxford, 1985), pp. 100–3; E. P. Thompson, *Customs in Common* (Harmondsworth, 1991), pp. 467–531; Fox, 'Ballads, Libels and Popular Ridicule'.

[16] Foyster, *Manhood*, p. 108.   [17] *Horn Exalted*, p. 13.

that marriage was a 'bottomlesse pit, out of which no repentance can bayle you', Francis Osborne likened the condition of married men to the fate of Actaeon, liable to be 'torne [apart] by our Families'. References to the moon also associated cuckolds' horns with 'lunacy' – husbands driven to jealous distraction by worries about their wives' conduct were described as 'horn mad'.[18]

Horns gave the cuckolded husband a bestial character. Plays and ballads frequently likened cuckolds to 'passive' beasts, either complacent towards, or stupidly unaware of their spouses' infidelities. Domesticated horned animals, such as cattle or sheep, were 'tame, and easier to be govern'd', just as cuckolds, being 'loving and good natur'd', were easily deceived.[19] 'There is not in nature so tame and inoffensive a beast as a London cuckold,' remarks a character in Thomas Shadwell's bawdy comedy *Epsom Wells* (1673).[20] Yet a further resemblance between horned husbands and the devil meant that there was something monstrous about deceived men. A cuckold was a 'Civil[ised] Monster and a Rational Beast', wrote one pamphleteer in 1700, 'patched up between Action and Forbearance, which by his Impotence and his wife's Incontinence is soon brought to perfection'.[21] It was this association with monstrosity which provides the key to understanding why cuckoldry might be regarded with fear but also generate derisive laughter. The monstrous horned husband symbolised the horror of dehumanisation brought about by the failure of manly reason and loss of control over his wife's body. Since Aristotle, there had been a close connection between laughter and deformity. Thomas Hobbes, for instance, wrote in *Leviathan* that laughter derived from 'the apprehension of some deformed thing in another'.[22] Horns wrote the cuckold's infamy on his body and provided a catalyst for laughing at him.

However, although cuckoldry might be represented as a degrading experience, there were a number of means by which it was thought its effects on a man's self-esteem might be mitigated. A series of proverbial expressions that 'cuckolds come by destiny', or that marriage was a 'lottery' and, being 'made in heaven', was subject to providential influence, suggested that cuckoldry was

---

[18] Ibid., pp. 12, 23, 26; [Francis Osborne], *Advice to a Son; or Directions for Your Better Conduct through the Various and Most Important Encounters of this Life* (London, 1656), p. 55; Anne Parten, 'Falstaff's Horns: Masculine Inadequacy and Feminine Mirth in *The Merry Wives of Windsor*', *Studies in Philology*, 82 (1985), 184–99.

[19] *Horn Exalted*, p. 9.

[20] Thomas Shadwell, *Epsom Wells* (1673), in *The Complete Works of Thomas Shadwell*, ed. Montague Summers (5 vols., London, 1927), II, p. 117.

[21] *The Lively Character of a Contented and Discontented Cuckold* (London, 1700), p. 1.

[22] Thomas Hobbes, *Leviathan: Or the Matter, Forme and Power of a Commonwealth Ecclesiastical and Civil* (1651), ed. C. B. Macpherson (Harmondsworth, 1968), p. 125. See also Daniel Wickberg, *The Senses of Humor: Self and Laughter in Modern America* (Ithaca, NY and London, 1998), p. 47.

potentially the fate of Everyman but was essentially beyond men's control.[23] A man's patient bearing of his wife's faults was seen as a sure means of achieving salvation. 'Since Cuckolds all to Heaven go', ran the 'text' of a mock cuckold's sermon of 1704,

> Why should we grieve for being so?
> Exalt your Horns, lead patient lives,
> And praise the mercies of our wives.[24]

The simple fact that no man could ever be certain of his wife's fidelity or that his children were his own, generated a *frisson* which goes some way towards explaining the long-term popularity of cuckolds as a source of comic entertainment. William Hickes's popular collection of *Oxford Jests* contained numerous variations on this theme. One comic tale concerned a man who went hunting with his dog, which happened to be called 'Cuckold'. When they returned, the dog ran on ahead: '"Oh mother," said the man's son, "Cuckold's come." "Nay then," says the Mother, "your Father is not far off, I am sure."' In another story a man told his wife, 'that he heard for certain, that they were all counted cuckolds in their Town', apart from one man. Asking her who she thought it might be, she replied rather more equivocally than he would have liked, 'Faith ... Husband, I cannot think who it is.'[25]

While on the one hand such jokes and proverbs may have expressed male vulnerability, such ideas might be used on the contrary as an argument to diminish the sense of shame associated with the cuckoldry. Thus *The Horn Exalted* reassured its readers that, since cuckoldry was often a matter of 'misfortune', it was in essence no 'dishonour'.[26] Rather than going in constant 'fear' of the horns, being a cuckold was a condition that men were expected to be able to cope with and even laugh about; another proverb said that 'a malcontented cuckold has no wit'.[27] The 'fun and amusement' that William Schellinks observed on his visit to 'Cuckold's Haven' seem to be indicative of the good-humoured way in which imputations of cuckoldom could be taken once removed from the actual context of infidelity. Cuckoldry was not only something for which some men might be stigmatised, but also a joke in which all men might participate, however uneasily. It was frequently portrayed in popular literature as representing (albeit ironically) a bonding experience for men. Horned husbands were depicted as

---

[23] Tilley (ed.), *Dictionary of Proverbs*, nos. C889, M681, M682, M688, M680; *British Apollo*, i, 50, 4 Aug. 1708.

[24] 'Dr Make Horns', *The Cuckold's Sermon Preach'd at Fumbler's-Hall on Wednesday the 18th of October Being Horn-Fair Day* (London, 1704), title page.

[25] William Hickes, *Oxford Jests, Refined and Enlarged*, 13th edn (London, n.d. [c.1725]), pp. 52, 97. For earlier versions of the latter see John Taylor, *Wit and Mirth*, in *The Works of John Taylor the Water Poet, Reprinted from the Folio Edition of 1630* (London, 1868–9), p. 359.

[26] *Horn Exalted*, p. 77.   [27] Tilley (ed.), *Dictionary of Proverbs*, no. C883.

joining together as 'brethren' in 'clubs', 'societies' or mock chivalric 'forked orders', presenting the condition as an inclusive and unifying experience.[28]

Although in one sense cuckoldry was a leveller, liable to affect all walks of life 'from the throne to the cottage', there was a great deal of interest in comparing and contrasting different types of cuckold.[29] Though in practice people may have been less discerning in their treatment of cuckolded husbands, some social commentators argued that cuckoldry should not be viewed in monolithic terms, universally causing mockery and automatically damaging reputation, but more as a matter of degrees.[30] Throughout the seventeenth century chapbooks, ballads and almanacs employed familiar vocabularies of social differentiation to distinguish various 'orders', 'sorts' and 'degrees' of cuckold. *The Tincker of Turvey* (1630), a popular chapbook parody of *The Canterbury Tales*, listed 'eight orders of cuckolds'. They included 'a winking cuckold', who turned a blind eye to his wife's infidelity, an 'antedated cuckold', no doubt an ageing lecher with a young bride, and the more intriguing-sounding 'cuckold and no cuckold' – a man whose irrational jealousy made him assume the role of cuckold regardless of his wife's fidelity.[31] Likewise the *Poor Robin* almanac for 1699 listed in verse nine 'sorts' of cuckold:

> The Patient Cuckold he is first
> The Grumbling Cuckold one o'th' worst,
> The Loving Cuckold he is best,
> The Patient Cuckold lives at rest,
> The Frantick Cuckold giveth blows,
> The Ignorant Cuckold nothing knows,
> The Jealous Cuckold double twang'd.
> The Pimping Cuckold would be hang'd,
> The Skimington Cuckold he is one,
> And so I think their number's done.[32]

---

[28] E.g., *British Apollo*, i, 47, 23 July 1708; *General Summons for those Belonging to the Hen-Peckt Frigat, to Appear at Cuckold's Point*; *Bull-Feather Hall: Or, The Antiquity and Dignity of Horns, Amply Shown* (London, 1664); Coppelia Kahn, *Man's Estate: Masculine Identity in Shakespeare* (Berkelely, CA and London, 1981), pp. 124–5.

[29] [Edward Ward], *Nuptial Dialogues and Debates: Or, an Useful Prospect of the Felicities and Discomforts of a Marry'd Life, Incident to All Degrees from the Throne to the Cottage* (2 vols., London, 1710).

[30] Cf. Foyster, *Manhood*, p. 7.

[31] *The Tincker of Turvey* (London, 1630), Contents [no pagination]. For other examples see *Poor Robin's Jests, Or the Compleat Jester. The Second Part* (London, 1669), p. 31; *AM* XVII/11, q. 4, 7 May 1695. On languages of social differentiation see Keith Wrightson, '"Sorts of People" in Tudor and Stuart England', in Jonathan Barry and Christopher Brooks (eds.), *The Middling Sort of People: Culture, Society and Politics in England 1550–1800* (Basingstoke, 1994), pp. 28–51.

[32] *Poor Robin, 1699* (London, 1699). See also Bernard Capp, *Astrology and the Popular Press: English Almanacs 1500–1800* (London, 1979), p. 124.

This kind of classification was stimulated over the course of the seventeenth century by a developing intellectual interest in cross-cultural comparison and by the growing importance of 'manners' as a means of contrasting the customs of different societies and as a tool of social differentiation. Mock learned treatises such as *The Horn Exalted* demonstrated that just as there were many different kinds of horned beasts, each with its own anthropomorphic characteristics, so the world was populated by different kinds of horned men. The goat, it argued, symbolised lascivious men taking voyeuristic pleasure in their spouses' adultery, for 'when a goat is at any time prevented of his sport' by a rival, 'he opens his mouth and gapes, and shewes his teeth as if he laugh'd'. Bulls, on the other hand, apt to wear themselves out in search of fresh pastures, warned men that their own ramblings away from home in search of new mates and consequent neglect of their wives might lead to their horning.[33] Horns were ambiguous symbols. Comparison with other societies showed that they might have more positive connotations. Among 'Indians', the treatise argued, elephant horns were used as love tokens and signs of virility, while in Spain, Germany and Venice horns were emblems of political power.[34] Authorities on dream interpretation also concurred that if a man dreamt that a pair of horns grew out of his head, this signified not dishonour, but that he was headed for greatness, since 'Horns are generally esteemed both the Defence and Beauty of horned cattle; and therefore may well be thought to signify Dominion and Grandeur'. Instead, dream lore associated blocked noses with cuckoldry – sensory deprivation that made a man unable to smell a rat.[35] The Old Testament also associated horns with divinity and pre-eminence. Horns, as *The Horn Exalted* surmised, might thus symbolise 'both for honour and disgrace'.[36]

Though it may have provided cold comfort for actual men suffering the ignominy of their wives' infidelity, commentators clearly believed that some cuckolds were considered to be more despicable, and worthy of derision, than others. The worst variety was the 'pimping cuckold' – a man who conspired in his wife's adultery for profit. The root of this man's dishonour lay not so much in the ease with which he was dispossessed of his wife, as in the fact that he was guilty of aiding and abetting a sexual offence which was still liable for prosecution in the ecclesiastical courts. 'Wittols', willing or 'contented' cuckolds who did nothing to hinder their wives' infidelities, shaded into this category as well.[37] The distinction between 'wittol' and 'cuckold' was important.

---

[33] *Horn Exalted*, pp. 20, 22–3; cf. Keith Thomas, *Man and the Natural World: Changing Attitudes in England 1500–1800* (Harmondsworth, 1983), p. 38.

[34] *Horn Exalted*, pp. 10, 34.

[35] *Nocturnal Revels: Or, A Universal Dream Book* (2 vols., London, 1706–7), II, pp. 91, 123.

[36] Psalms lxxv. 10; Ruth Mellinkoff, *The Horned Moses in Medieval Art and Thought* (Berkeley, CA and London, 1970); *Horn Exalted*, p. 32.

[37] Martin Ingram, *Church Courts, Sex and Marriage in England, 1570–1640* (Cambridge, 1987), ch. 9; Foyster, *Manhood*, pp. 197–8.

Stigmatising with a special term the man who knew and accepted he was a cuckold, or even profited from it, seemed to alleviate some of the blame of other cuckolds who were either unaware of their wives' infidelity or unwilling to let it pass uncensured. Some commentators also believed that a husband's mistreatment of his wife, although providing no excuse for her adultery, might at least justify shame and reproach for her cuckolded spouse. Responding to a query about whether it was 'just that a poor innocent Cuckold should bear the infamy when the persons who confer it upon him seem to be only guilty', the editors of the *Athenian Mercury* stated that 'the husband deserves no infamy in the matter, excepting so far, as by his own perfidy, or ill treatment of his wife, he has been partly the cause of the address of another, who will be sure not to omit anything that lies in his power to add to her felicity'.[38]

Though it was believed that many cuckolded husbands were natural and deserving targets of ridicule, there were some famous examples of cuckolds who had managed to avoid its stigma. A repeated theme across a range of later seventeenth- and early eighteenth-century publications was that historically there had been many 'men of honour' whose eminence and authority had not been diminished by their being cuckolds. Answering the question, 'Whence comes the word Cuckoldry, and whether it is in all Cases so Infamous as is generally esteemed?', the editors of the *Athenian Mercury* wrote that cuckoldry was 'not that Dishonour as is usually thought, because not so esteemed universally'. Figures from Roman antiquity such as Pompey, Caesar, Augustus, Lucullus, Cato and others provided examples of men who had remained 'Honourable' in spite of their wives' adultery, having the 'fate' of cuckoldry, but not suffering its 'Infamy and Scandal'.[39] Similarly, in October 1739, the *Universal Spectator* advised a cuckolded husband that 'Pompey, the Conqueror of so many Kings; Cicero, the Father of Eloquence, and Caesar, Master of the Universe, had all of them Wives that prov'd errant Jilts; yet we don't find they thought themselves the worse for it, or flew into Extravagances like the petty Cuckolds of the present Times.'[40] The chorus of a popular mid-eighteenth-century song, 'He that a Cuckold is, let it not grieve him', urged that the cuckold's condition 'is not to be scorned', for 'Caesar and Pompey were both of them horned'.[41]

These examples suggest that a man's rank and social reputation could play a crucial role in determining whether he would be mocked as a cuckold. Remarking on the marriage of the Duke of Richmond to Charles II's mistress, Frances Stuart, in March 1667, Samuel Pepys noted that the duke's 'quality'

---

[38] *AM* XVII/11, q. 4, 7 May 1695.   [39] *AM* I/20, q. 1, n.d. [*c.* May 1691].
[40] Cited in the *Gentleman's Magazine*, ix, Oct. 1739, 530.
[41] *The Merry Man's Companion, And Evenings Agreeable Entertainer: Containing Near Six Hundred of the very Best and most Favourite Songs, Catches, Airs etc. Now in Vogue* (London, 1750), p. 157.

might stop people ridiculing the match, whereas 'had a meaner person married her, he would for certain have been reckoned a cuckold at first dash'.[42] But in this case it was the king's rank that was the real deciding factor. By marrying a royal mistress, and by implication inviting the king to make him a cuckold, Richmond might be viewed as seeking 'honour' and royal favour by his own horning. At the highest levels of society rank seemed to rewrite normal codes of sexual reputation.

Becoming obsessed with fears of cuckoldry – whether real or imagined – was presented as dangerous and debilitating to manly reason, preventing men from functioning properly in public life. Some argued that cuckoldry was essentially a state of mind, that 'he's no cuckold who not thinks he's such'.[43] Men who had a morbid fascination with cuckoldry were especially comical, as the numerous jealous husbands who populated Restoration comedy testified. The humour of representing jealous husbands derived from the irony that, no matter how severe their methods for keeping their wives chaste, they were ultimately bound to end in precisely the result they were trying to prevent. Following the conventional wisdom that 'cuckolds make themselves', plays mocked men who exercised their patriarchal role in a peculiarly heavy-handed manner, endorsing instead the view of Alithea in William Wycherley's *The Country Wife* (1675) that 'Women ... are truest still to those that trust 'em.'[44] A correspondent asking the *Athenian Mercury* in October 1692 whether he remained a cuckold even after the death of his unfaithful wife was told facetiously that such a question might demand an answer 'from the very Center of Metaphysicks', before being informed in much plainer terms that 'the Whore being dead which made the poor Querist a Cuckold, he ceases to bear that opprobrious name'.[45]

In cuckolding jokes the extent to which the husband deserved derision crucially depended upon how he reacted when faced with the realisation of his wife's infidelity. While cuckoldry challenged masculinity, it also gave deceived husbands an opportunity to act like real men and take suitable action. Ironically, therefore, the extreme circumstances of being made a cuckold provided an extraordinary occasion for a dramatic assertion of manhood. Being (quite literally) the climactic scene of many cuckolding narratives, the cuckold's discovery of his wife and her lover in the sexual act offered a crucial test of his resolve. The popular image of the lover caught with his trousers down offered two different kinds of laughter: on the one hand the cuckold-maker's raised buttocks presented a defiant, mocking gesture, literally showing bare-faced cheek

---

[42] Cited in Faramerz Dabhoiwala, 'The Construction of Honour, Reputation and Status in Late Seventeenth- and Early Eighteenth-Century England', *TRHS*, 6th ser., 6 (1996), 204.

[43] E.g., *Bull-Feather Hall*, p. 4; *Universal Spy; Or, The London Weekly Magazine*, XXV, 28 Sept. 1739, 244.

[44] Wycherley, *Country Wife*, V. iv. 384.   [45] *AM* VIII/11, q. 4, 4 Oct. 1692.

to the man he has cuckolded. But on the other hand they suggested vulnerability, presenting a target upon which the husband could wreak his revenge.
Thus one story reported in the humorous journal *Poor Robin's Intelligence* in
June 1676 related how a shoemaker of White Hart Yard in London discovered
his wife in bed with a lover. The husband's swift act of revenge, in which he
'handsomely curried [the workman's] hide and sent him packing', was treated
approvingly for it adeptly managed the situation in such a manner as 'neither
to publish his Wife's faults or his own shame' and made the cuckold-maker the
figure of fun.[46] Swift action proved that a man was not 'contented' with his
cuckoldom.

In contrast, husbands who displayed incompetence when faced with the
dreadful discovery, in particular those who publicised their shame through
their undisciplined reactions, were stock butts of laughter. Cuckolding humour
thrived on the number of ways in which a husband might bring his wife's adultery to the attention of the wider community. Another tale from *Poor Robin's
Intelligence* mocked a husband whose loud exclamations upon discovering his
wife in bed with her lover led to the 'great disturbance of the neighbourhood',
thus alerting others to his fate. Elsewhere, a tailor of Covent Garden found his
wife in bed with his journeyman and 'considering [that his wife] had such a
reputation in the Neighbour-hood that he doubted no body wou'd believe' that
she was adulterous, locked the errant couple in his bedchamber and fetched
several neighbours to witness the scene. While such a discovery might enable
the tailor to be proved 'a cuckold by witness', and thus provide a basis for future
legal action by which he might be 'reveng'd of his Chapman for having taken
toll without his leave', his actions only served to bring his own inadequacies,
the fact that he is but 'the ninety-ninth part of a man', to the attention of his
neighbours.[47]

CUCKOLDRY A LA MODE

The strength of patriarchal household prescription and the ensuing dilemma
facing men of balancing the duties of trust and mutual obligation outlined in
domestic advice literature with a culturally ingrained distrust of female sexuality, contributed to cuckoldry's enduring success as comedy. Mockery of
deceived or dominated husbands dramatised the incongruity between how marital relations ought to be conducted and how, in practice, they might turn out to
be.[48] There was also undoubtedly an element of *schadenfreude*, or what Hobbes

---

[46] *Poor Robin's Intelligence*, 26 June 1676.   [47] Ibid., 11 Sept. 1676; ibid., 17 July 1676.
[48] Anthony Fletcher, 'Men's Dilemma: the Future of Patriarchy in England, 1560–1660', *TRHS*,
6th ser., 4 (1994), 61–81; J. A. Sharpe, 'Plebeian Marriage in Stuart England: Some Evidence
from Popular Fiction', *TRHS*, 5th ser., 36 (1986), 87; Elizabeth Foyster, 'A Laughing Matter?
Marital Discord and Gender Control in Seventeenth-Century England', *Rural History*, 4 (1993),
5–21.

described as 'sudden glory', to laughing at the misfortunes of other men, tinged with patriarchal unease.[49] But cuckolding comedy also thrived on its ability to adapt familiar themes and tropes to contemporary concerns. There was no 'pure' form of the cuckolding joke. On the one hand, early modern humour worked through the constant retelling, adaptation and appropriation of stock characters, themes and plots – many of which had a heritage traceable to classical literature and medieval fables.[50] Repetition served the purpose of recognition essential to generating a comic register and conditioning a humorous response to marital discord. Language also played an important role in this respect. Cuckoldry developed its own terminology for adultery and its victims – cuckolds were variously described as members of a 'hornified brethren', a 'forked order', or as 'horn bearers', 'cornutos', 'fumblers' and 'fribbles', words which instantly signified a response to infidelity far removed from the pages of sermons or religious conduct literature. On the other hand, cuckoldry, like other topics of humour, also depended on what Ronald Paulson has termed the 'peripheral' elements of the comic structure, topical allusions to social life which contributed significantly to its interpretation.[51] Paraphrasing the eighteenth-century satirist Thomas Brown, cuckolding comedy worked by being something 'very Ancient, and yet always New'.[52]

Perhaps the most obvious way in which cuckolding humour established points of contact with the wider world was by setting its plots of marital discord in recognisable social milieux. Spatial signifiers had traditionally played an important role in comedy, giving comic stories a feeling of authenticity which supported humorists' claims that comedy mirrored life.[53] Ballad-writers had sometimes reinforced their claims to be telling the 'truth' by setting their narratives in specific locations – Samuel Pepys's collection of ballads included songs about cuckolds in Norfolk, Newcastle, Taunton, Lancashire and various parishes in and around London.[54] Though cuckoldry was never represented as an exclusively urban phenomenon, what is striking about the cuckold humour of the later seventeenth century is its distinctly metropolitan tone. Building on

---

[49] Foyster, *Manhood*, p. 114.

[50] Roger Thompson, *Unfit for Modest Ears: a Study of Pornographic, Obscene and Bawdy Works Written or Published in England in the Second Half of the Seventeenth Century* (Basingstoke, 1979), pp. 96–7; [Edward Ward], *Female Policy Detected: Or, the Arts of a Designing Woman Laid Open* (London, 1712), pp. 56–8.

[51] Ronald Paulson, *Popular and Polite Art in the Age of Hogarth and Fielding* (Notre Dame, IN and London, 1979), p. 76.

[52] Thomas Brown, *Amusements Serious and Comical, Calculated for the Meridian of London* (London, 1700), p. 7. See also Johan Verberckmoes, *Laughter, Jestbooks and Society in the Spanish Netherlands* (Basingstoke, 1999), p. 28.

[53] Mariet Westermann, *The Amusements of Jan Steen: Comic Painting in the Seventeenth Century* (Zwolle, 1997), p. 115.

[54] *The Pepys Ballads*, ed. W. G. Day (5 vols., Cambridge, 1987), I, pp. 400, 402, 408; IV, pp. 122, 123, 125, 127, 134, 141, 145, 147, 150, 152.

the success of Renaissance 'city' comedies, the capital became increasingly important as a site for cuckold humour as the seventeenth century progressed, as London's role as the social hub of the nation developed.[55] The outwitting of the husband by his errant wife and her wily lover had traditionally been at the crux of this humour, and laughter was elicited by the seemingly infinite number of ways in which this could be achieved. Cuckolding humour thrived in an atmosphere where the possibilities for deception were rife. Underlying the popularity of cuckolding humour in this period was a widely held assumption that with the advent of fashionable urban society opportunities for committing adultery were on the increase.

Metropolitan society appeared to offer new freedoms for women to develop social lives away from their homes and their husbands' gaze. Evidence from letters and diaries show that genteel women visited parks, promenades and pleasure gardens unchaperoned by their husbands or male relatives. They also went to the theatre or concert hall with other women and paid regular visits to the houses of their friends and acquaintances, which might occasionally cause their husbands some disquiet.[56] In comic literature, the emerging network of pleasure gardens, theatres, music houses and assemblies represented increased liberty for wives (and some husbands) to deceive their spouses, while the annual onset of the London 'season' revitalised opportunities for erotic encounters with strangers of a kind ill-afforded by country living. Lady Cockwood in Sir George Etherege's play *She Would if She Could* (1668) listed 'the Plays, [St James's] Park, and Mulberry Garden' as places where a wife might go to 'indulge the unlawful passion of some young gallant'. The play also contains an assignation scene set at New Spring Garden.[57] Such locations became notorious in satirical literature as the hunting grounds for sexually rapacious young men, and as places where a wanton wife might go to find an 'Am'rous Beau'.[58] The vogue for women to attend such places wearing masks, a fashion aped by prostitutes, contributed further to their reputation as sites for extra-marital engagement under the protection of anonymity.[59]

The fashionable milieu of Restoration comedy was a *moral* as well as a topographic universe, the 'Town' it described existing as much as an imagined

---

[55] Theodore B. Leinward, *The City Staged: Jacobean Comedy, 1603–1613* (Madison, WI and London, 1986); John Twyning, *London Dispossessed: Literature and Social Space in the Early Modern City* (Basingstoke, 1998), p. 13.

[56] Joyce Ellis, '"On the Town": Women in Augustan England', *History Today*, December (1995), pp. 20–7; Susan E. Whyman, *Sociability and Power in Late-Stuart England: the Cultural World of the Verneys 1660–1720* (Oxford, 1999), pp. 93, 141; David Roberts, *The Ladies: Female Patronage of Restoration Drama* (Oxford, 1989), ch. 2.

[57] Etherege, *She Would if She Could*, III. iii. 340–1.

[58] Ibid., I. i. 154–61; [Edward Ward], *The Modern World Disrob'd: Or, Both Sexes Stript of their Pretended Vertue* (London, 1708), p. 202.

[59] Terry Castle, *Masquerade and Civilisation: the Carnivalesque in Eighteenth-Century English Culture and Fiction* (Stanford, CA, 1986), p. 39.

space of sexual opportunity as it did as a concrete reality.[60] It comprised not only the gentrified West End of London but also the expanding spa resorts of Epsom, Tunbridge and Bath. Epsom Wells was described as a place where 'Gallants are generally more free, and expect less ceremony in order to a familiarity' than other places, a space where the elite might taste the sexual freedoms commonly associated with the lower orders, allowing 'Ladies and Gentlemen [to] walk and prate up acquaintance, as fast as if it were in a Tavern'.[61] The 'Town', characterised by its extravagance and luxurious consumption, was also constructed in opposition to the 'City', its more industrious, yet money-grabbing and hypocritical neighbour. The 'Town' was a place where human relations had become subsumed to market forces, a world in which sex was both a unit of currency and a mode of consumption.

Cuckolding humour of the Restoration typically associated metropolitan women's sexual desire with social competitiveness and display. At a time when the urban middling sort was becoming increasingly wealthy and hungry for the material trappings of status, humorists portrayed citizens' wives in endless pursuit of 'modish' and 'fashionable' things. Taking a fashionable town 'gallant' was described as a means for merchants' and tradesmens' wives to enhance their own status.[62] The connection between cuckoldry and social advancement is captured brilliantly in descriptions of citizens' wives 'honouring' their husbands by their adulteries, 'dubbing' them 'knights of the forked order'. Such terms satirised the social pretensions of the new urban 'pseudo-gentry' emerging after the Restoration, middling men who purchased knighthoods and aped the manners of their landed superiors.[63] In its issue for 22 May 1676, *Poor Robin's Intelligence* reported 'news' from Blackfriars of a tailor whose 'A-la-mode' wife, 'scorning that her husband should walk the streets without the usual adornments of his neighbours', takes a lover to earn her spouse some horns so he might join the 'Highgate Levellers', a fraternity of cuckolds.[64] Courtly dramatists of the Restoration frequently used this theme to mock the pretensions of bourgeois *nouveaux riches*, but the image of the cuckolded citizen held important warnings for the middling sort themselves. The erotic appeal of the 'town' gallant to citizens' wives visualised the allure of emulation and

---

[60] John Spurr, *England in the 1670s: 'This Masquerading Age'* (Oxford, 2000), p. 161.

[61] *Poor Robin's Intelligence*, 3 July 1676; Charles Sedley, *Bellamira* (1687), in *The Poetical Works and Dramatic Works of Sir Charles Sedley*, ed. V. de Sola Pinto (2 vols., London, 1928), II, p. 49.

[62] E.g., Thomas Shadwell, *The Virtuoso* (1676), in *The Complete Works of Thomas Shadwell*, II, p. 151; *Poor Robin's Intelligence*, 22 May 1676, 14 Aug. 1676; [Ward], *Modern World Disrob'd*, p. 110.

[63] Alan Everitt, 'Social Mobility in Early Modern England', *PP*, 33 (1966), 56–73; Peter Earle, *The Making of the English Middle Class: Business, Society and Family Life in London, 1660–1730* (London, 1989), pp. 5–10.

[64] *Poor Robin's Intelligence*, 22 May 1676; the fraternity, and its annual parade, is described in *Bull-Feather Hall*, pp. 9–16.

extravagant consumption that could lead eventually to financial ruin or public disgrace. When a 'jolly wife, and a buxome widdow' of Aldersgate Street scorn 'the Mechanick Divertisements of Stool Ball' for 'the more Modish entertainments of Dancing and Revelling' with 'a couple of their gallants', ending with some nocturnal 'frollicking upon the bed of nature' in the Fields, they are arrested as prostitutes and dispatched to Bridewell.[65]

Fictionalised London life was as duplicitous as it was competitive. The stage was instrumental in constructing a view of a fashionable society obsessed with outward appearances, a world in which people, like players, were constantly playing roles. This was a fickle and claustrophobic world populated by people content with the 'appearance of things', in which character and value were drawn from the 'Airs you make in Publick' and the variable opinion of others.[66] The anonymity of urban life and the transience brought about by the London season increased the possibility that appearances were dissembled.

Comic dramatists had long seen their role as holding up to contempt deceitful characters, as the anti-puritan satires of Ben Jonson and his contemporaries illustrated.[67] In a few comedies of the later seventeenth century the layers of deception and dissimulation required to cuckold a husband were used to explore more 'libertine' ideas about the validity of moral codes and to examine the ways in which outward allegiance to norms of conduct might be used to more devious purposes. Allegiance to traditional sources of authority had been challenged by the upheavals of the Civil War and put to the test by ever increasing recourse to loyalty oaths during the 1640s and '50s.[68] The antinomianism of certain radical religious sects had brought into question the customary boundaries of sin and morality by claiming that they were simply human constructs.[69] After the Restoration the influence of continental 'libertine' ideas on a small but prominent group of court 'wits', together with King Charles II's open adulteries and (to some critics) treacherous flouting of the marriage vows, raised more general debate about the validity of traditional institutions of moral authority, such as marriage.[70] Libertines viewed marital vows as merely conventional restraints

---

[65] *Poor Robin's Intelligence*, 1 May 1676.

[66] Deborah C. Payne, 'Reading the Signs in *The Country Wife*', *Studies in English Literature 1500–1900*, 26 (1986), 403–19; Botica, 'Audience, Playhouse and Play', p. 241; Charles Burnaby, *The Reform'd Wife* (London, 1700), I. i. p. 3.

[67] Patrick Collinson, 'The Theatre Constructs Puritanism', in David L. Smith, Richard Strier and David Bevington (eds.), *The Theatrical City: Culture, Theatre and Politics in London, 1576–1649* (Cambridge, 1995), pp. 157–69.

[68] Keith Thomas, 'Cases of Conscience in Seventeenth-Century England', in John Morrill, Paul Slack and Daniel Woolf (eds.), *Public Duty and Private Conscience in Seventeenth-Century England: Essays Presented to G. E. Aylmer* (Oxford, 1993), p. 43; John Spurr, 'Perjury, Profanity and Politics', *The Seventeenth Century*, 8 (1993), 29–50.

[69] Christopher Hill, *The World Turned Upside Down: Radical Ideas During the English Revolution* (London, 1972), ch. 8.

[70] Rachel Weil, 'Sometimes a Scepter is only a Scepter: Pornography and Politics in Restoration England', in Lynn Hunt (ed.), *The Invention of Pornography: Obscenity and the Origins of Modernity 1500–1800* (New York, 1993), pp. 125–53; Spurr, *England in the 1670s*, ch. 7.

on the fulfilment of natural urges. The theatre's rakes rail against marriage as the 'worst of prisons' or an 'Ecclesiastical Mouse-trap', while female characters complain that the conventional prescriptions for chastity were contrary to what 'Nature had intended'.[71] Since most plays ended with a conventional marriage, dramatists saw their job as not so much to challenge the institution of marriage *per se*, as to demystify its relationships and the codes of behaviour that were supposed to support it. Cuckolding plots, in which motive was traditionally lustful and in which there were multiple layers of disguise and dissimulation, provided a fertile ground for some dramatists to explore the ramifications of libertine ideas, juxtaposing natural human sexual urges against the institutional restrictions of marriage and sexual honour.[72]

The most vivid exploration of these ideas occurs in Wycherley's *The Country Wife* (1675). Horner, the play's rakish anti-hero, significantly describes himself as a 'machiavel in love', and through his carefully contrived adulterous assignations with the wife of Sir Jasper Fidget and her companions, he explores the nexus between personal worth and public esteem.[73] With the help of a compliant doctor, he spreads the false rumour about the town that he has been rendered impotent by medication for venereal disease contracted during a recent visit to France. By assuming the 'reputation of a eunuch' – significantly a physical rather than a moral state – Horner takes on a position from which to abuse credulous husbands and disabuse their wives with secrecy and impunity. 'Women of honour', he argues, 'are only chary of their reputation, not their Persons, and 'tis scandal they wou'd avoid, not Men.'[74] In a social world primed by gossip, in which the fickle 'opinion of others' was the mediator of moral standards, adultery only became serious when publicly exposed. There's 'no sin', argues Horner, 'but giving scandal'.[75] The women to whom Horner reveals his designs agree that 'the crime's the less, when 'tis not known' and that a 'woman of honour loses no honour with a private person'. In this way, the maintenance of a demure and chaste reputation acts as a cover for cuckoldry, a means 'to deceive the world with less suspicion' and to 'enjoy the better, and more privately those you love'.[76]

Thereafter, the use of a good or virtuous reputation as a smokescreen to wickedness became a common, sardonic point of reference in cuckolding comedies on and off the stage. 'Reputation's a Jest', observes Railton at the

---

[71] Thomas Shadwell, *Epsom Wells*, in *The Complete Works of Thomas Shadwell*, II, 117; Shadwell, *The Virtuoso*, II, 143.
[72] Maximillian Novak, *William Congreve* (New York, 1971), pp. 42–5; Dale Underwood, *Etherege and the Seventeenth-Century Comedy of Manners* (New Haven, CT, 1957), pp. 10–40; James Grantham Turner, 'The Properties of Libertinism', in Robert P. Maccubin (ed.), *'Tis Nature's Fault: Unauthorized Sexuality During the Enlightenment* (Cambridge, 1987), pp. 75–87; Susan Staves, *Players' Scepters: Fictions of Authority in the Restoration* (Lincoln, NE and London, 1979), chs. 3 and 5.
[73] Wycherley, *Country Wife*, IV. iii. 63–4.   [74] Ibid., I. i. 154–6.
[75] Ibid., IV. iii. 23.   [76] Ibid., II. i. 382–3, 387; V. iv. 95, 117.

start of Thomas Baker's play *The Humour of the Age* (1701), pointing to its instability as an indication of real worth. 'Virtue each libertine's Pretence is grown', observes Freeman in the same play, 'The better to keep Vice from being known.' In Baker's *An Act at Oxford* (1704), the rakish student Bloom, when trying to seduce Arabella, the wife of the reforming justice Deputy Driver, assures her, 'we'll be both virtuous, that is, we'll be secret, and the world shall ne'er know the Contrary'.[77] When it came to cuckoldry, 'casuists agree', remarked the satirist Ned Ward in his burlesque verse *The Northern Cuckold* (1721), 'The shame of being catch'd therein/ Is ten times greater than the sin.'[78] Some satirists, mocking the 'hypocrisy' of the puritan regimes of the Interregnum, sardonically dated the vogue for dissimulation back to the 1650 Adultery Act whose draconian provisions had simply encouraged greater secrecy and deceit in the conduct of extra-marital affairs. By making it 'death' to 'boast' of one's affairs, noted the puritan Sir Timothy Treat-all in Aphra Behn's *The City Heiress* (1682), the law had simply encouraged more clandestine arrangements to ensure that there was 'no scandal'.[79] The drama's rakes and libertines enshrined in their words and actions this archly pragmatic approach to morality.

The allied belief that metropolitan manners might be used to disguise illicit intentions acted as a premise to a series of jokes based around the misinterpretation of social civilities. This was satirised in plays such as *The Country Wife* and *The London Cuckolds* where jealous husbands take naive country girls for brides on the grounds that their simple rustic manners made it easier to determine whether they were, in the words of the cuckold Pinchwife, 'foyl'd or unsound'.[80] Playwrights seized on the potential for jealousy and confusion caused by the meeting of different codes of behaviour, reworking the age-old clash between rustic and urbane manners. In *The London Cuckolds* Alderman Wiseacre's comically naive young wife, Peggy, permits the genteel rake, Ramble, to touch her hand when she curtsies to greet him. Her jealous husband is enraged at her letting such a dissolute man touch her, but she replies with seeming innocence that, 'he was a gentleman, and my aunt told me I must make a curtsy to gentlefolks'.[81]

The fine line between social and sexual kissing was also exploited for comic effect. 'What, invite your wife to kiss men? Monstrous! Are you not ashamed?' remarks Pinchwife, disgusted at another character's willingness to allow men of

[77] Thomas Baker, *The Humour of the Age* (London, 1701), I. i. p. 3; IV. ii. p. 53; Baker, *An Act at Oxford* (London, 1704), III, p. 25. See also Arthur Bedford, *A Serious Remonstrance In Behalf of the Christian Religion, Against the Horrid Blasphemies and Impieties Which are Still Used in the English Play-Houses* (London, 1719), ch. 11.

[78] [Edward Ward], *The Northern Cuckold: Or, the Garden House Intrigue* (London, 1721), p. 9.

[79] Aphra Behn, *The City Heiress* (1682), in *The Works of Aphra Behn*, ed. Montague Summers (6 vols., London, 1915), II, p. 206.

[80] Wycherley, *Country Wife*, I. i. 352.   [81] Ravenscroft, *London Cuckolds*, II. i. p. 474.

the town to greet his wife-to-be in this manner. 'These little freedoms now make people foolishly question women's virtue,' remarks Sir Lively Cringe in Charles Burnaby's comedy *The Modish Husband* (1702), as Lord Promise kisses his wife's hand, comically unaware that his lordship's motives are far from polite.[82] The provision of hospitality, especially food, supplied another contested aspect of civility in cuckolding humour.[83] The sharing of food between the wife and her lover symbolised the sharing of their bodies in the act of cuckoldry and was a common means of signalling adulterous intention. For instance, the eponymous hero of Thomas Rawlins's intricate comedy of misunderstanding, *Tom Essence*, is driven wild with jealousy when he observes his wife offering a drink to the gallant, Courtly. Such 'familiarity' in Tom's suspicious mind can only mean one thing, namely that Courtly 'lyes with my Wife'. Ultimately Tom's jealousy is proved to be groundless, but he ends the play by advising his wife to 'Use freedom with discretion, and you'le see/ Tom Essence understands Civility.'[84] Behind this playful comedy of misunderstanding was a more serious social message, that these social niceties were more than merely etiquette and played an important role in maintaining the moral integrity of the sociable world.

The sense of displacement engendered by a fickle and anonymous urban environment, in which strangers could not be trusted and social conventions seemed increasingly doubtful and ambiguous, was amplified by the dramatists' use of characterisation. Much has been written about the cuckold's relationship with his wife, yet the central axis in many plays, ballads and stories was the contrast between the husband and his wife's lover.[85] Cuckoldry upset indices of status and authority between men as well as inverting relations between man and wife, creating in the process new 'dominant' and 'subordinate' masculinities.[86] The lover's triumph, frequently represented in the language of military victory, established a new hierarchy of men, based not on rank, wealth, patriarchal respectability or the dignity of a particular trade or calling, but on sexual attractiveness and sexual performance. Sex was not just a leveller, but also a means of inscribing difference between male bodies.

Through the theme of cuckoldry, dramatists explored the increasingly fluid social relations of the later seventeenth-century urban scene. While the classic

---

[82] Wycherley, *Country Wife*, III. ii. 323–4; Charles Burnaby, *The Modish Husband* (London, 1702), I, p. 13.

[83] Gowing, *Domestic Dangers*, p. 150; Foyster, *Manhood*, pp. 128–9. See also chapter 5 below.

[84] [Thomas Rawlins], *Tom Essence: Or, the Modish Wife* (London, 1677), III. i. p. 28; V. iii. p. 67. See also *The Honest London Spy, Discovering the Base and Subtle Intreagues of the Town* (London, 1706), p. 67.

[85] Gershon Legman, *Rationale of the Dirty Joke: an Analysis of Sexual Humour* (London, 1969), pp. 695–7.

[86] Kahn, *Man's Estate*, pp. 120, 144, 150; Foyster, *Manhood*, p. 5. For 'dominant' and 'subordinate' masculinities, see John Tosh, 'What Should Historians do with Masculinity? Reflections on Nineteenth-Century Britain', *History Workshop Journal*, 33 (1994), p. 191.

cuckolding plot in Restoration comedy involved the horning of a wealthy citizen by an aristocratic rake, on closer examination both cuckold and cuckold-maker lack a proper place in the social order. The common description of Restoration rakes as 'ranging' or 'rambling' men, indicated by their names such as 'Wildish', 'Townley' or 'Ranger', testified both to their unfettered sexual desires and to their lack of fixture in the social hierarchy. The sexual innuendo that the cuckold-maker Mr Ramble in *The London Cuckolds* was a 'young active fellow fit for employment', also drew attention to his idleness and lack of a determined place in society.[87] Some stage plays represented cuckold-makers as demobbed soldiers, as returned travellers, like Horner in *The Country Wife*, or as younger sons of the elite whose social position was often uncertain.[88] The Restoration 'town gallant' was a 'pretender' to gentility and good breeding, rather than a true gentleman.[89] In contrast, their victims were men who had achieved, through wealth and marriage, the trappings of respectability, but by their carelessness, stupidity, impotence and incompetence lacked the control over their wives that would earn them proper respect. In a society where claims to status were becoming increasingly competitive and based on a range of cultural attributes, cuckolding humour was a prime site for debating contemporary male conduct, manners and styles of deportment.[90]

Physical attributes, contrasting strength, movement and size of bodies, provided means for writing relations between men in cuckolding humour. The doubtful manliness of the cuckold contrasted with the loud proclamation of manhood by gallants, justifying their conquests as behaving 'like a man'.[91] While husbands were characterised by 'tameness', docility and inactivity, the role of the lover was 'not to be express'd but in action'.[92] The movement of husbands is constrained and awkward, sometimes confined by their domineering wives to 'sneaking' around the house, whereas lovers demonstrate great agility, scaling walls, climbing through windows and dashing into closets when disturbed. They are men about town, ranging freely through the urban environment.[93] The description of impotent husbands as 'fumblers' also connoted insecure movement. Animalistic metaphors were used to underscore the rake's boisterous sexuality. Hence lovers were like 'unruly colts' who might

---

[87] Ravenscroft, *London Cuckolds*, III. i. p. 480. See also Karl E. Westhauser, 'The Power of Conversation: the Evolution of Modern Social Relations in Augustan London', PhD thesis, Brown University (1994), p. 95.

[88] E.g., Thomas Otway, *The Souldiers' Fortune* (1681), in *The Works of Thomas Otway*, ed. J. C. Ghosh (2 vols., Oxford, 1932).

[89] *The Character of a Town-Gallant; Exposing the Extravagant Fopperies of Some Vain Self-Conceited Pretenders to Gentility and Good Breeding* (London, 1675).

[90] For the wider context see Anna Bryson, *From Courtesy to Civility: Changing Codes of Conduct in Early Modern England* (Oxford, 1998), ch. 7.

[91] Ravenscroft, *London Cuckolds*, V. iv. p. 540.   [92] Shadwell, *The Virtuoso*, III. p. 151.

[93] *The XV Comforts of Rash and Inconsiderate Marriage* (London, 1682), p. 83; [Rawlins], *Tom Essence*, I. ii. p. 15; Etherege, *She Would if She Could*, V. i. 178–80; cf. ibid., I. i. 154–61.

'leap into other men's pastures'. Alternatively, they were like soldiers, 'men of dispatch', ready to 'storm' a woman's 'fortifications'. Such metaphors filled the language of sexual conquest across the spectrum of cuckolding literature.[94]

Fashionable dress provided another point of contrast. In comic narratives as in life, clothing did not simply adorn the body, but acted metonymically as 'components in a language' for communicating status and refinement.[95] Although official regulation of dress had ceased with the lapsing of the sumptuary laws in 1604, the idea that dress should reinforce and visualise hierarchy, order and respect remained an important principle in conduct literature throughout the later seventeenth and early eighteenth centuries.[96] However, in later seventeenth-century metropolitan society expanding opportunities for conspicuous display increased the importance of cultural attributes in the acquisition of status and so destabilised customary sumptuary distinctions.[97] The wearing of fashionable clothing, as Peter Borsay has observed, because of its protean nature facilitated freer access to status.[98] Furthermore, in the intensifying debates about the effects of 'luxury' and consumption in this period, critics viewed 'fashion' as not only trivialising moral teachings but setting up rival and dangerously appealing codes of behaviour. The image of adultery as a 'fashionable vice' was enshrined in the later seventeenth century, some commentators arguing that sexual immorality had become 'a sin grown so in fashion' that 'the great custom of fashion, has overgrown the sense of the sin'.[99] Working in competition with more worthy forms of identification, fashion provided an important site in cuckolding narratives for setting up inverted indices of masculine status and sexual morality.

Late seventeenth-century drama and social documentary stressed the importance for men of obtaining a balance between extravagant dress or excessive

---

[94] E.g., Otway, *The Souldier's Fortune*, II. 68–9; Shadwell, *Epsom Wells*, V. i. p. 165.

[95] Marcia Pointon, *Hanging the Head: Portraiture and Social Formation in Eighteenth-Century England* (New Haven, CT and London, 1993), pp. 112–13.

[96] N. B. Harte, 'State Control of Dress and Social Change in Pre-Industrial England', in D. C. Coleman and A. H. John (eds.), *Trade, Government and Economy in Pre-Industrial England: Essays Presented to F. J. Fisher* (London, 1976), pp. 132–65; Fenela Childs, 'Prescriptions for Manners in English Courtesy Literature 1690–1760, and their Social Implications', DPhil thesis, University of Oxford (1984), pp. 151–4.

[97] Neil McKendrick, 'The Commercialization of Fashion', in Neil McKendrick, John Brewer and J. H. Plumb (eds.), *The Birth of a Consumer Society: the Commercialization of Eighteenth-Century England* (London, 1982), pp. 34–99; Lorna Weatherill, 'Consumer Behaviour, Textiles and Dress in the Late Seventeenth and Early Eighteenth Centuries', *Textile History*, 22 (1991), 297–310.

[98] Peter Borsay, *The English Urban Renaissance: Culture and Society in the Provincial Town, 1660–1770* (Oxford, 1989), pp. 237–41; Dabhoiwala, 'Construction of Honour', 209.

[99] Francis Boyle, *Discourses Useful For the Vain Modish Ladies and Their Gallants* (London, 1696), p. 113. See also John Sekora, *Luxury: the Concept in Western Thought* (London, 1977); Erin Mackie, *Market A La Mode: Fashion, Commodity and Gender in the Tatler and the Spectator* (Baltimore, MD and London, 1997).

attention to grooming, liable to be stigmatised as effeminate and foppish, and slovenliness, associated with rustic vulgarity or servility.[100] Slovenliness was sometimes portrayed as a characteristic of the married state, as husbands became too care-worn or weighed down by the responsibilities of matrimony to bother dressing to impress. In this respect, sexual and social satire were inextricably linked. An unfashionable or unkempt appearance made men liable to be made cuckolds as their wives sought lovers who cut more impressive figures. Jack Pinchwife in Wycherley's play *The Country Wife* is instantly recognisable as a married man 'by the grumness of [his] countenance and the slovenlyness of [his] habit'.[101] 'The married man', states Doralice in John Dryden's 1671 comedy *Marriage A-la-Mode*, having in mind her own husband Rhodophil,

> is the creature of the world the most out of fashion. His behaviour is dumpish, his discourse his wife and family, his habit is so much neglected it looks as if that were married too: his hat is married, his peruke is married, his breeches are married, and if we could look within his breeches, we should find him married there too.[102]

The clothes of the ineffectual husband, being 'neglected', 'slovenly' and out of fashion, visualised his loss of authority and public respect, while the pun on 'marred' suggests his lack of sexual vigour.[103] Not just on stage, but across a range of comic literature, the sharp fashionable appearance of lovers was part their erotic appeal. Hence the lover in one later seventeenth-century ballad sports 'fine breeches' and a 'coat with Golden Lace'.[104] In another story the lover's 'beau' attire makes him look 'well mann'd below'.[105] The role of clothing as an erotic marker between husband and lover is perhaps most strikingly illustrated by a cuckolding story printed in *The Honest London Spy* (1706), in which a widower relates to a bachelor and a married man how he was deceived by his first wife. He describes how he became suspicious of his wife's conduct after receiving an anonymous letter tipping him off that she was using her daily visits to church as a cover for going to work at a fashionable brothel. In order to catch her at her tricks, the husband takes on the trappings and persona of a lover. Dress is integral to his new identity, and he describes buying 'a very beauish suit of Apparel, wig and other Accoutrements'. In this guise he goes to the brothel, and meeting his wife, 'we both address'd our selves to the Business which we came about'. The husband's virility is enhanced by his new persona, their 'amorous Engagements' are 'renew'd' over again. Later that evening, resuming

---

[100] Philip Carter, *Men and the Emergence of Polite Society: Britain 1660–1800* (London, 2001), ch. 4.

[101] *XV Comforts*, p. 54; Wycherley, *Country Wife*, I. i. 328–9.

[102] John Dryden, *Marriage A-La-Mode* (1671), ed. David Crane (London, 1991), V. i. 238–43.

[103] Childs, 'Prescriptions for Manners', pp. 154, 155.

[104] *The London Cuckold: Or an Antient Citizen's Head Well Fitted With a Flourishing Pair of Fashionable Horns* (London, n.d. [*c.*1680]).

[105] [Ward], *The Northern Cuckold*, p. 15.

his normal dowdy attire, he naturally 'had a mind to try whether we cou'd with the same vigour manage matters at home, as we had done abroad: But our Embraces in reality were much more dull and insipid'.[106]

THE POLITICS OF HOUSEHOLD AND NEIGHBOURHOOD

Cuckoldry's disruption of relations of authority made it a particularly fruitful means of exploring the sense of displacement engendered by later seventeenth-century fashionable society. But cuckolding humour had other characteristics and developed other motifs. *Poor Robin's Intelligence*, published weekly from 28 March 1676 to 6 November 1677, occupied an overlapping cultural space with the stage, yet presented a different version of metropolitan sexual politics, centred on the world of the household-workshop rather than polite society.[107] The 'Poor Robin' of its title evoked a familiar jest figure whose name was associated with a wide range of cheap print of the later seventeenth century. These included a hugely successful almanac written by William Winstanley, a collection of jests, and satirical characters of scolds, the Dutch and the French.[108] The content of *Poor Robin's Intelligence* was standard jestbook fare: quack doctors, fops, prostitutes and their gullible clients, naive country folk visiting the city for the first time, religious sects, domineering wives and, of course, cuckolds populated its pages.

Yet its format was more original. The second part of its title evoked the developing newspaper press and the journal presented comic tales in the convention of news. In this respect it bore an affinity with satirical newsbooks that had flourished in the absence of censorship during the 1640s and '50s.[109] It designated each story with a time and place, giving familiar stories of domestic discord a new immediacy and relevance. Not all its locations were real – for instance on 15 May 1676 the paper reported news of a worrying outbreak of 'horn plague' in 'Cuckoldshire' – but most of the action reported was situated in identifiable parishes, streets and alleys.[110] It was the product of a metropolitan popular culture that was becoming increasingly spatially aware and obsessed in

---

[106] *Honest London Spy*, pp. 96, 98, 102, 107. Cf. Lyndal Roper, *Oedipus and the Devil: Witchcraft, Sexuality and Religion in Early Modern Europe* (London and New York, 1994), pp. 117–19.

[107] The paper reappeared in 1679–80 as *Poor Robin's Intelligence Newly Reviv'd* and in 1688 as *Poor Robin's Public and Private Occurrences*.

[108] H. Ecroyd Smith, 'Poor Robin', *Notes and Queries*, 6th ser., 7 (28 April 1883), 321–2; Capp, *Astrology and the Popular Press*, pp. 124–5. Tim Hitchcock notes that 'Poor Robin' was sexual slang for the penis: *English Sexualities, 1700–1800* (Basingstoke, 1997), p. 117, n. 15.

[109] David Underdown, *A Freeborn People: Politics and the Nation in Seventeenth-Century England* (Oxford, 1996), pp. 102–4.

[110] *Poor Robin's Intelligence*, 15 May 1676. 'Cuckoldshire' is revisited in the issue for 4 June 1677.

the period of rebuilding following the Great Fire.[111] The conceit that the events described were taking place in the next street or parish became part of the joke and emphasised that the neighbourhoods were full of cuckolds and that opportunities for cuckoldry lay all around. When in May 1677 the paper advertised a prize fight that was due to take place between a cuckolded parson and his wife's lover next 'Horn-fair-day', the paper believed that 'if all Cuckolds and Cuckold-makers should go to see 'um' the 'streets would be as empty as in the great sickness'.[112]

Poor Robin's Intelligence was concerned above all with the sexual behaviour of small tradesmen, artisans and shopkeepers residing in the parishes of the City of London, the expanding eastern suburbs, and formerly gentrified West End parishes such as Covent Garden, which were now seeing an influx of poorer craftsmen.[113] Although the audience is impossible to ascertain with much certainty, it seems plausible to suggest that the paper was aimed at precisely the same groups of increasingly literate urban tradesmen and their apprentices whom it satirised. This may be surmised from an abundance of jibes that poked fun at particular kinds of trades. Stories about leather-stitchers for whom 'the horns and the hide do . . . follow one another' and a woollen-sempster forced into 'Herculean proofs of his virility' owing to the 'reproach of impotence' that is frequently 'cast upon men of that function', seem designed for an audience for whom occupational identity was a source of pride. Shoemakers, fish merchants, cobblers, glaziers, joiners and, above all, tailors (considered to be a rather effeminate trade) and their wives are among the *dramatis personae* of the paper's matrimonial comedy.[114] The paper seemed to offer a resource of jokes that might express differences and rivalries, but also foster cohesion among working men by the shared experience of cuckoldry and popular misogyny.

The matrimonial humour in *Poor Robin's Intelligence* was particularly focused on men for whom the possibility of achieving the levels of independence necessary to become householders and enter the exclusive club of patriarchal society was a serious career goal. For these men, a wife was portrayed as an object of status or an accoutrement of respectability. Thus a story appearing on 30 January 1677 related the case of a 'young merchant of knick-trades' who, 'wanting still one necessary Toy, called a Wife', embarked on a series of luckless courtships with ladies of 'quality', before, in some desperation, settling down

---

[111] Cynthia Wall, *The Literary and Cultural Spaces of Restoration London* (Cambridge, 1998).

[112] *Poor Robin's Intelligence*, 15 May 1677.

[113] For example, matrimonial intrigue or conflict takes place in Clerkenwell and Aldersgate Street (1 May 1676), Covent Garden (17 July 1676) and Shoreditch (24 July 1676).

[114] *Poor Robin's Intelligence*, 3 July 1676; 18 Sept. 1676. The mocking of particular trades with the symbols of cuckoldry was a feature of civic festivities and protest: Tim Harris, *London Crowds in the Reign of Charles II: Propaganda and Politics from the Restoration until the Exclusion Crisis* (Cambridge, 1987), p. 45.

with a local dishwasher who turned out to be pregnant by another man.[115] The message was that marital choices, like economic affairs, had to be managed with prudence.

The married state, which was ideally supposed to bequeath new independence and responsibilities, was ironically translated into comic discourse as a pathway to servility and failing sexual prowess. Familiar comic tropes such as bullied husbands and their shrewish wives competing for the upper hand in marriage make frequent appearances in the paper. News from Goswell Street dated 29 April 1676 reported a wife's beating of her drunken husband and, having 'got the masterdome', she immediately fetched her spouse's 'Sunday-Breeches' and put them on as a 'Trophy of her Man-hood'.[116] Patriarchal and civic responsibility was portrayed as a source of male vulnerability, leading men to neglect their wives. In the issue for 11 September 1676 a glass joiner of Queen Street while serving on the watch inadvertently tells one of his colleagues where 'he had laid the key of his wife's chamber', which leads to his horning.[117]

While this man's carelessness might appear in the dubious logic of comic discourse to 'justify' his fate, it is hard to find much comfort in the story of an 'honest labouring man' of Grub Street, which appeared on 25 September 1676. 'Being often obliged' by his occupation to 'lye abroad', the poor man came home unexpectedly one day to find his wife in bed with a lover, a 'stout fellow'. While the two men fought, the cuckold's wife ran away with the household savings, 'leaving the poor Cornuto with equal grief to bewail the loss of his money, and the growth of his horns'. At one level, this story seemed highly conservative in its message, highlighting the wife's greed and insatiable lust which renders her incapable of keeping any 'fasting nights' while her husband was absent and warning men of the untrustworthiness of women. Male readers may have felt some sympathy for the 'poor' and 'honest' cuckold, for it demonstrated the impossibility of controlling female sexuality. But for young unmarried men reading these comic tales it sent out an ambivalent message which may have served less to reinforce patriarchal values, than to cast doubts about normal modes of respectability by indicating that becoming head of a household was no sure means of achieving satisfying manhood.[118]

Running through these tales was a powerful message emphasising the interconnectedness of worldly success and domestic harmony and how much the former relied on the latter.[119] The sexual act was commonly described using the language of 'work' or 'business'. Thus a tailor's wife seeks out an 'able

[115] *Poor Robin's Intelligence*, 30 Jan. 1677.   [116] Ibid., 1 May 1676.
[117] Ibid., 11 Sept. 1676.   [118] Ibid., 25 Sept. 1676.
[119] Margaret R. Hunt, *The Middling Sort: Commerce, Gender and the Family in England 1680–1780* (Berkeley and Los Angeles, CA, 1996), pp. 50, 67 and *passim*.

workman' to 'take measure' of her better than her husband; in other stories lovers 'manage the[ir] business' carefully while the cuckolded husband minds his economic affairs. This language, together with a range of intricate plot devices, explored sexual danger and authority in the middling household where workspace and domestic space were necessarily, but sometimes uncomfortably, close.[120] Under the legitimate veil of employment, which included board and lodging, dangerous male interlopers were brought into the household. Hence, in the story of the tailor cuckold and his fashionable wife, the scheming mistress arranges for her lover to be appointed as her husband's journeyman.[121] The mutability of space in artisans' houses served as a metaphor for the uncertainty of domestic authority. In a tale concerning a cuckolded shoemaker of White Hart Yard, aspects of which we have already explored, the husband makes shoes while his wife entertains a mysterious male visitor, who 'knew the length of her foot as well as her husband', in her bedchamber. The privileged access she allows her 'workman' to the most intimate space of the household presents a transgression of the inter-linked codes of space and authority and prefigures the sexual favours she is about to grant him.[122] In many stories the underling in the workshop, the apprentice or the journeyman, becomes master in the bedroom. In a society where young men, through the terms of their apprenticeship and struggle for financial independence, had to defer marriage (and legitimate sexual relations) until their late twenties, stories of young subordinates cuckolding their masters offered fantasies of relieving the sexual tensions that built up within households.

RETHINKING CUCKOLDRY

A sign of cuckolding humour's popularity in Restoration England was that few felt the need to account for cuckoldry's appeal as a topic of humour, or to justify the mockery of deceived husbands. Such things could be taken for granted. Nevertheless, there were some dissenting voices. Churchmen, following St Paul's injunctions against 'foolish talking' and jesting, had long condemned frivolous laughter and cruel derision. *The Whole Duty of Man* attacked the mockery of the cuckold on the grounds that it was uncharitable and 'very unjust he should fall under reproach, only because he is injured'.[123] Moreover, as we have seen, the measure of shame attached to cuckoldry had long been viewed (at least theoretically) as a matter of degree – the extent to which individuals

---

[120] Jennifer Melville, 'The Use and Organisation of Domestic Space in Late Seventeenth-Century London', PhD thesis, University of Cambridge (1999) p. 207.

[121] *Poor Robin's Intelligence*, 22 May 1676; 14 Aug. 1676.

[122] Ibid., 26 June 1676.

[123] [Richard Allestree], *The Whole Duty of Man Necessary for all Families* (London, 1660), p. 228. See also Isaac Barrow, *Several Sermons Against Evil Speaking* (London, 1678), p. 49.

connived in their own horning and the nature of their reactions on discovery were crucial in determining how dishonoured they were. From the end of the seventeenth century a series of cultural developments brought these distinctions into sharper focus, permitting a serious rethinking of cuckoldry and male sexual reputation.

The stereotype of the cuckolded husband as a figure of ridicule and contempt was harder to sustain once the circumstances of infidelity were explored. From the 1690s, the voices of 'real-life' cuckolded husbands were broadcast to the reading public in London and provincial towns through the publication of their letters seeking the advice of the editors of the emerging periodical press. Publications such as the *Athenian Mercury* and the *British Apollo*, by allowing correspondents the opportunity to locate infidelity in their own particular circumstances, allowed a more 'realistic' portrayal of the dilemmas facing the deceived husband. The cuckolded men who appeared in correspondence printed in the *Athenian Mercury* came from diverse backgrounds including gentlemen, middling and plebeian men cuckolded by their neighbours, and other men made cuckolds by their social superiors. Their questions reveal a concern with how to maintain a dignified demeanour in the light of their spouses' adultery and also sought advice on the most effective means of revenge. Many letters expressed strong feelings of frustration, generally shared by the paper's editors, with the ineffectiveness of the courts in providing proper satisfaction for wronged husbands – the law's inadequacies merely adding to their sense of impotence.[124]

Some letters purported to be sent in by concerned friends of the cuckolded man and others presented cuckoldry in a hypothetical manner, possibly reflecting the pain and embarrassment suffered by men discussing this issue that even the cover of anonymity could not assuage. However, some correspondents supplied moving first-person accounts of their wives' infidelity, their letters serving as a form of catharsis or emotional detoxification in the wake of a loved one's betrayal. A sailor described in the *Athenian Mercury* for Tuesday 20 August 1695 how three years previously he had married a 'young and handsome' woman, 'purely out of love', but while he 'loved her intirely', she quickly 'grew cold in her carriage' towards him. Despite his trying 'all the endearing ways imaginable to reclaim her' from her 'giddy' behaviour, she would insolently 'put her fingers in her ears' when he tried to reason with her. Discovering her adultery with one of his shipmates, he chose to pardon her in the hope that she would reform her conduct, but to no avail, for she continued her infidelity 'and vows she cares not if all the world knew it, and seems not in the least sorry for it'. The correspondent also complained that she 'contradicts me in almost everything I do or say; frownes, chides, and gives me ill language before any company; and has often swore to my face she hates me as a toad, and wishes me dead'.

---

[124] E.g., *AM* II/3, q. 2, 3 June 1691; *Ladies Mercury*, I/3, q. 2, 10 March 1693.

So notorious had she become that all the correspondents' friends knew of her behaviour, making him 'asham'd to see them'. The sailor's sense of emotional betrayal emerges most poignantly in the final lines of his letter. Having 'all along exercised patience to a miracle' he could 'bear [it] no longer' and therefore sought advice on whether he might divorce her and marry another or, if that were not possible, help on 'how I must carry my self towards her, for to my shame I love her still'.[125]

In their self-fashioning, the cuckolded correspondents to the *Athenian Mercury* emphasised that they had behaved with propriety and discretion right to the bitter end. Husbands portrayed themselves as behaving lovingly towards their errant spouses and showing a willingness to forgive their actions. When the wife of one correspondent 'kept company three months with an ill man' from whom she caught a venereal infection, her spouse describes how he 'freely forgave her, spar'd no cost for a Chyrurgeon, and kep[t] it private'.[126] In plays and ballads the cuckolded husband who turned a blind eye to his wife's infidelities, or displayed too readily a willingness to excuse her actions, was a figure of fun. However, to these correspondents, the power and willingness to forgive was a display of strength rather than weakness. It showed the husband to be reacting in a reasonable manner, contrasting with the wife's abandonment to lust and inability to hear sense – illustrated most dramatically by the sailor's wife covering her ears when he tried to admonish her. Showing an ability to forgive their wives was a means by which these men were able to claim the moral high ground, and by their desire to keep the matter 'private' for as long as possible they aligned themselves with images of ideal husbands from conduct literature who were enjoined to do all things possible to protect their wives' faults from public scrutiny.[127] Behaving in this way was essential to maintaining the cuckold's sense of dignity.

Many letters were motivated by concern for economic well-being and fear of the financial implications of a wife's adultery, suggesting that economic and sexual credit were not easily separable. Correspondents feared they would be 'run in Debt', face a 'decay in Trade' or a 'sudden ruin' by their wives' behaviour. In the event of a wife eloping with another man it was actually considered prudent for the husband to publicly reveal himself, perhaps not specifically as a cuckold, but as a wronged husband. The capacity of an eloped wife to run up debts in her husband's name had the potential to damage credit networks. Given the importance of household authority in establishing the creditworthiness of men of the middling sort in particular, rumours of his wife's adultery had the potential to weaken a man's hand in business dealings. For instance, when gossip spread that his wife had eloped with his attorney, John Sayer of

---

[125] *AM* VIII/11, q. 3, 20 Aug. 1695.   [126] *AM* VI/6, q. 5, 20 Feb. 1692.
[127] William Gouge, *Of Domesticall Duties* (London, 1622), pp. 247–8; Richard Baxter, *A Christian Directory: Or, A Summ of Practical Theologie and Cases of Conscience* (London, 1673), p. 527.

Biddlesdon in Buckinghamshire apparently found that his 'credit with his wife did not encourage anyone else to deal with him on the square'.[128] If his wife eloped, therefore, it was important for a man to give notice of the event to disavow any debts his spouse might incur. From the late seventeenth century a growing number of advertisements were placed in the London press, and later in provincial papers, for this purpose.[129] The *Athenian Mercury* advised one deserted husband to place an advertisement in the London *Gazette*, 'declaring for Reasons best known to your self, that no one give Credit to [his wife], either as to Money or Commodities, as also give notice that all your Creditors (if any) do forthwith in some short time bring in all their Bills, Bonds, Obligations, &c. to whom you now stand indebted'. It also told the correspondent that he should 'for preventing other mischiefs, send us in the Names of such persons, the place where they live, and their Employ, whom you suspect of any ill design, and you shall hear further from us'.[130] Exposure was recommended not simply as a practical necessity in an economy based so heavily on obligation, but as a means of transferring the shame of publicity from the deceived husband to his wife and her lover. Fashioned in this way, revealing his spouse's infidelity became a means of *saving* a man's credit rather than damaging it.

Rather than portraying themselves as victims of scheming adulteresses, some correspondents instead chose to emphasise the underhand behaviour of the men who had made them cuckolds, bitterly presenting images of happy marriages destroyed by dangerous outsiders who had little concern with patriarchal household stability or conventional morality. One letter told how an aristocratic rake had 'under the Cover and Vail of power ... decoy'd a Gentleman's wife away from him'. When the wronged husband demanded the return of his spouse, the 'great man order[ed] some persons to carry away the Gentleman by force, and kept him for several hours'. Another correspondent described how he was 'decoy'd to a Breakfast' by the associates of his wife's lover to give the adulterous couple time to elope.[131] Such letters, tinged with an indignant sense of social injustice, sought to garner sympathy by articulating a different set of anxieties to those customarily linked with cuckoldry – the dangers of men's sexuality to relations of friendship and authority and the abuse of power. In the process, the matter of betrayal shifted from the marital relationship, where the husband was always vulnerable to imputations that his spouse was unfaithful because she was unfulfilled sexually, to the arena of social relations between men where the conduct of the cuckold-maker was more at issue.

---

[128] *A Full Account of the Case of John Sayer Esq.* (London, 1713), p. 5; Craig Muldrew, 'Interpreting the Market: the Ethics of Credit and Community Relations in Early Modern England', *Social History*, 18 (1993), 163–83.

[129] Joanne Bailey, 'Breaking the Conjugal Vows: Marriage and Marriage Breakdown in the North of England, 1660–1800', PhD thesis, University of Durham (1999), pp. 39–41.

[130] *AM* VI/6, q. 5, 20 Feb. 1692.

[131] *AM* III/7, q. 2, 18 Aug. 1691, VI/6, q. 5, 20 Feb. 1692.

The implicit shifting of the blame for adultery away from the inherent lustfulness of wives to unscrupulous male seducers in these letters was matched by other cultural developments that further challenged the basis of traditional cuckolding humour. From the 1680s, moral critics of the theatre and female playgoers started to protest against plays in which wives were displayed as indiscriminately adulterous as a dishonour and 'misrepresentation' of the female sex who deserved to be treated with greater 'complaisance' and politeness. Placed under pressure by attacks on its licentiousness led by Jeremy Collier's *Short View of the Immorality and Profaneness of the English Stage* (1698), and the attempts of the Societies for the Reformation of Manners to have playhouses suppressed, the early eighteenth-century theatre was forced to clean up its act.[132] The sex comedies of the 1670s in which, as one contemporary wearily observed, each married man 'must be a cuckold', now had to contend with new 'humane' or 'sentimental' comedies which gave strong examples of conjugal virtue.[133] When Colley Cibber adapted Sir John Vanbrugh's unfinished play *The Provoked Husband* in 1728, he stopped short of the conventional route of making the profligate Lady Townly cuckold her husband, on the grounds that it would be 'uncivil' and offensive to decorum to present a 'modern belle' in such a way.[134] Women were increasingly cast in passive, chaste roles, whose exemplary conduct was used to reform male manners. New plays increasingly drew attention to the injuries caused by a husband's rather than a wife's adultery. In Cibber's *The Careless Husband* (1705), the shining virtue of Lady Easy shames her adulterous husband into mending his ways. 'From that virtue found', he confesses, 'I blushed, and truly loved.'[135] Rather than holding up to derision incorrigible examples of failure, the representation of strong examples of conjugal virtue came to be seen in drama as the best way to reform the 'licentious irregularities that too often break in upon the peace and happiness of the married state'.[136] Reconciliation therefore became a much more pronounced theme in the sentimental matrimonial drama of the early eighteenth century and so adultery was more lamented than laughed at.

The emergence of 'sentimental' comedy was symptomatic of the polite world's growing efforts to distance itself from 'vulgar' cuckolding humour.

[132] Quoting from Jeremy Collier, *A Short View of the Immorality and Profaneness of the English Stage* (London, 1698), p. 8. See also Roberts, *The Ladies*, p. 144; Robert D. Hume, *The Rakish Stage: Studies in English Drama, 1660–1800* (Carbondale, IL, 1983), pp. 60–1; Joseph Wood Krutch, *Comedy and Conscience After the Restoration* (New York and London, 1961).

[133] Thomas Southerne, *The Wives' Excuse; Or Cuckolds Make Themselves* (1691), in *The Works of Thomas Southerne*, ed. Robert Jordan and Harold Love (2 vols. Oxford, 1988), I, p. 311.

[134] Sir John Vanbrugh and Colley Cibber, *The Provoked Husband, Or a Journey to London* (1728), ed. Peter Dixon (London, 1975), Epilogue, p. 153.

[135] Colley Cibber, *The Careless Husband* (1705), ed. William W. Appleton (London, 1967), V. vii. 328.

[136] Vanbrugh and Cibber, *Provoked Husband*, 'To the Queen', p. 3.

Elsewhere, a popular etiquette book for would-be gentlemen, *The Man of Manners: Or, Plebeian Polish'd* (1735), guided its readers to avoid starting dinner-table conversations with the jocular question 'Who can think of a cuckold?'[137] Joseph Addison, whose *Spectator* papers have been seen as a barometer of changing genteel opinion, regarded cuckolding plots of Restoration comedy as monotonous, 'ill-bred' and the products of a 'tast[e]less age'. What made cuckolding humour so offensive to him was that it had become utterly indiscriminating – a characteristic, according to Cicero, of crude and vulgar jesting. 'If an Alderman appears upon the stage', he complained, 'you may be sure it is in order to be cuckolded.' The same might be said for 'Knights and Baronets, Country-Squires, and Justices of the Quorum' or indeed any husband 'that is a little grave or elderly'.[138] Mocking the misfortunes of others was 'ungenerous' of spirit and wholly inconducive to the principles of accommodation that underpinned politeness. Rather than being the butt of mockery and derision, Addison argued that the cuckolded husband should be regarded as an 'innocent, unhappy creature' deserving compassion.[139]

All this evidence suggests that by the eighteenth century, certainly among the formers of polite opinion, it was considered distasteful and socially unacceptable to laugh at deceived husbands.[140] However, in spite of the shifting focus of new matrimonial drama and the arguments of reformers, older sex comedies remained an important part of the eighteenth-century theatrical repertoire. *The Country Wife* was revived no fewer than sixty-three times between 1701 and 1729, and a further forty-seven times between 1730 and 1740. This compares with only two known performances of the play from the time of its debut in January 1675 to 1700. Another cuckolding classic, Shadwell's *Epsom Wells* enjoyed a new popularity in the early eighteenth century with eighteen performances registered between 1708 and 1715.[141] Many of these eighteenth-century revivals were benefit performances, intended to raise money for actors or companies, suggesting that cuckolding comedies retained a crowd-drawing appeal. Even an advocate of social decorum such as Richard Steele could derive 'delight' from the skilful portrayal of cuckolds on stage. After viewing one of the four performances of *Epsom Wells* in April 1709, he declared that the comedian

---

[137] *The Man of Manners: Or, Plebeian Polish'd* (London, 1735), p. 5.

[138] *Spectator*, IV, p. 68 (1 Aug. 1712). See also M. A. Screech, *Laughter at the Foot of the Cross* (Harmondsworth, 1997), p. 137.

[139] *Spectator*, II, pp. 466–7; IV, p. 68.

[140] Keith Thomas, 'The Place of Laughter in Tudor and Stuart England', *Times Literary Supplement*, 21 January (1977), pp. 80–1; Stuart Tave, *The Amiable Humorist: a Study in the Comic Theory of the Eighteenth and Early Nineteenth Centuries* (Chicago, IL and London, 1960); L. Norrel, 'The Cuckold in Restoration Comedy', PhD thesis, Florida State University (1962), ch. 5.

[141] Data derived from William Van Lennep, Emmett L. Avery, Arthur H. Scouten, George Winchester Stone and Charles Beecher Hogan (eds.) *The London Stage, 1660–1800* (5 vols., Carbondale, IL, 1960–8), I–III.

William Bullock had played the henpecked cuckold Mr Biskett 'with such a Natural Air and Propriety of Folly', that in a scene where he is beaten, 'one cannot help wishing the Whip in one's own hand so richly does he seem to deserve his Chastisement'.[142] Cuckolds remained popular figures in ballads and jestbooks, even those ostensibly aimed at 'People of the best taste'.[143] The man who conspired in his wife's adultery for profit continued to be mocked remorselessly in literary and satirical publications, prints and the press throughout the eighteenth century.[144] The cuckold's death as a comic figure should not be exaggerated. But there can be little doubt that by the eighteenth century cuckoldry was portrayed as a more complex phenomenon.

Why, then, did early modern audiences laugh at cuckoldry and how did perceptions of it change over time? It is difficult to avoid the notion that the preponderance of jokes about faithless wives and men's inability to control them in the seventeenth century spoke to deep cultural concerns about the limits of patriarchal authority. Such humour may have worked as a 'safety valve' allowing men to express and confront their fears while simultaneously reasserting the principle that women should be chaste and submissive.[145] But this alone fails to fully comprehend the complexity of cuckoldry as a cultural theme, nor does it take into account its different meanings. Although there is no doubt that cuckoldry was seen as shameful and damaging to manliness, it was not regarded in monolithic terms. Writers paid a good deal of attention to the degrees of shame attached to cuckoldry, building on the longer-standing distinction between cuckold and wittol. This provided a means of trying to make sense of the ignominy caused to a man by his wife's adultery, of testing the limits and interrogating the meanings of dishonour. The proliferation of these more complex, inquisitive treatises on cuckoldry in the later seventeenth century was consistent with the wider interrogation of the meanings of marriage and infidelity in this period. Opinions on cuckoldry varied considerably, from those who saw it ironically as a cohesive social bond, to others who used it to expose social tensions and division.

However, from the last decade of the seventeenth century cuckolding comedy faced a hitherto unprecedented volume of criticism, much of it directed against the stage. Moralists argued that cuckold plays brought marriage into contempt and fostered disrespect towards male authority figures – the frequent butts of matrimonial humour. Both moralists and female playgoers argued that cuckold

---

[142] *Tatler*, I, p. 68.

[143] For instance, *Pinkethman's Jests: Or, Wit Refin'd. Being a New-Year's Gift for young Gentlemen and Ladies* (London, 1721), pp. 22, 23, 29, 36, 48, 63, 83, 87, 98, 100, 102.

[144] Peter Wagner, *Eros Revived: Erotica of the Enlightenment in England and America* (London, 1990), pp. 113–32. See also chapter 6 below.

[145] Alison Sinclair, *The Deceived Husband: a Kleinian Approach to the Literature of Infidelity* (Oxford, 1993), p. 28; Thomas, 'Place of Laughter', p. 78; Foyster, 'A Laughing Matter?', p. 9.

plays were offensive to women, indiscriminately casting wives as lustful whores and failing to treat women with the 'complaisance' and decency that their sex deserved. To those who saw women as by nature the more chaste and virtuous sex, cuckolding comedies looked dangerously outmoded. Furthermore, exponents of polite manners argued that it was crude, insensitive and ungenerous to expose men's marital misfortunes to derision. In an attempt to distance elite sensibilities and tastes from those of the 'vulgar' multitude, writers like Joseph Addison attempted to redefine the boundaries of acceptable laughter as a tool of social and cultural polarisation. At the same time, correspondents to the *Athenian Mercury* saw cuckoldry in terms of personal misfortune rather than as an occasion for public derision. Their letters, often tinged with sadness, anger and frustration, sought a more pragmatic sympathy for the cuckold's plight. These predominantly middling sort correspondents were concerned above all that their livelihoods would not suffer by their wives' behaviour – for them, the emotional and the economic were not easily divisible. Cuckoldry was still shameful and damaging to manliness and economic standing, but the shame expressed in these letters seemed to come primarily from *within*. Layered with personal circumstances, cuckoldry was cast more as a personal misfortune, although clearly one which (if not managed carefully) might have a wider impact. The proliferation of these more complex, sensitive portrayals of cuckoldry after 1688 is significant and is congruent with new political arguments regarding the family as a 'private' institution emerging at this time. However, the continuation of cuckolding humour into the eighteenth century shows us that the acceptance of these ideas was not universal and there were still contexts in which the deceived husband could be seen as worthy of mockery and contempt – especially if his behaviour was hypocritical or if he connived in his wife's adultery. In fine, there may have been a greater willingness on the part of writers and audiences to view cuckoldry as tragedy rather than comedy, but there were still many shades of opinion. For the truly tragic effects of adultery, we have to look elsewhere.

4. Sex, death and betrayal: adultery and murder

In the summer of 1679 a pamphlet was printed in London relating the sordid life of a Dorset bricklayer named James Robinson. Despite being born of 'good Parents' and 'well Educated in consideration of such an Employ', Robinson developed from an early age a 'head-strong humour', which led him into the debauched company of 'leud and wicked women'. At length his parents persuaded him to marry a 'beautiful and civil Maiden', hoping that her virtuous entreaties and the duties of conjugal fidelity would 'wean him from his darling vice'. But Robinson was soon led astray 'by the Devil' and by 'the insnaring delusions of a wicked Harlot'. Together the 'Secret Caball contrived between himself, his Mistris and Infernal Friend' plotted the murder of his wife by breaking her neck. Disguising the killing in such a way as to make it look as though his wife had died accidentally by falling out of bed, Robinson 'passed free from Justice'. But his success was short lived. Debating with his 'Gang' of alehouse companions one evening the various merits of rival ways to silence a scolding wife's tongue and put her 'to eternal silence', 'his own tongue betrayed his life, for says he, Turn but a Scolding Wives Neck round, and her Continual Clapper will no more allarm you, tho' it be placed right again; and to secure yourselves from the suspicion of the people, you may give out that she Dyed of sudden Fits.' Suspicions soon followed that his wife might have met her death in this way and Robinson was arrested. Brought before the local Justice of the Peace, he strenuously protested his innocence, declaring that 'if he was guilty, Divine Vengeance might light upon him, and that he might Rott alive'. Once again loose talk was to cost him dear, 'for on a sudden all his limbs began to swell with exceeding pain, and to rot by degrees'. Such torments at length persuaded him to make a full confession and repent his life of sin. The account ended with a description of Robinson's execution on 5 August in the hope that his 'lamentable Example' would warn all 'desperate and wicked minded persons' against 'dy[e]ing their impious hands in

Innocent Blood, lest Heavens vengeance find them out, though ne'r so secretly contrived'.[1]

The manifold ways in which adulterous passions could end in bloodshed were a topic of enduring fascination in early modern England. As 'secret crimes', adultery and murder bore similar characteristics. Conducting an affair behind a spouse's back and plotting a murder both involved elements of deception, treachery and betrayal. An account of one woman's duplicitous love affairs and eventual poisoning of her husband in 1684 was published as a means of exposing the general threats of 'Dissimulation, Treachery and Cruelty to Neighbours and Lovers, Bloody and Treasonous Practices against Parents and Husbands'.[2] Commentators could cite biblical precedents – such as the slaying of the Shechemites as punishment for Shechem's rape of Dinah, Absolom's ordering the murder of Amnon after he had ravished Tamar and the story of David and Bathsheba – to prove, as the theologian Immanuel Bourne put it, that 'In this Life this Sin of Adultery and Fornication oftentimes is an occasion of Murder'.[3]

This chapter examines the links between adultery and murder in later seventeenth- and early eighteenth-century England by analysing the popular literature of domestic homicide. Pamphlet accounts of familial murder, such as the tale of James Robinson, laid bare the bloody consequences of conjugal disintegration. From the sixteenth century through to the eighteenth, they served up tales of obsession, duplicity, morbid jealousy and vengeful crimes of passion, often, as was the case here, laid out in a comforting framework of providential discovery and divine justice. As one of the primary ways in which the reading public learned of the marital breakdown of named individuals, these publications demand attention for the light they shed on the fashioning of personal experience into culturally determined narratives of crime and sexual deviance. Crime pamphlets therefore provide an important means of studying the application of ideals and discourses concerning marriage explored in previous chapters. This chapter reveals the strategies of presenting adultery within the conventions of murder narratives. It explores the ways in which adultery could lead to violence and analyses the meanings of crimes of passion, assessing the extent to which the murder of an unfaithful spouse or a rival might be justified on the grounds of provocation. Finally, the chapter examines how the reporting of crimes of adulterous passions changed over time as crime writing diversified.

---

[1] *The Strange and Wonderful Relation of a Barbarous Murder Committed by James Robi[n]son, A Brick-Layer, Upon the Body of His Own Wife* (London, 1679), pp. 1–4.

[2] John Newton, *The Penitent Recognition of Joseph's Brethren: a Sermon Occasion'd by Elizabeth Ridgeway* (London, 1684), p. 12.

[3] Immanuel Bourne, *A Gold Chain of Directions with Twenty Gold-Links of Love, to Preserve Love Firm between Husband and Wife during their Lives* (London, 1669), p. 70; William Fleetwood, *A Funeral Sermon Upon Mr Noble* (London, 1713), p. 9. See also Tessa Watt, *Cheap Print and Popular Piety, 1550–1640* (Cambridge, 1991), pp. 117–19, 126.

If it is accepted that murder literature 'affords us considerable insights into contemporary views on, and experiences of, marital breakdown', it must also be recognised that different types of domestic murder offered different perspectives on households destroyed by unrestrained passions.[4] Adultery played a significant, yet largely unexceptional, role in many murder pamphlets as one sin among many that might lead a person from the path of righteousness down the slippery slope of moral decline that led to homicide. Stories of murders of new-born illegitimate children, where the effects of illicit sex were most tangible, raised questions about seduction and moral responsibility and were used to highlight the dangers of fornication. Although the majority of these cases involved single women, and therefore less obviously concerned the household disordered by marital infidelity, they were still sometimes presented by pamphleteers as general 'Warning[s] to Adulterers and Adulteresses to repent of, and forsake their crimes'.[5]

It was in narratives of spouse murder that the terrible effects of adultery were most painfully relayed. Cases where murder was motivated by jealousy, or revenge in response to the other spouse's infidelity, raised important legal and moral questions about provocation and responsibility – the extent to which killing might be justified by concepts of honour. A different set of concerns was raised by cases where adulterous husbands or wives were incited to kill their partners because they had become an obstacle to the illicit relationship. Crucially, the perception of spouse murder was shaped by the special legal categorisation of husband-murder as an act of 'petty treason', carrying especially strong overtones of domestic disorder and disobedience. While husbands found guilty of killing their wives faced death by hanging, women who killed their partners faced the more severe penalty of being burnt at the stake.[6] Murder narratives therefore brought into sharp focus the gendered nature of domestic authority.

---

[4] J. A. Sharpe, 'Domestic Homicide in Early Modern England', *Historical Journal*, 24 (1981), 41; cf. Mark Jackson, *New-Born Child Murder: Women, Illegitimacy and the Courts in Eighteenth-Century England* (Manchester, 1996), pp. 6–7.

[5] *Fair Warning to Murderers of Infants: Being An Account of the Tryal, Condemnation and Execution of Mary Goodenough at the Assizes Held in Oxon., in February 1691/2* (London, 1692), sig. A2. On infanticide as a crime associated with single women, see J. M. Beattie, *Crime and the Courts in England 1660–1800* (Oxford, 1986), pp. 113–24; Peter C. Hoffer and N. E. H. Hull, *Murdering Mothers: Infanticide in England and New England 1558–1803* (New York and London, 1984); Jackson, *New-Born Child Murder*; Keith Wrightson, 'Infanticide in Earlier Seventeenth-Century England', *Local Population Studies*, 15 (1975), 10–22; Laura Gowing, 'Secret Births and Infanticide in Seventeenth-Century England', *PP*, 156 (1997), 67–115.

[6] Frances E. Dolan, *Dangerous Familiars: Representations of Domestic Crime in England, 1550–1700* (Ithaca, NY and London, 1994), ch. 1; Garthine Walker, '"Demons in Female Form": Representations of Women and Gender in Murder Pamphlets of the Late Sixteenth and Early Seventeenth Centuries', in William Zunder and Suzanne Trill (eds.), *Writing and the English Renaissance* (London and New York, 1996), p. 131; Walker, 'Crime, Gender and Social Order in Early Modern Cheshire', PhD thesis, University of Liverpool (1994), p. 145; Laura Gowing, *Domestic Dangers: Women, Words and Sex in Early Modern London* (Oxford, 1996), pp. 202, 205; Beattie, *Crime and the Courts*, p. 100.

Although early modern crime statistics are always haunted by the 'dark figures' of unreported offences and unsurviving records, all the available evidence suggests that murder within the family was a fairly rare occurrence.[7] In Essex between 1560 and 1709, according to Sharpe's calculations, 59 out of a total of 327 homicide indictments involved the killing of spouses or blood relatives.[8] Beattie's evidence from the Surrey Assize proceedings suggests that familial murder accounted for 14 of a total of 39 homicide indictments filed between 1678 and 1774, a period when, more generally, the number of indictments for violent crime was falling.[9] While published accounts of domestic murder represented only a sample of the total output of crime writing in this period, the very rarity of the offence, together with the particular issues and emotions it raised, made its reporting particularly sensational. Murder pamphlets emphasised the heinousness of extra-marital sex to domestic relations by associating it with murder, and vice versa. Taken together, these narratives provide a fascinating route into the world of adulterous passions gone horribly awry.

SELLING SEX AND VIOLENCE: THE LITERATURE OF MURDER

Since the content of murder pamphlets is closely related to their form, it is necessary at the outset to examine briefly the conventions, authorship and readership of these texts. Whether their purpose was to legitimise state power and promote consensual attitudes to the law or to serve as weapons of propaganda by opposing religious parties, to provide moral *exempla* or lurid titillation (or both simultaneously), accounts of murders and executions were immensely popular in early modern England.[10] The standard mode of reporting established by the early seventeenth century was an eight-page pamphlet, in which murders were related within a standard paradigm of sin, crime and repentance. Typically selling for 2d unbound, it has been suggested that the typical purchasers of

---

[7] However, J. S. Cockburn has argued that the figures may underestimate the number of violent crimes involving family members: 'Patterns of Violence in English Society: Homicide in Kent 1560–1985', *PP*, 130 (1991), 95–6.

[8] Sharpe, 'Domestic Homicide', p. 34. On the low proportion of indictments for homicide compared with those for other felonies across the early modern period more generally see J. A. Sharpe, *Crime in Early Modern England 1550–1750* (London and New York, 1984), pp. 55, 60–2.

[9] Beattie, *Crime and the Courts*, p. 105.

[10] For debates on the political functions of murder literature see J. A. Sharpe, '"Last Dying Speeches": Religion, Ideology and Public Execution in Seventeenth Century England', *PP*, 107 (1985), 144–67; Peter Lake, 'Deeds Against Nature: Cheap Print, Protestantism and Murder in Early Seventeenth Century England', in Kevin Sharpe and Peter Lake (eds.), *Culture and Politics in Early Stuart England* (Basingstoke, 1994), pp. 257–83; Malcolm Gaskill, 'Reporting Murder: Fiction in the Archives in Early Modern England', *Social History*, 23 (1998), 1–30; Gaskill, 'The Displacement of Providence: Policing and Prosecution in Seventeenth- and Eighteenth-Century England', *Continuity and Change*, 11 (1996), 341–74.

the murder pamphlet were members of the urban middling sort, particularly London craftsmen, merchants and their households who had attained reasonable levels of literacy and had enough disposable income to spend on cheap literature, together with a few members of the gentry. Broadside accounts relaying felons' 'dying speeches' made on the scaffold before execution and ballads were cheaper forms of murder literature, possibly reaching a wider audience.[11]

After the Restoration, especially during the lapse of the Licensing Act between 1679 and 1685, the literature of murder proliferated, as new media stimulated public interest in crime reporting. The law courts became an important source of 'home news' for the London and, later, the provincial press.[12] Metropolitan newspapers of the Restoration reported details of violent deaths from the Bills of Mortality, and in some cases kept the public informed of the search for murderers, their examinations, trials and executions, sometimes generating renewed interest in cases when new evidence was brought to light.[13] A new kind of serial publication, the *Old Bailey Sessions Papers*, reporting crimes that came before the London criminal courts, began to be published from the 1670s. Appearing eight times a year, these accounts developed a more dispassionate, self-consciously factual and legalistic perspective on crime. They concentrated more on trial proceedings and processes of judicial decision-making than on the broader lessons individual cases might teach a sinful world.[14] At the same time, interest in the lives of criminals, the diverse ways in which they fell into lives of crime, and their penitence in prison, was stimulated by new biographical publications emerging in this period. Highly popular was the serialised *Account* of prisoners' lives written by the Ordinary (chaplain) of Newgate gaol, which sold for between 3d and 6d and had a print run of thousands.[15] Out of this type of publication emerged the eighteenth-century genre of lengthy and detailed criminal biographies, many of which ran into multiple editions. With their probing of the character and motivations of the criminal, these publications played a significant role in the development of the novel and other forms of biographical and autobiographical writing.[16]

---

[11] Dolan, *Dangerous Familiars*, pp. 7–8; Sharpe, 'Domestic Homicide', p. 40. See also Watt, *Cheap Print and Popular Piety*, pp. 260–64.

[12] James Sutherland, *The Restoration Newspaper and its Development* (Cambridge, 1986), pp. 52–79; G. A. Cranfield, *The Development of the Provincial Newspaper 1700–1760* (Oxford, 1962), p. 65.

[13] Sutherland, *Restoration Newspaper*, p. 59.

[14] Michael Harris, 'Trials and Criminal Biographies: a Case Study in Distribution', in Robin Myers and Michael Harris (eds.), *Sale and Distribution of Books from 1700* (Oxford, 1982), pp. 1–36.

[15] Ibid., pp. 18–19; P. Linebaugh, 'The Ordinary of Newgate and his *Account*', in J. S. Cockburn (ed.), *Crime in England 1550–1800* (London, 1977), pp. 246–69.

[16] The relationship between murder pamphlets and novels is discussed in Ian Bell, *Literature and Crime in Augustan England* (London, 1991); Lincoln Faller, *Turned to Account: the Forms and Functions of Criminal Biography in Late Seventeenth- and Early Eighteenth-Century England* (Cambridge, 1987); Philip Rawlings, *Drunks, Whores and Idle Apprentices: Criminal Biographies of the Eighteenth Century* (London, 1992).

These developments had important consequences for the ways in which pamphlets represented their subject matter. In the first place, the growth of competition generated by this process seems to have altered the timing of the composition of murder literature, bringing the publications closer temporally to the events they described. While pamphlets had normally appeared after the trial and execution, they increasingly began to be published in the period between sentencing and execution and even, in some particularly sensational cases, before the trial itself. In 1680 the hacking to death and dismembering of Walter Osgood, a Southwark hatter, by his unfaithful wife, Margaret, aroused such horror that a publication was rushed out before the case reached court, pre-empting other publications on the trial. Details of the case were derived from the Justice of the Peace's pre-trial hearing, and extraneous details of the Osgoods' unhappy marriage were supplied by interviews with neighbours. One 'ancient Neighbour' attested that 'they seldome went to bed without a storm of Oaths and mutual curses'.[17] Aside from the demands of competition, speed of publication had important consequences for the didactic message of the texts. The immediacy of the texts permitted their authors to conceive of the reader as being involved in the narratives, so that readers would identify themselves with the events and personalities described and take warning from them, whilst at the same time remaining separate, voyeuristically watching the terrible events as they unfolded before their eyes.[18]

Although the identity of writers of many murder pamphlets remains obscure, it would appear that clergymen played a prominent role in fashioning narratives of murder and repentance throughout the seventeenth century.[19] Their exclusive access to prisoners awaiting execution to prepare their souls for a penitent end put them in an advantageous position to produce these accounts.[20] The Ordinary of Newgate's *Account* was financially successful, indicating that the writing of such narratives might, like the performance of clandestine marriage ceremonies, provide a lucrative source of additional income for London's prison chaplains from the end of the seventeenth century.[21] Other accounts, most notably 'dying speeches', claimed to be written by the malefactors themselves, but these too were probably shaped by the ministers attending the prisoners or by those attending the execution who sought to profit from public

---

[17] *Dreadful News from Southwark: Or a True Account of the Most Horrid Murder Committed by Margaret Osgood, on Her Husband Walter Osgood a Hatmaker* (n.p., n.d. [c.1680]), p. 2.

[18] Lennard Davis, *Factual Fictions: the Origins of the English Novel* (New York, 1983) esp. pp. 58–67.

[19] See Sharpe, '"Last Dying Speeches"'; Lake, 'Deeds Against Nature', p. 260.

[20] For examples of cases of spouse murder written by ministers see Newton, *Penitent Recognition of Joseph's Brethren*; Samuel Smith, *The Behaviour of Edward Kirk, After His Condemnation for Murdering His Wife* (London, 1684).

[21] Linebaugh, 'The Ordinary of Newgate and his *Account*', p. 250.

interest in the final words of the condemned.[22] The involvement of clergy helps to explain the moralistic tone of many publications and their similarity with sermons and religious conduct literature. However, the mounting pressure to produce pamphlets quickly may have increased the number of narratives produced by unknown hack writers employed by publishers to sit in the courtroom and note down the more sensational cases. The presence of 'brachygraphy men' sitting in the courtroom taking shorthand notes to turn into 'scurvy pamphlets and lewd ballads' had been noted by early seventeenth-century commentators. The role of these shorthand writers was to become more prominent in the increasingly competitive later seventeenth-century marketplace for print culture.[23]

Authors of pamphlet and ballad accounts of murders were at pains to stress that their publications were 'full', 'just', 'exact' and, above all, 'true'. The moral message of the pamphlets derived its power precisely from the premise that the people described in the accounts were real and that the events had actually taken place, giving them an immediacy and relevance sometimes lacking from traditional religious conduct literature. But notwithstanding these protestations, the factual veracity of murder pamphlets must be viewed with some scepticism. While it is unhelpful to generalise about the 'truth content' of individual cases, it is undoubtedly true that the act of reporting cases, of shaping events into a narrative that would fit real events into a form which would tell a morally satisfying story of sinful decline and divine judgement, did involve a greater or lesser degree of refashioning or even outright fabrication.[24] Printed accounts of murder are not so much records of reality as 'evidence of the processes of cultural formation and transformation', best seen as 'fictional' rather than journalistic texts.[25]

Authors of murder pamphlets were faced with a paradox: on the one hand these publications thrived on the unusual nature of the crimes they depicted, emphasising the 'barbarous and inhumane' aspects of murder and the 'wicked and most unnatural' characters of murderers.[26] Yet for their didactic message to work the content of the pamphlets had to be moulded in such a way as to make the bloody events appear relevant to everyone and for readers to identify with the figure of the murderer. This involved a process which David Lindley has termed a 'kind of narrative back formation' whereby incidents were selected from the earlier life of the felon and presented in a form which would

---

[22] Sharpe, '"Last Dying Speeches"', *passim*.

[23] John Webster, *The Devil's Law Case* (1623), ed. Frances A. Shirley (Rochester, NY, 1972), IV. ii. 30, 34. Brachygraphy was a form of shorthand writing.

[24] Gaskill, 'Reporting Murder', p. 6.

[25] Dolan, *Dangerous Familiars*, p. 3; Walker, '"Demons in Female Form"', p. 124.

[26] E.g., *The Whole Tryals, With the Examination and Condemnation of John Taylor and John Flint* (London, 1706), p. 2; *A True Relation of the Most Horrible Murther, Committed By Thomas White* (London, 1682), p. 4.

explain his or her final actions.[27] No detail was merely incidental, and once someone was fixed as a murderer or as an accomplice to murder, a range of cultural assumptions could be brought into play to construct a character suitable to their role. The pattern was of a 'domino effect' of multiplying sin in which homicide became predictable and inevitable.[28] By focusing upon the events which led up to murder, authors were able to avoid the 'problem' of the anomalous nature of familial and other forms of murder by revealing 'those Seeds of Corruption which are implanted in us all' which, if not 'sufficiently checked', might have the same dreadful outcome.[29] In constructing events to illustrate a cultural and moral commonplace, that one sin led to another, pamphlets articulated a set of 'moral truths' about crime and its consequences recognisable to all.[30]

FASHIONING ADULTERY AND MURDER: PROVOCATION AND BETRAYAL

What role, then, did adultery play in murder narratives and how did stories of violent death fashion adulterous passions? Meanings of murder were derived from the manner and circumstances of death. Murder methods conveyed most powerfully the destruction of values inherent in the crime and depiction of deaths in narratives of spouse murder were frequently contrived in such a way that would connote a terrible betrayal of intimacy. Death ushered in under the veil of affection gave narratives of spouse-murder their horrific force. The image of Judas's kiss of betrayal, often found in stories of wife-murder, was a powerful expression of infidelity, emphasising that the breach of wedlock not only broke the perfect friendship that was supposed to exist between man and wife, but also broke the special covenant with God established by the marriage vows. It was said of John Marketman, a naval surgeon from West Ham (Essex), that he took his wife 'about the neck Judas like as if he intended to kiss her' before thrusting a knife deep into her heart.[31] In a ballad account of John Chambers, 'The Bloody-minded Husband', who had his servant shoot his wife so that he might enjoy 'sinful pleasures' with his 'wanton Harlot', Chambers is depicted as making to 'salute' his wife as she lay dying:

[27] David Lindley, *The Trials of Frances Howard: Fact and Fiction at the Court of King James* (London and New York, 1993), p. 44.

[28] Cynthia Herrup, 'Law and Morality in Seventeenth-Century England', *PP*, 106 (1985), 109.

[29] *Serious Admonitions to Youth, in a Short Account of the Life, Trial, Condemnation and Execution of Mrs Mary Channing* (London, 1706), p. 4.

[30] Gaskill, 'Reporting Murder', pp. 5–6 and *passim*; Natalie Zemon Davis, *Fiction in the Archives: Pardon Tales and their Tellers in Sixteenth-Century France* (Stanford, CA, 1987), p. 4.

[31] *The True Narrative of the Execution of John Marketman, Chyrurgion, of West Ham in Essex, for Committing a Horrible and Bloody Murther Upon the Body of His Wife* (n.p., n.d. [1680]), p. 3.

> But she (alas) refus'd his Judas kiss,
> And with her dying voice, she told him this;
> By Murther now you have procur'd my death,
> And with those words she yielded up her breath.[32]

Different, but no less deceitful, was the way in which Thomas White, a Shropshire ironworker's clerk, dispatched his wife in 1682. White had contracted the pox thanks to 'the Abuse of Himself with lewd Women', and had passed it on to his wife. When she complained about her infection, White threatened that 'if she in any way should make it farther known, he would be her Death, and that She nor her Children should never be the better for his Estate', upon which she fled for her own safety. At length, White feigned reconciliation and gave his wife 'Promises not to do her any harm'. However, 'this wicked and most unnatural wretch having a scimitar by his side, so secretly and by degrees got it out of his Scabberd' and passing the point of its blade 'through the Pocket-Hole of his Coat...as he sate close by Her' stabbed her in the right breast 'upon which she died immediately'.[33] In this way the mode of death powerfully reinforced the sense of betrayal and the destruction of love inherent in White's prior acts of adultery.

Another form of death carrying powerful overtones of treachery was poisoning. Poison was popularly seen as a woman's weapon, both practically as the preparation of food and drink was part of women's domestic work, and symbolically, representing women's supposed natural duplicity. Murder by poisoning was both stealthy and underhand, but also represented a breach of everyday trust and a deadly abuse of household responsibility.[34] Authors of murder pamphlets went to elaborate lengths to describe the ways in which poison was secreted in the victuals of the unsuspecting victim. John Newton's account of a Leicestershire murderess, Elizabeth Ridgway, related how she had purchased poison from a shop in Ashby de la Zouch which she had mixed with broth and given to her husband on his return from work.[35] But later seventeenth-century murder pamphlets and ballads presented poisoning as a weapon used by husbands as well as wives. There were times during illness or childbirth, when the wife was not in full command of the resources of her household and depended on the help of others. John Cupper murdered his wife, Hannah, shortly after she had given birth. After she had 'lain in her month' and was still in a vulnerable state, Cupper, with the help of Judith Brown, his servant and mistress, fed her small portions of poison in her milk and beer, finally procuring her death by giving her a large dose of 'White Arsenick in Milk'.[36] The exceptional

[32] The Pepys Ballads, ed. Hyder Rollins (8 vols., Cambridge, MA, 1931), III, pp. 203–4.
[33] True Relation of the Most Horrible Murther, Committed by Thomas White, pp. 2, 4.
[34] Walker, 'Crime, Gender and Social Order', pp. 147–8.
[35] Newton, Penitent Recognition of Joseph's Brethren, p. 8.
[36] William Smith, A Just Account of the Horrid Contrivance of John Cupper and Judith Brown His Servant, in Poysoning His Wife (London, 1684), p. 8.

conditions of defencelessness in which John Cupper tended his wife amplified the horror of this particular case. Edmund Allen, a notorious bigamist and inveterate wencher, was also portrayed as killing his wife by poisoning her 'under the pretence of more than usual love'.[37] Narratives of poisoning turned the household into a dangerous and paranoid environment, in which relationships properly based on trust could be horrifically betrayed and domestic intimacy was insidiously abused.

One of the chief reasons why adultery-related homicide generated such interest was because it fed into wider concerns that, in what was for the majority of people a divorceless society, adulterous lovers might use foul means to break the marriage knot. 'If you like another Partner in the Way of Marriage', wrote William Fleetwood, 'the way is open to your Escape and Satisfaction by the many Secret Instruments of Death and Dispatch.'[38] Thus it was reported in 1686 that Esther Ives and John Noyse, a cooper from Romsey in Hampshire, had strangled Esther's husband, William, in order 'to make a freer way for their unlawful lust; Or as it is conjectured, being rid of him, they might marry'. Indeed, it was precisely because Ives and Noyse were 'known to be People of bad Conversation' that the constable called to investigate William Ives's death made a more rigorous search of the corpse in order to establish that foul play had been involved.[39] Likewise in 1713 Richard Noble, found guilty of murdering John Sayer, his lover's husband, denied in his speech upon receiving sentence the rumour that he killed Sayer in order to 'remove him out of the World to enjoy his wife (as was suggested) without Molestation'.[40] Laura Gowing has astutely observed that in the early seventeenth-century metropolis, where remarriage after widowhood was common, suspicions about murder as a pragmatic crime would have been particularly resonant.[41] Although by the later seventeenth century rates of remarriage in the capital were falling, the secrecy and uncertainty surrounding marriage formation aroused by the growing number of clandestine unions made sure that it remained a topical theme.[42]

While these accounts highlighted the extraordinary lengths some people might go to in order to remove obstacles to their unlawful passions, narratives describing the death of an adulterous partner or their lover raised a different set of questions about the extent to which homicide was a justifiable, or at least excusable, remedy for injured spouses. There is no doubt that revenge killing was a popular literary theme, especially in moralising cautionary tales. We have already seen how moralists were able to draw on a large repertoire of grisly tales

---

[37] *Pepys Ballads*, ed. Rollins, VII, p. 90.   [38] Fleetwood, *Funeral Sermon upon Mr Noble*, p. 9.

[39] *A Full and True Account of a Most Barbarous and Bloody Murther Committed by Esther Ives, with the Assistance of John Noyse a Cooper* (London, 1686), pp. 4, 5.

[40] *A Full Account of the Case of John Sayer Esq. . . . Second Edition With Additions* (London, 1713), p. 37. This case is examined in more detail below.

[41] Gowing, *Domestic Dangers*, p. 205.

[42] Jeremy Boulton, 'London Widowhood Revisited: the Decline of Female Remarriage in the Seventeenth and Eighteenth Centuries', *Continuity and Change*, 5 (1990), 323–55.

of adulterers meeting peculiarly messy ends to indicate God's punishment of sinners. Many of these stories made the cuckolded husband the primary agent of retributive justice. *A Caveat for Sinners*, a broadside against adultery published in 1683, began with a 'Turkish History' of 'one Garella Mulchassa' who, 'living in Adultery with Amulla, at last Poysons him, and commits Adultery with Leonardo, whom she endeavoured to Stiffle, but he escaped and stabs her; She is Strangled by the command of her Husband, and he fley'd alive.' The story was illustrated with five woodcuts, four of which depicted scenes of death and mutilation to drive home the message: the scene of the lovers in bed together was followed by Garella giving Amulla the bowl of poison, his death, Garella being stabbed and strangled, Leonardo being flayed alive, and finally a bonus image – apparently unconnected to the story but consistent with the theme of violent reprisal – of an adulterer having his tongue bored.[43]

John Reynolds's ever-popular *God's Revenge Against the Crying and Execrable Sin of Adultery*, though dating from the early seventeenth century, was reprinted in 1669 and 1708 with illustrations and was replete with gory and exotic stories of intrigue in which adulterous passions led to murder. In 'Castrucchio and Gloriana: An Italian History', a husband returns home to find his wife in bed with her lover and wreaks a terrible revenge by stabbing the gallant to death. Upon presenting proof that Castrucchio was 'in Bed with his Lady' to the 'Officers of Justice', his actions were described as 'severe, but just Revenge'. Given this endorsement, he proceeds to force his wife to eat her lover's heart which, being laced with poison, kills her – all of which could have been avoided, the account concluded, had 'humble Vertue' been more the subject of her meditations 'than Covetousness or Ambition'.[44]

Debates about the justification of, or at least excuse for, homicide in cases of adultery at this time focused exclusively on the husband's right to avenge himself if he caught another man in the act of committing adultery with his wife. Legal argument took it for granted that wives were the property of their husbands and as such were incapable of agency. Consequently, there was no hope of mitigation for the wife who murdered her husband or his mistress after discovering them together. There emerged during the seventeenth century a series of categories of provocation that might reduce the charge of murder to the lesser crime of manslaughter. These included hot-blooded intentional killing that resulted from a grossly insulting assault, witnessing a friend, relative or kinsman being attacked or an Englishman unlawfully deprived of his liberty and, crucially, seeing a man in the act of adultery with one's wife. It was

---

[43] R. B., *A Caveat for Sinners, Or, A Warning to Swearers, Blasphemers, and Adulterers* (London, 1683).

[44] John Reynolds, *God's Revenge Against the Crying and Execrable Sin of Adultery, Expressed in Ten Several Tragical Histories* (London, 1706 edn), pp. 30–1. On Reynolds's work see Alexandra Walsham, *Providence in Early Modern England* (Oxford, 1999), pp. 112–14.

important that retribution was instantaneous and based on undeniable proof such as catching the lovers in the sexual act, in order for it to be seen as an understandable (if extreme) response to an outrageous affront. Reflection or delay before acting risked the husband's behaviour being construed as vindictive. The first manslaughter verdict on these grounds was given in 1617 to a man who killed his wife's lover by throwing a joint-stool at him.[45] In 1707 Lord Chief Justice Holt upheld this principle on the grounds that 'adultery is the highest invasion of property . . . if a thief comes to rob another, it is lawful to kill him'.[46] The provocation thus derived from notions of patriarchal propriety and the outrageous affront to a man's honour, which demanded immediate retributive justice. This was the serious side to the jokes, examined in the previous chapter, which gleefully celebrated the actions of husbands who enacted violent revenge on their rivals.

In truth, it seems that very few cases of this nature actually came to court.[47] Moreover, opinion on crimes of passion was divided. The law seemed to uphold aspects of an honour code that was at odds with Christian morality.[48] By the late seventeenth century, this code of honour was increasingly open to criticism. As moral opposition to duelling began to solidify during this period, didactic literature urged cuckolds to refrain from taking violent reprisals against gallants.[49] In June 1691 the *Athenian Mercury* argued that it 'seems absurd for a Gentleman to hazard his life' in the interests of seeking 'an Honourable satisfaction of the Adulterer', since it offered no real means of undoing the damage that had already been done. He should therefore 'slight and scorn' his wife's lover and let them know they were 'not worth our concern' and 'trust their Punishment to t'other world'.[50] By the eighteenth century the basis of the law of provocation was changing. Manslaughter verdicts in cases of adultery were increasingly brought on the grounds that in the heat of jealous anger occasioned by the discovery, the husband had lost his self-control, momentarily causing him to be ruled by his passions. Husbands who took violent reprisals against gallants taken in the act of adultery could still expect a more lenient verdict, but it was no longer underpinned by a code of honorific violence.[51]

---

[45] Jeremy Horder, *Provocation and Responsibility* (Oxford, 1992), pp. 24, 39.

[46] Ibid., p. 39, quoting from *R v. Mawgridge* (1707).

[47] Beattie, *Crime and the Courts*, p. 95, but cf. Elizabeth A. Foyster, *Manhood in Early Modern England: Honour, Sex and Marriage* (London, 1999), pp. 177–93.

[48] Mervyn James, 'English Politics and the Concept of Honour, 1485–1642', *PP*, Supplement no. 3 (1978); Anna Bryson, *From Courtesy to Civility: Changing Codes of Conduct in Early Modern England* (Oxford, 1998), pp. 232–41.

[49] Donna T. Andrew, 'The Code of Honour and its Critics: the Opposition to Duelling in England, 1700–1850', *Social History*, 5 (1980), 409–34.

[50] *AM* II/3, q. 2, 3 June 1691. Similar advice is given in *British Apollo*, iii, 83, 6 Oct. 1710.

[51] Horder, *Provocation and Responsibility*, pp. 87–8 and ch. 5 *passim*. For a later case study see Martin J. Weiner, 'The Sad Story of George Hall: Adultery, Murder and the Politics of Mercy in Mid-Victorian England', *Social History*, 24 (1999), 174–95.

The point of the moralistic stories of revenge found in Reynolds's output and elsewhere was not to encourage husbands to take the law into their own hands, but to prove that all infidelity risked terrible consequences – the goriness of these stories prefigured the agonies that awaited adulterers in hell. While it was recognised that in some circumstances it might be acceptable to display some leniency towards the man who took revenge on his wife's lover, few went so far as to advocate the killing of an unfaithful wife. Reynolds's stories highlighted to an English audience the essential difference of continental manners and concepts of honour. The slaying of the wife and lover by the injured husband was regarded more as a 'sad and lamentable' consequence of adultery than as something celebrated as a form of legitimate retaliation.[52] English protestant conduct literature urged husbands to forgive their errant wives and refrain from all but 'moderate' correction. Excessive violence by husbands was seen as irrational and shameful.[53] Murder pamphlets presented stories of husbands killing their supposedly adulterous wives as tales of dangerous and debilitating jealousy, rather than honourable killing. An 'inveterate and corroding humour', jealousy was portrayed as having a deleterious effect, kindling a 'sullen and secret Fire' which 'burnt inwardly and consum'd' the husband's 'quiet', leaving him powerless to resist the instigations of the devil.[54]

Such may be seen in the case of John Marketman, the most extensively reported example of a husband murdering his adulterous wife published in the later seventeenth century. Marketman apparently returned from sea in 1680 to hear that in his absence his spouse had been 'over lavish of her Favours to a Neighbour of hers', a shoemaker named George Bonah.[55] One pamphlet reported that on his arrival he had 'surprized her too familiar' with Bonah 'whereupon he in a Rage threatned her'. Although on this occasion he was eventually pacified, he retained an 'inward hatred' of his wife for her infidelity. At length, Marketman, 'with a seemed Reconciliation', invited his wife to come home from the neighbour's house where she had been sheltering, and making as if to embrace her 'he stab'd her with a Knife under her Right Breast', whereof she died.[56] Although the question of provocation was raised in some narratives of the case it is presented rather as something which damaged Marketman's spiritual

---

[52] Reynolds, *God's Revenge*, p. 68; cf. Walker, 'Crime, Gender and Social Order', p. 166.

[53] Elizabeth A. Foyster, 'Male Honour, Social Control and Wife Beating in Late Stuart England', *TRHS*, 6th ser., 6 (1996), 215–24.

[54] *Whole Tryals, With the Examination and Condemnation of John Taylor and John Flint*, p. 2.

[55] *The Full and True Relation of All the Proceedings at the Assizes Holden at Chelmsford, for the Countie of Essex* (n.p., n.d. [c.1680]), p. 2. For other accounts of this trial see *True Narrative of the Execution of John Marketman; A Full and True Account of the Penitence of John Marketman During His Imprisonment in Chelmsford Gaol for Murthering His Wife* (London, 1680); *The Wonders of Free Grace* (London, 1690), pp. 81–102; George Meriton, *Immorality, Debauchery and Profaneness Exposed to the Reproof of Scripture and the Censure of Law* (London, 1698), p. 118. Aspects of the case are also discussed in Sharpe, ' "Last Dying Speeches" ', 144–6.

[56] *Full and True Relation of All the Proceedings at the Assizes Holden at Chelmsford*, p. 2.

immune system, causing him to lose his resistance to sinful infection, rather than spurring him to excusable actions. One account reported that Marketman 'oftentimes was affronted and jeered' about his wife's familiarity with Bonah, which weakened his resolve against the 'Temptation of Satan', who 'infused into his heart desire of Revenge and did strongly animate him to this prodigious Cruelty'.[57] Because Marketman's behaviour stemmed from a brooding jealousy, rather than an immediate and 'appropriate' honorific response to his apparent cuckoldry, some pamphlets came to doubt whether Marketman had really caught his wife in bed with Bonah. One account speculated whether he might have been 'debauched and distempered in Drink' at the time and thus in no fit condition to make a reasonable assessment of the situation![58] Ultimately, any claims to justification collapsed in the face of the cold-blooded stealth and deception exercised by Marketman in the killing of his wife. His own dying speech made little reference to his wife's adultery, instead confessing his own sexual lapses which not only included 'fornication and adultery', but also 'those more secret Acts of committing folly by myself', which had no doubt provided some relief during his time aboard ship.[59] At every turn, his behaviour was dishonourable.

However, one pamphlet account did recognise that while the murderous effects of Marketman's jealousy were wrong, he did have a reasonable grievance against George Bonah, and endorsed this by printing a letter purportedly sent by Marketman to his wife's lover shortly before his execution. Bonah is reproached in the strongest terms, being accused of corrupting Marketman's wife for the satisfaction of his 'Brutish Lust' and 'robbing her [of her] Credit making her a Reproach amongst all honest persons', whilst 'depriving her of all that happiness of life which ariseth from the mutual kindness, which is between Man and Wife'. In response to his critics, Marketman presented evidence of their affair, of nocturnal liaisons and secret correspondence much as a husband might do in a marital separation suit. He also claimed that Bonah had tried to have him arrested for spurious debts and to blackmail him into signing over his wife's property to him 'or else be reduced into a condition of nothing but Poverty and Misery'. One Friday evening, he additionally complained, he had been beaten out of his own house at his wife's instigation so she could be 'entertained in your company, the whole night; since which I never had an Hours content'. Not only did Bonah dishonour Marketman by committing adultery with his wife, but he also used the affair to take other liberties, in the process heightening the offence. Having informed Bonah, and the world, of this 'injustice' which amounted to 'no less than Lust and perjury', Marketman concluded his missive by pointedly

---

[57] *True Narrative of the Execution of John Marketman*, p. 2.

[58] Ibid., p. 2; cf. *Full and True Relation of All the Proceedings at the Assizes Holden at Chelmsford*, p. 2.

[59] 'The Speech of John Marketman On the Ladder Before His Execution', repr. in *Full and True Account of the Penitence of John Marketman*, pp. 4, 7.

forgiving the 'injury' done to him and urged Bonah to 'unfeignedly Repent of all your Sins, that God may have Mercy on your Soul'. The retributive justice that Marketman had failed to mete out when he first caught Bonah in bed with his wife was administered belatedly in print rather than with the sword.[60]

GENDER AND THE POLITICS OF DOMESTIC TREACHERY

In the early modern period, as today, husbands were statistically more likely to kill their wives than vice versa.[61] Yet partly because of their rarity, cases of women murdering their spouses aroused special horror. 'Murder at all times is a black and crying sin', wrote the author of *Dreadful News from Southwark*, relating Margaret Osgood's crime, 'but to find it perpetuated deliberately, and by one of the *softer sex*, and by a Wife upon her Husband, and without any proportionate provocation, and to be persisted in, stood unto, and in effect justified, this seems to be the height of malice, and a feared Impiety.'[62] Such a crime offended against all the notions of modesty and decorum conduct book writers projected on to ideal women. However, biblical precedent that 'there is no wrath above the wrath of a woman' served as a reminder of women's susceptibility to violent outburst.[63] The violent crimes of women upset both the gender order and the hierarchy of the household and part of the restorative function of pamphlets was to reinscribe the principles of patriarchal household government. The Reverend John Newton informed Elizabeth Ridgway that her crime was made doubly shocking by the fact that she was responsible not only for killing 'a Man made in the likeness of God', but for murdering 'a Husband set over you as your Soveraign Head'.[64] Although it was recognised that Sarah Elston, convicted in 1678 of stabbing her husband with a pair of scissors, had suffered from her spouse's 'ill husbandry, cross carriage [and] ill company', her case was still used to stress the importance of unquestioning wifely submissiveness. In her printed dying speech she urged all women to 'take warning by her':

> to live in Love and Peace with their Husbands if it be possible; at least to avoid their Fury by going out of the way for the present, when they are in a rage, rather than to stand bandying of words, or teazing them with reproachful Language; which she acknowledged had oft been her own fault: That they should remember that their Husband is their Head, and that the Apostle

---

[60] *Full and True Account of the Penitence of John Marketman*, pp. 12–14; see also Horder, *Provocation and Responsibility*, pp. 48–9.
[61] Walker, '"Demons in Female Form"', p. 136 and *passim*.
[62] *Dreadful News from Southwark*, p. 1 (my emphasis).
[63] Davis, *Fiction in the Archives*, p. 79 and ch. 3 *passim*.
[64] Newton, *Penitent Recognition of Joseph's Brethren*, p. 27.

requires them to be obedient to them in every thing; and this not onely to the kinde and indulgent, but even the peevish and froward ought to have the same observance.[65]

In a cruel statement of society's double standards, instead of being recognised as a victim of domestic abuse, Sarah was made to apologise for her own 'abuse' of the correct duties of a wife.

In narratives of petty treason, cuckoldry was portrayed as a portent of the catastrophic events that lay in store for the injured husband. Mary Channing, a Dorset gentlewoman executed in March 1706 for the murder of her husband, was reported as declaring before her marriage that she would 'make him a cuckold' or some other 'dreadful Calamity' might occur.[66] In the pamphlet narratives a wife's power to cuckold her husband became synonymous with her power to kill him. 'Murder was the culmination of the economic, material, and physical consequences of adultery', argues Gowing, 'it was the last danger that adulterous women posed to their husbands.'[67] Pamphlet accounts of petty treason depicted with some relish wives usurping their husbands' domestic authority, replacing them in the marriage bed with lovers and flagrantly casting off all sense of 'duty'. Mary Channing 'express'd a more than ordinary kindness' for one Mr Nail, a former suitor, providing him with 'a plentiful and costly Entertainment' and obliging her husband 'to quit his own Bed to let him lie in it, whilst he himself was forc'd to make use of a Neighbour's' and she (so she claimed) 'would be contented with the Maid's [bed]'. This 'excess of Civility' kindled rumours of a 'criminal conversation' between Mary and her visitor.[68]

Pamphleteers tried to make familiar what was a very uncommon crime by retailing stereotypes of dangerous femininity, and by filling their stories with timeworn images of female agency run amok. Popular literature had long represented adulterous wives as verbally abusive or violent.[69] 'No wild beast is so cruel as an incensed woman,' warned the author of *Dreadful News from Southwark*, as the narrative depicted Margaret Osgood mutilating her powerless husband, 'regardless of her own Duty'.[70] Authors did everything possible to outrage their audience's sensibilities. Where the murderess hailed from the upper echelons of society, commentators spared few details of her social indiscretions and immodesty in company, which confirmed her as a deviant female in public as much as her sexual transgressions did in private. The genteel Mary Channing's contempt for her tradesman husband that culminated in adultery and murder is rendered all the more unjust by her inability to behave in a manner appropriate to her breeding. 'At several private Entertainments where she

---

[65] *A Warning for Bad Wives: Or, the Manner of the Burning of Sarah Elston* (London, 1678), pp. 2, 6.
[66] *Serious Admonitions to Youth*, p. 13.   [67] Gowing, *Domestic Dangers*, p. 202.
[68] *Serious Admonitions to Youth*, p. 28.   [69] Foyster, *Manhood*, pp. 104–7.
[70] *Dreadful News from Southwark*, p. 3.

was within a few Weeks before she dispatch'd her Husband', it was reported, 'her Discourse was so Lewd, and her Actions so Indecent, that even the Men who were present were asham'd of her Company, and reprov'd her for such a Conversation.'[71] The incivility of Mary Channing embellished her dramatic slide into moral depravity.

Although drawing quantitative data from such ephemeral sources as murder pamphlets poses problems, all evidence suggests that cases of petty treason were reported especially avidly in this literature during the fifty years prior to the outbreak of the Civil War.[72] Murder pamphlets of this period joined in the broader project of securing patriarchal authority by presenting horror stories of female domestic insubordination.[73] In contrast, although sensational cases such as the ones already mentioned were liable to provoke considerable media interest after 1660, suggesting continuing patriarchal anxieties, the majority of cases of spouse murder reported in later seventeenth-century pamphlets concerned the death of wives at the hands of their husbands. Frances Dolan has argued that the upheavals of the Civil War, together with desires to limit the power of the Restoration monarchy and mounting fears of arbitrary government, generated wider interest in the power of all patriarchs, including the nature of authority within the family. This focused attention on cases of domestic tyranny and the abuses of authority by men who killed their household subordinates.[74] Nevertheless, as Dolan herself admits, few pamphleteers were brave enough to use domestic homicide to make explicit attacks on the limits of state power.[75] The late seventeenth-century proliferation of crime writing, and the increasing pressure it placed on publishers to bring out more factually accurate and representative accounts of murder, may provide an alternative explanation. The fact that there were more pamphlets concerned with husbands murdering their wives may reflect, with a greater degree of accuracy, the 'reality' of spouse murder.

However, representations of male household murderers necessarily brought into question the politics of domestic authority. The tone of pamphlets describing adulterous and murderous men was more muted than the sensational reporting of wifely petty treason. Yet they still managed to convey a good deal of disappointment with the husband's dereliction of duty. If women who murdered their husbands committed crimes against obedience, men who murdered their domestic subordinates were guilty of terrible breaches of responsibility or abusing their privileged positions in the household order. In the example of the

[71] *Serious Admonitions to Youth*, pp. 26–7.   [72] Dolan, *Dangerous Familiars*, pp. 89–90.

[73] See also Anthony Fletcher, 'The Protestant Idea of Marriage in Early Modern England', in Anthony Fletcher and Peter Roberts (eds.), *Religion, Culture and Society in Early Modern Britain: Essays in Honour of Patrick Collinson* (Cambridge, 1994), pp. 161–81; David Underdown, 'The Taming of the Scold: the Enforcement of Patriarchal Authority in Early Modern England', in Anthony Fletcher and John Stevenson (eds.), *Order and Disorder in Early Modern England* (Cambridge, 1985), pp. 116–36.

[74] Dolan, *Dangerous Familiars*, p. 97 and ch. 3 *passim*.   [75] Ibid., p. 99.

wife-murderer Thomas White, noted his biographer, 'you see a Man, who by the Laws of God and Common Natural Duty, was Bound by all lawful means to take care for the Welfare and Preservation both of the Souls and Bodies of his Wife and Children, Contriving and Resolving the Ruine of Both'.[76]

The most fascinating politicisation of men's adulterous passions occurred in January 1679 with the trial and execution of a married Shropshire clergyman, Robert Foulkes, for murdering his newborn bastard child. The case was highly unusual, not just because of Foulkes's profession, but also for his being found guilty of a felony normally associated with single women.[77] The murder was the culmination of a long-term affair with Anne Atkinson, an unmarried woman from his parish, Stanton Lacy, which had been investigated by the Hereford consistory court. When Anne became pregnant, Foulkes took her to London where the couple took lodgings in York Buildings off the Strand. It was here that the baby was born in November 1678 and, shortly afterwards, strangled by Foulkes and crammed down a privy. The vicar returned to Shropshire alone, but was arrested and brought back to London where he was tried and convicted of murder at the Middlesex sessions of 15 January 1679.[78]

In any period, a crime as shocking as this would have aroused public interest, but from the perspective of Foulkes's Anglican superiors, this publicity could hardly have come at a worse time. The scoffing of wits and sceptics at the moral authority of religion had been getting louder during the 1660s and '70s, and the rising problem of protestant nonconformity brought into question the hegemony of the established church. Even more seriously, the recent revelation of the Popish Plot and the murder of the investigating magistrate Sir Edmundberry Godfrey, supposedly at the hands of Jesuits, heightened fears that the church's enemies were gaining in strength.[79] The last thing a beleaguered church needed was an adulterous, infanticidal Anglican minister stealing the headlines.

Pamphleteers represented Foulkes's adultery as a gross abuse of his patri-archal and parochial responsibilities. When they discussed the nature of the relationship between Foulkes and his lover, they commonly believed that the

---

[76] *True Relation of the Most Horrible Murther, Committed by Thomas White*, pp. 2, 3.

[77] But for another case of infanticide involving a minister see Peter Lake, '"A Charitable Christian Hatred": the Godly and their Enemies in the 1630s', in Christopher Durston and Jacqueline Eales (eds.), *The Culture of English Puritanism, 1560–1700* (Basingstoke, 1996), pp. 145–83.

[78] *The Execution of Mr Rob Foulks, Late Minister of Stanton-Lacy in Shropshire* (London, 1679), p. 3. See also *A True and Perfect Relation of the Tryal and Condemnation, Execution and Last Speech of that Unfortunate Gentleman Mr Robert Foulks* (London, 1679); *The Shropshire Amazement* (London, n.d. [c.1708?]); London Metropolitan Archives (LMA), MJ/SR 1556 Middlesex Sessions Roll, 15 Jan. 1679. The background to this case is explored in David M. Turner, '"Nothing is so Secret but shall be Revealed": the Scandalous Life of Robert Foulkes', in Tim Hitchcock and Michele Cohen (eds.), *English Masculinities, 1660–1800* (London, 1999), pp. 169–92.

[79] John Spurr, *The Restoration Church of England, 1646–1689* (New Haven, CT and London, 1991), pp. 68–76 and ch. 2 *passim*.

vicar had been 'left Guardian' to an orphaned 'young gentlewoman', who lived in his house as a 'Servant or Boarder'. One pamphlet depicted Foulkes as 'making use of some Authority' derived from 'that trust' between guardian and ward, to 'debauch her to his bed'.[80] Whether or not this was an accurate depiction of their relationship, it served to set the adultery in a familiar household setting, emphasising the dangers of male lusts to the principles of mutuality and trust that cemented relations between the dominant and subordinate in domestic relations. The trust of Anne's father in leaving his daughter to the upbringing of a figure of religious authority made Foulkes's sexual conquest even more scandalous and threatened to undermine the moral authority of the clergy in general.

In response the church launched a remarkable damage limitation exercise masterminded by William Lloyd, then Dean of Bangor, who had recently established his credentials as a defender of the established faith in his sermon at the funeral of Sir Edmundberry Godfrey.[81] Through the intervention of the Bishop of London, Foulkes's execution was delayed until 31 January, in which time, under Lloyd's guidance, he was transformed into a national icon of penitence for sexual sin.

The focal point of this transformation, which also included prayers being said for Foulkes across London's churches on the eve of his execution, the fast day commemorating the Royal Martyr, was a remarkable autobiographical sermon, *An Alarme for Sinners*. Such was its power that it became a key reference work in later seventeenth-century campaigns to reform male sexual manners.[82] According to Foulkes, its purpose was to 'glorifie God' and to 'wipe off all I could of the Scandal and Reproach which my Vicious Life and Ignominious Death reflected upon my Function'. Foulkes began his narrative from a position of abjection, relating how, notwithstanding God's favour towards him, he had allowed himself to become corrupted and allowed an 'unclean' and 'filthy' devil to take command of his 'swept and garnished soul'. One by one, the ties that bound him to civil society were broken away as Foulkes described how he violated first his baptismal vows followed quickly by his 'Ordination Engagements, and the Faith of Wedlock' as he 'delivered' himself to 'work all uncleanness with greediness'. At last, with a conscience 'so feared and past fearing' he was driven to murder his own base issue.[83]

Yet Foulkes was at pains to stress that his temptation was one that could befall anyone. He declared himself guilty of 'the too too fashionable sin of uncleanness', which was 'so remarkably the sin of this present age'.[84] After his initial account of his slide into sin, Foulkes's tone became more robust, mounting

---

[80] *A True and Perfect Relation*, p. 5. See also, *Shropshire Amazement*, p. 2.

[81] Spurr, *Restoration Church*, p. 76.

[82] See, for instance, *Wonders of Free Grace*, pp. 37–52; *AM* IV/16, 21 Nov. 1691; [John Dunton], *The Hazard of a Death-Bed Repentance* (London, 1708), p. 19.

[83] Robert Foulkes, *An Alarme for Sinners* (London, 1679), pp. 5, 9.   [84] Ibid., pp. 6, 14.

a vigorous defence against some of the rival pamphlet accounts and the wilder stories that had surfaced at his trial. He denied that his lover had ever been left to his charge, stating that 'her Father was a Gentleman whom I never saw, or had the least Intercourse with'. He also refuted the scandalous rumours that had circulated at his trial that he had tried to 'vitiate her at Nine years old' or that he had purposely 'corrupted her Judgement, and misinformed her Conscience to believe that Polygamy was Lawful'.[85] Foulkes had been convicted on the confession of his partner, and throughout the narrative his sense of betrayal was palpable. His contempt for her was overwhelming – she was presented as a de-personalised signifier of sexual temptation, the 'whorish woman' of Proverbs vi, whose 'charms' were liable to 'ensnare' unwary men leading them to 'thraldom' and 'slavery'.[86] Elsewhere she appeared as a monstrous embodiment of female sexuality, the tempting 'cockatrice' who had to be 'crush[ed]'.[87] Such a woman, Foulkes advised his male readers, was liable to 'waste your Estate, divide your Family, ruin your Health, destroy your Soul and', he added pointedly, 'if ever you need her friendship, she will most perfidiously betray you'.[88]

In a remarkable finale, Foulkes left a set of 'dying directions' to his wife and children, cast as the silent victims of his failure of patriarchal duty. He commended to his wife the religious upbringing of his children, but also urged her to be 'governed' in all things by her brother. He also advised his eldest daughter, Elizabeth, to 'remember Modesty and Chastity are great Ornaments of a Woman' and to 'observe what ruin and destruction Whoredom makes in the world'.[89] In his dying statement, Foulkes was given one last, extraordinary chance to act with the patriarchal responsibility that had eluded him during his 'vicious life'. What began as a story of a tragic betrayal of authority and responsibility, ended as a reinforcement of the patriarchal status quo. Such was the restorative function of the seventeenth-century murder narrative.

'DYING FOR THE SAKE OF HIS MISTRESS'

Readers of Robert Foulkes's *Alarme for Sinners* could be left with no illusions that adultery was not a heinous crime that invited terrible consequences. Every detail of the murder suggested squalor and depravity. However, as the period progressed, representations of adultery and murder were changing. Competition between publishers led to more innovative and inventive attempts to discuss criminal lives. New genres of representing murder displaced traditional prov-idential modes of explanation from their narratives.[90] Authors themselves be-came increasingly conscious that the hackneyed messages of murder pamphlets

---

[85] Ibid., pp. 20–1.   [86] Ibid., p. 14.   [87] Ibid., p. 10.
[88] Ibid., p. 6.   [89] Ibid., pp. 28, 30.
[90] This theme is explored in more detail in Gaskill, 'Displacement of Providence' and in his *Crime and Mentalities in Early Modern England* (Cambridge, 2000), ch. 7.

no longer satisfied the demands of a more enquiring readership who might peruse these texts 'with no more concern, than Persons in Health read Quack-Doctors Bills, and make no better use of them'.[91] By the eighteenth century new modes of fashioning murder were apparent, which drew on melodrama and romance, and tried to develop the personalities of those involved, exploring motive in more subtle ways. One final case study reveals particularly vividly how older methods of representing adultery and murder were being broken down under the pressure of both cultural and market forces.

In the afternoon of Thursday 29 January 1713, a Buckinghamshire landowner named John Sayer was slain by his attorney, Richard Noble. Noble was also the lover of Sayer's wife, Mary, and the couple had eloped together some eighteen months previously. After running up a series of debts in John's name, the fugitive couple ended up lodging at the house of Joseph Twyford in the Mint, where they were eventually tracked down. John Sayer secured a warrant from a Justice of the Peace to compel his wife to come back to live with him, she 'being gone from him and living in a loose disorderly manner'.[92] Accompanied by two constables and six assistants, Sayer burst into the room where his wife and Noble were at that moment dining. A struggle broke out and John Sayer was fatally stabbed in his left side near the heart. Richard Noble, Mary Sayer and her mother, Mary Salisbury, who was also present, were arrested and brought to trial at Kingston Assizes on Friday 13 March, Noble being accused of wilful murder and the women of aiding and abetting. The women were acquitted, but notwithstanding his plea of self-defence, Noble was convicted and sentenced to be hanged at Tyburn on Saturday 28 March.[93]

The case was widely reported in the press and, in the month following the trial, numerous pamphlets were published.[94] These included reports of the trial proceedings, copies of Noble's speech on receiving sentence, his last dying speech and a funeral sermon on Noble written by the eminent Anglican divine, William Fleetwood. There were also a series of lengthier accounts ranging in price from 6d to a shilling giving extensive details of the affair between Noble and Mary Sayer.[95] Publishers vied with each other to publish the definitive

---

[91] *Fair Warning to Murderers of Infants*, sig. A2.

[92] A *Full Account of the Case of John Sayer Esq.* (London, 1713), p. 9. Subsequent accounts reported that Sayer's warrant was to force Noble to surrender himself to face an action for criminal conversation: *A Full and Faithful Account of the Intrigue Between Mr Noble and Mrs Sayer* (London, 1713), p. 8.

[93] A *Complete Collection of State Trials*, ed. T. B. Howell (33 vols., London, 1809–28), XV, pp. 731–62.

[94] For newspaper reports of the case and its aftermath see the *Evening Post*, 561, 14 Mar. 1713; 562, 17 Mar. 1713; 568, 31 Mar. 1713; *Dawks's Newsletter*, 17 Mar. 1713; 26 Mar. 1713; 28 Mar. 1713; 31 Mar. 1713; *British Mercury*, 402, 18 Mar. 1713.

[95] *Full Account of the Case of John Sayer Esq.*; *Full Account of the Case of John Sayer Esq.... Second Edition*; *Full and Faithful Account of the Intrigue Between Mr Noble and Mrs Sayer*; Fleetwood, *Funeral Sermon*; *The Whole and True Tryals and Condemnation of*

version of events, turning out 'corrected' and 'enlarged' editions of their original pamphlets and using newspaper advertisements to discredit their rivals. Anne Baldwin's advertisement for the second edition of *The Case of Mr Sayer* announced that, so 'the publick may not be impos'd on by any Spurious and Pyratical Edition of this Case', the 'Affidavits, Depositions, Original Papers, Letters etc., relating to it are Lodg'd in the Hands of Mrs Baldwin, the proofs of which will be so convincing, as to leave no room for Counterfeits' – probably referring to an advertisement for an account of the case published by John Morphew which claimed to be based on 'several original papers'.[96] The details of the story seemed to be taking precedence over the moral message. Rumours also spread about the incident and the characters involved. Jonathan Swift exploited this atmosphere of speculation for an ingenious April Fool's Day prank in which he contrived to spread a rumour about London that Noble's body had gone missing after the execution, being 'recovered by His Friends, and then seised again by the Sheriff and is now in a Messenger's hands at the Black Swan in Holborn'.[97]

The popularity of this case had much to do with the genteel background of its participants. John Sayer's estates were worth some £1,800 a year, while his wife was worth some £3,000, and there were many references to the material consequences of adultery.[98] Using his legal skills, Noble had contrived a private separation agreement between Mary Sayer and her husband and then used underhand methods to have John imprisoned for debt while the lovers enjoyed the fruits of his estate. John was systematically stripped of everything he owned, as Noble got possession not just of his wife, but also of his property and estate and he even, to complete his rival's emasculation, took to wearing his 'cloaths, sword and watch, strutting about in Mr Sayer's Roquelaur which cost 26 Guineas'.[99] Some pamphlets speculated on Mary Sayer's connections with ladies at court, while Noble, accomplished in the genteel arts of dancing and fencing, was a true product of polite society.[100] The juxtaposition of the superior manners, wealth and breeding of the characters involved, with the sordid

all the Prisoners Who were Try'd at Kingston... With a Full and Particular Account of Mr Noble, Mrs Sayer and Mrs Salisbury, For the Murder of 'Squire Sayer (London, 1713); A Full and True Account [of Richard Noble] Etc. (n.p., n.d. [c.1713]); Mr Noble's Speech, To the Lord Chief-Justice Parker, Before He Received Sentence of Death (London, 1713); The True Copy of the Original Paper Signed by Mr Richard Noble, Which He Designed for His Last Speech (London, 1713); The Case of Mr Richard Noble Impartially Consider'd: Abstracting from the Man, or Crime, But Meerly as to the Law (London, 1713).

[96] *Post Boy*, 2790, 28 Mar. 1713; cf. ibid., 2789, 26 Mar. 1713.

[97] Jonathan Swift, *Journal to Stella*, ed. Harold Williams (2 vols., Oxford, 1948), II, p. 650.

[98] *Full Account of the Case of John Sayer Esq.*, pp. 3–4.

[99] *Full Account of the Case of John Sayer Esq.... Second Edition*, p. 12. A roquelaur was a short cloak.

[100] *Full and Faithful Account of the Intrigue Between Mr Noble and Mrs Sayer*, p. 5; *A Full and True Account Etc.*, pp. 3–4.

act of murder, taking place at the epicentre of London's criminal underworld, made for compelling reading.

The case was also politically important. John Sayer's sister was married to Dr Thomas Bray, founder of the Society for Promoting Christian Knowledge and a leading figure in campaigns for the 'Advancement of the Purity of Religion and Manners'.[101] Bray's letter to Noble urging his repentance for his 'Treachery, Adultery and Murder' was published and helped to connect this case to the ongoing campaign for the reformation of manners.[102] Different groups tried to make political capital out of the trial. Noble had to deny from the scaffold that he was a 'free-thinker'.[103] Even though the pamphlets played down party political matters, the Whig publisher Anne Baldwin could not resist repeating an unsubstantiated rumour that Noble was a 'staunch Tory' and *ipso facto* a 'Jacobite'.[104] Beyond this, a good deal of interest in the case derived from a palpable sense that justice had not been done in the original trial. It appears that an appeal was lodged against the acquittal of Mary Sayer and some of the pamphlets clearly emphasised her guilt and her shameless and ungrateful treatment of her husband.[105] If Mary Sayer's involvement in her husband's murder could not be proved in court, then at least the pamphlets could imply her guilt by detailing her matrimonial treachery.

What is striking about the reporting of the case, in particular the lengthier pamphlet accounts of the affair between Richard Noble and Mary Sayer, is the way in which competing discourses about crime and illicit sexuality could coexist in the same narrative.[106] 'We ought to look upon all the Events in this Affair, as the Righteous Hand of God', began the preface to *A Full and Faithful Account of the Intrigue Between Mr Noble and Mrs Sayer*, 'and to praise his Name for exerting it in so visible a manner against such crying sins as Adultery and Murder.' Yet a few pages later, the case was presented in the dramatic metaphor of a 'Tragedy', offering the classic Aristotelian combination of 'Pleasure and Instruction'. The open admission that a reader might derive 'pleasure' from the narrative marked a significant departure from murder narratives of the later seventeenth century.[107] The title and format of this publication, which ran to over fifty pages, deliberately invoked scandalous novellas of intrigues and gallantry coming into vogue during the early decades of the eighteenth century.

---

[101] *Full and Faithful Account of the Intrigue Between Mr Noble and Mrs Sayer*, p. 35.
[102] Ibid., p. 37.   [103] Ibid., p. 53.   [104] Ibid., p. 26.
[105] On the appeal see *Evening Post*, 561, 14 Mar. 1713; *Full Account of the Case of John Sayer Esq.*, p. 20.
[106] This is most striking in the series of publications produced for the bookseller Anne Baldwin upon which the following analysis is largely based: *Full Account of the Case of John Sayer Esq.*; *Full Account of the Case of John Sayer Esq. . . . Second Edition*; *Full and Faithful Account of the Intrigue Between Mr Noble and Mrs Sayer.*
[107] *Full and Faithful Account of the Intrigue Between Mr Noble and Mrs Sayer*, Preface [no pagination].

While earlier murder pamphlets had tended to give little detail of the actual conduct of illicit affairs, concentrating instead more exclusively on the symbolic aspects of adultery and betrayal, some of the accounts of this case presented lavish details of the 'Artifice' used by Mary Sayer to 'blind the Family in her Amours'. Like an unfaithful wife in a cuckolding drama, Mary is depicted negotiating the landscape of fashionable London in pursuit of her love affairs, travelling in coaches and chairs to secret assignations in places such as Oxenden chapel in the West End, Hyde Park and Mayfair which 'all the world knows was a Place of Intrigue'. The account also gave details of the false names – Mervyn, Morley and Jordan – used by Richard and Mary during their fugitive period.[108] Evidence given at the trial was embellished with rumour to glamorise the adulterous liaison.[109]

Proceeding from the belief that retroactive justice needed to be done, many pamphlets launched on a thorough and highly conventional character assassination of Mary Sayer, highlighting her impolite lack of 'decency' and feminine modesty. From an early age she apparently displayed 'a liveliness of humour' which she was unable to keep 'within bounds' thus causing her 'the Indecency of being always the first Mover in the Affair of Love'.[110] In 'civil company' she could not refrain from 'talking of what wou'd put other Ladies to the Blush', which eventually 'occasion'd all her sober Acquaintance to leave off visiting her'. At length, the narrative continued, 'she had a Name for that and Intriguing so notorious, that when ever she went to Church, the Ladies that were in the Pew, she wou'd have sat in, left it'.[111] The pamphlets also made much of her decision when she gave birth to Noble's bastard child in November 1712 to be delivered by a man, reputedly telling a female midwife, Mrs Scoffen, that 'she was always laid by men, and she thought it more their business than a woman's'.[112] At that time the use of male practitioners in childbirth was still highly unorthodox, usually being called upon only in the last resort when all hopes of a live birth had vanished and technological intervention was required to remove the dead infant from the womb.[113] To choose a man-midwife from the outset carried strong overtones of indecency and immodesty, and suggested ulterior sexual motives.[114]

---

[108] Ibid., pp. 5–6, 11, 12.

[109] *Full Account of John Sayer Esq . . . . Second Edition*, pp. 41–2; *Complete Collection of State Trials*, ed. Howell, XV, p. 736.

[110] *Full Account of the Case of John Sayer Esq.*, p. 4.

[111] *Full and Faithful Account of the Intrigue Between Mr Noble and Mrs Sayer*, p. 12.

[112] *Full Account of the Case of John Sayer Esq. . . . Second Edition*, p. 10.

[113] Adrian Wilson, 'Participant or Patient? Seventeenth-Century Childbirth from the Mother's Point of View', in Roy Porter (ed.), *Patients and Practitioners: Lay Perceptions of Medicine in Pre-Industrial Society* (Cambridge, 1985), pp. 129–44; Wilson, *The Making of Man-Midwifery: Childbirth in England 1660–1770* (London, 1995).

[114] Roy Porter, 'A Touch of Danger: the Man-Midwife as Sexual Predator', in G. S. Rousseau and Roy Porter (eds.), *Sexual Underworlds of the Enlightenment* (Manchester, 1987), pp. 206–32.

If the portrayal of Mary Sayer relied on conventional stereotypes of deviant wifely behaviour, the representation of the men in the case was more ambivalent. John Sayer comes across as a kindly figure, 'of a singular, easy, quiet Temper, and honest Principles, both as to his Neighbours and the Publick', ever willing to forgive his wife, even giving her adultery the 'soft name' of 'misconduct' to avoid conflict.[115] Yet he is a flawed character, often portrayed as ineffectual or lacking judgement. He is 'fond' of his wife 'almost to Doating, blind to all her weaknesses'. Reduced by his wife's indifference to seek sexual satisfaction in a piece of 'Town Gallantry' with a Mayfair prostitute, he contracts the pox which renders him impotent and therefore unable to control his wife sexually. Furthermore, his agreement to a swingeing private separation agreement with his wife, contrived by Noble, served only to 'confirm his Cuckoldom by a Covenant'.[116]

What links John Sayer and Richard Noble together is their shared manipulation by Mary. Both allow themselves to be dominated by her, though in significantly different ways. John is henpecked, not just by his wife but also by his mother-in-law and sister-in-law, and struggles to make himself heard over a cacophony of female tongues. 'One may imagine what a comfortable life he led', noted one pamphlet somewhat sardonically, 'there a mother-in-law rattling in his Ears a Peal of Raillery on his Insufficiency; there a wife treating him as the vilest wretch upon Earth; and a Third backing them, in the most provoking manner.'[117] Noble, in contrast, is portrayed as being like a pet to Mary. Given the nickname 'Puppy', he travels round like a lap-dog or retainer in her 'Equipage'. Yet if John Sayer's subordination confirms his inadequacy, Noble seems to be happy in the service of his mistress. More than just an asset to be shown off, he was a 'tenant at will' of her body.[118] It was through his sexual prowess and brilliant legal skills that Mary was able to escape from her unfulfilling marriage.[119]

Mary's ultimate ingratitude towards her devoted lover, rejoicing at her acquittal and apparently giving Noble little thought as he languished in gaol, forms the basis for a romanticised portrayal of the young lawyer. In spite of his ironic claim to 'be careful not to give way in the least to Fancy, nor to mingle any of the Beauties of fiction with the Truth of History', the author of *The Case of John Sayer* presented Noble in romantic terms. He first appears as 'Paris' or like the 'Phrygian Shepherd, surrounded by so many Nymphs'.[120] In an expanded

---

For another contemporary pamphlet impugning the morals of women who chose to use men-midwives see *Capt. Leeson's Case: Being an Account of his Tryal for Committing a Rape Upon the Body of Mrs May a Married Woman of 35 Years of Age* (London, 1715), pp. 7, 15.

[115] *Full Account of the Case of John Sayer Esq.*, p. 3; *Full and Faithful Account of the Intrigue Between Mr Noble and Mrs Sayer*, p. 6.

[116] *Full Account of the Case of John Sayer Esq.*, pp. 4, 7.

[117] Ibid., p. 5.   [118] Ibid., p. 8.   [119] Ibid., p. 7.   [120] Ibid., pp. 6, 7.

second edition to the pamphlet the author hinted that a longer account of Noble's affairs 'might display several Scenes, that wou'd make a Thousand Lovers envy Noble's Fortune', at least until 'the Hour of his Imprisonment'.[121]

When that hour came, Noble became a tragic, almost heroic, figure. The author of *A Full and Faithful Account of the Intrigue Between Mr Noble and Mrs Sayer* described Noble's repentence as 'strong and affecting' and criticised the 'inhumanity' of his gaolers for clapping him in irons.[122] Noble was a tragic figure not simply because his lust was a fatal flaw which set him upon the slippery slope of moral decline, but because his love for Mary Sayer was ultimately unfulfilled and ended in betrayal. His speech upon receiving the death sentence was described as 'very moving', which 'coming from the mouth of a Man in his Sad Circumstances, drew Tears from the Spectators, especially from the Fair Sex, some of whom 'tis possible consider'd him not only as a dying Man, but dying for the sake of his Mistress'.[123] It was a story that could leave no one unmoved. 'Those who think Tears are Womanish', wrote one pamphleteer, 'will surely reckon compassion to be a Folly, and it is not to such that I write.'[124]

Richard Noble's depiction as a tragic and romantic anti-hero was significantly removed from the depiction of malefactors in seventeenth-century moralising tracts. In spite of the author's desire to distance himself from 'Womanish' sentiment, his and other descriptions of Noble seem designed to appeal in particular to a growing female readership. The affinity between Richard Noble's representation and the depiction of dashing highwaymen, other notorious felons renowned for attracting the 'fondness' of 'Ladies', is striking.[125] Pamphleteers were now finding themselves torn between conflicting representational styles: between traditional frameworks of morality and causation and the need to appeal to the 'pleasure' of an expanding readership; and between the images of whoredom and moral decline and the glamorous modern world of 'intrigue' and 'gallantry'. Adultery was still cast as a source of disorder, but the emphasis was much more on the circumstances of the individuals involved rather than on treating them simply as moral exemplars. Put another way, revelation of the 'private' details of the case seemed to take priority in some publications above the more 'public' moral message. The mode of reporting in this case would set a precedent followed, as we shall see in chapter 6, in eighteenth-century reports of trials for criminal conversation. By the eighteenth century, it seemed, the hard moral edge of traditional narratives of adulterous homicide was being softened by the tears of sentiment.

---

[121] *Full Account of the Case of John Sayer Esq. . . . Second Edition*, p. 8.
[122] *Full and Faithful Account of the Intrigue Between Mr Noble and Mrs Sayer*, pp. 28, 29.
[123] *Full Account of the Case of John Sayer Esq.*, p. 19.
[124] *Full and Faithful Account of the Intrigue Between Mr Noble and Mrs Sayer*, p. 41.
[125] E.g., *The Memoirs of Monsieur du Val* (1670), in *The Harleian Miscellany* (12 vols., London, 1808–11), VII, pp. 392–402.

Murder literature presented early modern audiences with compelling visions of conjugal relations in a state of collapse. Their narratives exemplified the bloody destruction of ideals of domestic order and exposed a sinister side to cuckoldry. Although modes of representing adultery and murder were becoming increasingly hybrid by the eighteenth century, consistent with the explosion of print culture and its destabilisation of traditional narratives of illicit behaviour, marital breakdown was overwhelmingly presented in this literature within the discursive framework of crime and disorder. Murder narratives presented the most powerful expression of the idea explored in the period's sermons and conduct literature that adultery was a powerful sin that could bring about the ruin of men, women and their families. In particular, the notion that adultery powerfully destroyed love, trust and mutual respect between husband and wife was powerfully conveyed by the stealthy methods of murder employed in domestic homicides.

However, because domestic order had different meanings and consequences for men and women, their adulteries and murders were represented in different ways. It was when matrimonial disintegration was viewed *in extremis* that gendered perspectives on marital relations became most nakedly visible. Though women who killed their spouses were less represented in this period than before the Civil War, their cases were particularly shocking as new ideals of women as 'gentler' and more naturally passive began to take hold. Women like Margaret Osgood, Mary Channing and Mary Sayer (guilty more by public opinion than by law), who cuckolded then killed their spouses, aroused particular revulsion because their behaviour upset conventions and was cast as domestic rebellion. However, pamphlets also provided compelling reinforcement for the notion that men's adulterous passions could destroy households. They provided evidence of the abuse of domestic authority and cast this in terms of a failure of responsibility. Though men in some circumstances could claim they were provoked by their spouses' adultery this matter was treated ambivalently in murder literature since it conflicted with notions of order and morality. The final chapters of this book examine other ways in which legal and moral discourses came together to fashion adultery in different forms of matrimonial litigation, beginning with marital separation suits brought before the ecclesiastical courts.

5. Sex, proof and suspicion: adultery in the church courts

The law played an important role in both shaping and mediating understandings of sex, marriage and gender relations in early modern England. Studying patterns of matrimonial litigation sheds light on the practical options available to men and women in the face of their partner's adultery, while attention to their pleading strategies tells us more about expectations of marriage and the ways in which they were shaped by gender. The product of real marriages in crisis, the evidence presented to court allows us to witness adultery as social drama, its capacity to disrupt the everyday comforts of mutuality, hierarchy, precedence, work and spatial integrity vividly acted out before us. Here, stories about infidelity were fashioned from the words of the people whose lives were most closely affected by it – husbands, wives, household servants, kin and neighbours.

The final chapters of this book compare different legal responses to adultery and cultures of matrimonial litigation. Focusing on marital separation suits brought before the church courts, this chapter explores the ways in which ecclesiastical law defined adulterous behaviour and, using the statements of litigants and witnesses, examines how adulterous affairs were uncovered. An analysis of church court records brings us into a world of conjugal infidelity more firmly grounded in material actuality and lived experience than the printed materials examined in previous chapters. However, the words of participants in the legal process were no less subject to mediation and cultural construction than other genres of fashioning adultery. It has now been well established by historians that court testimonies were the results of a collaborative process consisting of questions and cross-examination by lawyers and shaped into legally meaningful form by the clerks of the court.[1] Evidence presented to the court was not a

---

[1] Interest in the formation of court records has burgeoned in recent years: see (for example) Laura Gowing, *Domestic Dangers: Women, Words and Sex in Early Modern London* (Oxford, 1996), pp. 41–50; Miranda Chaytor, 'Husband(ry): Narratives of Rape in the Seventeenth Century', *Gender and History*, 7 (1995), 378–407; Garthine Walker, 'Rereading Rape and Sexual Violence in Early Modern England', *Gender and History*, 10 (1998), 1–25; Tim Stretton, *Women Waging*

straightforward relation of 'fact', but situated observations that served legally purposeful strategies. Careful consideration must therefore be given to the forms and conventions of bringing evidence of adultery to court. Court records no more reveal the hidden 'truth' of marital breakdown than do murder pamphlets or cuckold comedies. Nevertheless, the rich social detail of testimonies enables us to ask questions about adultery and marital relations the answers to which cannot be derived, or at least are not readily accessible, from other sources. Particular attention is paid in this chapter to the ways in which adulterous affairs became visible to others. As we shall see, the problems of securing direct proof of illicit sexual relations meant that separation suits frequently relied on a variety of circumstantial evidence. This evidence may be used to explore issues that have not yet received much attention in historical studies of matrimonial litigation. Though considered legally inferior by the judicial authorities, circumstantial evidence offers the historian an important insight into how, on a practical day-to-day basis, breaches of codes of sociability and civility and extraordinary 'freedoms' and 'familiarity' manifested themselves and raised suspicion about immorality. Furthermore, through the records of suspicion, it is possible to build up a picture of how love affairs were conducted, allowing us in turn to speculate about what they may have meant to those involved.

Inevitably, questions must be asked about how representative of marital breakdown this material is. While launching a separation suit was a far less extreme response to adultery than the murders examined in the previous chapter, it was still very much a minority response to marital breakdown.[2] Litigation was a costly and cumbersome process. Since the best that the church courts could offer was a separation from bed and board, it may seem surprising to modern eyes that anyone was prepared to follow this course of action at all.[3] Bearing in mind that litigation has a culture of its own and that bringing a dispute before a judge could be a means of settling wider conflicts, the starting point for any discussion of marital separation must be the circumstances under which adultery came to court. At the outset, therefore, let us examine the social background of litigants and their pleading strategies.

Law in Elizabethan England (Cambridge, 1998), pp. 13–18 and ch. 8. Historical interest in this issue has been influenced by a wider 'linguistic turn' in legal studies. See W. Lance Bennett and Martha S. Feldman, *Reconstructing Reality in the Courtroom* (London and New York, 1981); Bernard S. Jackson, 'Narrative Models in Legal Proof', in David Ray Papke (ed.), *Narrative and the Legal Discourse: a Reader in Storytelling and the Law* (Liverpool, 1991), pp. 158–78.

[2] Martin Ingram, *Church Courts, Sex and Marriage in England, 1570–1640* (Cambridge, 1987), pp. 181–2; Gowing, *Domestic Dangers*, p. 182.

[3] Although judicial separation was sometimes referred to as 'divorce' in the church courts, legally separated spouses were unable to remarry unless they proceeded to obtain a full divorce by private act of Parliament: Lawrence Stone, *Road to Divorce: England 1530–1987* (Oxford, 1990), pp. 301–22; Sybil Wolfram, 'Divorce in England 1700–1857', *Oxford Journal of Legal Studies*, 5 (1985), 155–86.

BRINGING ADULTERY TO COURT

Ecclesiastical law took a limited view of the causes of matrimonial breakdown. Separation was permitted on the grounds of adultery or life-threatening cruelty, or a combination of the two. Neither allowed the couple to remarry. That was only possible if marriage was annulled on the grounds of some irregularity, such as an unlawful marriage contract, or impotence, which prevented the union from being consummated. Adultery might play a role in other matrimonial causes. Most notably, in suits for the restitution of conjugal rights, brought to compel cohabitation after an elopement or unauthorised separation, a counter-plea of adultery or cruelty could be made which, if successful, could effectively change the action into a cause for separation.[4]

Separation suits could be brought in any ecclesiastical court. However, after the Restoration the bulk of this business became concentrated in the larger courts – the York consistory court in the northern province and the London consistory court and (especially) the Court of Arches in the south.[5] The Court of Arches was the pinnacle of ecclesiastical jurisdiction, situated in the headquarters of the civil lawyers at Doctors' Commons. Its main role was to hear appeals arising from cases contested in lower church courts. However, it also acted as a court of first instance for a number of 'peculiar' parishes falling outside the jurisdiction of the Bishop of London and sometimes took over suits begun in lower ecclesiastical courts that proved too complex for these jurisdictions to handle effectively.[6] The superior legal expertise available in the Court of Arches did not come cheaply. In the separation case brought by Sir George Barlow against his wife, which began in 1705 and meandered on inconclusively until 1707 when an out of court settlement seems to have been reached, the cumulative fees amounted to over £100.[7] Hardly surprising then that, by Stone's calculations, some 47 per cent of plaintiffs who brought matrimonial cases to the court in the period 1660–99 were well-heeled gentry, professionals or merchants, with a further 38 per cent coming from substantial middling backgrounds.[8]

---

[4] Stone, *Road to Divorce*, pp. 192–5; Ingram, *Church Courts*, pp. 145–6, 171–8,181–4.

[5] For the north see Joanne Bailey, 'Breaking the Conjugal Vows: Marriage and Marriage Breakdown in the North of England, 1660–1800', PhD thesis, University of Durham (1999).

[6] Stone, *Road to Divorce*, pp. 33–44; G. D. Squibb, *Doctors' Commons: a History of the College of Advocates and Doctors of Law* (London, 1977); M. Doreen Slatter, 'The Records of the Court of Arches', *Journal of Ecclesiastical History*, 4 (1953), 139–53; T. E. James, 'The Court of Arches during the Eighteenth Century: Its Matrimonial Jurisdiction', *American Journal of Legal History*, 5 (1961), 55–66.

[7] LPL, J6/68 (*Barlow v. Barlow*, Bill of Costs, 28 June 1706); J7/13 (*Barlow v. Barlow*, Bill of Costs, 18 June 1707). See also Stone, *Road to Divorce*, pp. 186–90.

[8] Ibid., p. 427 (table 1.6). In Scotland, by contrast, where the Commissary Court offered full divorces, the social background of litigants may have been more diverse: Leah Leneman, *Alienated Affections: the Scottish Experience of Divorce and Separation 1684–1830* (Edinburgh, 1998), ch. 1.

After the Restoration, as with other ecclesiastical jurisdictions, the Court of Arches was filled with a backlog of cases that had built up during the Interregnum when the church courts had been suppressed.[9] Stone calculated that the Court of Arches heard some 378 matrimonial suits between 1660 and 1679.[10] The period of Republican rule itself generated matrimonial business for the court as some wives who had married at this time claimed that their husbands had subsequently declared the unions to be invalid and had taken another partner.[11] After 1680 the number of separation cases brought per decade dropped considerably, consistent with a broader decline of civil litigation in all courts at this time. It has been estimated that matrimonial cases of all kinds accounted for just 10 per cent of the business of the Court of Arches in the period 1660–1760. Many of these cases seem to have been settled out of court by informal agreement.[12]

Historians have identified significant gender differences in patterns of litigation. In spite of the fact that both men and women had the right to bring suits for separation in the church courts on the grounds of their partner's infidelity, the overwhelming majority of separation suits for adultery were brought by men against their wives. When wives tried formally to separate from their husbands, they did so largely on the grounds of cruelty. In so far as women did accuse their husbands of adultery in court, these charges were usually bound up with additional charges of cruelty. This apparent double standard is regarded by Gowing as a reflection of the premise that 'men and women's sexual behaviour had incomparably different meanings'.[13] However, although this gendered pattern of litigation was repeated in the later seventeenth-century courts, the issues are not quite as clear-cut as Gowing and others have allowed.[14] First, since legal definitions of cruelty included the transmission of venereal disease from one partner to another, the sexual conduct of husbands may have been at issue in some cruelty suits. Second, it is important to recognise that there may well have been differences in patterns of litigation between ecclesiastical jurisdictions. Though the majority of cases in the Court of Arches ostensibly concerned

---

[9] Stone, *Road to Divorce*, p. 33–4; Faramerz Dabhoiwala, 'Prostitution and Police in London, *c*.1660–*c*.1760', DPhil thesis, University of Oxford (1995), pp. 94–7 and ch. 4 *passim*.

[10] Stone, *Road to Divorce*, p. 424 (table 1.1).

[11] For instance, LPL, E4/126 (*Plummer v. Plummer*, 1671); E12/59 (*Butler v. Butler*, Personal Answers of John Butler, 12 Nov. 1697). On this latter case see Rachel Weil, *Political Passions: Gender, the Family and Political Argument in England, 1680–1714* (Manchester, 1999), p. 127.

[12] Stone, *Road to Divorce*, p. 34. See also C. W. Brooks, 'Interpersonal Conflict and Social Tension: Civil Litigation in England, 1640–1830', in A. L. Beier, David Cannadine and James M. Rosenheim (eds.), *The First Modern Society: Essays in English History in Honour of Lawrence Stone* (Cambridge, 1989), pp. 357–99.

[13] Gowing, *Domestic Dangers*, p. 180. A similar pattern of cases emerges from the seventeenth-century Norwich consistory court: Susan Dwyer Amussen, *An Ordered Society: Gender and Class in Early Modern England* (Oxford, 1988), p. 127.

[14] On the gendered profile of matrimonial litigation in the north of England between 1660 and 1800, see Bailey, 'Breaking the Conjugal Vows', p. 52.

female adultery, the appeal structure of the court may have given women litigants more scope to defend their names and impugn their husbands' conduct.
Foyster has shown that women initiated a significant minority of adultery cases
in the later seventeenth-century Court of Arches as a means of challenging
verdicts made against them in the lower ecclesiastical courts. The wealthier
backgrounds of these women may have allowed them to draw on the help of
relatives to challenge their husbands' versions of events and to make allegations of their own. By pursuing their cases to the legally sophisticated Court of
Arches, women may have been acting on the hope that they would receive a
fairer hearing than in the lower courts.[15]

Indeed, evidence from law reports reveals that the Court of Arches could be
quite favourable towards injured wives. In a case of 1723 the court upheld a suit
for separation brought by Mary Strudwicke on the grounds of her husband's
adultery, against her spouse's counter-allegation that since the adultery took
place he and his wife had had the 'carnal knowledge of each others bodies'. In
law, sex between husband and wife after the discovery of adultery signalled a
reconciliation, which was legally capable of halting a suit of separation. The
Judge of the Arches rejected the husband's allegation on the basis that 'The
Contrivance or Sollicitation of the Wife would not except the Husband from
being Criminal'.[16] If it was tacitly acknowledged that a wife should suffer her
husband's infidelity with greater forbearance than a husband should his wife's,
this also meant that 'reconciliation' could be interpreted more leniently for
wives married to adulterous husbands – a double standard which in this case
worked in Mary Strudwicke's favour.[17]

While for some women (and men) the prospect of having the intimate details
of their sex lives brought out in court was no doubt distressing, others seem to
have welcomed the opportunity litigation gave them to state their side of the
story and to bring counter-allegations of their spouses' infidelity. Legal records
provide striking evidence that women litigants were not prepared to accept any
sexual double standards. Unlike secular jurisdictions, where married women
lacked legal agency and were incapable of bringing suits in their own name, the
church courts gave women a unique opportunity to express their grievances.[18]

---

[15] Elizabeth A. Foyster, *Manhood in Early Modern England: Honour, Sex and Marriage* (London, 1999), pp. 82–3.

[16] Lincoln's Inn Library, MS Misc. 147 (Reports of Ecclesiastical Cases in the Court of Delegates and the Court of Arches between about 1714 and 1728, digested under titles by Dr Exton Sayer), p. 99. See also H[enry] C[onset], *The Practice of the Spiritual or Ecclesiastical Courts* (London, 1685), p. 281.

[17] This principle was also applied in Scottish divorce cases in this period: Leneman, *Alienated Affections*, pp. 77–8.

[18] The proportion of women litigants in the church courts may have been increasing more generally in this period: see Tim Meldrum, 'A Women's Court in London: Defamation at the Bishop of London's Consistory Court, 1700–1745', *The London Journal*, 19 (1994), 1–20; Stone, *Road to Divorce*, p. 187.

For instance, in 1688 Alexander Denton of Hillesden in Buckinghamshire successfully sued his neighbour Thomas Smith in the Court of Common Pleas
for having 'conversed scandalously and incontinently' with his wife, Hester.
But in order to pre-empt any further action on the part of her husband, Hester
Denton went on to counter-allege cruelty at the Court of Arches, hoping also
to use the litigation to clear her name. In the preceding suit, she maintained,
'there were some false Reflections cast on . . . [her] honour and reputation by
some persons out of malice or corruption yet as shee believeth nothing justly
proved against her'.[19] In spite of the verdict given for her husband elsewhere,
there was no legal impediment to her taking this action, for a prior verdict in
a rival jurisdiction bore no weight on subsequent hearings in an ecclesiastical
court.[20]

Female defendants in separation cases frequently made counter-accusations
of their husbands' adultery. When Dorothy Skelton was accused by her husband
of committing adultery with 'diverse and sundry persons', she responded by
formally accusing her husband of infidelity with one Elizabeth Appletree – a
claim she was able to support with the testimony of five witnesses.[21] A common
strategy of accused wives was to allege that their husbands had been unfaithful
with maidservants, exploiting a familiar leitmotif of predatory male sexuality.[22] In this way, wives were able to portray themselves as displaced both in
their husbands' affections and in the household order. Given the complex nature of household loyalties, it may also have been in some women's minds
that certain servants might be persuaded or bribed to testify in their favour.
Whatever their motives, women who counter-alleged their husband's adultery
were acting in full knowledge that the ecclesiastical law stipulated that, if the
person bringing a separation suit was also found to be adulterous, the case
would be dismissed.[23] The counter-allegation of adultery was a weapon by
which some wives might force their husbands to a workable reconciliation or
an out of court settlement. On occasion it might even form the basis for promoting a suit in Chancery for a separate maintenance.[24] These women, faced

---

[19] LPL, E9/38 (*Denton v. Denton*, Allegation on the part of Alexander Denton, 1690); Ee 7 (*Denton v. Denton*, Personal Answers of Hester Denton, Hilary Term 1690), fo. 44.

[20] Thomas Poynter, *A Concise View of the Doctrine and Practice of the Ecclesiastical Courts in Doctors Commons* (London, 1824), p. 199.

[21] LPL, E 5/20 (*Skelton v. Skelton*, Libel on the part of Captain Charles Skelton, 23 Oct. 1673); E 5/128 (*Skelton v. Skelton*, Allegation on the part of Dorothy Skelton, 20 Jan. 1674).

[22] E.g., LPL, E12/75 (*Hockmore v. Hockmore*, Allegation on the part of Mary Hockmore, n.d. [*c.*1698]); Ee 9 (*Gouldney v. Gouldney*, Personal Answers of Elizabeth Gouldney, n.d. [*c.*1732]), fo. 191/1v.

[23] C[onset], *Practice of the Spiritual and Ecclesiastical Courts*, p. 280.

[24] Amy Louise Erickson, *Women and Property in Early Modern England* (London, 1993), pp. 124–7. See also LPL, Bbb 826/8 (*Hockmore v. Hockmore*, Deposition of Richard Stephens, 30 Aug. 1698).

with the prospect of destitution and losing access to their children, had little time for the advice of some conduct writers to demurely accept their husbands' faults.[25]

Female defendants were also adept in using articles of exception and interrogatories (cross-examination of witnesses) to discredit those who gave evidence against them, accusing them of telling tales, being addicted to scandalous gossip or worse. One witness brought to testify against Winifred Barlow had the credit of her testimony challenged by the claim that she was a 'very great lyer' being a 'Tale bearer and a Carryer of Storyes from one house to another . . . adde[ing] to them in their carriage and by her relating of them'.[26] In another case, the evidence of the servant-witness Martha Ryland was contested on the grounds of her propensity for drunkenness and the telling of defamatory stories. A fellow witness deposed that when Martha Ryland had been drinking,

> shee is very passionate and apt to give ill language and in those Passions she behaves herselfe like a Mad Woman And [Anna Tustin] . . . sayth that she hath heard [th]e said Martha very much defame a Lady with whom shee had formerly liv'd and say That [th]e said Lady lov'd a Gentleman that us'd to come to her and was much pleas'd with his Company.[27]

Some wives even made allegations about the morals of their imputed lovers, especially where they were suspected of adultery with a social inferior. Dorothy Skelton, daughter of King Charles II's physician, Edward D'Aubrey, impugned the sexual honesty of her suspected lover, Charles Brooks, a footman to Lord Brounker, describing him as a 'loose, scandalous and lascivious person'. She declared that she 'would not prostitute her self to the lust of soe base a fellow', adding that he was 'a little weasl'd faced fellow . . . of a most ugly face and body'.[28]

In making and responding to allegations, husbands and wives aligned themselves with archetypes, presenting their partners' behaviour in diametrically opposing terms.[29] Statements of litigants in separation cases articulated gendered expectations of marriage. Husbands bringing cases of adultery against their wives describe themselves as treating their spouses with 'much love and respect' or behaving in a 'kind, tender, indulgent and affectionate manner'.[30] They are protective of their wives and 'unwilling to beleeve any ill' against them

---

[25] Cf. George Savile, *The Works of George Savile, Marquis of Halifax*, ed. Mark N. Brown (3 vols., Oxford, 1989), II, pp. 372–3.

[26] LPL, Bbb 914/1 (*Barlow v. Barlow*, Articles of Exception brought by Dame Winifred Barlow, 24 Apr. 1706); Bbb 914 (*Barlow v. Barlow*, Deposition of Henry Walker, 18 May 1706).

[27] LPL, Eee 7 (*Denton v. Denton*, Deposition of Anna Tustin, 6 Feb. 1690), fo. 78v.

[28] LPL, E5/128 (*Skelton v. Skelton*, Allegation on the part of Dorothy Skelton, 20 Jan. 1674).

[29] Similar strategies were used in civil courts: Stretton, *Women Waging Law*, pp. 190–6.

[30] LPL, Ee 4 (*Skelton v. Skelton*, Personal Answers of Captain Charles Skelton, 9 July 1674), fo. 288; E30/75 (*Gouldney v. Gouldney*, Libel on the part of Henry Gouldney, 1732).

'untill it was so evidently manifested'.[31] In contrast, their wives are represented as scolding or disobedient and behaving with 'great unkindnesse and disrespect' or being 'affronting and undutifull'. Alexander Denton complained that his wife 'abused him, both by words and actions both in publick and private and would make mouths at him, and affront him, and wou'd . . . refuse to let him kiss her'.[32] Charges of adultery were often reinforced in husbands' statements with accusations of profligacy and failure to perform sexual services, 'the conjugal rites due from a wife to a husband'.[33] In return for their kindness, husbands expected obedience, duty and unrestricted access to their spouses' bodies.

Wives defending themselves against accusations of adultery or impugning their husbands' conduct used the submissive role that was expected of them to their own ends. They presented themselves as good housekeepers and good mothers. Hester Denton claimed to have 'managed the affaires of [her husband's] family with great ease, prudence and paines and industry and thrift and with great respect and duty to him'. In spite of overwhelming evidence to the contrary, Mary Hockmore protested that she 'behaved herself with all due respect' towards her husband, carefully managing 'his family and domestick affairs' and being 'a very tender mother' to their five children.[34] Wives also insisted that their conduct was 'virtuous', 'sober' and 'honest'.[35] They accused their husbands of being cruel and irresponsible in their domestic relations. Aside from consorting with 'diverse Lude and unchast women', Dorothy Woodward accused her husband, Thomas, of treating her 'with much and unhuman severity, giving of her many Blowes Bruses cutts and wounds with his hands and other weapons or Instruments in divers places of her head and Body' in a manner wholly 'contrary to the holy Law or state of Wedlocke'.[36] Hester Denton stated that her husband had, 'without provocation', threatened to turn her out of doors without even 'a farthing to keep her from starveing'. Contrary to her spouse's self-presentation as a model husband, Elizabeth Gouldney alleged that he 'behaved himselfe in an unkind, disaffectionate and incontinent manner by keeping company with several lewd women'.[37]

---

[31] LPL, Ee 4 (*Skelton v. Skelton*, Personal Answers of Captain Charles Skelton, 12 Aug. 1674), fo. 302v.

[32] LPL, E9/38 (*Denton v. Denton*, Allegation on the part of Alexander Denton, n.d. [*c*.1690]).

[33] LPL, Bbb 826/10 (*Hockmore v. Hockmore*, Libel on the part of William Hockmore n.d. [*c*.1698]); E9/38 (*Denton v. Denton*, Allegation on the part of Alexander Denton, n.d. [*c*.1690]).

[34] LPL, E9/53 (*Denton v. Denton*, Libel on the part of Hester Denton, n.d. [*c*.1690]); E12/75 (*Hockmore v. Hockmore*, Allegation on the part of Mary Hockmore n.d. [*c*.1698]).

[35] For instance: LPL, Bbb1004/2 (*Bernard v. Bernard*, Allegation on the part of Martha Bernard, 4 July 1712); Bbb 1031/1 (*Bave v. Bave*, Allegation on the part of Winifred Bave, 20 Feb. 1716); D1805 (*Rudd v. Rudd*, Allegation on the part of Lettice Rudd, 1730), fo. 451.

[36] LPL, E4/102 (*Woodward v. Woodward*, Libel on the part of Dorothy Woodward, undated [*c*.1666?]).

[37] LPL, E9/53 (*Denton v. Denton*, Libel on the part of Hester Denton, n.d. [*c*.1690]); Ee 9 (*Gouldney v. Gouldney*, Personal Answers of Elizabeth Gouldney, n.d. [*c*.1732]), fo. 191/1v.

Some men claimed that they sought a separation as a means of restoring honour and reputation lost through their wives' adultery. Captain Charles Skelton justified bringing a suit against his wife in 1673 as a response to the 'great dishonor' done to his family and the 'particular abuse and disreputation' brought upon himself by his spouse's scandalous behaviour.[38] Women, by contrast, did not suggest that their honour had been damaged by their spouses' adultery, but were keen to present themselves as wronged women, complaining that their husbands' allegations of adultery had damaged their character and reputation. In particular, they were concerned about the effects of their husbands' allegations on their position of respect in the household. Hester Denton complained that her husband had called her 'whore, jade, bitch', almost on a daily basis, 'both before strangers and their menial servants', which had made her life 'a burden to her'.[39]

Through the conventions of the law and the formulaic language of the courts, husbands and wives tried to convey the pain of estranged affections and the stresses of marital disharmony. But reading between the lines of these statements, there seems to be rather more at stake in some suits than marital breakdown alone. What emerges particularly strongly is the role of money as a motivating factor.[40] For a husband the principal advantage of bringing a suit for separation was its potential reward of freeing him from debts run up by his wife in his name. He would be released from the obligation of paying his wife alimony if the separation was predicated on the grounds of her elopement or adultery.[41] She, in contrast, stood to lose everything – her maintenance, portion and access to her children.[42]

It is apparent that many cases were motivated by disputes arising from the financial negotiations and transactions which played a significant, if not wholly determining, role in the formation of marriage for the middling sort and above. The late payment of a wife's portion, or the delivery of a financial settlement not up to the expectations of the husband or his family, motivated a number of separation suits.[43] Charles Bave, a physician from Bath, stressed his disappointment in his wife's 'fortune' of £250 to emphasise his financial difficulties caused by his wife's elopement and cohabitation with other men.[44] Sir George Barlow's suit against his wife, Winifred, in 1704 followed an unsuccessful attempt to

---

[38] LPL, Ee 4 (*Skelton v. Skelton*, Personal Answers of Captain Charles Skelton, 12 Aug. 1674), fo. 303.

[39] LPL, E9/53 (*Denton v. Denton*, Libel on the part of Hester Denton, n.d. [c.1690]).

[40] The financial considerations underlying separation suits in the early seventeenth century are discussed in Ingram, *Church Courts*, p. 184.

[41] John Godolphin, *Repertorium Canonicum: Or, An Abridgement of the Ecclesiastical Laws of this Realm Consistent with the Temporal* (London, 1687), p. 508.

[42] Stone, *Road to Divorce*, p. 193; Bailey, 'Breaking the Conjugal Vows', p. 101.

[43] Margaret R. Hunt, *The Middling Sort: Commerce, Gender and the Family in England 1680–1780* (Berkeley and Los Angeles, CA, 1996), pp. 154–5.

[44] LPL, Bbb 1028/4 (*Bave v. Bave*, Personal Answers of Charles Bave, Trinity Term, 1715).

compel payment of her portion in the Court of Chancery.[45] The prospect of having lurid allegations of Winifred's extra-marital couplings and immodest behaviour brought out in court may have been intended to put pressure on her family to accommodate themselves to Sir George's demands. In such cases litigation served less as a means of breaking marriage, than as a threat to compel payment or a method of reaching a settlement. Occasionally too, separation litigation might be instigated by parents to split up a young couple who had married clandestinely without their permission and they could go to considerable lengths to find, or even manufacture, sufficient proofs of infidelity on which to launch a suit.[46]

The complicated circumstances lying behind legal action are vividly revealed in the separation suit contested between Henry Bernard and his wife, Martha, in 1712. Martha Bernard left her husband's house in London in January 1704, two years after their marriage, and went back to live in her home parish of Llandrinio in Montgomeryshire. It appears that Henry Bernard was initially content to allow his wife to live her own life, allowing her to keep the rents and profits of the estate in Llandrinio worth £40 a year, which by rights should have passed to him as part of their marriage settlement. He also asked few questions about her relationship with a Shrewsbury man, Jesse Okell.[47] Henry was finally spurred into bringing a formal separation out of financial necessity in 1712. There survives a set of letters sent by Martha to her husband, and subsequently exhibited as evidence, which suggest the complex negotiations which preceded the case. The letters present only Martha's side of the correspondence, but nevertheless provide tantalising hints of the strategic manoeuvres behind separation litigation.

Henry seems to have laid the grounds for a separation suit by orchestrating the spreading of 'grose and scandallus' rumours about his wife's infidelity. With the help of his sister, he apparently spread the fame that Martha was 'the most lustfull wretch liveing' and that 'thirty times lying with [her] in a week would not content [her]'. In contrast, Martha was keen to secure a private 'agreement' provided it could be reached without 'chary or trouble'. She said she would allow him to keep property of hers worth £400 in return for half her portion, and placed the matter in the hands of her attorney. When these negotiations broke down, Henry next tried to assert his power over his wife by having her arrested for stealing his goods. While bitterly resentful of her husband's underhand conduct, Martha nevertheless became more willing to

---

[45] LPL, Bbb 904 (*Barlow v. Barlow*, Allegation on the part of Dame Winifred Barlow, 27 July 1705); cf. Bbb 905/3 (*Barlow v. Barlow*, Personal Answers of Sir George Barlow, 25 Feb. 1706); Eee 9 (*Barlow v. Barlow*, Deposition of Thomas Heneage, 12 June 1705), fo. 52.

[46] E.g., LPL, D1805 (*Rudd v. Rudd*, Allegation on the part of Lettice Rudd, Michaelmas Term, 1730), ff. 448v–64v. However, the most common means of challenging a clandestine marriage was to secure an annulment. See Alison Wall, 'For Love, Money, or Politics? A Clandestine Marriage and the Elizabethan Court of Arches', *Historical Journal*, 38 (1995), 511–33.

[47] LPL, Bbb 999/6 (*Bernard v. Bernard*, Libel on the part of Henry Bernard, undated, *c.*1712).

accede to his demands. In a further letter she agreed to do everything she could to facilitate his separation suit in the Court of Arches provided that he did not take the matter further and seek a parliamentary divorce. 'A devorce', she wrote, 'cuts me to the h[e]art when I think on it: to resi[g]n my right to any other woman.'[48]

However, whether fearing her husband's capacity for double dealing or perhaps still being hopeful of reaching a better settlement out of court, Martha ultimately resisted his attempts to manufacture evidence of her adultery. Anne Prince recalled in the Court of Arches how in the autumn of 1712 a group of three men, who had apparently come from London, paid a visit to her house in Shrewsbury where Martha was residing. She overheard the men whispering conspiratorially that 'one of us must throw [Martha Bernard] on the bed and lye with her and the other two must be witnesses'. Fearing a rape, she hid Martha in 'an inner roome' and called the constable. When the men tried to break into the house a fracas ensued, and Anne remembered taking a spit and hitting one of the assailants over the head which 'struck of[f] his hat and periwig', forcing the men to flee.[49] Martha's letters show the extent to which some wives were prepared to stand up to their husbands' demands in separation agreements, resisting attempts to impugn their reputations and sticking tenaciously to what they understood to be their rights and dues. 'If you are resolute of beginning law', Martha warned her husband, 'you may conclude I will endeavour to end it.'[50] While the flouting of patriarchal codes, insatiate female sexuality and the dishonour of cuckoldry might provide the idiom in which separation suits were contested, the pragmatic side of litigation shows just how far these issues were complicated by material and strategic considerations. There was evidently more at stake in bringing a separation suit than the issue of infidelity alone.

PROVING ADULTERY

To secure a separation, adultery had to be proved either by 'witnesses' to the sexual act, 'or at least by vehement presumption, and publick fame'.[51] Direct proof of adultery or some strong tangible evidence of guilt such as pregnancy or catching venereal disease, preferably accompanied by a confession on the part of the guilty party, provided the strongest grounds for breaking marriage. However, this sort of material was not often forthcoming. Adultery and

---

[48] LPL, Bbb 1004 (*Bernard v. Bernard*, Letters from Martha Bernard to Henry Bernard, undated).
[49] LPL, Bbb 1004/6 (*Bernard v. Bernard*, Deposition of Anne Prince, n.d. [*c*.1712]). For another attempt to manufacture evidence of adultery in this way see Bbb 1004/6 (*Bernard v. Bernard*, Deposition of Elizabeth Martin, n.d. [*c*.1712]).
[50] LPL, Bbb 1004 (*Bernard v. Bernard*, Letters from Martha Bernard to Henry Bernard, undated).
[51] C[onset], *Practice of the Spiritual or Ecclesiastical Courts*, p. 280.

fornication, lamented the legal commentator John Ayliffe, being 'Acts of Darkness and great Secrecy', were consequently 'very hard and difficult to prove'. Even to observe a man and woman apparently performing a sexual act might be misleading since the man might be impotent or the woman frigid. All evidence of adultery was therefore to some degree 'presumptive', evaluated on the 'proximity and nearness of the Acts'. Strong proofs of adultery included witnessing 'the Man's lying on the Woman's Body with her Coats up', viewing the man and woman 'both together naked and undress'd in some secret place ... or else from seeing them in Bed together and the like'.[52]

In common with all other representations of adultery in this period, the law defined marital infidelity in resolutely heterosexual terms. Notwithstanding evidence from criminal records, which suggests that many participants in London's nascent male homosexual subculture were married, accusations of sodomy were scarce in matrimonial litigation.[53] Ecclesiastical law made no provision for separation on the grounds of homosexuality.[54] In any case, since the penalties for sodomy were so severe, being punishable by death for both parties, evidence for such behaviour was even more difficult to obtain than for adultery.[55] Female same-sex relations lacked recognition in the eyes of the law and as such could not be used as grounds for separation. Yet sexual contact with other women might on rare occasions be cited as additional evidence of a wife's licentious character. Among the extraordinary allegations made against Dame Winifred Barlow was the claim that sometime during the summer of 1699 she had sexually assaulted her maidservant, Dorothy Prickett, by throwing her on to a bed and endeavouring to 'force something up into [her] Body'. In her own testimony, Dorothy claimed that her mistress had thrust her hands under her clothes and 'sayd she must fuck [her] and that it would be a pleasure to her'. Such evidence was used to cast Winifred as 'a wicked lewd person', but despite her alleged admission to Dorothy that sex with her would give her 'pleasure', there was no suggestion from her husband's lawyers that she had any developed sexual preferences for women. In George Barlow's version of events, this fumbling sexual encounter with Dorothy Prickett would not lead Winifred to further lesbian passions, but to the only recognised way of satisfying her over-developed libido – sex with other men.[56]

[52] John Ayliffe, *Parergon Juris Canonici Anglicani: Or a Commentary By Way of Supplement to the Canons and Constitutions of the Church of England* (London, 1726), pp. 44–5.

[53] Tim Hitchcock, *English Sexualities, 1700–1800* (Basingstoke, 1997), p. 69.

[54] Stone, *Road to Divorce*, p. 193.

[55] Hitchcock, *English Sexualities*, pp. 60–1; Tim Meldrum, *Domestic Service and Gender 1660–1750: Life and Work in the London Household* (London, 2000), pp. 117–18.

[56] LPL, E15/37 (*Barlow v. Barlow*, Libel on the part of George Barlow, n.d. [c.1705]); Bbb 903 (*Barlow v. Barlow*, Deposition of Dorothy Prickett, 18 Oct. 1705). See also Bbb 903 (*Barlow v. Barlow*, Deposition of Elizabeth Matthias, 18 Oct. 1705); more generally, Hitchcock, *English Sexualities*, p. 78.

Witnessing illicit sex normally followed a set of pre-determined and time-worn forms which were enshrined in legal textbooks. Depositions hinged on legally sanctioned acts of clandestine surveillance: peering through cracks in walls, chinks in curtains or hangings, or the keyholes of locked doors.[57] To distance their spying from voyeurism or mere 'curiosity', which was condemned in moral prescription, witnesses sometimes placed their statements within the context of investigating a crime and informal policing.[58] Thomas Wagstaff, an apprentice in the house in the parish of St Giles in the Fields where Winifred Bave lodged in 1714, explained his decision to spy on the lodger's activities through a window one evening on the grounds that he had suspected 'that there was an unlawful familiarity' taking place between Mrs Bave and one Mr Collins, which he ought to investigate.[59]

Increasingly in this period, attempts were made by wealthier litigants and their lawyers to instigate a more professional approach to the gathering of evidence and its delivery in court. Servants in some aristocratic households were encouraged to keep written memoranda recording sightings of adultery which might form the basis of testimonies in court.[60] A more rigorous approach to establishing proof is also evident in the practice adopted by some wealthy husbands in the eighteenth century of employing amateur 'detectives' to locate their eloped spouses and gather incriminating evidence. Following the elopement of his wife, Elizabeth, with one Audley Harvey, Henry Gouldney, an attorney from Chippenham in Wiltshire, employed a number of men to track down the errant couple. The investigators, who included Richard Taverner, a farmer, Thomas Plumley, described as a 'yeoman', and the weaver Nathaniel Nutt, made a number of enquiries at inns before finally tracking down the fugitive couple to the house of Sara and William Bartlett in the village of North Bradley. Plumley and Nutt were sent to the house to divert Harvey's attention by pretending to make a social visit, while Taverner crept up to a downstairs window where he saw 'Mrs Gouldney donning her Cloaths and dressing herself'. Having established that Audley Harvey and Elizabeth Gouldney were together in the same house, Taverner and his colleagues returned to Chippenham to inform Henry Gouldney and pick up their reward. Several weeks later, Henry Gouldney sent Taverner and two bailiffs to arrest Audley Harvey on an action of criminal conversation.[61] This more rigorous approach to collecting evidence of adultery

[57] Ayliffe, *Parergon*, p. 50; cf. Ingram, *Church Courts*, p. 245.

[58] Cf. *The Universal Monitor: Or, a General Dictionary of Moral and Divine Precepts* (London, 1702), p. 200.

[59] LPL, Eee 11 (*Bave v. Bave*, Deposition of Thomas Wagstaff, 1 June 1715), fo. 183.

[60] Lawrence Stone, *Uncertain Unions and Broken Lives: Marriage and Divorce in England 1660–1857* (Oxford, 1995), pp. 395–6.

[61] LPL, Bbb 1246/12 (*Gouldney v. Gouldney*, Deposition of Richard Taverner, 30 Aug. 1732); Bbb 1246/5 (*Gouldney v. Gouldney*, Deposition of Thomas Plumley, 29 Aug. 1732). This case is discussed further in chapter 6 below.

is consistent with the more forensic approach to gathering evidence visible in other areas of eighteenth-century policing.[62]

There are also signs that some litigants were prepared to invest a good deal of time and money in the pre-trial examination and briefing of witnesses to establish their testimonies. Anne Oneat, brought to testify on behalf of Sir John Rudd in his separation suit, recalled on cross-examination that in March 1730 one Mary Steward paid her a visit at her lodgings at the Cock and Magpie in Lambeth. Mary and Anne were old acquaintances, having once lodged together at the house of Mrs Sweetman in Princes Street off Drury Lane, where Lettice Rudd also lodged with her lover, John Smith. Mary appears to have been employed as a go-between liaising with Sir John's lawyers and prospective witnesses. After winning Anne's confidence through a number of social visits, in which gossip about the Rudds' marital difficulties appears to have been exchanged, she arranged a meeting with one Mr Richards in his chambers at Doctors' Commons, where more formal enquiries were made about what Anne knew about Lettice Rudd's adultery. Although Anne testified that this meeting stopped short of prescribing what she should say in court, such contact was no doubt important in shaping the evidence subsequently delivered.[63]

In spite of such initiatives, problems of securing direct evidence of adultery proved difficult to overcome, meaning that many cases relied to a greater or lesser extent on a variety of presumptive evidence. Ecclesiastical law allowed a range of incidental factors to be considered as evidence of immorality based on suspicious circumstances, public notoriety and the character and reputation of the accused.[64] The act of a man and woman being alone in 'a suspected Place, kissing and embracing each other in a very immodest Posture' was sufficient to raise 'vehement Suspicion', especially if the man and woman had been 'both suspected before of Incontinency'. Witnesses were therefore encouraged to give evidence not simply of penetrative sexual activity, but of such behaviour that was recognisable as 'the Preludes of Debauchery, and of a libidinous Conversation'.[65] Concepts of civility were highly serviceable in enmeshing suspected persons in a web of incriminating evidence. Over the course of the seventeenth century, as Martin Ingram has shown, such concepts were 'slowly added to

---

[62] Malcolm Gaskill, 'The Displacement of Providence: Policing and Prosecution in Seventeenth- and Eighteenth-Century England', *Continuity and Change*, 11 (1996), 341–74; Barbara J. Shapiro, *Probability and Certainty in Seventeenth-Century England: a Study of the Relationships Between Natural Science, History, Law, and Literature* (Princeton, NJ, 1983), *passim*.

[63] LPL, D1805 (*Rudd v. Rudd*, Deposition of Anne Oneat, 22 June 1730), ff. 217v–219v.

[64] Charles Donahue Jr., 'Proof by Witnesses in the Church Courts of Medieval England: an Imperfect Reception of the Learned Law', in Morris S. Arnold, Thomas A. Cveer, Sally A. Sailly and Stephen D. White (eds.), *On the Laws and Customs of England: Essays in Honor of Samuel E. Thorne* (Chapel Hill, NC, 1981), pp. 127–58; Barbara J. Shapiro, *'Beyond Reasonable Doubt' and 'Probable Cause': Historical Perspectives on the Anglo-American Law of Evidence* (Berkeley, CA and Oxford, 1991), pp. 48, 49, 121, 201–17.

[65] Ayliffe, *Parergon*, p. 45.

existing linguistic repertoires' of illicit sex used by the courts.[66] By the end of the century, libels and allegations in adultery suits were littered with references to 'very indecent' behaviour or body language, to 'uncivil' conduct, 'extraordinary familiarities' and to 'conversation' which was 'scandalous' or 'criminal'.[67] William Stapleton alleged in 1693 that his wife had deserted him some seven or eight years previously to live in 'a very uncivill and scandalous manner', being 'much addicted' to drunkenness, visiting 'houses of very ill fame' and consorting with 'uncivill, unchast and dishonest persons'.[68] Similarly, Thomas Woodward was believed to have consorted with 'Mary Smart wife of Thomas Smart, Elizabeth Ball and others in an undecent and suspicious manner'.[69] The remainder of this chapter explores in more detail the kind of behaviour that might arouse suspicions and what this reveals about the conduct of illicit relations.

COMMITTING ADULTERY: SPACE, SECRECY AND UNLAWFUL INTIMACY

Since adultery was deemed to take place in 'private and suspicious' (or 'suspected') places, location played a crucial role in defining illicit intimacy in depositional material. Through the late seventeenth and early eighteenth centuries the concept of 'privacy' and the adjective 'private' were developing a number of meanings in different social and cultural contexts. The word 'private' could be used variously to refer to individual wealth and economic enterprise (as opposed to that of the state), to denote institutions offering selective rather than general membership and to characterise individual beliefs and conscience.[70] In the records of adultery litigation 'private' was synonymous with the shameful desire to keep illicit goings on hidden from public view, presenting affairs as

---

[66] Martin Ingram, 'Sexual Manners: the Other Face of Civility in Early Modern England', in Peter Burke, Brian Harrison and Paul Slack (eds.), *Civil Histories: Essays Presented to Sir Keith Thomas* (Oxford, 2000), p. 98.

[67] E.g., LPL, E9/38 (*Denton v. Denton*, Allegation on the part of Alexander Denton, 1690); E30/75 (*Gouldney v. Gouldney*, Libel on the part of Henry Gouldney, 1732); London Metropolitan Archives (LMA), DL/C/156 (*Dormer v. Dormer*, Libel on the part of John Dormer, 1715) fo. 34v.

[68] LPL, E 11/10 (*Stapleton v. Stapleton*, Libel on the part of William Stapleton, 9 Feb. 1693).

[69] LPL, Eee 4 (*Woodward v. Woodward*, Deposition of Hester Swann, 18 Jan. 1671), fo. 526v.

[70] Linda A. Pollock, 'Living on the Stage of the World: the Concept of Privacy Among the Elite of Early Modern England', in Adrian Wilson (ed.), *Rethinking Social History: English Society 1570–1920 and its Interpretation* (Manchester, 1993), pp. 78–96; John Brewer, 'This, That and the Other: Public, Social and Private in the Seventeenth and Eighteenth Centuries', in Dario Castiglione and Lesley Sharpe (eds.), *Shifting the Boundaries: Transformations of the Languages of Public and Private in the Eighteenth Century* (Exeter, 1995), pp. 1–21; Lawrence E. Klein, 'Gender and the Public/Private Distinction in the Eighteenth Century: Some Questions about Evidence and Analytic Procedure', *Eighteenth-Century Studies*, 29 (1995), 97–109; Jennifer Melville, 'The Use and Organisation of Domestic Space in Late Seventeenth-Century London', PhD thesis, University of Cambridge (1999), ch. 3.

furtive and secretive.[71] This use of the word 'private' tied in with the definition of adultery in legal theory, as well as in wider social discourse, as a crime of 'secrecy'.[72]

In legal records, the word 'private' described both spatial arrangements and certain types of clandestine behaviour in which the key criterion was that a suspected couple were 'alone' together. Lovers went about their liaisons in a 'private manner' in 'private rooms and chambers'. The basic principle on which a room was adjudged to be 'private' in legal theory was whether the door was shut. Closed doors created an enclosed intimate space. Refusal to open a door when challenged led to the inference that the occupants of a room were up to no good and was occasionally the prelude to the door being broken down to discover the adulterous lovers within.[73] In the houses of the wealthier middling sort and gentry, where doors were often fitted with locks, distinctions were sometimes made between closed doors which were actually locked and those that were merely latched. Visiting the house of Sir George and Dame Winifred Barlow one summer morning, Anne Yarnold, who described herself as 'pretty well acquainted with the [Barlow] family', lifted up the latch of Winifred Barlow's bedchamber to find her sitting in bed eating sugared lemons with Hugh Philips (one of her suspected lovers), Philips's sister and a kinswoman. Although the incident was unusual and supported other rumours of Winifred's overfamiliarity with Hugh Philips, the presence of the other women and, significantly, the fact that the door was 'latched but not locked' made the circumstances less suspicious.[74]

Spatial intimacy was swayed by patterns of consumption as furniture and hangings began to play an important role in demarcating public and private spaces within the houses of wealthier people. Unsurprisingly, rooms containing beds were considered more private and 'secret' than others as the bedchamber slowly became redefined as an exclusively private space. In sixteenth- and early seventeenth-century houses bedchambers still retained their medieval use as reception rooms.[75] Remnants of this practice are still visible in the later seventeenth century, especially when families took temporary lodgings, such as when visiting London for the season. In May or June 1687, for instance, Alexander and Hester Denton left their country estate at Hillesden in Buckinghamshire to take rooms for several weeks at the house of one Mr Graves in King Street, Bloomsbury. Because of the lack of space, one witness deposed, 'it was usual for Visitants to goe into [th]e Dyneing Room and so through into

---

[71] Brewer, 'This, That and the Other', p. 9; Ingram, *Church Courts*, pp. 244–5.
[72] Ayliffe, *Parergon*, p. 44.
[73] E.g., LPL, Bbb 826/8 (*Hockmore v. Hockmore*, Deposition of William Battishill, 30 Aug. 1698).
[74] LPL, Bbb 903 (*Barlow v. Barlow*, Deposition of Anne Yarnold, 16 Oct. 1705).
[75] Pollock, 'Living on the Stage of the World', p. 82; John E. Crowley, *The Invention of Comfort: Sensibilities and Design in Early Modern Britain and Early America* (Baltimore, MD, 2000), p. 7.

UNIVERSITY OF
WOLVERHAMPTON

UNIVERSITY OF WOLVERHAMPTON
Harrison Library

Customer name: WOAKES, RACHEL
Customer ID: 63002396

Items that you have loaned

Title:
 Fashioning adultery : gender, sex, and civility
 in England, 1660-1740 /
ID: 23822465
Due: 01/11/2018 23:59

Title: Hamlet /
ID: 23134933
Due: 01/11/2018 23:59

Title: Hamlet, William Shakespeare /
ID: 08392773
Due: 01/11/2018 23:59

Total items: 3
Account balance: £0.00
24/10/2018 13:51
Loaned: 8
Overdue: 0
Hold requests: 0
Ready for collection: 0

Thank you for using Self Service.
A copy of this receipt has been emailed to you.

You can check your account online at
www.wlv.ac.uk/lib

Books will automatically renew unless
requested by another borrower. Overdue books
are fined at £1 per day

ye Bedchamber and to sit upon [th]e Bed'. When another witness testifies to Hester Denton and her lover, Thomas Smith, actually committing adultery at Mr Graves's lodgings, the sexual act is described as taking place in a more secluded 'little room' beyond the bedchamber normally used as a dressing room or store room.[76]

Curtains were also coming to play a more conspicuous role in establishing illicit intimacy. On the evidence of probate inventories, window curtains seem to have become increasingly common and spread over a broader social range of dwellings in the period from 1675 to 1725.[77] This was especially true in towns where the closer proximity of inhabitants stimulated a greater desire for seclusion – residents of eighteenth-century Bristol, for example, were five times more likely to own window curtains than their rustic neighbours.[78] Nevertheless, some depositions show that in spite of their growing popularity, curtains might still connote an unusual desire for privacy, particularly in the eyes of poorer witnesses. While staying in London with her husband in 1696, Mary Hockmore made several visits to her lover, Edward Ford, at his lodgings in the house of Rive Morgan, a Westminster victualler. Morgan recalled in court how Mary had complained to him 'by reason of his haveing noe curtaines to [th]e window' of Ford's room and demanded 'w[ha]t reasons why there were none'.[79] Since Mary was the wife of a prosperous Devonshire gentleman, the incident gives a telling indication of how expectations of intimacy and material comfort were shaped by rank.

In the habitations of the wealthy, bed curtains provided an extra veil of intimacy within the bedchamber.[80] The combination of locked doors and bed curtains in creating layers of concealment for an adulterous couple is vividly illustrated in a statement made by Elizabeth Matthias, a carpenter's wife, in the case against Winifred Barlow. At harvest time in 1698, Elizabeth recalled, she had been sent on an errand to buy some provisions for Sir George's family at Narberth market. On returning to the house and not finding her mistress in the parlour as she had expected, Elizabeth went upstairs to Winifred's chamber. The room had three doors, 'each opening on a different stair case', and Elizabeth, 'endeavouring to open the door of [th]e s[ai]d chamber so most used found the s[ai]d door was bolted on [th]e inside', upon which she returned to the parlour and climbed one of the other staircases to try a different door into Winifred's room. This door was shut but unlocked and Elizabeth entered the

---

[76] LPL, Eee 7 (*Denton v. Denton*, Deposition of Margaret Townsend, 4 Feb. 1690), fo. 67v; Eee 7 (*Denton v. Denton*, Deposition of Anna Tustin, 6 Feb. 1690), ff. 74r–75r.

[77] Lorna Weatherill, *Consumer Behaviour and Material Culture in Britain 1660–1760* (London and New York, 1988), p. 40.

[78] Carl B. Estabrook, *Urbane and Rustic England: Cultural Ties and Social Spheres in the Provinces 1660–1780* (Manchester, 1998), p. 149.

[79] LPL, Eee 8 (*Hockmore v. Hockmore*, Deposition of Rive Morgan, 9 Aug. 1698), fo. 614.

[80] Weatherill, *Consumer Behaviour and Material Culture*, p. 161.

bedchamber, which appeared to be deserted, yet the 'curteins of the bed [were] drawn close all around the bed'. Her curiosity raised, Elizabeth proceeded to open the curtain 'on that side [of] the bed which stood next [to] [th]e chamber door [th]e dep[onen]t went in at' and there she saw

> the s[ai]d Lady [Barlow] lying on the s[ai]d bed and upon the dep[onen]t's opening the curtains saw...Hugh Philips get from off [th]e s[ai]d Lady Barlow on whom he lay and he then layd down w[i]th his face to [th]e...bed and the dep[onen]t then also saw the s[ai]d Lady put or thrust down her petticoats over her leggs upon which the dep[onen]t went...out [of] [th]e... Chamber.[81]

As domestic space in larger houses became increasingly demarcated and rooms acquired more specialised use, so different types of intimacy became associated with specific locations. While sexual intercourse was coming to be more exclusively associated with the bedchamber, other spaces connoted different sorts of interaction between the sexes. During the later seventeenth century, the parlour in such houses was changing from a withdrawing space (often containing a bed) to a living room used to entertain guests.[82] In 1687 Thomas Smith visited the house of Hester Denton at Hillesden in Buckinghamshire during her husband's absence. Martha Ryland, a maidservant, deposed that Hester Denton came downstairs and met Smith and took him into the parlour, shutting the door after her. Suspicious at this unusual behaviour, Martha peered through a hole in the door and saw

> Hester Denton seat her selfe in a chayr and the said Mr Smith came p[re]sently to her And standing over her with his face towards hers seated himself in her lap and continued as shee believes a quarter of an hour in that posture kissing and stroaking her upon ye face and sometimes clucking [sic] her under ye chin.[83]

The behaviour of Hester Denton and Thomas Smith, which clearly transgressed the normal amount of familiarity allowed on social visits, is rendered even more suspicious by its location in a room associated with sociability.

Other living spaces such as dining rooms, which in wealthier households also contained upholstered furniture, might be used for kissing and fondling. In the early eighteenth century, servants in the house of John and Diana Dormer reported numerous sightings of their mistress entertaining her lover, the footman Thomas Jones, in the dining room on the first floor of the Dormers' London dwelling in Albermarle Street. One afternoon another footman, Charles Whiston, came into the dining room (which also functioned as a sitting room)

---

[81] LPL, Bbb 903 (*Barlow v. Barlow*, Deposition of Elizabeth Matthias, 16 Oct. 1705).

[82] Weatherill, *Consumer Behaviour and Material Culture*, pp. 11–12; Frank E. Brown, 'Continuity and Change in the Urban House: Developments in Domestic Space Organisation in Seventeenth-Century London', *Comparative Studies in Society and History*, 28 (1986), 583–4, 588.

[83] LPL, Eee 7 (*Denton v. Denton*, Deposition of Martha Ryland, 8 Feb. 1690), fo. 81.

and there saw 'the said Diana then sitting on a Couch in the said roome and him the said Thomas Jones then haveing the small of her leggs in his hands and turning her body thereby to lay her along the couch and the said Thomas Jones being soe surprised by this Dep[onen]t turned away'.[84] On a different occasion, passing the open door of the dining room, another footman, James Warham, saw reflected in a mirror 'the said Diana there sitting upon a blew and white velvet couch or squabb and he the said Thomas Jones standing by and close to her and stooping with his face towards hers as if it were to kisse her'.[85] The emergence of increasingly comfortable living spaces was evidently exploited by lovers for physical intimacy.

Transgressions of spatial codes were most sharply visible in cases of employer–servant sexual relations. We saw in chapter 3 how the close proximity of living space and work space in London's poorer artisanal households acted as a premise for a series of cuckolding tales in *Poor Robin's Intelligence* and other publications. But in the houses of the wealthier people who could afford the costs of matrimonial litigation, increased segregation between employers and servants was becoming apparent. In London in particular, the architectural stan-dardisation imposed on the layout of new houses erected after the Rebuilding Act of 1667 made for greater distinction between the living and sleeping spaces and spheres of activity of masters and servants.[86] The delineation of servants' living quarters at the top of houses in garrets, and the social segregation of movement typified by the distinction between the main and back staircases, helped to create separate spatial zones within these households.[87] Spatial seg-regation and social zoning generated a new set of concerns in the evidence of employer–servant sexual relations brought before the courts, especially in cases hinging on the patriarchal nightmare of adultery between a mistress and a male servant.

The adulterous relationship between Diana Dormer and Thomas Jones pro-vides a particularly vivid illustration of these themes. By contemporary stan-dards, the case was highly notorious and became a matter of public interest after John Dormer brought an action of criminal conversation against Jones in 1715, which, as we shall see in the next chapter, was the subject of various pamphlet accounts.[88] Shortly after this trial, Diana Dormer brought a case for

---

[84] LMA, DL/C/255 (*Dormer v. Dormer*, Deposition of Charles Whiston, 24 Mar. 1715), fo. 159.

[85] Ibid. (Deposition of James Warham, 16 Feb. 1715), fo. 80v.

[86] Peter Earle, *The Making of the English Middle Class: Business, Society and Family Life in London, 1660–1730* (London, 1989), p. 207; Meldrum, *Domestic Service and Gender*, p. 81 and ch. 4 *passim*; Melville, 'Use and Organisation of Domestic Space', ch. 5.

[87] Similar 'zoning' was apparent in country houses, which increasingly adopted back stair-cases after the Restoration: Mark Girouard, *Life in the English Country House: a Social and Architectural History* (New Haven, CT and London, 1978), p. 138.

[88] For an analysis of this case within the broader context of master–servant sexual relations see Meldrum, *Domestic Service and Gender*, pp. 80, 83, 119–20.

restitution of conjugal rights in the London consistory court, but over thirty witnesses were brought to testify against her, many of whom were domestic servants who recalled their mistress's illicit sexual transactions in and around the Dormers' houses in Albemarle Street in the fashionable West End of London and (less frequently) at the family estate at Rousham in Oxfordshire. The adultery between Diana Dormer and Thomas Jones antagonised many servants in the household on account of their mistress's favouritism and Jones's behaving in a manner deemed to be above his station.[89] Jones's impudence was manifested particularly clearly by his abuse of the spatial codes of the household. When John Dormer was absent from home, Jones would go 'directly up the fore stairs with much impudence and assureance and into such roome where [Diana Dormer] was then said to bee'. In the household rules, going up the main stairs was strictly 'prohibited to the servants'.[90] Jones's flouting of spatial conventions powerfully underscored his disruption of the domestic hierarchy inherent in cuckolding his master.[91]

Evidence brought to the court in this case vividly shows how large houses offered numerous opportunities for illicit liaisons. The housemaid, Elizabeth Evans, reported that Thomas Jones and Diana Dormer 'were daily in each others' company in most roomes' of the house at Albemarle Street.[92] It was Jones's duty as footman to make tea and coffee at the request of his master and mistress and it was from this legitimate form of interaction that more illicit liaisons sometimes took shape. Alice Hogger, a chambermaid, observed that her mistress would send for Jones to come to her in her bedchamber in the morning 'under pretence of making her Tea or giving her her breakfast'.[93] Tea seems to have been served on the first floor of the house in a gallery.[94] Most references to Thomas Jones and Diana Dormer being alone together relate to this floor, where there was also a parlour or dining room adjacent to, and connecting with, Diana's bedchamber. They were also observed to be alone in Diana's dressing room on the same storey, sometimes referred to merely as a 'closett', which was also accessed through the bedchamber. On the second floor of the house, they were seen to be together in the nursery room and a 'little bedchamber' next to it, and in what was described as a 'sweet meate closett' and the closet where Diana kept her clothes, or 'linnen-roome'[95] At the top of the house, 'up three pair of staires', Diana and Thomas were occasionally reported to be alone in a room described as a 'Garrett... next to... Thomas Jones his Lodging roome', in which, ominously,

[89] Ibid., p. 58.
[90] LMA, DL/C/255 (*Dormer v. Dormer*, Deposition of Richard Morris, 19 Mar. 1715), fo. 145v; ibid. (Deposition of Francis Warmington, 17 May 1715), fo. 181.
[91] See also Meldrum, *Domestic Service and Gender*, p. 83.
[92] LMA, DL/C/255 (*Dormer v. Dormer*, Deposition of Elizabeth Evans, 3 Mar. 1715), fo. 84v.
[93] Ibid. (Deposition of Alice Hogger, 18 Mar. 1715), fo. 141v.
[94] Ibid. (Deposition of Mary Green, 5 Mar. 1715), fo. 99.
[95] Ibid. (Deposition of Mary Green, 5 Mar. 1715), fo. 99.

'there was a bed'.[96] At Rousham, although less evidence is available, a similar pattern of room use emerges, based primarily around a similar first-floor suite of a dining room with adjacent bedroom, dressing room or closet. Less often, Diana Dormer and Thomas Jones were found alone together in the ground-floor parlour and second-floor 'linnen-room' at Rousham.[97]

Practical considerations concerning the likelihood of discovery and the ease of escape or concealment if disturbed seem to have played an important role in their choice of rooms for staging their affair. The fact that Diana's bedchamber had access to the backstairs afforded her lover an escape route, with the extra advantage that this was a staircase unlikely to be used by his master.[98] Servants reported that Jones was often seen to 'slip' or 'skulke' down these stairs and make away.[99] The rooms on the second floor of the Dormer residence in Albemarle Street presented different opportunities for seclusion. Thomas Jones's eventual dismissal from service in 1711, when the affair was discovered by John Dormer, coincided with Diana giving birth to a daughter and they continued to meet most often in the nursery of the house. As a female and maternal space, this was another part of the house where John Dormer was unlikely to go, reducing the risk of detection.[100] More generally, the closets on this floor offered small and secretive locations for expressing affection. One morning in 1709, the housemaid Mary Green observed Thomas Jones to come to Diana in her 'sweet-meate closett' on this floor and there to 'putt his hand about her waste and turne her round in a very familiar manner'.[101] On stage, closets often functioned as hiding places for lovers, and witnesses in separation suits reported similar uses. In the Hockmore case of 1698, for instance, the servant Mary Lynton recalled seeing Charles Manley, one of her mistress's lovers, 'two or three times to shutt into a closett' when disturbed in Mary Hockmore's bedchamber.[102]

Cultural anxieties about the use of new opportunities for fashionable sociability for arranging and carrying out liaisons are partly borne out by the evidence from adultery litigation. A large social event such as the funeral of the Duke of Buckingham in 1687 provided the perfect subterfuge for Hester Denton to surreptitiously meet Thomas Smith, at Westminster Abbey. The couple then took a coach to Lincoln's Inn where they deposited Hester's three female chaperones before driving off into the metropolis alone.[103] The temptations of Restoration

---

[96] Ibid. (Deposition of Thomas Levin, 16 Mar. 1715), fo. 129v; ibid. (Deposition of Thomas Edwards, 24 Mar. 1715), fo. 151v.

[97] Ibid. (Deposition of Thomas Levin, 16 Mar. 1715), fo. 129v.

[98] Ibid. (Deposition of James Warham, 16 Feb. 1715), fo. 80v.

[99] Ibid. (Deposition of Theodora Patrick, 15 Mar. 1715), fo. 118v.

[100] Ibid. (Deposition of Elizabeth Evans, 3 Mar. 1715), ff. 84v, 85v.

[101] Ibid. (Deposition of Mary Green, 5 Mar. 1715), fo. 99.

[102] LPL, Bbb 826/8 (*Hockmore v. Hockmore*, Deposition of Mary Lynton, 30 Aug. 1698).

[103] LPL, Eee 7 (*Denton v. Denton*, Deposition of Margaret Townsend, 4 Feb. 1690), fo. 67v.

London led some husbands to try to send their wives into the country when they could not be around to keep an eye on them. When Captain Charles Skelton went to sea, he ordered his wife to go to her uncle's house in Norfolk, but she refused, preferring to stay in London where she 'took her extravagant courses and kept very ill company', arranging a host of illicit sexual transactions in the taverns and bawdy houses around Tower Hill.[104]

While lodging in London in 1714, Winifred Bave sometimes met her lover, Mr Clark, at the bagnio, a fashionable gathering point, on one occasion leaving the key to her lodgings there for him to pick up.[105] Such uses of the bagnio, which had originally been intended to 'relieve the Diseased', would confirm its popular reputation in the eighteenth century as a place where, as one periodical account put it, 'the two Sexes may have such Accommodation as their Vices require'.[106] By the eighteenth century modish spa towns such as Bath also figured in court records as presenting opportunities for adulterous liaisons. Winifred Barlow alleged that her husband had used a visit to Bath in 1700 to consort with 'Lewd debauched and incontinent women' from whom he supposedly caught 'the foule disease called the French pox'.[107] A summer visit to Bath in 1713 enabled Diana Dormer to renew her acquaintance with Thomas Jones. Visiting the abbey cloisters, Diana slipped away from the female servants who chaperoned her to have a 'private conversation' with her lover.[108]

Making visits to provincial towns with their husbands for important events in the social calendar gave wives opportunities to steal away and rendezvous with gallants. Visiting Exeter with her husband for the assizes, Mary Hockmore slipped away while her spouse was engaged in business to liaise with her Swiss mercenary lover, Killcutt.[109] The anonymity of town life was tempting to adulterous country dwellers. On another occasion, Mary Hockmore threatened her husband that she would leave his house in rural Devon and set up a new existence in London, declaring that 'there I'le live, and I'le bring thee a child every yeere if the Art of man can gett them, and thou shalt maintayne them all, And I will run thee in debt untill I have ruined thee, if I Damne both Body and Soule to effect it'.[110]

[104] LPL, E 5/20 (*Skelton v. Skelton*, Libel on the part of Captain Charles Skelton, 23 Oct. 1673); Ee 4 (Personal Answers of Captain Charles Skelton, 9 July 1674), fo. 288v.

[105] LPL, Eee 11 (*Bave v. Bave*, Deposition of Thomas Wagstaff, 1 June 1715), fo. 183v.

[106] *Universal Spy; Or, The London Weekly Magazine*, 18, 10 Aug. 1739, 173.

[107] LPL, Bbb 903/4 (*Barlow v. Barlow*, Interrogatories on the part of Winifred Barlow, n.d. [*c*.1705]).

[108] LMA, DL/C/255 (*Dormer v. Dormer*, Deposition of Richard Hayes, 17 May 1714), fo. 178; ibid. (Deposition of Joseph Morrice, 25 Mar. 1715), ff. 162v–163r.

[109] LPL, Bbb 826/8 (*Hockmore v. Hockmore*, Deposition of Mary Seller, 30 Aug. 1698). On the assizes as social occasions see J. M. Beattie, *Crime and the Courts in England 1660–1800* (Oxford, 1986), p. 330; Amanda Vickery, *The Gentleman's Daughter: Women's Lives in Georgian England* (New Haven, CT and London, 1998), p. 261.

[110] LPL, Bbb 826/10 (*Hockmore v. Hockmore*, Libel on the part of William Hockmore, 1698); Bbb 826/8 (*Hockmore v. Hockmore*, Deposition of Richard Stephens, 30 Aug. 1698).

The capital's reputation as a place where men and women could leave their spouses and set up new lives with lovers, sometimes under new identities, was confirmed by other cases. For instance, in May 1708 Jonathan Collins, a barrister, left his wife, Sara, to cohabit with a widow, Martha Burt, in Putney and other places in London and rural Surrey and Middlesex, as 'man and wife'.[111] Inns and taverns afforded lodgings to eloped couples and more generally provided places for lovers to meet, both in towns and on country roads.[112] One such liaison is vividly described by Elizabeth Thomas, a server at the Pageant Tavern in Charing Cross, who recalled an illicit meeting which took place there between Dorothy Skelton and 'a person resembling a Captain' in July 1672. The couple paid for the use of a 'lower room' where they first 'called for wine, brandy and a tart'. Bringing them their provisions, Elizabeth observed that the captain 'used uncivill postures with the said Mrs Skelton by lascivious kissing and putting his hand into his cutpece [*sic*]'. The captain then threatened Elizabeth that if she did not leave the room 'he should be rude with her, meaning as [Elizabeth] conceived that he would violently thrust her out', whereupon she went out into the yard and spied on the couple's sexual couplings 'through a little chink of the window'.[113] Such locations, where few questions seem to have been asked about a couple's marital status, provided ideal opportunities for lovers to carry on their adulterous relations unchallenged beyond the more dangerous confines of the household and its systems of surveillance.

'EXTRAORDINARY FAMILIARITIES' AND THE MEANINGS OF ADULTERY

Just as they were painstakingly aware of the minutiae of spatial detail, witnesses in adultery suits were sensitised to the smallest inferences of suspicion in the conduct and deportment of suspected persons. Not just sex, but all manner of physical intimacy was described in statements made before the courts, revealing a wide variety of 'adulterous' conduct. Such evidence illustrates vividly the kind of 'uncivil' behaviour that helped to support accusations of adultery and the forms that excessive 'freedoms' or 'familiarities' could take. Ironically, evidence brought to blacken the character of the accused may provide hints at what enjoyment was to be had from having an affair. The chapter concludes

---

[111] LPL, E18/25 (*Collins v. Collins*, Libel on the part of Sarah Collins, n.d. [*c*.1706]); for another example see Bbb 826/10 (*Hockmore v. Hockmore*, Libel on the part of William Hockmore, 1690).

[112] E.g., LPL, Eee 7 (*Stapleton v. Stapleton*, Deposition of Catherine Edwards, 9 Feb. 1693), fo. 521v; ibid. (Deposition of Anne Stevens, 9 Feb. 1693), fo. 524; Bbb 999/5 (*Bernard v. Bernard*, Deposition of John Drayton, 2 May 1712); Bbb 1246/7 (*Gouldney v. Gouldney*, Deposition of Ambrose Dunn, 29 Aug. 1732).

[113] LPL, Eee 5 (*Skelton v. Skelton*, Deposition of Elizabeth Thomas, 13 Nov. 1673), fo. 62v.

by examining this evidence in more detail and asks what it reveals about the meanings of the relationships described.

Many witnesses described imputed lovers apparently enjoying physical intimacy other than sexual contact. This is borne out in descriptions of Hester Denton's love affair with Thomas Smith. There is much evidence that Hester valued her lover's companionship and made great efforts to accommodate him when he visited the Dentons' house at Hillesden, sometimes at the expense of caring for her own husband. The cookmaid, Martha Ryland, recalled in her testimony that her mistress would order her to prepare a 'Calves head hasht sometimes fatt Chickens Ducks Turkeys Fish Cheesecakes Tarts Soups and other things w[hi]ch were not ordinary at other times'. In contrast, when she asked her mistress on other occasions what she should prepare for Alexander Denton, 'the said Hester has slightingly answered what dost tell me of thy master let him take what there is in ye house'.[114] On another occasion, when Alexander Denton asked for a 'dish of milk', his wife 'hath gone to ye Dayry Mayd and order'd her to scim it saying it was good enough for him'.[115] The contrast between lavish provision for a lover and meagre scraps for the husband vividly demonstrated the misplacement of a wife's loyalties and abuse of her domestic duties in organising meals. Whereas long-established rules of hospitality and principles of good manners dictated that guests, particularly neighbouring gentry like Thomas Smith, should be provided for to the best of a household's ability, good manners dictated that guests should not usurp the role of the host by 'commanding the resources of the establishment'.[116]

Hester's 'familiarity and kindnesse' for Thomas Smith also revealed itself to Alexander Denton's clerk, Humphrey Drake, who had seen her go 'out of a warm Room where she hath been to a Cold Room where . . . Mr Smith was on purpose . . . for the enjoyment of . . . Mr Smith's Company'.[117] When they were in London, Smith was observed to 'kisse and embrace' Hester, with his 'armes sometimes about her Neck and at other times about her waist'.[118] Alongside these physical intimacies, the lovers shared laughter together, again at the expense of Hester's husband. Valentine Budd, a servant in the Denton household, recalled an occasion when his master came home from hunting and joined his wife and Thomas Smith who were already at dinner. When Alexander Denton asked his wife to 'cutt him something' to eat, she only did so at 'twice or thrice asking and then slightingly flung it on his plate'. She then proceeded to make 'mouths' at her husband as he ate, all the time 'looking at Mr Smith who hath

[114] LPL, Eee 7 (*Denton v. Denton*, Deposition of Martha Ryland, 8 Feb. 1690), ff. 81, 81v.
[115] Ibid. (Deposition of Valentine Budd, 11 Feb. 1690), fo. 85v.
[116] Felicity Heal, 'Hospitality and Honor in Early Modern England', *Food and Foodways*, 1 (1987), 323.
[117] LPL, Eee 7 (*Denton v. Denton*, Deposition of Humphrey Drake, 10 Feb. 1690), fo. 83.
[118] Ibid. (Deposition of Mary Blitham, 11 Feb. 1690), fo. 92v.

likewise laugh'd and pointed at [Alexander Denton] . . . whilst he was eating'. The mocking laughter and gestures, together with Hester's seeking the approval of her lover rather than of her husband, made this scene highly resonant with symbols of the inversion of household order.[119]

Other evidence brought in adultery trials seemed to convey a desire on the part of the suspected wife for the attention of men and a desire to shock others by breaking social conventions. Dame Winifred Barlow, against whom an especially wide range of incriminating social *faux pas* was alleged, was accused of greeting the gentlemen who visited her husband's house 'very indiscreetly' by giving them 'too great a freedome by kissing them after a wanton manner'.[120] Thomas Davies observed Hugh Philips to 'kiss . . . Lady Barlow very lovingly and otherwise than after [th]e usuall way of saluting a woman'.[121] On another occasion, Winifred's over-familiarity was noticed at a card game when the servant John Barden observed that one of the players, Captain Passinger, was permitted to 'sit with his arms about . . . Dame Winifred's waist as they and others sat playing'.[122] It was reported that when Charles Rich visited the Barlows' house he and Winifred would sit in the parlour 'shaking hands together and talking and whispering together after a very familiar and free manner'.[123] Thomas Davies deposed that William Rochford, a local ferryman, had boasted to him that 'he could have a kiss of the s[ai]d Lady Barlow when he pleased and that he was used to put a silver penny in a little purse within her stayes and could look for [th]e same when he pleased and that when he could not find it he was to have twenty kisses'.[124] Much was made in this case of Winifred's exhibitionism and apparent love of unseemly pranks. Henry Bowen, the Barlows' household chaplain, recalled that when various neighbouring gentlemen were being entertained at the house during the evening time she would walk about the house in her night clothes which, as he informed her, was 'inbecomeing' (*sic*) a woman of her station.[125] Many witnesses testified to her habitual drunkenness, which led her to cast off normal constraints of bodily control and social decorum. Drink 'brought on her violent fitts' in which she 'could not help herself', made her vomit in company and behave 'wantonly and foolishly'. Walter Middleton, her husband's grandfather, deposed that when 'merry' with drink Winifred was 'of a very free temper' and had 'kissed' him, calling him 'her little grandfather' and joking with him that he had been 'an old whoremonger'.[126]

[119] Ibid. (Deposition of Valentine Budd, 11 Feb. 1690), fo. 84v.
[120] LPL, E 15/37 (*Barlow v. Barlow*, Libel on the part of Sir George Barlow, 1705).
[121] LPL, Bbb 903 (*Barlow v. Barlow*, Deposition of Thomas Davies, 18 Oct. 1705).
[122] Ibid. (Deposition of John Barden, 15 Oct. 1705).
[123] Ibid. (Deposition of Henry Bowen, 13 Oct. 1705).
[124] Ibid. (Deposition of Thomas Davies, 18 Oct. 1705).
[125] Ibid. (Deposition of Henry Bowen, 13 Oct. 1705).
[126] Ibid. (Deposition of Walter Middleton, 13 Oct. 1705).

Winifred's maidservants also complained of their mistress's desire to offend their sensibilities. One, Sarah Long, testified that during the summer of 1703, in the presence of herself and two other serving women, Winifred removed all her clothes to take a bath. In her own version of events, Winifred justified this action as a desire to maintain cleanliness and propriety consistent with what was expected of women of her rank, arguing that it was 'usuall . . . in very hott weather' for 'Ladies and Gentlewomen' to take baths.[127] Sarah Long, in contrast, interpreted the incident in terms of shamelessness and exhibitionism, recalling that Winifred seemed to revel in her bodily exposure, taking time to comb and powder 'the hair of her private parts'. When asked to put her shift back on, Winifred apparently retorted that Sarah was a 'damned old Bitch and bid [her] hold her tongue'.[128] In the hands of Sir George Barlow's counsel, this was compelling evidence of his wife's lascivious nature, but read against the grain it appears to place Winifred's love affairs in the context of a desire for fun, attention and intimacy and an eagerness to throw off the stultifying conventions of genteel life on a Welsh country estate.

Social status is a critical factor in evaluating evidence of illicit familiarity. It was the social expectations loaded on gentlewomen like Hester Denton or Winifred Barlow of modesty, demureness and setting a good example to others that made their transgressions particularly visible. It was women of this status too who, regardless of the risks involved, seemed most likely to indulge in affairs for 'fun' – pleasure of various kinds, emotional fulfilment and intimacy that was probably lacking in their own marriages – rather than economic advantage. The stylised nature of court depositions and the exceptional nature of the cases that proceeded this far should caution us against reading too much into this material – motive cannot be read unproblematically from the pages of court records. None the less, descriptions of providing gifts, favours, touching, kissing and other intimacies suggest some of the wider expectations and experiences of love affairs for women that went beyond their husbands' narratives that they were motivated by the need to satiate their lascivious desires. Sexual pleasure may well have been important for these women, but so too appears to be the attentiveness of lovers and other shared pleasures, both emotional and physical.

What of the men involved? Evidence of men as pleasure seekers, boasting of their sexual prowess especially to other men in taverns, is not difficult to find in

---

[127] LPL, Bbb 914/1 (*Barlow v. Barlow*, Articles of Exception on the part of Winifred Barlow, 24 April 1706). On the changing politics of bathing see Keith Thomas, 'Cleanliness and Godliness in Early Modern England', in Anthony Fletcher and Peter Roberts (eds.), *Religion, Culture and Society in Early Modern Britain: Essays in Honour of Patrick Collinson* (Cambridge, 1994), pp. 58–9, 70–1.

[128] LPL, Bbb 903 (*Barlow v. Barlow*, Deposition of Sarah Long, 15 Oct. 1705).

legal records from the seventeenth and eighteenth centuries.[129] Audley Harvey proudly told an alehouse companion that he had slept with Elizabeth Gouldney at her house in her husband's absence and that he had 'fuckt her five times the said Night'.[130] In an even more spectacular display of bravado, Thomas Jones exposed himself in an alehouse shortly before Christmas in 1713 and told his companion, a fellow servant called James Webster, that his 'prick was his plough and that it had been in severall ladyes bellyes and especially Mrs Dormer'.[131] But sexual pleasure might also be associated with other benefits. Relationships with higher status women carried economic advantages for some men and there is much evidence of women demonstrating their feelings for their lovers by giving them gifts. Jesse Okell, for example, received a present of a ring from his lover, Martha Bernard. She also gave him a nightgown 'which upon a quarrel betwixt them she took from him again'.[132] For male servants sexually involved with their mistresses, the affair could be a means of increasing their status within the household. Thomas Jones used his relationship with his mistress as a pretext for swaggering about the house and ordering around his fellow servants. The housemaid Elizabeth Evans deposed that whenever Jones had 'any quarrels or differences with his fellow servants' he reported them to Diana Dormer who promptly dismissed them. Alice Rigby was sent packing for 'refusing to wash Tom Jones's Stockings' and when Mary Davis the laundry maid complained to her mistress of Jones's abusing her, Diana supposedly replied that 'if Tom Jones used them all . . . like Doggs, they should take it, and if they did not like it they might goe'.[133]

In some cases, there are signs that men's behaviour may have been infused with a desire to humiliate or subordinate the cuckolded husband. A particularly lurid example occurs in the Hockmore separation case. At a social gathering held at the house of Francis Risdon at Sandwell in Devon, attended by the Hockmores and many of their gentry neighbours, William Hockmore was humiliated by Edward Ford and Nicholas Cove, his wife's imputed lovers. They spent the evening being 'very familiar' with Mary Hockmore, 'kissing' and toying with her, seemingly oblivious to their fellow guests. Later, at supper, Cove took to

[129] G. R. Quaife, *Wanton Wenches and Wayward Wives: Peasants and Illicit Sex in Early Seventeenth-Century England* (London, 1979), p. 53; Laura Gowing, 'Gender and the Language of Insult in Early Modern London', *History Workshop Journal*, 35 (1993), 7; Meldrum, 'A Women's Court in London', 10–11.

[130] LPL, Bbb 1246/7 (*Gouldney v. Gouldney*, Deposition of Ambrose Dunn, 29 Aug. 1732).

[131] LMA, DL/C/255 (*Dormer v. Dormer*, Deposition of James Webster, 12 Apr. 1715), fo. 168v. This pithy phrase drew on a familiar metaphor for adultery, 'to plough another man's field', dating back to Chaucer: Kathryn Jacobs, 'Rewriting the Marital Contract: Adultery in *The Canterbury Tales*', *The Chaucer Review*, 29 (1995), 343.

[132] LPL, Bbb 999/5 (*Bernard v. Bernard*, Deposition of Jesse Okell senior, 2 May 1712).

[133] LMA, DL/C/255 (*Dormer v. Dormer*, Deposition of Elizabeth Evans, 3 Mar. 1715), fo. 84; ibid. (Deposition of Thomas Levin, 16 Mar. 1715), fo. 130.

'jeering' William Hockmore about his wife, openly teasing him that he would soon 'fitt him' with cuckold's horns.[134] Thomas Smith's participation in the mockery of his friend Alexander Denton, already described, seems also to fit this pattern. Likewise Thomas Jones is portrayed as taking exceptional delight in his sexual triumph over his master, singing 'Roome for Cuckolds, here comes a Company' outside his master's house in Albemarle Street.[135] Though men are presented in depositions as enjoying shared physical intimacies with their lovers, the issue of power was important in their behaviour. Many of the accounts of non-sexual physical contact found in witness testimonies describe possessive gestures – Jones, for example, was described on several occasions as standing holding his mistress round the waist or with his hands on her hips, conveying a sense of sexual ownership.[136] As in cuckolding dramas on stage, men's sexuality appears closely bound up with questions of status and authority.

In conclusion, the law attempted to simplify experiences of marital breakdown so that they might be presented in a way that would satisfy the rules of evidence needed to procure a separation. By allowing couples to separate solely on the grounds of adultery and/or cruelty, the law took a limited view of the causes of marital failure. However, reading the statements of litigants and witnesses from the edges or against the grain, a more complex picture of marital breakdown and its meanings emerges. It becomes evident that suits could be motivated by broader factors than the actual adultery complained of. Launching a separation suit might be a means of broader conflict resolution in which adultery appears less as a cause than as a means to an end. The evidence of adultery trials likewise raises questions about the acceptance of the sexual double standard. Although the majority of separation cases on the grounds of infidelity concerned the adultery of wives, women litigants were often willing to challenge their husbands' behaviour and to resist their husbands' attempts to blacken their name. Such material provides a useful reminder that precept and practice could differ.

Beyond this, records of marital separation reveal much about the broader factors that helped to fashion adultery in this period. If conduct writers increasingly conceptualised adultery in terms of its transgression of the rules of civility and sociability, statements of litigants and witnesses richly demonstrate these concerns in the context of lived experience. Such rules played an increasingly heavy role in defining people's relations with their social and physical environment, but the evidence revealed in court materials shows the manifold ways in which these rules could be challenged – from the drama of disobedience acted out at

---

[134] LPL, Bbb 826/8 (*Hockmore v. Hockmore*, Deposition of William Battishill, 30 Aug. 1698).

[135] LMA, DL/C/255 (*Dormer v. Dormer*, Deposition of Francis Warrington, 24 May 1715), fo. 183.

[136] E.g., ibid. (Deposition of Mary Green, 5 Mar. 1715), fo. 99; ibid. (Deposition of Alice Hogger, 18 Mar. 1715), fo. 142.

Alexander Denton's dinner table, to the independence of spirit demonstrated by Martha Bernard in refusing to accept her husband's terms of separation. The records of suspicion reveal not only the strategies of concealment and disguise used by lovers, but also the telltale signs that conveyed adulterous desires to others. From this evidence it becomes possible to probe the meanings of affairs more deeply as witnesses give tantalising hints of the varieties of intimacy that were important to lovers, and the kind of frustrations that could be relieved by love affairs. Though this evidence cannot be taken at face value and the exceptional nature of the material precludes any generalisation, it becomes apparent that standard historical explanations of women embarking on affairs mainly for pragmatic or prudential reasons and of men as feckless pleasure seekers fail to comprehend the range of emotions raised by such relationships or how needs might differ according to status.[137] The final chapter of this book explores ways in which status and concepts of civility determined the meaning of adultery further through analysis of a new type of matrimonial litigation – actions for criminal conversation.

[137] Cf. Robert B. Shoemaker, *Gender in English Society, 1650–1850: the Emergence of Separate Spheres?* (London and New York, 1998), p. 75; Bailey, 'Breaking the Conjugal Vows', pp. 90–2.

6. *Criminal conversation*

The term 'criminal conversation' was one of the most evocative means of describing adultery in early eighteenth-century England. It was also the name
given to a new form of civil action brought to the courts of King's Bench or
Common Pleas, by which a cuckolded husband could sue his wife's lover for
the 'loss of comfort and society' he had suffered by the infidelity. If adultery could be adequately proved, he could claim damages for the insult to
his honour, or the mental disquiet he had suffered. It did not automatically
lead to a separation (which still had to be sued for in the church courts),
nor did it provide any answers to the problem of remarriage after adultery
for the innocent party. Yet it did offer injured husbands a potentially powerful means of revenging themselves by inflicting financial humiliation on their
rivals.

Emerging during the late seventeenth century at a time when the costs of
waging law were increasing, this response to infidelity was slow to catch on,
being prohibitively expensive for the majority of men. Stone has calculated that
between 1680 and 1740 there were only twenty-three recorded cases of criminal
conversation (or crim. con. as it was popularly known) brought to trial. He has
therefore categorised the period before 1760 as an 'era of stagnation' in the
development of the action, standing in marked contrast to the explosion of
cases in the closing decades of the eighteenth century. During the 1790s, when
the action reached its apogee, some seventy-three suits were contested in the
courts.[1] The spectacular growth of crim. con. as the eighteenth century drew
to a close attracted enormous public interest, much of it prurient, evinced by
a mass of sensational periodical accounts, collections of trials, biographies of
the infamous, and satirical prints.[2]

---

[1] Lawrence Stone, *Road to Divorce: England 1530–1987* (Oxford, 1990), pp. 246, 430 (table 9.1).

[2] Ibid., pp. 248–55; Peter Wagner, *Eros Revived: Erotica of the Enlightenment in England and America* (London, 1990), pp. 113–32; Donna T. Andrew, ' "Adultery A-La-Mode": Privilege, the Law and Attitudes to Adultery 1770–1809', *History*, 82 (1997), 18–19; Katherine Binhammer,

This final chapter explores the early history of crim. con., the publicity these trials generated and the questions they raised. Though the earlier period has no doubt suffered in comparison with later developments, the slow adoption of crim. con. by injured husbands in the period before the mid-eighteenth century, and its confinement to the wealthier sort, should not belie its importance. As one legal historian has observed in a different context, 'the significance of a branch of the law is not dependent on the frequency of litigation'.[3] The cultural importance of criminal conversation, as both a legal action and a term for labelling vice, far outweighed the number of cases in this period. As previous chapters have argued, the late seventeenth and early eighteenth centuries, far from being an 'era of stagnation', were a time when the meanings of infidelity underwent significant changes, influenced by new notions of social differentiation, gender and manners. The lively publicity surrounding these trials provides an intriguing intersection of literary and legal cultures and is highly revealing of new ways of representing adultery and debates about the meaning of infidelity that were developing by the eighteenth century. In the first place, crim. con. cases raised important questions about whether adultery was a 'private tragedy' or matter for public regulation. Secondly, they brought into sharp focus the question about who was most to blame for adultery – the woman, for tempting, or her partner, for his sexual rapaciousness – at a time when understandings of male and female sexual nature were changing. Beyond this, they provide further evidence of the manifold ways in which social circumstances and concepts of civility gave sexual contact meaning. These actions went beyond establishing whether adultery had taken place (important as this was), to assessing the ways in which affairs had been conducted and how this contributed to the insult suffered by the cuckolded husband. Finally, the trials give a new perspective on the options available to the injured husband and shed further light on how his predicament was viewed. True enough, crim. con. gave him a new opportunity for restoring his lost manhood, but it also placed him in a vulnerable position, liable to have his wife's sexual indiscretions laid bare in open court (not to mention the embarrassment this could cause her) and laying himself open to accusations of vindictive, unscrupulous behaviour or even prostituting his wife for unlawful gain. Embarking on litigation was always a gamble: for all concerned, this was a response to infidelity in which the stakes were high.

'The Sex Panic of the 1790s', *Journal of the History of Sexuality*, 6 (1991), 409–34; Cindy McCreery, 'Keeping Up with the Bon Ton: the *Tête-à-Tête* Series in the *Town and Country Magazine*', in Hannah Barker and Elaire Chalus (eds.), *Gender in Eighteenth-Century England: Roles, Representations and Responsibilities* (London, 1997), pp. 207–29.

[3] S. D. Waddams, *Sexual Slander in Nineteenth-Century England: Defamation in the Ecclesiastical Courts, 1815–1855* (Toronto and London, 2000), p. 179.

THE EMERGENCE OF THE ACTION

The first crim. con. trials seem to have been recorded during the 1680s, but prior to this there were a number of means whereby a married man could sue another at common law for interfering in his marital relations. In the first place, he could bring a case against a man for injuring or assaulting his wife in such a way that he lost her 'help or companionship'. He could also sue a man for seducing or enticing his wife away from him by which means he lost her economic assistance. Both actions bore technical and procedural similarities with various legal remedies available to a master for injuring or enticing away a servant and they reflected the importance of the household as a unit of production.[4] There are other instances, found throughout the seventeenth and early eighteenth centuries, in which a cuckolded husband informally demanded compensation from his wife's lover. This type of bartering might take the form of a payment made by the lover in return for the husband's agreeing not to take the matter further by means of a formal prosecution in the ecclesiastical courts, or suing for damages at common law. Husbands may also have sought to exact payments from lovers using the threat of adverse publicity. There are some indications that bartering may have become more common in the later seventeenth and early eighteenth centuries as actions for crim. con. emerged.[5] Such agreements and financial payments offered the cuckolded husband a chance to reassert his power and turn the tables on his wife's lover.

Formal prosecutions of this nature appear to have been brought to the courts initially as actions for assault and battery. These suits were satirised by dramatists during the 1670s, sensing, no doubt, an opportunity for crude sexual innuendo. The cuckolded citizens Bisket and Fribble, characters in Thomas Shadwell's play *Epsom Wells* (1673), threaten to sue the rakes Cuff and Kick 'upon an Action of Assault and Battery' after surprising them in 'indecent postures' with their wives.[6] Similarly, the hero of Rawlins's play *Tom Essence* (1677), believing his wife to have fallen under the malign influences of a genteel seducer, decides to enter 'an Action of Battery against [the imputed lover], for violently assaulting the body of Dorothy Essence, my Wife; and my Lawyer tells me, I shall have swinging damages for every bout I can prove he has

---

[4] J. H. Baker, *An Introduction to English Legal History*, 3rd edn (London, 1990), p. 519. See also Garthine Walker, '"Strange Kind of Stealing": Abduction in Early Modern Wales', in Michael Roberts and Simone Clarke (eds.), *Women and Gender in Early Modern Wales* (Cardiff, 2000), pp. 50–74.

[5] Martin Ingram, *Church Courts, Sex and Marriage in England, 1570–1640* (Cambridge, 1987), p. 284; Stone, *Road to Divorce*, pp. 244–5.

[6] Thomas Shadwell, *Epsom Wells* (1673), in *The Complete Works of Thomas Shadwell*, ed. Montague Summers (5 vols., London, 1927), II, pp. 176, 179.

assaulted her'.[7] By the eighteenth century, the more refined term 'criminal conversation' was commonly used to define this form of trespass, possibly as a means of encouraging a politer sort of litigant who might have been deterred by the crudeness of the term 'assault and battery', or to distinguish the action from rape. However, in legal terms at least, cases continued to be framed as actions for assault, or related themes such as 'insult'. Thus John Dormer brought an action against his footman Thomas Jones in 1715 for 'insulting' his wife by 'Force and Arms', while in 1741 J. G. Biker sued the man-midwife Dr Morley for making 'an Assault upon Katherine, the Plaintiff's Wife', alleging that he had 'ravished, debauched, lay with and carnally knew' her.[8]

Describing adultery as a form of 'assault and battery' committed by 'force of arms' was first and foremost a convenient legal fiction used to bring the action to court and have it tried before a jury. Adultery was a form of 'assault and battery' in the sense that it involved unlawful touching and threatened unwarranted physical contact. The wording of writs in this way also founded the suit on a sexual predatory action, in which the agency and blame lay solely with the lover.[9] But although the 'assault' was committed on the wife's body, in actions for crim. con. she was consigned to a passive role, for the husband sued for his own 'injury' or 'affront' rather than on behalf of his spouse. Cuckoldry was regarded as a matter between men in these lawsuits. The husband's injury was defined as the 'loss of comfort and society' he had suffered during the period of his wife's infidelity, but could also refer to the 'uneasiness' or 'disappointment' he experienced as a result of discovering that his wife was unfaithful.[10] A husband's complaint that he had 'lost the Benefit of [his wife's] Company' could be interpreted in a number of ways: it might imply emotional estrangement or loss of sexual services, but the word 'benefit' still carried economic overtones and recognised that the adultery of his wife could damage a man's standing in the world.[11] Some titled plaintiffs claimed that damages should be based on consequences of the adultery that were still to come, namely the threat to the husband's 'posterity' posed by the possibility of his wife giving birth to a spurious heir.[12]

---

[7] [Thomas Rawlins], *Tom Essence: Or, the Modish Wife* (London, 1677), IV. iii., p. 46. For other literary allusions to this action see Gellert Spencer Allemann, *Matrimonial Law and the Materials of Restoration Comedy* (Philadelphia, 1942), pp. 138–40.

[8] *Cases of Divorce for Several Causes* (London, 1715), p. 47; *The Tryal Between J. G. Biker, Plaintiff; and M. Morley, Doctor of Physic, Defendant; For Criminal Conversation with the Plaintiff's Wife* (London, 1741), p. 1.

[9] Binhammer, 'Sex Panic of the 1790s', 427.

[10] *An Account of the Tryal of Richard Lyddel, Esq.; . . . For Carrying on a Criminal Conversation with the Late Lady Abergavenny* (London, 1730), p. 3.

[11] *Observations on the Tryal of Thomas Jones the Foot-Boy* (London, 1715), p. 9.

[12] *The Tryal Between Sir W[illiam] M[orice] Baronet, Plaintiff, and Lord A[ugu]st[u]s F[i]tzR[o]y, Defendant, for Criminal Conversation* (London, 1742), p. 2.

The language of 'affront' and 'insult' in writs for crim. con. made this legal action similar to actions for defamation in the common law courts in which damages were awarded for injurious words held to undermine a man's right to respect. Actions for criminal conversation and types of defamation suit, in particular the action for *scandalum magnatum* – the defamation of eminent persons, specifically peers of the realm – apparently followed similar principles in the assessment of damages. Lassiter had shown that English jurists of the sixteenth and seventeenth centuries frequently upheld the principle that legal remedies for defamatory words depended not simply on the nature of the words themselves, but also on the 'quality of the person of whom the words [were] spoken'. Large sums of damages, such as the £1,000 awarded to the Earl of Shaftesbury in the 1670s, increased the public profile of the action in the later seventeenth century.[13] In her analysis of damages in actions for crim. con. in the late seventeenth and eighteenth centuries, Susan Staves has similarly suggested that awards were calculated on a form of sliding scale according to the rank of the plaintiff. Thus while all men stood to lose face by cuckoldry, the degree of loss to be compensated varied according to rank – the higher the plaintiff's social status, the more money he could demand, and usually won.[14]

This reasoning is reflected in published cases of crim. con. from the early eighteenth century. In 1730, the Earl of Abergavenny sued his erstwhile friend Richard Lyddel Esq. for £50,000 in an action for crim. con. and was eventually awarded £10,000 in damages.[15] A less socially exalted litigant, Squire John Dormer was awarded £5,000 in 1715; the same amount was awarded to a baronet (slightly higher in rank) in 1742.[16] A few cases were brought by men of the middling sort to whom lesser sums were awarded. A London mercer was awarded £500 in a suit of 1730. In the same year the *Grub Street Journal* reported that one 'Mr Huttle', a baker of St James's Westminster, had successfully sued 'Mr Shuttleworth, one of the Beadles of the said Parish' for £100.[17] Counsel made a good deal of the plaintiff's social status in their arguments to juries, maintaining that perceptions of adultery should be differentiated according to the background of those involved. However, important as it was, rank was not the sole factor determining damages. As we shall see, matters such as the degree of the husband's contrivance in his own cuckoldry, or the scandalous

[13] John C. Lassiter, 'Defamation of Peers: the Rise and Decline of the Action for *Scandalum Magnatum*', *American Journal of Legal History*, 22 (1978), 216, 226.

[14] Susan Staves, 'Money for Honor: Damages for Criminal Conversation', *Eighteenth-Century Culture*, 11 (1982), 270, 284.

[15] *St James's Evening Post* , 4 Feb. 1730.

[16] *Weekly Packet*, 137, 19 Feb. 1715; *Tryal Between Sir W[illiam] M[orice] Baronet, Plaintiff, and Lord A[ugu]st[i] F[i]tzR[o]y*, p. 50.

[17] *The Tryal Before the Lord Chief Justice R-y---d at the Guild Hall Between Mr J- C- a Mercer at Aldgate and Mr J. E-- for Criminal Conversation* (London, n.d. [1730]); *Grub Street Journal*, 6, 12 Feb. 1730.

manner in which the defendant debauched the plaintiff's wife were significant considerations when the case for damages was made to the jury.

Why did the action for criminal conversation emerge in the late seventeenth century? The genesis of this litigation has been seen as part of a broader 'commercialisation' of sexual honour in this period.[18] Certainly, the period's satirical literature was full of examples of schemes for cashing in on marriage and adultery. In March 1710 Defoe's *Review* ran a mock report of the foundation of an office selling licences for the 'Toleration of Vice', to which punters could pay between £20 and £200 for various adulterous privileges.[19] 'It is a stock-jobbing age', remarks a character in Henry Fielding's comedy *The Modern Husband* (1731), 'everything has its price; marriage is traffic throughout; as most of us bargain to be husbands, so some of us bargain to be cuckolds; and he would be as much laughed at, who preferred his love to his interest.'[20] Set in the aftermath of the South Sea Bubble, this play paints a picture of a world in which marriage, honour and reputation have become wholly governed by market forces. The play's central character, Mr Modern, facing ruin from his wife's gambling debts and lavish consumption, encourages her familiarity with Bellamant with a view to suing him for crim. con. to replenish his finances. Fielding's society is one where honour and reputation have become divorced from any ethical or emotional sense of worth. When his wife complains, with (false) protestations of her virtue, Modern replies that 'to me virtue has appeared nothing more than a sound, and reputation as its echo'.[21] The play is typical of the cynicism that dogged crim. con. in the early eighteenth century. As the prologue proclaimed:

> To-night (yet strangers to the scene) you'll view
> A pair of Monsters most entirely new!
> Two characters scarce ever found in life,
> A willing cuckold – sells his willing wife![22]

There is no doubt that criminal conversation suits contributed to a raft of cultural anxieties generated by the explosion of financial capitalism. However, to fully understand the emergence of crim. con., we need to place it in the context of broader changes in the policing of sexual morality and the ongoing search for an effective means of bringing adulterers to justice, set against the backdrop of the declining efficiency of the church courts. In Restoration London, where the secular authorities quickly overtook the church courts in

---

[18] Stone, *Road to Divorce*, p. 237; but cf. Elizabeth A. Foyster, *Manhood in Early Modern England: Honour, Sex and Marriage* (London, 1999), p. 176.

[19] *Review*, VI, 143, 7 Mar. 1710, pp. 571–2. See also ibid., VI, 141, 2 Mar. 1710, pp. 563–4.

[20] Henry Fielding, *The Modern Husband* (1731), in *The Works of Henry Fielding Esq.*, ed. Leslie Stephen (10 vols., London, 1882), II, pp. 99–100.

[21] Ibid., p. 81.   [22] Ibid., p. 74.

the regulation of vice, there was a scattering of private initiatives brought by husbands, wives and parents (at their own expense) against seducers and other immoral persons in the Middlesex Quarter Sessions and other local jurisdictions.[23] The advent of crim. con. should be seen in this transitional judicial context. The very name of the action emphasised the criminality of illicit familiarity, and prosecutions were justified on the grounds that adultery was a crime that needed to be punished. A broadsheet likened the punitive damages (£5,000) awarded to John Dormer against his servant Thomas Jones in 1715 to a form of 'corporal Punishment', which is 'justly inflicted by the Severity of Criminals found guilty of Adultery and Fornication'.[24] At the very least, it was a sum that Jones had little hope of paying and, had he not escaped from the courtroom, would have led to a lengthy term in the debtors' prison.

Although crim. con. was undeniably a 'private' action to gain financial compensation for the personal 'insult' or 'affront' suffered by the wronged husband, some lawyers were reluctant to present it in these terms, casting it instead as an adjunct to 'public' campaigns to regulate vice. The counsel for the plaintiff in the case brought by Lord Abergavenny against Richard Lyddel in 1730 justified the setting of damages at a level which would ruin the defendant, by arguing that a severe 'Pecuniary Punishment' was a modern equivalent of the principle in Mosaic law that an adulterer deserved to be 'put to Death'.[25] Although by 1730 the idea that adulterers should literally be put to death was no longer popular, the notion that adultery deserved to be treated harshly certainly remained resonant, and reference to the death penalty provided a means for underscoring these arguments. The £10,000 damages brought against Lyddel certainly represented a far more severe punishment for adultery than anything available in the ecclesiastical or criminal courts and, unable to pay, Lyddel had been forced to flee the country.[26] Counsel acting for Sir William Morice in his case against Lord Augustus Fitzroy told the jury that the injury caused by adultery was so great that no sum awarded could adequately provide 'Satisfaction or Compensation' for the plaintiff; rather a suitable amount should be awarded that could be 'given as a Punishment... for the Sake of the Publick, and for Example's Sake, in order to restrain others from committing such a heinous and injurious offence'.[27]

---

[23] Faramerz Dabhoiwala, 'Prostitution and Police in London c.1660–c.1760', DPhil thesis, University of Oxford (1995), p. 131. See also Robert B. Shoemaker, *Prosecution and Punishment: Petty Crime and the Law in London and Rural Middlesex, c.1660–1725* (Cambridge, 1991), pp. 127–8, 140–6; and more generally, C. W. Brooks, 'Interpersonal Conflict and Social Tension: Civil Litigation in England, 1640–1830', in A. L. Beier, David Cannadine and James M. Rosenheim (eds.), *The First Modern Society: Essays in English History in Honour of Lawrence Stone* (Cambridge, 1989), p. 393.

[24] *The Whole Tryal, Examination and Conviction of Thomas Jones, Footman to Esquire Dormer* (London, 1715).

[25] *An Account of the Tryal of Richard Lyddel*, p. 8.

[26] *Memoirs of the Society of Grub Street* (2 vols., London, 1737), I, p. 91.

[27] *The Tryal Between Sir W[illiam] M[orice] Baronet... and Lord A[ugu]st[u]s F[i]tzR[o]y*, p. 49.

The strategy was subtle, intended to make the jury feel more comfortable about awarding high damages by persuading it that it was acting for the public good rather than for Morice's personal financial advantage. Nevertheless, the publicity given to these opinions in trial pamphlets kept alive the idea that adultery was a matter of public importance. Infrequent as these trials were, the damages awarded in these cases were high enough to be of symbolic importance, sending out the message that adultery was still liable to severe sanction.[28]

In contrast, defence counsel did all they could to diminish the public significance of these cases and called for a sense of perspective. Cases where the plaintiff's motives could be cast as doubtful or unscrupulous revealed serious problems in presenting crim. con. as a tool for publicly regulating sexual immorality. This point was clearly made in 1739 by an attorney in a suit brought by the comedian Theophilus Cibber against William Sloper for criminal conversation with his wife, Susannah. Sloper's lawyer did not try to deny the adultery between Susannah and his client, instead basing the case to undermine the plaintiff's claim to damages on his apparent connivance in the affair. Although, the attorney told the jury, he did not wish to act as an 'Advocate for the Immorality of the Action', the key issue was only 'whether the Defendant has injur'd the Plaintiff' since crim. con. 'is not a Prosecution for the Publick or to punish the Immorality'. Because it was believed that the defendant had been aided or encouraged in his affair by the plaintiff himself, Sloper was not deemed worthy of serious punishment and was fined a mere £10 – a sum intended to ridicule the plaintiff (who had originally asked for £5,000) rather than upbraid the defendant.[29] The principle of public moral regulation followed by the church courts (at least in theory) was that all those who committed adultery were considered equally sinful and criminal and deserving of punishment. In crim. con. actions, because damages were awarded according to the degree of affront suffered by the husband, influenced by a variety of factors from the plaintiff's rank to the degree of connivance, adultery was not judged by a single moral standard but on the basis of how if affected others.

PAMPHLETS, PUBLICITY AND THE RHETORIC OF SCANDAL

Since prosecutions for crim. con. were not routine, trials generated huge public interest when they occurred. Such a 'great Concourse of People' gathered outside Westminster Hall hoping to get in to see the trial between Lord Abergavenny and Richard Lyddel on Monday 16 February 1730, that the Speaker of the House of Commons was impeded on his way to Parliament and 'a Fellow was order'd

[28] Cf. Dabhoiwala, 'Prostitution and Police', p. 61; Randolph Trumbach, *Sex and the Gender Revolution, Volume I: Heterosexuality and the Third Gender in Enlightenment London* (Chicago, IL and London, 1998), p. 29.

[29] *The Tryal of a Cause for Criminal Conversation, Between Theophilus Cibber, Gent. Plaintiff, and William Sloper, Esq. Defendant* (London, 1739), p. 32.

into Custody for rudely pressing on him and tearing his Gown'.[30] Between 1692 and 1742, seven major trials for crim. con. were subject to detailed coverage in pamphlets.[31] Typically these consisted of a transcript or summary of the trial proceedings, often (though not universally) with a degree of editorial comment. Prices for an unbound, single trial pamphlet varied between 6d and 1s, placing these publications in the same price bracket as murder pamphlets and other cheap print.[32] All of these major cases involved plaintiffs or defendants from the upper ranks of society contesting large sums of damages. As with modern media scandals, public fascination in these cases derived in no small measure from the tension existing between the 'projected aura' of persons of rank and status through their material wealth and cultivated manners, and the 'disclosed realities of their private lives'.[33] The Abergavenny case revealed, in the words of one pamphlet, how a 'worthy Gentleman, after living several Years in the utmost Harmony with his Spouse, had her torn from his Embraces and publickly proved in open Court as lascivious as the most Common Prostitute'.[34] Cases involving less exalted litigants were not neglected, but received much briefer coverage – a half-sheet publication at most, or a newspaper report.[35]

The first trial to receive major publicity was the case brought by the Duke of Norfolk against his wife's lover, Sir John Jermaine, in 1692. The protracted attempts of the duke to obtain a divorce were the subject of a series of publications during the 1690s, some of which seem to have been published at the duke's behest as a dubious means of shaming his adulterous spouse and her lover and garnering sympathy for his cause.[36] The court proceedings were published verbatim, exposing in explicit detail the minutiae of the duchess's liaisons with her lover.[37] Whatever Norfolk intended by the publication of the proceedings, the transcript also served well as a law report and would have been of interest to legal professionals. For others, reading the evidence produced in court offered a tantalising glimpse into the world of aristocratic vice, from the glamorous disguises

---

[30] *Whitehall Evening-Post*, 1179, 17 Feb. 1730.

[31] The relevant cases are: *Norfolk v. Jermaine* (1692); *Dormer v. Jones* (1715); *Abergavenny v. Lyddel* (1730); *Gouldney v. Harvey* (1732); *Cibber v. Sloper* (1738, 1739); *Biker v. Morley* (1741); *Morice v. Fitzroy* (1742).

[32] See, for instance, the advertisements in *St James's Evening Post*, 2308, 26 Feb. 1730; *Daily Post-Boy*, 6543, 28 Feb. 1730.

[33] John B. Thompson, 'Scandal and Social Theory', in James Lull and Stephen Hinerman (eds.), *Media Scandals: Morality and Desire in the Popular Culture Marketplace* (Cambridge, 1997), p. 55.

[34] 'Francis Truelove', *The Comforts of Matrimony; Exemplified in the Memorable Trial, Lately had upon an Action Brought by Theo[philus] C[ibbe]r against [William] S[loper] Esq.* (London, 1739), p. 7.

[35] E.g., *Tryal Before the Lord Chief Justice R-y---d at the Guild Hall Between Mr J- C- a Mercer at Aldgate and Mr J. E-- for Criminal Conversation*; *Grub Street Journal*, 6, 12 Feb. 1730.

[36] Stone, *Road to Divorce*, pp. 251, 313–17. See for example, *His Grace the Duke of Norfolk's Charge Against the Dutchess, Before the House of Lords* (London, 1692).

[37] *The Tryal Between Henry Duke of Norfolk, Plaintiff, and John Jermaine Defendant, in an Action of Trespass* (London, 1692).

used by the duchess, such as her dressing 'in Man's apparel, a Blew Coat and Perruke' to secretly visit Jermaine's apartment, down to more tawdry descriptions of ruffled beds and soiled sheets. Such evidence served both to confirm the mystique of the upper classes and to remind others that they were as messily human as everyone else.[38] Parallels with cuckolding dramas in the theatre are also apparent. The format of the report somewhat resembled a play script with the examination of witnesses reading like a dialogue and eloquent speeches placed in the mouths of the opposing counsel – this was courtroom drama indeed.[39]

Although matrimonial cases and sensational adultery trials were published on a decidedly *ad hoc* basis in the first half of the eighteenth century, there can be little doubt that the publication of the court proceedings in the Norfolk case revealed new possibilities to be exploited by unscrupulous hacks operating in an increasingly competitive marketplace. The lapsing of the Licensing Act in 1695 arguably made the publication of court proceedings easier, diminishing the risk of censorship. Congreve speculated upon the alarming consequences of new forms of trial reporting in his play *The Way of the World* (1700). When Mrs Fainall vows to contest her husband's suit for separation brought on the spurious grounds of her alleged adultery with Mirabell, she is warned that the salacious details of her presumed infamy brought out in the courtroom will

> be exposed by the shorthand writers to the public press; and from thence be transferred to the hands, nay into the throats and lungs of hawkers, with voices more licentious that the loud flounder man's, or the woman who cries grey peas. And this you must hear till you are stunned; nay, you must hear nothing else for some days.[40]

Publication of matrimonial cases inevitably led to accusations of scandal-mongering.[41] The fact that pamphlets were able to publish materials exhibited in open court provided a means of legitimising the publication of sexually explicit witness statements, love letters and other evidence – an opportunity not lost on the entrepreneurial publisher Edmund Curll, whose compilation of *Cases of Divorce for Several Causes* was published in 1715. Curll defended the publishing of these cases, which included the crim. con. suit contested between John Dormer and Thomas Jones, together with trials for bigamy and annulment on the grounds of impotence, as 'nothing more . . . than a faithful Relation of Facts' and placed the responsibility of interpretation solely on the reader's personal conscience.[42] He added that the issues raised by such cases 'conduce to the mutual Happiness of the Nuptial State', and were thus 'Matters of the greatest

---

[38] Ibid., p. 11; *His Grace the Duke of Norfolk's Charge Against the Dutchess*, p. 10.
[39] See also Staves, 'Money for Honor', 283.
[40] William Congreve, *The Way of the World* (1700), ed. Katherine M. Lynch (London, 1965), V. 214–20.
[41] [Edmund Curll], *Curlicism Display'd: Or, an Appeal to the Church* (London, 1718), p. 26; Ralph Straus, *The Unspeakable Curll* (London, 1927), pp. 79–81.
[42] *Cases of Divorce for Several Causes*, Preface [no pagination].

Importance to Society'. Such publications were therefore 'directly calculated for Antidotes against Debauchery and Unnatural Lewdness, and not for Incentives to them'.[43] With the compilation retailing at 2s 6d bound, which would have put it out of the price range of the young apprentices or servants deemed most easily corruptible by salacious material, Curll seems to have had a professional audience in mind, principally lawyers or medical men. While undoubtedly offering cheap thrills under the cover of respectability, rather than being merely pornography, *Cases of Divorce* and publications like it fit into a more widespread public culture of sexual debate in early eighteenth-century England.[44]

Editorial comment, where it occurred, was often characterised by a keen sense of moral outrage. This was encouraged by the nature of the trials themselves. The rarity of cases lent themselves to being portrayed as exceptionally bad cases of adultery. The rhetoric of lawyers, in particular counsel for the plaintiff, likewise exaggerated the shocking nature of the adultery in order to persuade the jury to award higher damages. 'I do not think it is in the Power of Language to make the Plaintiff's Case more calamitous than it really is,' commented one barrister in a trial of 1742.[45] The early case brought by John Dormer against Thomas Jones in 1715 aroused an equal measure of fascination and revulsion, concerning as it did the socially taboo topic of mistress–servant adultery. Some cheaper publications reporting the trial adopted a strident tone of moral condemnation drawing on religious discourses of sexual sin. A broadsheet entitled *The Whole Tryal, Examination and Conviction of Thomas Jones, Footman to Esquire Dormer* saw in the case a providential warning of the 'Rewards of Iniquity' and ended with a reiteration of the Seventh Commandment probably intended as a specific warning to servants and apprentices not to follow the pattern of debauchery set by Jones.[46] It emphasised the 'outrageous manner' in which Jones had behaved, even beating and abusing his mistress, ending its account with Jones being flung into gaol, carefully omitting to mention the footman's final act of defiance, whereby he fled the courtroom and absconded to the Mint, London's sanctuary for debtors and criminals.[47]

However, other publications recognised that shocking revelations carried their own pleasure and developed a particularly hyperbolic mode of introducing the trials. 'In matters of Incontinence and Adultery few or no Examples are to be found so impious in their Nature, and so flagrant in their circumstances, as that which is now to be submitted to the Reader's perusal,' began the account of

---

[43] [Curll], *Curlicism Display'd*, p. 26.
[44] Tim Hitchcock, *English Sexualities, 1700–1800* (Basingstoke, 1997), pp. 16–17. For imitations see (e.g.)*The Cases of Polygamy, Concubinage, Adultery, Divorce, etc.* (London, 1732).
[45] *The Tryal Between Sir W[illiam] M[orice] Baronet . . . and Lord A[ugu]st[u]s F[i]tzR[o]y*, p. 45.
[46] *The Whole Tryal, Examination and Conviction of Thomas Jones.*
[47] Cf. *Weekly Packet*, 137, 19 Feb. 1715.

the Dormer trial in Curll's *Cases of Divorce*, inviting the audience to read on.[48] Another account of this case justified its existence on the basis of the enormous 'Amusement and Speculation' generated by this particular trial, and presented itself as serving the public interest, arguing that it 'would not be amiss to offer to the World a small taste of the whole Transactions, as deliver'd in Evidence upon the Hearing'.[49] Modes of revelation employed by such pamphlets contributed to the rhetoric of scandal. When described in the press, hitherto 'normal' modes of surveillance commonly used to detect adultery, such as eavesdropping by servants and others, took on more of a voyeuristic feel. Pamphlets fed a desire on the part of readers to implicate themselves in the revealing of the intimate lives of others, not just for any moral lessons that might be drawn, but because it was transgressive and exciting.[50]

In crim. con. trials personalities and events quickly became subsumed into stereotyped patterns of character and behaviour. None of the main actors was allowed to give testimony in these trials, and in their absence counsels for the plaintiff and the defence sought to reduce the individuals involved into pre-existing roles which illustrated universal 'truths'. These constructions of character were developed in the publicity surrounding trials. Moreover, the verdicts reached in the trials gave narratives of crim. con. a sense of closure, facilitating moral judgement and readily created heroes and villains. In the conservative and moralising literature inspired by the Dormer trial, the differences between the master and his treacherous servant were written on their bodies. In contrast to the commonplace cultural description of cuckolded husbands as ugly and dowdy and cuckold-makers as fashionable and dashing, these were bodies on which hierarchies were to be restored rather than inverted. Thus one pamphlet emphasised that Dormer was a man to whom 'Nature, as well as [material] Fortune' had been 'extremely kind', providing him with a 'sweet and winning Aspect, a gentle and easy Deportment' which made him 'in every respect a finish'd and accomplish'd Gentleman'.[51] Jones, by contrast, as the editor of another transcript of the trial pointed out, 'deriv'd his Birth from the Dregs of the Populace', adding that 'If the Master was most acceptable for the Comliness of his Person, the Beauties of his Mind, and the Affability of his Temper: The Servant was distinguishable for his Deformity of Body and Soul'.[52] This commentator praised Dormer's legal action against Jones on the grounds that it restored social hierarchy, for a man of the plaintiff's status could not suffer 'such a base Proletarian as Jones to triumph over the Misfortunes of his Bed'.[53]

[48] *Cases of Divorce for Several Causes*, p. 41.

[49] *Observations on the Tryal of Thomas Jones the Foot-Boy*, p. 5.

[50] For similar comments, based on press reports of nineteenth-century divorce trials, see Barbara Leckie, *Culture and Adultery: the Novel, the Newspaper and the Law, 1857–1914* (Philadelphia, PA, 1999), pp. 90–1.

[51] *Observations on the Tryal of Thomas Jones the Foot-Boy*, p. 6.

[52] *Cases of Divorce for Several Causes*, p. 45.   [53] Ibid., p. 46.

Adultery was frequently described as taking place suddenly without much warning and to the great 'shock' or 'astonishment' of the husband and other onlookers. Narratives of scandal thrived on the element of surprise and sudden changes of fortune or behaviour. John Dormer's wife, Diana, like a bolting horse 'suddenly leapt the Fence of Virtue and Chastity'. Lady Morice, in spite of her 'refined Understanding, Wit and Beauty' and apparently perfect marriage, suffered a similarly dramatic fall from grace. 'But alas!', sighed the author of the account of her husband's crim. con. action, 'how frail is human Nature! For, notwithstanding the happy situation she was placed in, she fell a Victim to the crafty Snares of the Defendant.'[54]

The product was a mode of representation significantly removed from traditional means of explaining moral decline as a slow descent of the subject down a slippery slope of sin. The providential element was displaced by a more melodramatic, and distinctly secular, portrayal of domestic relations in crisis that owed more to other genres of scandalous prose fiction such as the 'secret history' and *roman à clef* which were becoming popular during the early eighteenth century.[55] Proceedings in the trial for crim. con. between Henry Gouldney and Audley Harvey in 1732 were even published in the *Pall-Mall Miscellany*, a collection of songs, poems and novellas about love and marriage published with the aim of providing 'Wit, Satyr and Spleen'.[56] Borrowing a technique from popular fiction, the names of participants in the trials were often disguised by the replacement of letters in their name with a dash, even though it was frequently obvious who they were. Although the trials were public occasions, this technique allowed readers to indulge the fantasy that they were privy to secret knowledge. The tension between the publicity of the trials and the intimate details of people's 'private' lives they revealed made these pamphlets so compelling.

The Abergavenny trial of 1730 provides a fascinating case study of the type of public interest crim. con. trials might arouse and the responses they provoked. Lady Abergavenny died shortly after her husband discovered her affair with Richard Lyddel, and these tragic circumstances coloured public perceptions of his subsequent pursuit of his wife's lover for damages. Lady Abergavenny's demise, though most likely resulting from complications in childbirth, was represented publicly as a product of her 'grief and shame', casting her as the epitome of lost female virtue.[57] A set of verses in the *Grub Street Journal*

---

[54] *The Tryal Between Sir W[illiam] M[orice] Baronet. . . and Lord A[ugu]st[u]s F[i]tzR[o]y*, p. v.

[55] J. J. Richetti, *Popular Fiction Before Richardson: Narrative Patterns 1700–1739* (Oxford, 1969), pp. 120–60; Wagner, *Eros Revived*, pp. 87–112; Annabel Patterson, ' "Secret History": Liberal Politics and the 1832 Reform Bill', *Literature and History*, 3rd ser., 7 (1998), 33–52.

[56] *The Pall-Mall Miscellany* (London, n.d. [1732]), Preface.

[57] Historical Manuscripts Commission, *Egmont MSS, Diary* (3 vols., London, 1920–3), I, p. 50.

reflected on her tragic fate and urged young people to take pity on her plight and learn from her remorse:

> Let them recount, what deep, what num'rous sighs
> Spring from her breast, what torrents drown'd from her eyes;
> When pale, dishevell'd, prostrate upon the floor,
> Her fate she wail'd, and curs'd her natal hour:
> 'Twixt glimm'ring hope perplex'd, and dark despair,
> Begged that the silent grave might end her care.[58]

Another series of poems presented her as the unhappy nymph 'Calista'. The model was the tragic heroine of Nicholas Rowe's play *The Fair Penitent* (1703), who killed herself out of remorse for her affair with the rake Lothario and betrayal of her husband-to-be, Altamont.[59] These verses presented Lady Abergavenny as a sentimental figure, abused by all the men in her life, and ostensibly aimed to defend her against the 'malignant Blasts of sland'rous tongues' arising from the circumstances of her life and death. She is presented as a victim of the cruel ravisher 'Lorenzo', an 'Inhumane Wretch', represented as the worst of all villains.[60]

Unlike the conciliatory and gentle character in Rowe's play, the 'Altamont' of these verses receives little sympathy. In *A Poem Sacred to the Memory of the Honourable Lady Aber-----y*, he is represented as her 'Stern Lord', harsh, unforgiving and consumed by a 'Fierce Jealousy'. In a rival poem, *An Epistle from Calista to Altamont*, 'Calista' casts doubts on her husband's severe response to his cuckolding by pointing out that the 'misfortune' of cuckoldry was hardly unique to him.[61] The tragic death of Lady Abergavenny cast her husband's motives in pursuing Lyddel for damages into serious doubt. Viscount Percival noted in his diary that a 'great many' people blamed Lord Abergavenny 'for prosecuting the gentleman, since his lady died for that fact'.[62] Lord Abergavenny lost face not so much by the fact of his cuckoldry, but for pursuing his vindictiveness against Lyddel through the courts. The reactions to this case show that even a successful suit for crim. con. was no means of restoring a cuckolded husband's honour. His actions might be construed as, at the very least, ill-judged, at worst, dishonourable. Such was the popularity of the image of Lady Abergavenny as

---

[58] *Memoirs of the Society of Grub Street*, I, pp. 91–2.

[59] Nicholas Rowe, *The Fair Penitent* (1703), ed. Malcolm Goldstein (London, 1969). The name 'Calista' derives from that of the nymph of classical mythology whose unchastity with Zeus also led to an untimely demise: *The Oxford Classical Dictionary*, ed. N. G. L. Hammond and H. H. Scullard (Oxford, 1970), s.v. 'Callisto'.

[60] *A Poem, Sacred to the Memory of the Honourable Lady Aber-----ny. Humbly Inscrib'd to the Quality of Great-Britain* (London, 1729), p. 4.

[61] Ibid.; *An Epistle From Calista to Altamont* (London, 1729), p. 4.

[62] Historical Manuscripts Commission, *Egmont MSS, Diary*, I, p. 50.

Calista that two performances of *The Fair Penitent* were staged 'at the particular Desire of several Ladies of Quality' in the week following the trial, to sell-out audiences.[63]

CONTESTING CULPABILITY

Blame, then, was a multi-faceted issue in trials for crim. con. It was not sufficient for the plaintiff to prove just that the act of adultery had taken place – he also had to demonstrate that he had been affronted by the defendant's behaviour. If it could be proved that the defendant had been 'tempted' by the plaintiff's wife, or, more often, if the husband had connived in his own cuckoldry, his claims to affront were fatally flawed and the damages awarded might be derisory. What was crucially at stake in crim. con. trials was not just the fact of the adultery, but the manner in which it was committed. The opposing arguments of counsel in these trials exposed questions of culpability and the meanings of marital breakdown to the severest scrutiny. In the process, reports of these trials contributed significantly to the increasingly inquisitive and challenging cultural climate in which sexuality was discussed in the early eighteenth century.

In this context, evidence of incivility and over-familiar behaviour acquired a new importance in establishing the seriousness of the defendant's actions. As we have seen, the very name 'criminal conversation' served to place the transgression of adultery firmly within the realm of polite social interaction. The plaintiff's counsel questioned witnesses particularly closely on the ways in which the defendant's behaviour breached normal codes of sociability and exploited more legitimate modes of social interaction, the aim being to highlight his deviousness. Testimony of the defendant's exploitation of normal modes of social interaction was brought to emphasise his tireless pursuit of the plaintiff's wife. Lord Augustus Fitzroy, defendant in a crim. con. action brought by Sir William Morice in 1742, was accused of practising all manner of 'Gallantries and Acts' to 'insinuate himself' into the 'esteem' of the plaintiff's wife. Thus, it was argued, the defendant 'was constantly an Attendant on this Lady, in all public Places; such as Plays, Operas, Assemblies, and other public Places of Resort; and was very particular in his Behaviour towards her, by addressing himself entirely to her, and leading her to her Chair or Coach'. He continued his pursuit of the object of his desires by making frequent social visits to her house, making a point of sitting very close to her on the couch and sometimes staying until four or five o'clock in the morning. 'Surely these Things will not be reckon'd on the Foot of common Visits', argued the plaintiff's counsel, 'for these Actions are enough to ruin the Character of any Woman; and when he

---

[63] William Van Lennep, Emett L. Avery, Arthur H. Scouten, George Winchester Stone and Charles Beecher Hogan (eds.), *The London Stage, 1660–1800* (5 vols., Carbondale, IL, 1960–8), III, p. 38.

could persuade her to do such Things, it was easy to bring her to do any Thing.' In response, Fitzroy's lawyer tried to normalise his client's social mores. His frequent visits to take tea with Lady Morice were described as nothing more than 'what is usual in the most reputable Families, where People receive Company and drink Tea'.[64]

Concepts of civility were also important in discussing the defendant's social relations with the plaintiff. What was at issue in trials for criminal conversation was less the adulterous wife's betrayal of her husband than the defendant's cheating of the plaintiff. The relationship between the husband and the lover was a crucial factor in determining the seriousness of the adultery. In the suit contested between Lord Abergavenny and Richard Lyddel, witnesses were asked to elaborate upon the social relations between the plaintiff and the defendant. Elizabeth Hopping, a serving maid, deposed that her master 'always received' Lyddel 'very joyfully' and invited him to stay at his house for as long as a week at a time. Mr Osman, Lord Abergavenny's steward, also emphasised that the two men's friendship was 'very great' and that 'his Lordship always received Mr Lyddel with a great deal of Pleasure and Satisfaction'. The witness believed that 'his Lordship's secrets were communicated' to Lyddel and declared that 'he never knew of greater Friendship and Intimacy' than theirs. Another witness added that until he saw it with his own eyes he could scarcely 'conceive that Mr Lyddel would be guilty of so foul a Crime' as adultery with the plaintiff's wife, such was the 'mutual Respect' between the two men.[65]

Placed in this context of 'Friendship and Intimacy', Lyddel's adultery with Lady Abergavenny was doubly heinous: not simply for its immorality, but for its transgression of the civilities offered by Lord Abergavenny to his friend. What was overwhelmingly at issue was the betrayal of trust between the two men. Lyddel's cuckolding of Lord Abergavenny was dishonourable not only on the grounds of its immorality, but also because it was ungentlemanly, breaching the trustworthiness which lay at the core of aristocratic codes of honour.[66] Thus the incivility of Lyddel's actions lay in the fact that they led him to behave in a manner ill-befitting a man claiming genteel status and friendship with a peer of the realm.[67] Descriptions of Lyddel sneaking off to Lady Abergavenny's chamber after being received by Lord Abergavenny in his apartment and of his 'too great' and 'unbefitting' familiarity with her, kissing her not only in her bedchamber where usually 'Visitors never came', but also in more 'public' spaces in the house such as the parlour, dining room and

[64] *Tryal Between Sir W[illiam] M[orice] Baronet . . . and Lord A[ugu]st[u]s F[i]tzR[o]y*, pp. 3, 4, 5, 14.

[65] *Account of the Tryal of Richard Lyddel*, pp. 3, 7.

[66] Mervyn James, 'English Politics and the Concept of Honour, 1485–1642', *PP*, Supplement no. 3 (1978), 28.

[67] George Mackenzie, *Moral Gallantry* (London, 1685), p. 9.

dressing room, powerfully underscored his flagrant cheating of his erstwhile friend.[68]

Cases like this raised questions about how sexuality affected relations of status and authority between men. Lyddel's deception of Lord Abergavenny was made all the more serious, and all the more rude and unmannerly, by his inferiority of rank which made his 'friendship' with Abergavenny and their 'mutual respect' all the more privileged. Thomas Jones's cuckolding of his master, John Dormer, was even more obviously despicable. But proving that the plaintiff had suffered disrespect appropriate to his rank was a more difficult matter in cases where he was of a lower social status than his wife's imputed lover. This is neatly illustrated by Cibber's case against Sloper in 1738. There were many aspects to this case, some of which have already attracted historical attention. The fact that Cibber and his wife were celebrated stage performers gave the case considerable publicity. Much was made, both in the courtroom and in subsequent pamphlets, of the fact that as performers Theophilus and Susannah Cibber were popularly held to possess lower moral standards than other members of society, stemming from older conceptions of actors and actresses as 'whores' and 'rogues'.[69]

However, the point to emphasise here is the fact that a man faced considerable difficulties getting his claims to a loss of honour taken seriously if the defendant was of higher social rank. Cibber's counsel employed the familiar strategy of alleging that Sloper, under the guise of the 'Civility' of social visits and 'the specious View of Friendship', had 'made use of all his Art to seduce and alienate the affection of the Plaintiff's wife from him'.[70] Although Cibber styled himself as a 'gentleman' in prosecuting the case, as an actor his claims to this status were highly dubious. His blustering and overblown manner was already well-known from his famous performance as Pistol in Shakespeare's *Henry IV* plays and he was sometimes illustrated in this guise in satirical prints accompanying the trial.[71] Sloper's lawyers were quick to ridicule his claims to be descended from William of Wickham. They effectively cast him not as an abused 'gentleman' but as a pretentious social climber, valuing money and alliance with the *beau monde* to such an extent that he would encourage his wife's affair with a wealthy young gentleman. William Murray, the future Lord Chief Justice Mansfield, representing Sloper, sardonically observed that Cibber's claims of noble ancestry would have been stronger had he 'observed

---

[68] *Account of the Tryal of Richard Lyddel*, p. 3.

[69] On the background and consequences of this case and the personalities involved see Kimberley Crouch, 'Attitudes Toward Actresses in Eighteenth-Century Britain', DPhil thesis, University of Oxford (1995), pp. 167–97; cf. Mary Nash, *The Provoked Wife: the Life and Times of Susannah Cibber* (London, 1977), pp. 108–67.

[70] E.g., 'Truelove', *Comforts of Matrimony*, p. 23.

[71] For instance, *A Collection of Remarkable Trials* (Glasgow, n.d. [c.1739]), Frontispiece; Nash, *The Provoked Wife*, p. 147 (depicting *Pistol's a Cuckold, or Adultery in Fashion*).

William of Wickham's Motto, that Morals make the Man', adding that the actual words are 'Manners make the Man; but Manners are there intended to signify Morals'.[72] Thus Cibber's social pretensions could be turned against him to ridicule his claims to 'affront'. Rather than being 'uneasy' at his wife's familiarity with Sloper, a wealthy young gentleman, it was suggested that Cibber 'esteemed it an honour done to him', believing that his wife's sexual kinship with Sloper would improve his own standing in the world.[73] With this kind of connivance, the claims that Sloper had abused Cibber's 'civility' towards him were exposed as fraudulent. Attention instead shifted to the plaintiff's own unscrupulous behaviour and bad sexual manners.

Consideration of the state of the plaintiff's marital relations also bore on the assessment of damages. Since the plaintiff aimed to prove that he had suffered from the loss of his wife's 'comfort and society', it was important to establish that his marital relations had been stable and loving before the incursions of the defendant. The plaintiff's marriage was typically distanced from the normal causes of marital disharmony, being portrayed as founded on mutual affection rather than financial considerations or parental pressure. Thus it was argued that John Dormer had shown 'Wisdom in the choice of a wife', eschewing 'the Baits and Allurements of Money' in favour of 'Beauty, good Humour and a suppos'd Innocence'.[74] The counsel for J. G. Biker similarly stated that he had 'thought himself happy, in the Possession of a Wife, young, beautiful, virtuous and affectionate', only to have his felicity dashed 'by the Discovery of a Piece of Management of the Defendant, in seducing [his wife] from those Paths of Virtue, in which she had been brought up from her Infancy'.[75] Henry Gouldney's lawyer also cited as 'peculiar Aggravations' to Audley Harvey's adultery with his client's wife, the facts that 'Mr Gouldney had been married to his Wife sixteen or seventeen Years, had had eight children by her' and 'always liv'd in very good Credit, and never let her want for any thing his Circumstances would admit of'.[76]

Such images of domestic harmony were inevitably challenged by the defendant. Lord Augustus Fitzroy's counsel painted a picture of William Morice's marriage in turmoil long before his client entered the scene. Morice's problems began, he argued, when his wife had refused to join her husband at his country seat, preferring instead to stay at Bath and 'keep company with vicious People', as a result of which he had turned her away from his doors. A letter was produced in which Morice told his wife that they 'might still have been happy' had she not stayed in Bath. No mention was made of Fitzroy. Thus, it was argued, Morice could not legitimately claim that his client had caused him

---

[72] *The Tryal of a Cause for Criminal Conversation*, p. 30.
[73] 'Truelove', *Comforts of Matrimony*, p. 15.   [74] *Cases of Divorce for Several Causes*, p. 43.
[75] *The Tryal Between J. G. Biker, Plaintiff; and M. Morley...Defendant*, p. 2.
[76] *Pall-Mall Miscellany*, p. 22.

to lose 'the Comfort and Society of his Wife' since he had lost that long ago and had contributed to this loss himself by turning his wife away.[77]

As this evidence shows, although crim. con. was cast first and foremost as a matter between men, the conduct of the adulterous wife was also significant. Ideally, the prosecution wanted to portray the adulterous wife as essentially virtuous prior to the arrival of the defendant in her life, at which point her resistance was broken down by his cunning wiles and deception. This strategy is evinced by the rhetoric used by William Morice's attorney in 1742. Having sketched an idyllic picture of the plaintiff's marital relations, in which his wife lacked nothing which 'could contribute to the Happiness of any Woman', he presented Lady Morice's subsequent unchastity as a matter of 'wonder' that she should 'abandon her Honour; be regardless of her Husband; and alienate her Affections from him'. Agency was shifted entirely to the lover for, as the barrister continued, all would be explained when the defendant's 'constant and unwearied Insinuations, in order to ensnare and vitiate the Lady' were revealed.[78] Such representations of women struck a chord with new understandings of gender roles and male and female sexual nature, which cast women in passive roles. Undoubtedly published crim. con. trials helped to propagate these new sensibilities of gender difference. However, lawyers often exaggerated and manipulated these cultural stereotypes in order to fix blame more securely on the male lover. The fact that women were *legally* passive in these cases undeniably added to their construction as sexually passive subjects.[79]

How were the allegations of the plaintiff defended? In some cases defendants simply denied the fact that adultery had taken place and brought their own witnesses to cast doubts on the veracity of the plaintiff's evidence.[80] Others suggested, somewhat disingenuously, that a verdict for the defendant would in fact better serve the interests of the husband. John Jermaine's lawyer argued that it 'will be more Honour to the Duke of Norfolk to have the Defendant Acquitted, than Satisfaction to him by giving him any Damages'.[81] Acquitting his client would restore the duke's honour completely by proving (or at least indicating) he was not a cuckold. A verdict for Norfolk, in contrast, would simply prove to the world that he wore the horns, an iniquity for which monetary damages offered little satisfaction. Some lawyers in denying their client's involvement in the case sought to recapture the ethical high ground by presenting the defendant's behaviour as more chivalrous than that of the

---

[77] *The Tryal Between Sir W[illiam] M[orice] Baronet...and Lord A[ugu]st[u]s F[i]tzR[o]y*, pp. 25, 32.

[78] Ibid., p. 2.

[79] Joanne Bailey, 'Breaking the Conjugal Vows: Marriage and Marriage Breakdown in the North of England, 1660–1800', PhD thesis, University of Durham (1999), p. 135.

[80] E.g., *Tryal Between J. G. Biker, Plaintiff; and M. Morley...Defendant*, pp. 17–28.

[81] *The Tryal Between Henry Duke of Norfolk...and John Jermaine...in an Action of Trespass*, p. 12.

plaintiff. The counsel for Lord Augustus Fitzroy urged the jury to bring a verdict for his client on the grounds that by doing so they would 'clear the Character of the Lady, which will be of greater Advantage to the Plaintiff, than his proving the Crime, or getting Damages'.[82]

In other cases and reports, the agency of the plaintiff's wife was treated more critically and problematically. Some early crim. con. publications found it difficult to accept that agency lay solely with the lover and castigated the wife for her lack of moral responsibility. The author of *Cases of Divorce for Several Causes* blamed Diana Dormer for the 'scandalous manner of her Prostitution to one of her most inferior servants', an act of 'ingratitude' to a man of such fine qualities as her husband which could only be explained by the 'infirmities' of her 'nature'.[83] In some trials the defendant's counsel openly attacked the character of the plaintiff's wife. Audley Harvey's attorney argued that Elizabeth Gouldney was 'an idle, loose Woman, and given to keep Company with other Men besides her Husband long before the Familiarity was said to have been between her and Mr Harvey', especially with the parson of Chippenham.[84] This put the prosecution in the tricky position of having to defend the sexual reputation of the plaintiff's wife while maintaining that she had still committed adultery with the defendant. Sergeant Baynes for the plaintiff argued that evidence of 'the Parson's being often in private with Mrs Gouldney' was no proof of 'their being ludicrous together; for, added he, I have a House my self in the Country and so ha[ve] a great many Gentlemen present, and . . . I take it to be an honour to have the Company of the Parson'.[85] The use of the word 'ludicrous' diminished the seriousness of Mrs Gouldney's alleged transgression by associating it with playfulness rather than immorality. The jury proved sympathetic to these arguments and, after an hour's deliberation, 'gave a Verdict for the Plaintiff, and One Thousand Pounds Damages'.[86]

A more common story told by the defence was that the plaintiff's wife had enticed or 'tempted' the defendant into sleeping with her. Richard Lyddel's attorney argued that Lady Abergavenny's 'coming into Mr Lyddel's chamber' made her become a 'Temptation to him, and was a Temptation hard to be resisted'. He blamed Lord Abergavenny for entrapment, on the grounds that, rather than acting to prevent any further liaison once he had been apprised of the affair, he had laid 'a Snare and Temptation' to 'draw' Lyddel 'into a Criminal Action'.[87] William Sloper's attorney similarly argued that his client had been tempted by Susannah Cibber who, 'being Mistress of the alluring Arts of the Stage, first engages the young Gentleman's Affection and draws him in, and

---

[82] *The Tryal Between Sir W[illiam] [M[orice] Baronet . . . and Lord A[ugu]st[u]s F[i]tzR[o]y*, p. 32.

[83] *Cases of Divorce for Several Causes*, pp. 41, 42.

[84] *Pall-Mall Miscellany*, p. 24.   [85] Ibid., p. 25.

[86] Ibid., p. 28.   [87] *Account of the Tryal of Richard Lyddel, Esq.*, p. 8.

this with the Husband's Privity and Assistance'.[88] While the tale of men being led astray by female wiles was an old one, in both these cases the women's agency is diminished. Rather than seducing men for their own pleasure, they are depicted as passive baits used by their husbands to lure young men. The act of adultery was still committed by the defendant, but by arguing that he was 'tempted' his actions were presented simply as obeying 'natural' urges that any 'normal' man might find hard to resist, thus avoiding personal responsibility for his behaviour.

CONCLUSION: JUDGING ADULTERY

The fashioning of adultery in trials for crim. con. and related publications seems to bring us a long way from the Christian precepts for judging conjugal infidelity expounded in sermons and books of marital advice. The factors which weighted blame for sexual sin in these traditional discourses, such as the 'degree or severity' of a person as a Christian, or the extent to which their sins took them away from the pathway of Christian knowledge, were conspicuous by their absence in crim. con. suits. Although trials still reiterated the principle that adultery was morally wrong, the sinfulness of adultery was not the real issue at stake here. In so far as the principle was used at all, it was frequently there to be cynically manipulated by lawyers to gain higher damages for their clients. Crim. con. abandoned the idea that adultery should be judged by universal moral standards and set a distinctly 'secular' agenda for discussing infidelity. The language of moral decline and the instigation of the devil was replaced by a secular language of affront, which made much use of concepts of civility and rudeness in analysing deviance – not in the way that church courts and moralists had done as an adjunct to religious languages of sexual sin, but as alternative moralities with their own distinctive codes of values.

Crim. con. provided lurid evidence of men's sexual rapacity, destroying the peace of families. Women, in contrast, were generally presented as passive objects of seduction. Trial publications did much to reinforce emerging understandings of male and female sexual nature. By the 1730s, even women who were alleged to have 'tempted' the defendants into committing adultery with them were frequently portrayed as being used by their husbands as part of a devious scheme to profit from their unchastity.[89] Cases also raised questions about the perception of cuckolded husbands. Trials for crim. con. reveal not so much a new-found 'sympathy' for the cuckolded husband, as a sense of empowerment, the chance to inflict potentially lasting damage on his rival. However, the usual criteria still applied. If a man was found to be complicit in his wife's affair, any

---

[88] *Tryal of a Cause for Criminal Conversation*, p. 31.
[89] E.g., 'Truelove', *Comforts of Matrimony*, p. 15.

claims to sympathy or respect vanished. Moreover, as the treatment of Lord Abergavenny in the press shows, the limits of public sympathy for a wronged husband might reveal themselves in other ways. It was the tragic demise of the tainted 'Calista' that captured public attention, not the vengeance of the proud 'Altamont'. As Abergavenny found out, there was a thin line between taking proper action to restore honour, and petty-minded vindictiveness – a trait that might almost be as dishonourable as being a cuckold itself.

Undeniably, what was at stake in these trials was the 'private injury' caused to a husband by cuckoldry. However, trial evidence shows that the transition towards seeing adultery as a 'private' matter was not straightforward. Lawyers' powerful appeal to juries to act in the public good shows how these cases provided a site for debating whether adultery was a public or private matter in the eighteenth century. Beyond this, the reporting of these trials contributed significantly to the visibility of adultery in the public sphere. A wealth of personal information about the conduct of affairs, normally confined to the courtroom, was now made available in print. Readers learnt little that was new about affairs and how they were conducted, but, primed by the experience of other emerging genres such as 'secret histories' and novels, they could feel that they were participants in the revealing of the scandalous and intimate details of the lives of others. This material contributed to the development of a cult of sexual celebrity in the eighteenth century. The concentration on the affairs of the elite did much to further the opinion that the *beau monde* lived by a code of sexual manners significantly removed from the rest of society. The Abergavenny trial prompted a satirical essay in the *Grub Street Journal* that challenged the 'injudicious verdict' reached in that case on the grounds that the jury had been composed largely of members of the middling sort who did not understand aristocratic sexual mores. Adultery, it sardonically suggested, was 'approved and practised by all who have any taste for politeness' and hence such cases should be tried before juries composed solely of gentlemen of large estates, 'who have been brought up in such free and polite maxims'.[90] Far from being insignificant, trials for criminal conversation were at the cusp of cultural change.

---

[90] *Memoirs of the Society of Grub Street*, I, p. 62.

Conclusion

[Adultery is] a Crime that breaks through all Covenants, confounds all Races and Families, disturbs and unsettles all Inheritances, and fills the whole World with Tumult and Madness and Confusion.[1]

The nature of [adultery] is political and variable; not physical and invariable ... its degree of civil or even moral turpitude depends on manners and opinions; on times and circumstances.[2]

In the eyes of seventeenth-century religious moralists, adultery was a great sin for which all those who committed it were considered equally deserving of punishment. Not only did it affect the individuals concerned and their families, but it was also a great offence to God and, due to the organic conception of society, threatened political as well as familial disorder. However, over the course of the later seventeenth and early eighteenth centuries, as previous chapters have shown, the unity of moral vision that underpinned these arguments began to break down. Changes in patterns of moral policing, in ideologies of the family and its relationship to structures of political authority, together with new thinking about gender roles and social differentiation raised questions about the validity of traditional understandings of marital infidelity. The language of sexual immorality, seen by moralists as a key guardian of moral standards, diversified and new forms of legal action developed which appeared to judge adultery more in terms of rank and the degree and type of injury it caused. The expansion of print acted as a catalyst for increased public debate about the social, moral and political implications of marital breakdown. A proliferation of genres opened up spaces for a reconsideration of traditional themes in new and innovative ways, encouraging subtler and more complex deliberations on the causes and consequences of infidelity. Though religious moralists had long

[1] J. S., *A Sermon Against Adultery* (London, 1672), p. 19.
[2] *Free Thoughts on Seduction, Adultery and Divorce* (London, 1771), p. 34.

194

recognised that there were differences between prescription and practice, as the period progressed there was a wider cultural recognition of a multiplicity of moral universes, governed not just by religious teaching but by fashion, customs and the conventions of different social environments. In the process, a growing tension developed between the enduring belief that marital infidelity was morally wrong and the awareness that its meanings were contingent on 'manners and opinions' and 'times and circumstances'.

Within this foment of ideas about infidelity, several important themes and related lines of development may be discerned. All these changes should be seen as shifts within existing frameworks of reference, rather than crude transformations in which one set of ideas was replaced by another. Nevertheless they had important and lasting consequences for the ways in which marital infidelity was conceptualised. In the first place, this book has shown how concepts of civility and politeness played an increasingly pronounced role in thinking about sexual and social conduct. Marriage had long been seen as a process by which sexual desire was tamed or transformed into higher forms of love or friendship, making it a powerful institution of civil society. As a corollary, sixteenth- and early seventeenth-century moralists had emphasised that sexual immorality had no place in civilised society and described adultery as 'bestial' or 'uncivil' conduct. However, the influence of notions of manners and social refinement on moral discourse became more marked in several distinct ways as the seventeenth century progressed. Most notably, these ideas were expressed linguistically through the development of new vocabularies of adultery. On the one hand, the soft words of civility, such as intrigue and gallantry, entered the sexual lexicon after the Restoration, and appeared to give a spurious respectability and romantic glamour to love affairs. Partly in response to these developments, periodicals, novels and other texts increasingly conceptualised infidelity through a proliferation of words that situated the transgression of adultery more firmly within the context of polite sociability – a notion encapsulated above all by the eighteenth-century description of adultery as 'criminal conversation'. Though it was intended to be consonant with religious teaching on sexual morality, this language conveyed increasing concern about the ways in which adultery affected personal social relations with others rather than the adulterers' offence to God. Adultery was conceptualised as being inconsistent with the project of social refinement, which placed an increasing premium on the cultivation of good manners through virtuous social interaction between the sexes.

Concepts of civility and politeness also played a significant role in prescriptions for conjugal fidelity. Moralists' appeals to the values of civilized societies in their warnings against adultery took on a new significance in the context of colonial expansion and the popularity of travellers' tales and proto-anthropological cross-cultural comparisons. Furthermore, in a new kind of conduct literature emerging after the Restoration aimed at fashioning the polite gentleman, adultery was portrayed as an offence against 'generosity' – a key value of politeness that viewed benevolence and the humane desire to do right by one's fellow man as key impulses to virtue. While religious moral teaching had emphasised the divine punishments that awaited adulterers, the tone of this new form of conduct literature was less coercive, recognising that the values of sociability might act as a different incentive to morality. A further manifestation of the links between incivility and immorality may be found in the legal sphere. Evidence of 'uncivil' behaviour or 'extraordinary familiarity' had long been used in marital separation suits brought before the church courts as a means of enmeshing suspected adulterers in a web of guilt. Though such evidence was of secondary legal importance, the practical problems of obtaining proof, especially in the context of increasing privacy within the homes of the wealthier sort, gave it a prominent role in these cases in this period. Even more significant was the role played by this kind of evidence in trials for criminal conversation. Since damages were awarded on the basis of the *manner* in which adultery had been committed (rather than the sinfulness of adultery *per se*), the incivility of the gallant's behaviour became a critical issue. As such, these notions established an alternative, distinctly secular, framework for judging infidelity.

The increased bearing of these concepts on discourses of adultery and sexual immorality owed much to the proliferation of guides to polite manners in this period. That ideas developed in the 'public sphere' of polite social interaction were increasingly applied to domestic relations and sexual behaviour indicates that historians need to broaden their understanding of the 'rise of politeness' beyond the world of the coffee house and the tea table and explore its impact on married life and personal conduct. Moreover, it is important to see these developments as part of an ongoing process that went beyond the period covered by this study. These concepts became even more pronounced in moral literature of the second half of the eighteenth century, although by this time languages of politeness were themselves becoming modified by the development of sentimental cultures of 'feeling' and sensibility.[3] In the new culture of feeling, which placed great importance on the expression of genuine emotion as a sign of true refinement, adulterous desires were condemned as 'simple or gross sensations', wholly incompatible with the refined sensibility of conjugal love.[4] The reformer John Bowles furthermore described adultery as a failure of 'moral sense', an important concept that combined Christian moral duty with sensitivity to the feelings and needs of others.[5] These developments take us

---

[3] John Mullan, *Sentiment and Sociability: the Language of Feeling in the Eighteenth Century* (Oxford, 1988); G. J. Barker-Benfield, *The Culture of Sensibility: Sex and Society in Eighteenth-Century Britain* (Chicago, IL and London, 1992); Philip Carter, *Men and the Emergence of Polite Society: Britain 1660–1800* (London, 2001), ch. 3.

[4] *Letters on Love, Marriage and Adultery* (London, 1789), p. 80.

[5] John Bowles, *Reflections on the Political and Moral State of Society at the Close of the Eighteenth Century* (London, 1800), p. 136.

beyond the scope of this survey. However, as sexual morality has so seldom featured in historical analyses of politeness and sensibility this further linguistic turn would repay further study.

One of the main consequences of the enhanced role of concepts of civility and politeness on discussions of adultery was to make for an increasingly socially diverse approach to matters of sex and morality. Calls for a more euphemistic language of sexual misconduct developing by the early eighteenth century were informed by the idea that respectable, well-bred persons needed to be addressed in different terms to the rest of society and needed to be taught about moral principles in a manner more appropriate to their refined nature. Women, in particular genteel ladies, also needed to be addressed with greater 'complaisance', according to new perceptions of them as the more delicate 'fair' sex. Some of these arguments, such as the claim made in *An Essay Upon Modern Gallantry* (1726) that 'pretty gentlemen' had 'stomachs too nice to digest any arguments made from religion', were undoubtedly satirical and cannot be taken as the view of the elite themselves.[6] Nevertheless, it is certainly noticeable that the language of 'whoredom', which had long served as a universal signifier of sexual sin, became much less common in depictions of upper-class adultery in the eighteenth century and came to be applied more specifically to prostitution, a vice increasingly associated with poverty.[7]

Furthermore, by the eighteenth century the language of gallantry had become synonymous with a code of elite sexual manners that was at odds with conventional moral teaching. The implications of this new terminology of adultery were two-fold and contradictory. On the one hand, 'gallantry' seemed to suggest a more tolerant perspective on fashionable vice, manifested by the recognition on the part of publishers and social commentators that there was a pleasure to be had from describing and reading about the 'extraordinary intrigues' and 'gallantries' enjoyed by 'celebrated' practitioners of love affairs. Such literature, together with the examples of famous adulterers whose lives and intrigues were immortalised in the press, fostered the notion common by the mid-eighteenth century that illicit sexual activity might provide a basis for fame and 'honour'.[8] On the other hand, representations of the elite as debauched and effeminate acted as a powerful means of differentiating social groups by moral standards. As the middle class developed its own distinctive social identity based on respectability, in which conjugal love and 'domesticity' were core values, so sexual mores increasingly became a focal point of social tension, marked by gathering criticisms of 'aristocratic vice' during the second half

---

[6] *An Essay Upon Modern Gallantry* (London, 1726), p. 10.
[7] Faramerz Dabhoiwala, 'Prostitution and Police in London, *c.*1660–*c.*1760', DPhil thesis, University of Oxford (1995), pp. 223–5.
[8] Faramerz Dabhoiwala, 'The Construction of Honour, Reputation and Status in Late Seventeenth- and Early Eighteenth-Century England', *TRHS*, 6th ser., 6 (1996), 211.

of the eighteenth century.[9] By this time, thinking about all aspects of sexual immorality was more sharply oriented around issues of class and gender. As Dabhoiwala has shown, in the developing philanthropic thought about prostitution that led to the foundation of charitable institutions like the Magdalen House (1758), streetwalking prostitutes were increasingly seen as victims of poverty, bawds and male seducers. These poor women were viewed as fundamentally different to aristocratic adulteresses, mistresses and scandalous 'demi-reps' whose behaviour was much more a matter of personal moral choice.[10] In this way, family relations and sexuality played an important role in forging group identities in eighteenth-century England.[11]

As the volume and variety of writing on extra-marital sex increased during the later seventeenth and early eighteenth centuries, so writers began to engage more critically with the circumstances of marital breakdown and consider more subtly the consequences of infidelity. In the process, older stereotypes began to collapse and traditional modes of representing the causes of adultery were challenged and modified. The conjectured readership of much of this writing was the urban middling sort for whom a successful marriage was crucial to worldly success, and there is an important parallel between the proliferation of writings on marital breakdown in this period and an expansion of trade publications exploring in greater detail the causes of business failure.[12] Periodicals such as the *Athenian Mercury* began to consider adultery as a social problem, and as something that might result from confusion about the laws regarding marriage formation. Stories of men who took mistresses because of the lack of effective divorce laws or destitute and deserted wives who began extra-marital unions out of economic 'necessity' and a desire to provide for their children provided more 'rational' perspectives on adultery and marital breakdown, modifying the customary religious teaching that all extra-marital sex resulted from unrestrained lusts. Such correspondence played a significant role in challenging ingrained assumptions about the nature of female sexuality: rather than presenting women as shameless adulteresses, wilfully cuckolding their husbands in order to satiate their unrestrained desires, these letters present a more rounded picture of the dilemmas facing women in this society. They also showed, in a manner later developed by Bernard Mandeville in his notorious *Fable of the Bees* (1714), that sexual 'vice' might be the product of virtuous intentions.[13] The dialogic form of question-and-answer periodicals provided a vehicle for demonstrating, in complex and challenging ways, tensions between the precepts of official morality and personal moral sympathy.

[9] Donna T. Andrew, '"Adultery A-La-Mode": Privilege, the Law and Attitudes to Adultery 1770–1809', *History*, 82 (1997), 5–23; Margaret R. Hunt, *The Middling Sort: Commerce, Gender and the Family in England 1680–1780* (Berkeley and Los Angeles, CA, 1996), ch. 8.
[10] Dabhoiwala, 'Prostitution and Police', pp. 223, 229.   [11] Hunt, *The Middling Sort*, p. 8.
[12] Ibid., pp. 35–7.   [13] Dabhoiwala, 'Prostitution and Police', pp. 183–6.

A more critical understanding of the circumstances of infidelity also raised questions about the extent to which cuckolded husbands deserved derision. Though mockery of cuckolds remained a persistent feature of popular culture throughout this period, there were subtler attempts to analyse the shame suffered by men as a result of wifely adultery and to explore ways in which its damage to reputation might by mitigated. The development of cultural spaces for deceived husbands to present their own stories of marriages disordered by adultery gave some support to Addison's argument that the cuckold was a 'poor innocent creature' deserving compassion. Placed in the context of personal pain, images of the cuckolded husband as a figure of fun became harder to sustain. Though the notion that cuckoldry was deeply humiliating and damaging to manhood remained strong throughout this period and beyond, in writings about cuckoldry this shame is increasingly conceptualised as coming primarily from within rather than as something automatically bestowed by the wider community. Building on the existing conceptualisation of cuckoldry as a matter of degrees, commentators increasingly acknowledged that its effect on a man's public reputation could be more mutable and contingent on circumstances. Its primary dangers lay in its capacity to damage economic credit and business dealings and commentators advised men to act quickly to minimise its effects.

However, it remains difficult to determine changing 'attitudes' towards cuckoldry from literary evidence. In spite of the development of 'softer' approaches to the problem of cuckoldry in this period, and an attempt by some commentators to identify cuckold humour more closely with the 'vulgar' tastes of the lower orders, there was something of a renaissance in mocking accounts and images of cuckolds in the later eighteenth century – not just in popular ballads, but also in satirical prints and magazines aimed at a more genteel audience.[14] Though there was a proliferation of meanings of cuckoldry in the eighteenth century, notions of a 'decline' in its comic potential need to be treated cautiously. Future research in this area would therefore benefit from taking a longer time perspective, to explore continuities and changes in representations of cuckoldry from the seventeenth to the nineteenth century.

This probing of the circumstances of adultery was part of a wider debate about whether adultery was a matter of personal conscience or public regulation, set against the backdrop of increasing public awareness of the limitations of the church courts as agents of moral policing. The matter was raised in stage comedies of the 1670s in which the fulfilment of natural urges was set against the restraining influences of hollow social convention. The debate intensified in

---

[14] See, for instance, Cindy McCreery, 'Keeping Up with the Bon Ton: the *Tête-à-Tête* Series in the *Town and Country Magazine*', in Hannah Barker and Elaine Chalus (eds.), *Gender in Eighteenth-Century England: Roles, Representations and Responsibilities* (London, 1997), pp. 207–29; Elizabeth A. Foyster, *Manhood in Early Modern England: Honour, Sex and Marriage* (London, 1999), p. 217.

the wake of the Glorious Revolution. The symbolic separation of the political and domestic spheres in the arguments used to depose James II made it arguably more difficult to justify the intervention of external authorities to regulate family relationships. Moreover, the granting of a limited liberty of conscience encouraged a more personal approach to questions of religion and morality, at a time when the expansion of print meant that the church no longer had a monopoly on the formation of public opinion on these matters. Though moralists and others continued to search for more effective public punishments for adultery – illustrated by the activities of the Societies for the Reformation of Manners and the debate among lawyers about the purpose of crim. con. – the emphasis seemed to be shifting gradually towards voluntary self-regulation. The increasingly prominent place of concepts of civility and politeness in moral discourse represented an important shift in this direction, urging greater self-control and fostering awareness of how one's behaviour affected others. Periodicals such as the *Athenian Mercury* and the *Spectator* acted as informal moral tribunals and constantly emphasised the need for self-reflection and personal reformation. The printing of personal testimony encouraged self-identification with problems, laying the basis for voluntary change.[15] These ideas were themselves nothing new – puritan conduct literature of the early seventeenth century had emphasised the importance of internalising moral precepts and self-control – but they acquired a new importance in the context of political and institutional changes.[16]

When these issues are examined in longer historical perspective, it is evident that by the eighteenth century there was a greater distinction between personal 'private' issues on the one hand and matters of public concern and intervention on the other.[17] However, the notion of a 'privatisation' of family relations and adultery is too slippery to adequately describe this process of development. Though there can be no doubt that, as the century progressed, middle-class ideology and sentimental fiction increasingly portrayed adultery as a tragedy acted out (and dealt with) behind closed doors, the notion that infidelity should be publicly punished was slow to disappear.[18] Later in the eighteenth century, amid concerns about the rising tide of divorces and the effeminate morals of the nation's rulers, heightened by the sense of national emergency engendered by a state of almost constant warfare between 1776 and 1815, calls were once again

---

[15] See also Isabel V. Hull, *Sexuality, State and Civil Society in Germany, 1700–1815* (Ithaca, NY, 1996), p. 262.

[16] Edmund Leites, *The Puritan Conscience and Modern Sexuality* (New Haven, CT and London, 1986).

[17] Dabhoiwala, 'Construction of Honour', 212.

[18] Tony Tanner, *Adultery and the Novel: Contract and Transgression* (Baltimore, MD and London, 1979), pp. 14–15; Randolph Trumbach, *Sex and the Gender Revolution, Volume I: Heterosexuality and the Third Gender in Enlightenment London* (Chicago, IL and London, 1998), p. 392.

heard for more effective public regulation of sexual immorality.[19] 'No vice can prove more fatal to dissolve the ties of society, to bring distrust and distress into families: no vice can be more infectious, and have a more dreadful influence on the rising population,' argued a tract of 1792, using language very similar to that used by seventeenth-century moralists. The same tract argued that the law of criminal conversation should be reformed to turn the damages awarded into a public fine so that it might 'operate to the prevention of the crime'.[20] Bills intended to make adultery a public crime were introduced into Parliament in 1779 and 1800.[21] Nevertheless, the extraordinary political crises of the American War of Independence and the French Revolution that gave rise to such legislative initiatives only served to emphasise that by this stage such measures were highly unusual. The trend towards decriminalisation of adultery visible in the late seventeenth and early eighteenth centuries would not be reversed.

Beyond charting shifting social and moral meanings of adultery, this book has also explored the ways in which debates about the meanings of illicit sexuality were influenced by changing understandings of gender relations and male and female sexual nature. Throughout its analysis, this book has emphasised that gendered perspectives on the causes and consequences of adultery were intimately bound up with questions of social status. In spite of commonplace notions of a sexual double standard, this book has shown that the question of how men's sexuality endangered patriarchal household relations was an issue of consuming interest in late seventeenth- and early eighteenth-century England. Building on the notion current in religious teaching that men bore greater responsibility for adulterous transgressions owing to their superior 'reason', writers in the later seventeenth century paid a good deal of attention to probing the limits of patriarchal authority in families set against a broader debate about the nature of all kinds of political authority in the aftermath of the Civil War and mounting concerns about 'arbitrary government'.[22]

One of the most significant features of discussions of men's sexuality in this period regarded the ways in which sexual relations with women acted as encoded representations of relations of status and authority between men. This was a crucial means by which male and female extra-marital sex was distinguished in this period and discussed in different terms. Literary discussions of male sexual mores frequently suggest that one of the most important features of adultery

---

[19] Lawrence Stone, *Road to Divorce: England 1530–1987* (Oxford, 1990), pp. 273–8; Katherine Binhammer, 'The Sex Panic of the 1790s', *Journal of the History of Sexuality*, 6 (1991), 409–34.

[20] *The Evils of Adultery and Prostitution; with an Inquiry into the Causes of their Present Alarming Increase* (London, 1792), pp. 3, 67.

[21] Andrew, ' "Adultery A-La-Mode" ', 11, 20.

[22] Susan Staves, *Players' Scepters: Fictions of Authority in the Restoration* (Lincoln, NE and London, 1979); Rachel Weil, 'Sometimes a Scepter is Only a Scepter: Pornography and Politics in Restoration England', in Lynn Hunt (ed.), *The Invention of Pornography: Obscenity and the Origins of Modernity 1500–1800* (New York, 1993), pp. 125–53.

for men was the deception or subordination of the husband. This is to be seen time and again in stories of apprentices or journeymen becoming master in the bedroom, or of men being cuckolded by friends or colleagues. Though a man's control of his wife was critically at issue in cuckoldry, the comparison between husband and gallant provided the axis of many seventeenth-century cuckolding narratives and this relationship was used to contrast styles of masculine deportment, fashion and manners. The social relationship between husband and gallant was also a significant factor in trials for criminal conversation. What was at stake in these cases was less the wife's betrayal of her husband than the lover's betrayal of his master or friend. All these factors contributed to shifting understandings of men as the more lustful sex, as sexual 'aggressors' whose desires not only threatened to destroy conjugal love and patriarchal domestic order but also damaged homosocial friendships and political relations between men themselves.[23] This connection between sexual rivalry and competitions for status and authority deserves greater attention from historians of early modern masculinities.

Occasionally, the sources represent a different side to male sexuality to the commonplace image of men as wilful seducers or pleasure seekers secure of their place in the sexual system. Although in the eighteenth century male reputation became less sensitive to sexual aspersions, this book has shown that the cultural expression of male anxieties about sexual behaviour remained important, even at a time when conceptions of deviant masculinity were shifting. It is clear that heterosexual relations were seen as presenting problems and scruples for men, which went beyond familiar concerns about cuckoldry or sexual performance. Correspondence to periodicals like the *Athenian Mercury* reveals men expressing concerns and doubts about their conduct. Rather than being confident sexual braggarts, their letters display anxieties about how others might perceive their actions, scruples of conscience and, sometimes, concern for the welfare and reputation of the women involved.

Nevertheless, over the course of the later seventeenth and early eighteenth centuries, the aggressive, predatory aspect of male sexuality became culturally more pronounced as new ideas of femininity began to cast women, formerly seen as the more lustful sex, in more passive roles. The notion that women were victims of male seduction was exaggerated in actions for criminal conversation owing to the doctrine of coverture that saw wives as the property of their husbands, therefore making them ineligible to give evidence in these trials. The extent to which women accepted or internalised these notions remains an issue for future research. However, reading carefully the statements of female defendants in the very different legal setting of the church courts, it becomes apparent that accused wives and their lawyers were not unwilling to employ images of victimhood to their own purposes and, faced with the prospect of losing

---

[23] Cf. Trumbach, *Sex and the Gender Revolution*, p. 394.

everything, were prepared to defend themselves vigorously against their husbands' charges. Instead of meekly accepting the double standard, these women showed themselves ready and willing to accuse their husbands of infidelity, often as a practical means of halting the suit and bringing their spouses to reach an informal out of court settlement. Furthermore, though the evidence produced in marital separation suits is opaque and motives cannot be read off the page, through this material it is possible to glimpse a more complex picture of how adultery came to court and to speculate about what affairs may have meant to those involved. For upper-class women who formed the majority of defendants in adultery suits, there are signs that physical intimacies, a desire for attention and attempts to escape boredom may have been important elements of love affairs alongside sexual attraction.

Considerations of space and the nature of the evidence mean that it has not been possible to give full attention to all aspects of the subject and questions remain for future research. In the first place, many of the developments described in this book had a distinctly urban, metropolitan feel to them. The market for more diverse, questioning approaches to infidelity may have been greater in London owing to the religious and social diversity of the capital. As this book has shown, the great curiosity about matters of sexual morality and the testing of the boundaries of acceptable conduct displayed in the printed literature of this period was motivated in large part by an urgent cultural desire to make sense of sexual and social mores in an increasingly complex and competitive society in which older values and meanings no longer seemed so fixed or easy to apply. Although cultural diffusion was a major feature of this period, the impact of new ideas on more stratified rural communities remains open to question. While the development of print culture may have acted as an agent of cultural homogenisation, the effect, with regards to ideas about sexual morality, may have been to emphasise differences between metropolitan and provincial mores.[24] The sexual manners of rural societies in this period require further research. Secondly, the sources used in this book place a great deal of emphasis on social differentiation of adultery from the top down. The cumulative effect of increasing attempts to differentiate middle-class moral values from those of the elite, as the eighteenth century progressed, was to obscure the meanings of adultery for the lower classes. This book has suggested ways in which motives for having affairs may have differed by class as well as gender. However, the question of how far developments in the conceptualisation of adultery explored in this book extended below the educated classes must remain open for future study.

---

[24] Note the comments of Carl B. Estabrook, *Urbane and Rustic England: Cultural Ties and Social Spheres in the Provinces 1660–1780* (Manchester, 1998), p. 197 and *passim*.

These limitations notwithstanding, this survey has attempted to deepen our understanding of the ways in which sexual and social mores inter-related in an under-researched period. Its forensic approach to its sources, examining how the form of different genres of texts influenced their content, has broader implications for the practice of cultural history. It suggests that as historians we need to revise our understanding of 'representation' and 'reality' as a dichotomous relationship to one which takes into account the variety of forms in which cultural reality is fashioned and the multiple 'points of contact' different types of text establish with the wider world. By dissecting cultural forms in this way and paying close attention to the structures and aesthetics of representation, we are able to arrive at a more textured understanding of extra-marital sex in this period, which better allows for the complex and uneven ways in which cultural meanings are constructed. Representations of adultery provided contemporaries with a means not only of making sense of the micro-dramas of disordered families and the pain of alienated affections, but also of comprehending broader cultural and political changes.

Bibliography

1 MANUSCRIPT SOURCES

London: British Library

Add. MS 22560   Diary of Rev. John Thomlinson

London: Lambeth Palace Library

Court of Arches MSS

Bbb 252, 826/7,   Commissions in partibus, 1671, 1698, 1705, 1706, 1707,
826/8, 826/10,   1712, 1715, 1716, 1732
903, 903/4,
903/5, 904,
905/3, 914,
914/1, 914/5,
914/6, 915/6,
924/1, 924/4,
999/5, 999/6
1004, 1004/1
1004/2, 1004/5
1004/6, 1028/1
1028/4, 1029/7
1029/8, 1031/1, 1031/4
1035/2, 1246/5,
1246/7, 1246/12

D 80, 1805, 2252   Process Books, 1722, 1727, 1730, 1738
1348, 1921

E 4/102, 4/157, 5/20,   Libels, Interrogatories and Allegations, 1666, 1673, 1674,
5/24, 5/27, 5/126, 5/128,   1690, 1693, 1698, 1705, 1706, 1707, 1708, 1722, 1732, 1738
9/38, 9/53, 11/7,
11/8, 11/9, 11/10,
12/75, 15/34,
15/35, 15/36, 15/37,
16/79, 17/10, 17/10a,
18/25, 26/151, 26/164,
30/75, 31/92, 33/111

205

Ee 3   Personal Answers Book, 1666–1672
Ee 4   Personal Answers Book, 1672–1681
Ee 7   Personal Answers Book, 1689–1694
Ee 8   Personal Answers Book, 1693–1716
Ee 9   Personal Answers Book, 1714–1732

Eee 4   Depositions Book, 1669–1673
Eee 5   Depositions Book, 1673–1676
Eee 7   Depositions Book, 1688–1694
Eee 9   Depositions Book, 1704–1706
Eee 10   Depositions Book, 1707–1713
Eee 11   Depositions Book, 1713–1716

G 102/96, 104/9   Miscellaneous Exhibits, 1732
104/21

J 6/68, 7/13,   Bills of Costs, 1706, 1707, 1712, 1715
7/102, 7/105,
8/83, 8/99

Jj 6/63   Bond, 1713

London: Lincoln's Inn Library

MS Misc. 147   Reports of Ecclesiastical Cases in the Court of Delegates and Court
               of Arches between about 1714 and 1728, digested under titles by
               Dr Exton Sayer

London: London Metropolitan Archives

London Consistory Court MSS

DL/C/156   Allegations, Libels and Sentences, March 1715–February 1717
DL/C/169   Allegations, Libels and Sentences, November 1738–December 1742
DL/C/172   Deposition Book, July 1738–July 1740
DL/C/199   Personal Answers Book, February 1703–December 1719
DL/C/255   Depositions Book, December 1714–December 1715
DL/C/549/ 61, Miscellaneous Matrimonial Cause Papers 1738–1739
62, 62, 94, 96,
97

Middlesex Sessions Papers

MJ/SR 1556 Middlesex Sessions Roll, 15 January 1679

2 PRINTED PRIMARY SOURCES: NEWSPAPER AND PERIODICAL PUBLICATIONS

Athenian Mercury
British Apollo
British Mercury
Daily Post-Boy

Dawks's Newsletter
Defoe's Review, ed. Arthur Wellesley Secord (9 vols., New York, 1938)
Evening Post
Female Tatler, ed. Fidelis Morgan (London, 1992)
Gentleman's Magazine
Grub Street Journal
Ladies Mercury
Monthly Miscellany: Or, Memoirs For the Curious (2 vols., London, 1708)
Night-Walker: Or, Evening Rambles in Search After Lewd Women with the Conferences
  held with them
Poor Robin's Intelligence
Poor Robin's Intelligence Newly Reviv'd
Poor Robin's Publick and Private Occurrences
Post Angel
Post Boy
St. James's Evening Post
Secret Mercury, Or, the Adventure of Seven Days
Spectator, ed. Donald F. Bond (5 vols., Oxford, 1965)
Tatler, ed. Donald F. Bond (3 vols., Oxford, 1987)
Universal Spectator, ed. Henry Stonecastle (2 vols., London, 1736)
Universal Spy; Or, The London Weekly Magazine
Weekly Packet
Whitehall Evening-Post

3 PRINTED PRIMARY SOURCES: OTHER WORKS

An Account of the Tryal of Richard Lyddel, Esq.;... For Carrying on a Criminal
  Conversation with the Late Lady Abergavenny (London, 1730).
The Adventuress; Or the Lady's Flight From Scotland Yard... To Which is Added, Several
  Entertaining Intrigues, and Extraordinary Pieces of British Gallantry (London, n.d.
  [*c*.1725?]).
Allestree, Richard, *The Government of the Tongue* (Oxford, 1674).
[Allestree, Richard], *The Government of the Thoughts: a Prefatory Discourse to the*
  Government of the Tongue (London, 1694).
  The Ladies Calling (Oxford, 1673).
  The Whole Duty of Man, Necessary for all Families (London, 1660).
Athenae Redivivae: Or the New Athenian Oracle (London, 1704).
Ayliffe, John, *Parergon Juris Canonici Anglicani: Or a Commentary By Way of*
  Supplement to the Canons and Constitutions of the Church of England (London,
  1726).
B., A., *A Letter of Advice Concerning Marriage* (London, 1676).
B., R., *A Caveat for Sinners, Or, A Warning to Swearers, Blasphemers, and Adulterers*
  (London, 1683).
Bailey, Nathan, *An Universal Etymological English Dictionary* (London, 1724).
Baker, Thomas, *An Act at Oxford* (London, 1704).
  The Humour of the Age (London, 1701).
Barrow, Isaac, *Several Sermons Against Evil-Speaking* (London, 1678).
  The Theological Works of Isaac Barrow, ed. Alexander Napier (9 vols., Cambridge,
  1859).

Baxter, Richard, *A Christian Directory: Or, A Summ of Practical Theologie and Cases of Conscience* (London, 1673).

Bayly, Lewis, *The Practice of Pietie: Directing a Christian How to Walke that He May Please God* (London, 1632 edn).

Beard, Thomas, *The Theatre of God's Judgements* (London, 1648).

Bedford, Arthur, *The Evil and Danger of Stage Plays: Shewing their Natural Tendency to Destroy Religion, and Introduce a General Corruption of Manners* (London, 1706).

　Serious Reflections on the Scandalous Abuse and Effects of the Stage (Bristol, 1705).

　A Serious Remonstrance In Behalf of the Christian Religion, Against the Horrid Blasphemies and Impieties Which are Still Used in the English Play-Houses (London, 1719).

Behn, Aphra, *The Works of Aphra Behn*, ed. Montague Summers (6 vols., London, 1915).

Berkeley, George, *Alciphron: Or, the Minute Philosopher* (2 vols., London, 1732).

Boswell, James, *Boswell's London Journal 1762–1763*, ed. Frederick A. Pottle (London, 1950).

Bourne, Immanuel, *A Gold Chain of Directions with Twenty Gold-Links of Love, to Preserve Love Firm between Husband and Wife during their Lives* (London, 1669).

Bowles, John, *Reflections on the Political and Moral State of Society at the Close of the Eighteenth Century* (London, 1800).

Boyle, Francis, *Discourses Useful For the Vain Modish Ladies and Their Gallants* (London, 1696).

A Brief Narrative of a Strange and Wonderful Old Woman that hath a Pair of Horns Growing Upon her Head (London, 1676).

Brown, Thomas, *Amusements Serious and Comical, Calculated for the Meridian of London* (London, 1700).

Bull-Feather Hall: Or, The Antiquity and Dignity of Horns, Amply Shown (London, 1664).

Burnaby, Charles, *The Modish Husband* (London, 1702).

　The Reform'd Wife (London, 1700).

Byrd, William, *The London Diary (1717–1721) and Other Writings*, ed. Louis B. Wright and Marion Tinling (New York, 1958).

Capt. Leeson's Case: Being an Account of his Tryal for Committing a Rape Upon the Body of Mrs May a Married Woman of 35 Years of Age (London, 1715).

[della Casa, Giovanni], *Galateo, Or Rather, a Treatise of the Manners and Behaviours it Behoveth a Man to Use and Eschewe, in His Familiar Conversation*, trans. Robert Peterson (London, 1576 edn).

　Galateo of Manners: Or, Instructions to a Young Gentleman How to Behave Himself in Conversation (London, 1703 edn).

The Case of Mr Richard Noble Impartially Consider'd: Abstracting from the Man, or Crime, But Meerly as to the Law (London, 1713).

Cases of Divorce for Several Causes (London, 1715).

The Cases of Polygamy, Concubinage, Adultery, Divorce, etc. (London, 1732).

'Castamore', *Conjugium Languens: or, the Natural, Civil and Religious Mischiefs Arising from Conjugal Infidelity and Impunity* (London, 1700).

The Character of a Town-Gallant; Exposing the Extravagant Fopperies of Some Vain Self-Conceited Pretenders to Gentility and Good Breeding (London, 1675).

The Character of a Towne-Misse (London, 1675).

Cibber, Colley, *The Careless Husband* (1705), ed. William W. Appleton (London, 1967).

Coles, Elisha, *An English Dictionary* (London, 1685).

A Collection of Miscellany Letters, Selected out of Mist's Weekly Journal (4 vols., London, 1722–7).

A Collection of Remarkable Trials (Glasgow, n.d. [*c*.1739]).

Collier, Jeremy, *A Short View of the Immorality and Profaneness of the English Stage* (London, 1698).

A Complete Collection of State Trials, ed. T. B. Howell (33 vols., London, 1809–28).

Congreve, William, *The Way of the World* (1700), ed. Katherine M. Lynch (London, 1965).

C[onset], H[enry], *The Practice of the Spiritual or Ecclesiastical Courts* (London, 1685).

Croft, Herbert, *A Sermon Preached before Right Honourable the Lords Assembled in Parliament, Upon the Fast-Day Appointed February 4 1673/4* (London, 1674).

[Curll, Edmund], *Curlicism Display'd: Or, an Appeal to the Church* (London, 1718).

D., B., *The Art of Courtship* (London, 1662).

Defoe, Daniel, *Conjugal Lewdness; Or, Matrimonial Whoredom. A Treatise Concerning the Use and Abuse of the Marriage Bed* (London, 1727).

The Fortunes and Misfortunes of the Famous Moll Flanders (1722), ed. G. A. Starr (Oxford, 1971).

The History and Remarkable Life of the Truly Honourable Col. Jacque Commonly Call'd Colonel Jack (1722), ed. Samuel Holt Monk (London, 1965).

Roxana: the Fortunate Mistress (1724), ed. John Mullan (Oxford, 1996).

[Defoe, Daniel], *An Essay Upon Projects* (London, 1697).

Serious Reflections During the Life and Surprising Adventures of Robinson Crusoe (London, 1720).

Dekker, Thomas, *The Gul's Horn-Book* (1609), ed. R. B. McKerrow (New York, 1971).

Dennis, John, *The Critical Works of John Dennis*, ed. E. Niles Hooker (2 vols., Baltimore, 1939).

Dirty Dogs For Dirty Puddings. Or, Memoirs of the Luscious Amours of... Several Persons of Both Sexes of Quality and Distinction (London, 1732).

'Dr Make Horns', *The Cuckold's Sermon Preach'd at Fumbler's-Hall on Wednesday the 18th of October Being Horn-Fair Day* (London, 1704).

Dreadful News from Southwark: Or a True Account of the Most Horrid Murder Committed by Margaret Osgood, on Her Husband Walter Osgood a Hatmaker (n.p., n.d. [*c*.1680]).

Dryden, John, *Marriage A-La-Mode* (1671), ed. David Crane (London, 1991).

Dunton, John, *The Life and Errors of John Dunton, Citizen of London*, ed. J. B. Nichols (2 vols., London, 1818).

[Dunton, John], *The Hazard of a Death-Bed Repentance* (London, 1708).

Dyche, Thomas, *A New General English Dictionary* (London, 1735).

Ellis, Clement, *The Gentile Sinner* (London, 1664).

England's Vanity: Or the Voice of God Against the Monstrous Sin of Pride in Dress and Apparel (London, 1683).

An Epistle From Calista to Altamont (London, 1729).

An Essay Towards a General History of Whoring (London, 1697).

An Essay Upon Modern Gallantry (London, 1726).

Etherege, George, *The Dramatic Works of Sir George Etherege*, ed. H. F. B. Brett-Smith (2 vols., London, 1927).

The Evils of Adultery and Prostitution; with an Inquiry into the Causes of their Present Alarming Increase (London, 1792).

The Execution of Mr Rob Foulks, Late Minister of Stanton-Lacy in Shropshire (London, 1679).

Fair Warning to Murderers of Infants: Being An Account of the Tryal, Condemnation and Execution of Mary Goodenough at the Assizes Held in Oxon., in February 1691/2 (London, 1692).

Fielding, Henry, *The Works of Henry Fielding Esq.*, ed. Leslie Stephen (10 vols., London, 1882).

Fleetwood, William, *A Funeral Sermon Upon Mr Noble* (London, 1713).

   The Relative Duties of Parents and Children, Husbands and Wives, Masters and Servants Consider'd in Sixteen Sermons (London, 1705).

Foulkes, Robert, *An Alarme for Sinners* (London, 1679).

Free Thoughts on Seduction, Adultery and Divorce (London, 1771).

A Full Account of the Case of John Sayer Esq. (London, 1713).

A Full Account of the Case of John Sayer Esq.... Second Edition With Additions (London, 1713).

A Full and Faithful Account of the Intrigue Between Mr Noble and Mrs Sayer (London, 1713).

A Full and True Account of a Most Barbarous and Bloody Murther Committed by Esther Ives, with the Assistance of John Noyse a Cooper (London, 1686).

A Full and True Account of the Penitence of John Marketman During His Imprisonment in Chelmsford Gaol for Murthering His Wife (London, 1680).

A Full and True Account [of Richard Noble] Etc. (n.p., n.d. [c.1713]).

The Full and True Relation of All the Proceedings at the Assizes Holden at Chelmsford, for the Countie of Essex (n.p., n.d. [c.1680]).

A General Summons for those Belonging to the Hen-Peckt Frigat, to Appear at Cuckold's Point on the 18th of this Instant October (London, n.d. [c.1680]).

A General Summons to all the Hornified Fumblers, To assemble at Horn Fair October 18 (London, n.d. [c.1830]).

Godolphin, John, *Repertorium Canonicum: Or, An Abridgement of the Ecclesiastical Laws of this Realm Consistent with the Temporal* (London, 1687).

Gouge, William, *Of Domesticall Duties* (London, 1622).

H., J., *Essays of Love and Marriage* (London, 1673).

H., N., *The Ladies Dictionary* (London, 1694).

The Harleian Miscellany (12 vols., London, 1808–11).

[Haywood, Eliza?], *Bath Intrigues: In Four Letters to a Friend in London* (London, 1725).

Hell Upon Earth: Or, the Town in an Uproar (London, 1729).

Hickes, William, *Oxford Jests, Refined and Enlarged*, 13th edn (London, n.d. [c.1725]).

His Grace the Duke of Norfolk's Charge Against the Dutchess, Before the House of Lords (London, 1692).

Historical Manuscripts Commission, *Egmont MSS, Diary* (3 vols., London, 1920–3).

Hobbes, Thomas, *Leviathan: Or the Matter, Forme, and Power of a Commonwealth Ecclesiastical and Civil* [1651], ed. C. B. Macpherson (Harmondsworth, 1968).

The Honest London Spy, Discovering the Base and Subtle Intreagues of the Town (London, 1706).

Hooton, Henry, *A Bridle for the Tongue* (London, 1709).

Hoppit, Julian (ed.), *Failed Legislation, 1660–1800: Extracted from the Commons and Lords Journals* (London and Rio Grande, OH, 1997).

The Horn Exalted, Or Roome for Cuckolds. Being a Treatise Concerning the Reason and Original of the Word Cuckold and Why Such are said to wear Horns (London, 1661).

Law, William, *The Absolute Unlawfulness of the Stage-Entertainment Fully Demonstrated* (London, 1726).

L[enton], F[rancis], *Characterisimi: Or, Lenton's Leasures Expressed in Essays and Characters* (London, 1631).

L'Estrange, Nicholas,'*Merry Passages and Jeasts': a Manuscript Jestbook of Sir Nicholas L'Estrange (1603–1655)*, ed. H. F. Lippincott (Salzburg, 1974).

A Letter To A Member of Parliament With Two Discourses Enclosed In It. I. The One Shewing the Reason Why a Law Should Pass to Punish Adultery With Death ([London?], 1675).

Letters on Love, Marriage and Adultery (London, 1789).

The Lively Character of a Contented and Discontented Cuckold (London, 1700).

Locke, John, *An Essay Concerning Human Understanding* (1690), ed. Roger Woolhouse (Harmondsworth, 1997).

The London Cuckold: Or an Antient Citizen's Head Well Fitted With a Flourishing Pair of Fashionable Horns (London, n.d. [*c*.1680]).

London in 1710, From the Travels of Zacharius Conrad von Uffenbach, trans. and ed. W. H. Quarrell and Margaret Mare (London, 1934).

M., A., *The Reformed Gentleman: Or, The Old English Morals Rescued from the Immoralities of the Present Age* (London, 1693).

Mackenzie, George, *Moral Gallantry* (London, 1685).

The Man of Manners: Or, Plebeian Polish'd (London, 1735).

Memoirs of the Society of Grub Street (2 vols., London, 1737).

Meriton, George, *Immorality, Debauchery and Profaneness Exposed to the Reproof of Scripture and the Censure of the Law* (London, 1698).

The Merry Man's Companion, And Evenings Agreeable Entertainer: Containing Near Six Hundred of the very Best and most Favourite Songs, Catches, Airs etc. Now in Vogue (London, 1750).

Mr Noble's Speech, To the Lord Chief-Justice Parker, Before He Received Sentence of Death (London, 1713).

Moxon, Mordecai, *The Character, Praise and Commendation of a Chaste and Virtuous Woman: in a Learned and Pious Discourse against Adultery* (London, 1708).

A Myraculous and Monstrous but yet most True and Certayne Discourse of a Woman... in the midst of whose Forehead (by the wonderful work of God) there groweth out a Crooked Horne of Four Inches Long (London, 1588).

N., A., *An Account of Marriage, or, the Interests of Marriage Considered and Defended against the Unjust Attacques of the Age* (London, 1672).

News from Covent-Garden: Or, the Town-Gallants Vindication (London, 1695).

Newton, John, *The Penitent Recognition of Joseph's Brethren: a Sermon Occasion'd by Elizabeth Ridgeway* (London, 1684).

Nocturnal Revels: Or, A Universal Dream Book (2 vols., London, 1706–7).

Observations on the Tryal of Thomas Jones the Foot-Boy (London, 1715).

Oldys, Alexander, *The Female Gallant: Or, the Wife's the Cuckold. A Novel* (London, 1692).

[Osborne, Francis], *Advice to a Son; or Directions for Your Better Conduct through the Various and Most Important Encounters of this Life* (London, 1656).

Ostervald, Jean Frederic, *The Nature of Uncleanness Consider'd* (London, 1708).

Otway, Thomas, *The Works of Thomas Otway*, ed. J. C. Ghosh (2 vols., Oxford, 1932).

The Pall-Mall Miscellany (London, n.d. [1732]).

Pepys, Samuel, *The Diary of Samuel Pepys*, ed. Robert Latham and William Matthews (11 vols., London, 1970–83).

The Pepys Ballads, ed. Hyder Rollins (8 vols., Cambridge, MA, 1931).

The Pepys Ballads, ed. W. G. Day (5 vols., Cambridge, 1987).

Percy, William, *The Cuckqueanes and Cuckolds Errants, or the Bearing Down the Inne*, ed. John Arthur Lloyd (London, 1824).

Pinkethman's Jests: Or, Wit Refin'd. Being a New-Year's Gift for young Gentlemen and Ladies (London, 1721).

A Poem, Sacred to the Memory of the Honourable Lady Aber-----ny. Humbly Inscrib'd to the Quality of Great-Britain (London, 1729).

Poor Robin, 1699 (London, 1699).

Poor Robin's Jests, Or the Compleat Jester. The Second Part (London, 1669).

Poynter, Thomas, *A Concise View of the Doctrine and Practice of the Ecclesiastical Courts in Doctors Commons* (London, 1824).

Ravenscroft, Edward, *The London Cuckolds* (1682), in *Restoration Comedy*, ed. A. Norman Jeffares (4 vols., London, 1974), II, pp. 435–552.

[Rawlins, Thomas], *Tom Essence: Or, the Modish Wife* (London, 1677).

Remarques on the Humours and Conversations of the Gallants of the Town (London, 1673).

Reynolds, John, *God's Revenge Against the Crying and Execrable Sin of Adultery, Expressed in Ten Several Tragical Histories* (London, 1706 edn).

Richardson, Samuel, *Pamela: Or, Virtue Rewarded* (1740) (2 vols., London, 1962).

Rowe, Nicholas, *The Fair Penitent* (1703), ed. Malcolm Goldstein (London, 1969).

Ryder, Dudley, *The Diary of Dudley Ryder 1715–1716*, ed. William Matthews (London, 1939).

Rye, William Brenchley (ed.), *England as seen by Foreigners in the Days of Elizabeth and James the First* (London, 1865).

S., J., *A Sermon Against Adultery* (London, 1672).

Satan's Harvest Home: Or, the Present State of Whorecraft, Adultery, Fornication, Procuring, Pimping, Sodomy and the Game at Flatts (London, 1749).

Savile, George, *The Works of George Savile, Marquis of Halifax*, ed. Mark N. Brown (3 vols., Oxford, 1989).

Schellinks, William,*The Journal of William Schellinks' Travels in England, 1661–1663*, trans. and ed. Maurice Exwood and H. L. Lehmann, Camden Society, 5th ser., 1 (London, 1993).

Sedley, Charles, *The Poetical Works and Dramatic Works of Sir Charles Sedley*, ed. V. de Sola Pinto (2 vols., London, 1928).

Serious Admonitions to Youth, in a Short Account of the Life, Trial, Condemnation and Execution of Mrs Mary Channing (London, 1706).

Shadwell, Thomas, *The Complete Works of Thomas Shadwell*, ed. Montague Summers (5 vols., London, 1927).

The Shropshire Amazement (London, n.d. [*c*.1708?]).

Smith, Alexander, *Court Intrigues: Or, an Account of the Secret Amours of Our British Nobility and Others* (London, 1730).

Smith, Samuel, *The Behaviour of Edward Kirk, After His Condemnation for Murdering His Wife* (London, 1684).

Smith, William, *A Just Account of the Horrid Contrivance of John Cupper and Judith Brown His Servant, in Poysoning His Wife* (London, 1684).

[Somers, John], *A Discourse Concerning Generosity* (London, 1695).

Southerne, Thomas, *The Works of Thomas Southerne*, ed. Robert Jordan and Harold Love (2 vols., Oxford, 1988).

The Strange and Wonderful Relation of a Barbarous Murder Committed by James Robi[n]son, A Brick-Layer, Upon the Body of His Own Wife (London, 1679).

Swift, Jonathan, *Journal to Stella*, ed. Harold Williams (2 vols., Oxford, 1948).

A Proposal for Correcting, Improving and Ascertaining the English Tongue (London, 1712).

Synodalia: A Collection of Articles of Religion, Canons and Proceedings of Convocation in the Province of Canterbury, from the Year 1547 to the Year 1717, ed. Edward Cardwell (2 vols., Oxford, 1842).

Taylor, Jeremy, *Holy Living* (1650), ed. P. G. Stanwood (Oxford, 1989).

Taylor, John, *The Works of John Taylor the Water Poet, Reprinted from the Folio Edition of 1630* (London, 1868–9).

Thomas, William, *Christian and Conjugall Counsell, Applyed Unto the Marriage State* (London, 1661).

Tillotson, John, *The Works of the Most Reverend Dr John Tillotson, Late Lord Archbishop of Canterbury*, ed. Ralph Barker (2 vols., London, 1712).

The Tincker of Turvey (London, 1630).

Towerson, Gabriel, *An Explication of the Decalogue of the Ten Commandments, with Reference to the Catechism of the Church of England* (London, 1676).

The True Copy of the Original Paper Signed by Mr Richard Noble, Which He Designed for His Last Speech (London, 1713).

The True Narrative of the Execution of John Marketman, Chyrurgion, of West Ham in Essex, for Committing a Horrible and Bloody Murther Upon the Body of His Wife (n.p., n.d. [1680]).

A True and Perfect Relation of the Tryal and Condemnation, Execution and Last Speech of that Unfortunate Gentleman Mr Robert Foulks (London, 1679).

A True Relation of the Inhumane and Unparallel'd Actions and Barbarous Murders of Negroes or Moors: Committed on three Englishmen in Old Calabar in Guinney (London, 1672).

A True Relation of the Most Horrible Murther, Committed By Thomas White (London, 1682).

'Truelove, Francis', *The Comforts of Matrimony; Exemplified in the Memorable Trial, Lately had upon an Action Brought by Theo[philus] C[ibbe]r against [William] S[loper] Esq.* (London, 1739).

The Tryal Before the Lord Chief Justice R-y---d at the Guild Hall Between Mr J- C- a Mercer at Aldgate and Mr J. E-- for Criminal Conversation (London, n.d. [1730]).

The Tryal Between Henry Duke of Norfolk, Plaintiff, and John Jermaine Defendant, in an Action of Trespass (London, 1692).

The Tryal Between J. G. Biker, Plaintiff; and M. Morley, Doctor of Physic, Defendant; For Criminal Conversation with the Plaintiff's Wife (London, 1741).

The Tryal Between Sir W[illiam] M[orice] Baronet, Plaintiff, and Lord A[ugu]st[u]s F[i]tzR[o]y, Defendant, for Criminal Conversation (London, 1742).

The Tryal of a Cause for Criminal Conversation, Between Theophilus Cibber, Gent. Plaintiff, and William Sloper, Esq. Defendant (London, 1739).

Turner, William, *A Compleat History of the Most Remarkable Providences, Both of Judgement and Mercy, Which have happened in the Present Age* (London, 1697).

Twelve Delightful Novels, Displaying the Stratagems of Love and Gallantry (London, 1719).

Two Books of Homilies Appointed to be Read in Churches, ed. John Griffiths (Oxford, 1859).

The Universal Monitor: Or, a General Dictionary of Moral and Divine Precepts (London, 1702).

Vanbrugh, Sir John and Colley Cibber, *The Provoked Husband, Or a Journey to London* (1728), ed. Peter Dixon (London, 1975).

Wanley, Nathaniel, *The Wonders of the Little World: Or, A General History of Men* (London, 1678).

[Ward, Edward], *Female Policy Detected: Or, the Arts of a Designing Woman Laid Open* (London, 1712).

   The Forgiving Husband, and Adulteress Wife: Or a Seasonable Present to the Unhappy Pair in Fanchurch Street (London, n.d. [*c.*1708]).

   The Modern World Disrob'd: Or, Both Sexes Stript of their Pretended Vertue (London, 1708).

   The Northern Cuckold: Or, the Garden House Intrigue (London, 1721).

   Nuptial Dialogues and Debates: Or, an Useful Prospect of the Felicities and Discomforts of a Marry'd Life, Incident to All Degrees from the Throne to the Cottage (2 vols., London, 1710).

A Warning for Bad Wives: Or, the Manner of the Burning of Sarah Elston (London, 1678).

Webbe, George, *The Arraignment of An Unruly Tongue* (London, 1619).

Webster, John, *The Devil's Law Case* (1623), ed. Frances A. Shirley (Rochester, NY, 1972).

The Whole and True Tryals and Condemnation of all the Prisoners Who were Try'd at Kingston... With a Full and Particular Account of Mr Noble, Mrs Sayer and Mrs Salisbury, For the Murder of 'Squire Sayer (London, 1713).

The Whole Tryal, Examination and Conviction of Thomas Jones, Footman to Esquire Dormer (London, 1715).

The Whole Tryals, With the Examination and Condemnation of John Taylor and John Flint (London, 1706).

Williams, Roger, *A Key Into the Language of America: Or, An Help to the Language of the Natives in that part of America called New England* (London, 1643).

The Wonders of Free Grace (London, 1690).

Wycherley, William, *The Plays of William Wycherley*, ed. Arthur Friedman (Oxford, 1979).

The XV Comforts of Rash and Inconsiderate Marriage (London, 1682).

4 PRINTED SECONDARY SOURCES

Allemann, Gellert Spencer, *Matrimonial Law and the Materials of Restoration Comedy* (Philadelphia, 1942).

Amussen, Susan Dwyer, *An Ordered Society: Gender and Class in Early Modern England* (Oxford, 1988).

   '"The Part of a Christian Man"': the Cultural Politics of Manhood in Early Modern England', in Susan D. Amussen and Mark A. Kishlansky (eds.), *Political Culture and Cultural Politics in Early Modern England: Essays Presented to David Underdown* (Manchester, 1995), pp. 213–33.

Andrew, Donna T., '"Adultery A-La-Mode": Privilege, the Law and Attitudes to Adultery 1770–1809', *History*, 82 (1997), 5–23.

   'The Code of Honour and its Critics: the Opposition to Duelling in England, 1700–1850', *Social History*, 5 (1980), 409–34.

Bahlman, Dudley, *The Moral Revolution of 1688* (New Haven, CT, 1957).

Bailey, Richard, *Images of English: a Cultural History of the Language* (Cambridge, 1992).

Baker, J. H., *An Introduction to English Legal History*, 3rd edn (London, 1990).

Barker-Benfield, G. J., *The Culture of Sensibility: Sex and Society in Eighteenth-Century Britain* (Chicago, IL and London, 1992).

Barry, Jonathan, 'Bourgeois Collectivism? Urban Association and the Middling Sort', in Jonathan Barry and Christopher Brooks (eds.), *The Middling Sort of People: Culture, Society and Politics in England 1550–1800* (Basingstoke, 1994), pp. 84–112.

'Literacy and Literature in Popular Culture: Reading and Writing in Historical Perspective', in Tim Harris (ed.), *Popular Culture in England, c.1500–1850* (Basingstoke, 1995), pp. 69–94.

Beattie, J. M., *Crime and the Courts in England 1660–1800* (Oxford, 1986).

Bell, Ian, *Literature and Crime in Augustan England* (London, 1991).

Bennett, W. Lance and Martha S. Feldman, *Reconstructing Reality in the Courtroom* (London and New York, 1981).

Berry, Helen, '"Nice and Curious Questions": Coffee Houses and the Representation of Women in John Dunton's *Athenian Mercury*', *The Seventeenth Century*, 12 (1997), 257–76.

Binhammer, Katherine, 'The Sex Panic of the 1790s', *Journal of the History of Sexuality*, 6 (1991), 409–34.

Borsay, Peter, *The English Urban Renaissance: Culture and Society in the Provincial Town, 1660–1700* (Oxford, 1989).

'The Restoration Town', in Lionel K. J. Glassey (ed.), *The Reigns of Charles II and James VII and II* (Basingstoke, 1997), pp. 171–90.

Boucé, Paul-Gabriel, 'Imagination, Pregnant Women and Monsters in Eighteenth-Century Britain and France', in G. S. Rousseau and Roy Porter (eds.), *Sexual Underworlds of the Enlightenment* (Manchester, 1987), pp. 86–100.

Boulton, Jeremy, 'Clandestine Marriages in London: an Examination of a Neglected Urban Variable', *Urban History*, 20 (1993), 191–210.

'Itching After Private Marryings? Marriage Customs in Seventeenth-Century London', *London Journal*, 16 (1991), 15–34.

'London Widowhood Revisited: the Decline of Female Remarriage in the Seventeenth and Eighteenth Centuries', *Continuity and Change*, 5 (1990), 323–55.

Brewer, John, '"The Most Polite Age and the Most Vicious": Attitudes towards Culture as a Commodity, 1660–1800', in Ann Bermingham and John Brewer (eds.), *The Consumption of Culture 1600–1800: Image, Object, Text* (London and New York, 1995), pp. 341–61.

The Pleasures of the Imagination: English Culture in the Eighteenth Century (London, 1997).

'This, That and the Other: Public, Social and Private in the Seventeenth and Eighteenth Centuries', in Dario Castiglione and Lesley Sharpe (eds.), *Shifting the Boundaries: Transformations of the Languages of Public and Private in the Eighteenth Century* (Exeter, 1995), pp. 1–21.

Brooks, C. W., 'Interpersonal Conflict and Social Tension: Civil Litigation in England, 1640–1830', in A. L. Beier, David Cannadine and James M. Rosenheim (eds.), *The First Modern Society: Essays in English History in Honour of Lawrence Stone* (Cambridge, 1989), pp. 357–99.

Brown, Frank E., 'Continuity and Change in the Urban House: Developments in Domestic Space Organisation in Seventeenth-Century London', *Comparative Studies in Society and History*, 28 (1986), 558–90.

Brown, Roger Lee, 'The Rise and Fall of the Fleet Marriages', in R. B. Outhwaite (ed.), *Marriage and Society: Studies in the Social History of Marriage* (London, 1981), pp. 117–36.

Brundage, James A., *Law, Sex and Christian Society in Medieval Europe* (Chicago, IL, 1987).

Bryson, Anna, *From Courtesy to Civility: Changing Codes of Conduct in Early Modern England* (Oxford, 1998).

Burke, Peter, *The Art of Conversation* (Cambridge, 1993).

    'A Civil Tongue: Language and Politeness in Early Modern Europe', in Peter Burke, Brian Harrison and Paul Slack (eds.), *Civil Histories: Essays Presented to Sir Keith Thomas* (Oxford, 2000), pp. 31–48.

Burke, Peter, Brian Harrison and Paul Slack (eds.), *Civil Histories: Essays Presented to Sir Keith Thomas* (Oxford, 2000).

Capp, Bernard, *Astrology and the Popular Press: English Almanacs 1500–1800* (London, 1979).

    'The Double Standard Revisited: Plebeian Women and Male Sexual Reputation in Early Modern England', *PP*, 162 (1999), 70–100.

Carter, Philip, *Men and the Emergence of Polite Society: Britain 1660–1800* (London, 2001).

Castle, Terry, *Masquerade and Civilisation: the Carnivalesque in Eighteenth-Century English Culture and Fiction* (Stanford, CA, 1986).

Chappell, Edwin, *The Secrecy of the Diary* ([London?], 1933).

Chartier, Roger, *Cultural History: Between Practices and Representations*, trans. Lydia G. Cochrane (Cambridge, 1988).

    'Culture as Appropriation: Popular Cultural Uses in Early Modern France', in Steven L. Kaplan (ed.), *Understanding Popular Culture: Europe from the Middle Ages to the Nineteenth Century* (Berlin, 1984), pp. 229–53.

    (ed.), *A History of Private Life, Volume III: Passions of the Renaissance* (Cambridge, MA and London, 1989).

    The Order of Books (Cambridge, 1994).

Chaytor, Miranda, 'Husband(ry): Narratives of Rape in the Seventeenth Century', *Gender and History*, 7 (1995), 378–407.

Claydon, Tony, *William III and the Godly Revolution* (Cambridge, 1996).

Clayton, Timothy, *The English Print 1688–1802* (New Haven, CT and London, 1992).

Cockburn, J. S., 'Patterns of Violence in English Society: Homicide in Kent 1560–1985', *PP*, 130 (1991), 70–106.

Cohen, Michele, *Fashioning Masculinity: National Identity and Language in the Eighteenth Century* (London, and New York, 1996).

Colley, Linda, 'Going Native, Telling Tales: Captivity, Collaboration and Empire', *PP*, 168 (2000), 170–93.

Collinson, Patrick, 'The Theatre Constructs Puritanism', in David L. Smith, Richard Strier and David Bevington (eds.), *The Theatrical City: Culture, Theatre and Politics in London, 1576–1649* (Cambridge, 1995), pp. 157–69.

Copley, Stephen, 'Commerce, Conversation and Politeness in the Early Eighteenth-Century Periodical', *British Journal for Eighteenth-Century Studies*, 18 (1995), 63–77.

Corfield, P. J., 'Introduction: Historians and Language', in P. J. Corfield (ed.), *Language, History and Class* (Oxford, 1991), pp. 1–29.

Cranfield, G. A., *The Development of the Provincial Newspaper 1700–1760* (Oxford, 1962).

Cressy, David, 'Literacy in Context: Meaning and Measurement in Early Modern England', in John Brewer and Roy Porter (eds.), *Consumption and the World of Goods* (London and New York, 1993), pp. 305–19.

Literacy and the Social Order: Reading and Writing in Tudor and Stuart England (Cambridge, 1980).

Crowley, John E., *The Invention of Comfort: Sensibilities and Design in Early Modern Britain and Early America* (Baltimore, MD, 2000).

Curtis, T. C. and W. A. Speck, 'The Societies for the Reformation of Manners: a Case Study in the Theory and Practice of Moral Reform', *Literature and History*, 3 (1976), 45–64.

Dabhoiwala, Faramerz, 'The Construction of Honour, Reputation and Status in Late Seventeenth- and Early Eighteenth-Century England', *TRHS*, 6th ser., 6 (1996), 201–13.

Darnton, Robert, *The Forbidden Best-Sellers of Pre-Revolutionary France* (London, 1996).

Davidoff, Leonore and Catherine Hall, *Family Fortunes: Men and Women of the English Middle Class, 1780–1850* (London, 1987).

Davies, Kathleen M., 'Continuity and Change in Literary Advice on Marriage', in R. B. Outhwaite (ed.), *Marriage and Society: Studies in the Social History of Marriage* (London, 1981), pp. 58–80.

Davis, Lennard, *Factual Fictions: the Origins of the English Novel* (New York, 1983).

Davis, Natalie Zemon, *Fiction in the Archives: Pardon Tales and their Tellers in Sixteenth-Century France* (Stanford, CA, 1987).

Dolan, Frances E., *Dangerous Familiars: Representations of Domestic Crime in England, 1550–1700* (Ithaca, NY and London, 1994).

Donahue Jr., Charles, 'Proof by Witnesses in the Church Courts of Medieval England: an Imperfect Reception of the Learned Law', in Morris S. Arnold, Thomas A. Green, Sally A. Scully and Stephen D. White (eds.), *On the Laws and Customs of England: Essays in Honor of Samuel E. Thorne* (Chapel Hill, NC, 1981), pp. 127–58.

Dubrow, Heather, *Genre* (London and New York, 1982).

Dunn, John, 'The Claim to Freedom of Conscience: Freedom of Speech, Freedom of Thought, Freedom of Worship?', in Ole Peter Grell, Jonathan I. Israel and Nicholas Tyacke (eds.), *From Persecution to Toleration: the Glorious Revolution and Religion in England* (Oxford, 1991), pp. 171–93.

Dyer, Richard, *The Matter of Images: Essays on Representations* (London and New York, 1993).

Earle, Peter, *A City Full of People: Men and Women of London 1650–1750* (London, 1994).

The Making of the English Middle Class: Business, Society and Family Life in London, 1660–1730 (London, 1989).

Elias, Norbert, *The Civilizing Process: the History of Manners* (1939), trans. Edmund Jephcott (Oxford, 1978).

Ellis, Joyce, '"On the Town": Women in Augustan England', *History Today*, December (1995), pp. 20–7.

Erickson, Amy Louise, *Women and Property in Early Modern England* (London, 1993).

Estabrook, Carl B., *Urbane and Rustic England: Cultural Ties and Social Spheres in the Provinces 1660–1780* (Manchester, 1998).

Everitt, Alan, 'Social Mobility in Early Modern England', *PP*, 33 (1966), 56–73.

Faller, Lincoln, *Turned to Account: the Forms and Functions of Criminal Biography in Late Seventeenth- and Early Eighteenth-Century England* (Cambridge, 1987).

Feather, John, *History of British Publishing* (London and New York, 1988).

Finlay, Roger and Beatrice Shearer, 'Population Growth and Suburban Expansion', in A. L. Beier and Roger Finlay (eds.), *London 1500–1700: the Making of the Metropolis* (London, 1986), pp. 37–59.

Fletcher, Anthony, *Gender, Sex and Subordination in England 1500–1800* (New Haven, CT and London, 1995).

'Men's Dilemma: the Future of Patriarchy in England, 1560–1660', *TRHS*, 6th ser., 4 (1994), 61–81.

'The Protestant Idea of Marriage in Early Modern England', in Anthony Fletcher and Peter Roberts (eds.), *Religion, Culture and Society in Early Modern Britain: Essays in Honour of Patrick Collinson* (Cambridge, 1994), pp. 161–81.

Fletcher, Anthony and John Stevenson, 'Introduction', in Anthony Fletcher and John Stevenson (eds.), *Order and Disorder in Early Modern England* (Cambridge, 1985), pp. 1–40.

Foucault, Michel, *The History of Sexuality, Volume I: An Introduction*, trans. Robert Hurley (Harmondsworth, 1978).

Fowler, Alistair, *Kinds of Literature: an Introduction to the Theory of Genres and Modes* (Oxford, 1982).

Fox, Adam, 'Ballads, Libels and Popular Ridicule in Jacobean England', *PP*, 145 (1994), 47–83.

'Custom, Memory and the Authority of Writing', in Paul Griffiths, Adam Fox and Steve Hindle (eds.), *The Experience of Authority in Early Modern England* (Basingstoke, 1996), pp. 89–116.

Oral and Literate Culture in England 1500–1700 (Oxford, 2000).

Foyster, Elizabeth A., 'A Laughing Matter? Marital Discord and Gender Control in Seventeenth-Century England', *Rural History*, 4 (1993), 5–21.

'Male Honour, Social Control and Wife Beating in Late Stuart England', *TRHS*, 6th ser., 6 (1996), 215–24.

Manhood in Early Modern England: Honour, Sex and Marriage (London, 1999).

'Silent Witnesses? Children and the Breakdown of Domestic and Social Order in Early Modern England', in Anthony Fletcher and Stephen Hussey (eds.), *Childhood in Question: Children, Parents and the State* (Manchester, 1999), pp. 57–73.

Gaskill, Malcolm, *Crime and Mentalities in Early Modern England* (Cambridge, 2000).

'The Displacement of Providence: Policing and Prosecution in Seventeenth- and Eighteenth-Century England', *Continuity and Change*, 11 (1996), 341–74.

'Reporting Murder: Fiction in the Archives in Early Modern England', *Social History*, 23 (1998), 1–30.

George, Charles H. and Katherine George, *The Protestant Mind of the English Reformation 1570–1640* (Princeton, NJ, 1961).

Gibson, Marion, *Reading Witchcraft: Stories of Early English Witches* (London and New York, 1999).

Gillis, John, 'Conjugal Settlements: Resort to Clandestine and Common Law Marriage in England and Wales 1650–1850', in John Bossy (ed.), *Disputes and Settlements: Law and Human Relations in the West* (Cambridge, 1983), pp. 261–84.

Girouard, Mark, *Life in the English Country House: a Social and Architectural History* (New Haven, CT and London, 1978).

Gowing, Laura, *Domestic Dangers: Women, Words and Sex in Early Modern London* (Oxford, 1996).

'Gender and the Language of Insult in Early Modern London', *History Workshop Journal*, 35 (1993), 1–21.

'Secret Births and Infanticide in Seventeenth-Century England', *PP*, 156 (1997), 67–115.

Harris, Michael, 'Timely Notices: the Uses of Advertising and its Relationship to News during the Late Seventeenth Century', in Joad Raymond (ed.), *News, Newspapers and Society in Early Modern Britain* (London, 1999), pp. 141–56.

'Trials and Criminal Biographies: a Case Study in Distribution', in Robin Myers and Michael Harris (eds.), *Sale and Distribution of Books from 1700* (Oxford, 1982), pp. 1–36.

Harris, Tim, *London Crowds in the Reign of Charles II: Propaganda and Politics from the Restoration until the Exclusion Crisis* (Cambridge, 1987).

'Problematising Popular Culture', in Tim Harris (ed.), *Popular Culture in England, c.1500–1850* (Basingstoke, 1995), pp. 1–27.

Harris, Tim, Paul Seaward and Mark Goldie (eds.), *The Politics of Religion in Restoration England* (Oxford, 1990).

Harte, N. B., 'State Control of Dress and Social Change in Pre-Industrial England', in D. C. Coleman and A. H. John (eds.), *Trade, Government and Economy in Pre-Industrial England: Essays Presented to F. J. Fisher* (London, 1976), pp. 132–65.

Hayton, David, 'Moral Reform and Country Politics in the Late Seventeenth-Century House of Commons', *PP*, 128 (1990), 48–91.

Heal, Felicity, 'Hospitality and Honor in Early Modern England', *Food and Foodways*, 1 (1987), 321–50.

Herrup, Cynthia, 'Law and Morality in Seventeenth-Century England', *PP*, 106 (1985), 102–23.

Hill, Christopher, *The World Turned Upside Down: Radical Ideas During the English Revolution* (London, 1972).

Hitchcock, Tim, *English Sexualities, 1700–1800* (Basingstoke, 1997).

'Redefining Sex in Eighteenth-Century England', *History Workshop Journal*, 41 (1996), 73–90.

Hoffer, Peter C. and N. E. H. Hull, *Murdering Mothers: Infanticide in England and New England 1558–1803* (New York and London, 1984).

Horder, Jeremy, *Provocation and Responsibility* (Oxford, 1992).

Houlbrooke, Ralph, *Death, Religion and the Family in England 1450–1750* (Oxford, 1998).

Howe, Elizabeth, *The First English Actresses: Women and Drama 1660–1700* (Cambridge, 1992).

Hughes, Derek, *English Drama, 1660–1700* (Oxford, 1996).

Hull, Isabel V., *Sexuality, State, and Civil Society in Germany, 1700–1815* (Ithaca, NY, 1996).

Hume, Robert D., *The Rakish Stage: Studies in English Drama 1660–1800* (Carbondale, IL, 1983).

'Texts Within Contexts: Notes Toward a Historical Method', *Philological Quarterly*, 71 (1992), 69–100.

Hunt, Margaret R., *The Middling Sort: Commerce, Gender and the Family in England 1680–1780* (Berkeley and Los Angeles, CA, 1996).

Ingram, Martin, *Church Courts, Sex and Marriage in England, 1570–1640* (Cambridge, 1987).

'Law, Litigants and the Construction of "Honour": Slander Suits in Early Modern England', in Peter Coss (ed.), *The Moral World of the Law* (Cambridge, 2000), pp. 134–60.

'Reformation of Manners in Early Modern England', in Paul Griffiths, Adam Fox and Steve Hindle (eds.), *The Experience of Authority in Early Modern England* (Basingstoke, 1996), pp. 47–88.

'Ridings, Rough Music and the "Reform of Popular Culture" in Early Modern England', *PP*, 105 (1984), 79–113.

'Sexual Manners: the Other Face of Civility in Early Modern England', in Peter Burke, Brian Harrison and Paul Slack (eds.), *Civil Histories: Essays Presented to Sir Keith Thomas* (Oxford, 2000), pp. 87–109.

Isaacs, Tina, 'The Anglican Hierarchy and the Reformation of Manners', *Journal of Ecclesiastical History*, 33 (1982), 391–411.

Jackson, Bernard S., 'Narrative Models in Legal Proof', in David Ray Papke (ed.), *Narrative and the Legal Discourse: a Reader in Storytelling and the Law* (Liverpool, 1991) pp. 158–78.

Jackson, Mark, *New-Born Child Murder: Women, Illegitimacy and the Courts in Eighteenth-Century England* (Manchester, 1996).

Jacobs, Kathryn, 'Rewriting the Marital Contract: Adultery in *The Canterbury Tales*', *The Chaucer Review*, 29 (1995), 337–47.

James, Mervyn, 'English Politics and the Concept of Honour, 1485–1642', *PP*, Supplement no. 3 (1978).

James, T. E., 'The Court of Arches during the Eighteenth Century: Its Matrimonial Jurisdiction', *American Journal of Legal History*, 5 (1961), 55–66.

Jones, Vivien, 'The Seductions of Conduct: Pleasure and Conduct Literature', in Roy Porter and Marie Mulvey Roberts (eds.), *Pleasure in the Eighteenth Century* (Basingstoke, 1996), pp. 108–32.

Kahn, Coppelia, *Man's Estate: Masculine Identity in Shakespeare* (Berkelely, CA and London, 1981).

Kamensky, Jane, *Governing the Tongue: the Politics of Speech in Early New England* (Oxford, 1997).

Kelly, Ann Cline, *Swift and the English Language* (Philadelphia, PA, 1988).

Kinnear, Mary, 'The Correction Court in the Diocese of Carlisle, 1704–1756', *Church History*, 59 (1990), 191–206.

Klein, Lawrence E., 'Gender, Conversation and the Public Sphere in Early Eighteenth-Century England', in Judith Still and Michael Worton (eds.), *Textuality and Sexuality: Reading Theories and Practices* (Manchester, 1993), pp. 100–15.

'Gender and the Public/Private Distinction in the Eighteenth Century: Some Questions about Evidence and Analytic Procedure', *Eighteenth-Century Studies*, 29 (1995), 97–109.

'Politeness for Plebes: Consumption and Social Identity in Early Eighteenth Century England', in Ann Bermingham and John Brewer (eds.), *The Consumption of Culture 1600–1800: Image, Object, Text* (London and New York, 1995), pp. 362–82.

Shaftesbury and the Culture of Politeness: Moral Discourse and Cultural Politics in Early Eighteenth-Century England (Cambridge, 1994).

Korobkin, Laura Hanft, *Criminal Conversations: Sentimentality and Nineteenth-Century Legal Stories of Adultery* (New York, 1998).

Krutch, Joseph Wood, *Comedy and Conscience After the Restoration* (New York and London, 1961).

Lake, Peter, '"A Charitable Christian Hatred": the Godly and their Enemies in the 1630s', in Christopher Durston and Jacqueline Eales (eds.), *The Culture of English Puritanism, 1560–1700* (Basingstoke, 1996), pp. 145–83.

'Deeds Against Nature: Cheap Print, Protestantism and Murder in Early Seventeenth Century England', in Kevin Sharpe and Peter Lake (eds.), *Culture and Politics in Early Stuart England* (Basingstoke, 1994), pp. 257–83.

Langford, Paul, *Englishness Identified: Manners and Character 1650–1850* (Oxford, 2000).

A Polite and Commercial People: England 1727–1783 (Oxford, 1989).

Laqueur, Thomas, *Making Sex: Body and Gender from the Greeks to Freud* (Cambridge, MA and London, 1990).

Laslett, Peter, *The World We Have Lost: Further Explored* (London, 1983).

'The Wrong Way Through the Telescope: a Note on Literary Evidence in Sociology and in Historical Sociology', *British Journal of Sociology*, 27 (1976), 319–42.

Lassiter, John C., 'Defamation of Peers: the Rise and Decline of the Action for *Scandalum Magnatum*', *American Journal of Legal History*, 22 (1978), 216–36.

Lawson, Annette, *Adultery: an Analysis of Love and Betrayal* (Oxford, 1989).

Leckie, Barbara, *Culture and Adultery: the Novel, the Newspaper and the Law, 1857–1914*, (Philadelphia, PA, 1999).

Legman, Gershon, *Rationale of the Dirty Joke: an Analysis of Sexual Humour* (London, 1969).

Leinward, Theodore B., *The City Staged: Jacobean Comedy, 1603–1613* (Madison, WI and London, 1986).

Leites, Edmund, 'Good Humor at Home, Good Humor Abroad: the Intimacies of Marriage and the Civilities of Social Life in the Ethic of Richard Steele', in Edward A. and Lillian D. Bloom (eds.), *Educating the Audience: Addison, Steele and Eighteenth-Century Culture* (Los Angeles, CA, 1984), pp. 51–89.

The Puritan Conscience and Modern Sexuality (New Haven, CT and London, 1986).

Lemmings, David, 'Marriage and the Law in the Eighteenth Century: Hardwicke's Marriage Act of 1753', *Historical Journal*, 39 (1996), 339–60.

Leneman, Leah, *Alienated Affections: the Scottish Experience of Divorce and Separation 1684–1830* (Edinburgh, 1998).

Lindley, David, *The Trials of Frances Howard: Fact and Fiction at the Court of King James* (London and New York, 1993).

Linebaugh, P., 'The Ordinary of Newgate and his *Account*', in J. S. Cockburn (ed.), *Crime in England 1550–1800* (London, 1977), pp. 246–69.

Love, Harold, 'Who were the Restoration Audience?', *Yearbook of English Studies*, 10 (1980), 21–44.

McCreery, Cindy, 'Keeping Up with the Bon Ton: the *Tête-à-Tête* Series in the *Town and Country Magazine*', in Hannah Barker and Elaine Chalus (eds.), *Gender in Eighteenth-Century England: Roles, Representations and Responsibilities* (London, 1997), pp. 207–29.

McEwen, Gilbert D., *The Oracle of the Coffee House: John Dunton's Athenian Mercury* (San Marino, CA, 1972).

McKeon, Michael, 'Historicizing Patriarchy: the Emergence of Gender Difference in England, 1660–1760', *Eighteenth-Century Studies*, 28 (1995), 295–322.

McKendrick, Neil, 'The Commercialization of Fashion', in Neil McKendrick, John Brewer and J. H. Plumb (eds.), *The Birth of a Consumer Society: the Commercialization of Eighteenth-Century England* (London, 1982), pp. 34–99.

Mackie, Erin, *Market A La Mode: Fashion, Commodity and Gender in the Tatler and the Spectator* (Baltimore, MD and London, 1997).

Maclean, Ian, *The Renaissance Notion of Woman: a Study in the Fortunes of Scholasticism and Medical Science in European Intellectual Life* (Cambridge, 1980).

Manley, Lawrence, 'From Matron to Monster: Tudor-Stuart London and the Languages of Urban Description', in Heather Dubrow and Richard Strier (eds.), *The Historical Renaissance: New Essays on Tudor and Stuart Literature and Culture* (Chicago, IL and London, 1988), pp. 347–74.

Meldrum, Tim, *Domestic Service and Gender 1660–1750: Life and Work in the London Household* (London, 2000).

‘A Women's Court in London: Defamation at the Bishop of London's Consistory Court, 1700–1745', *The London Journal*, 19 (1994), 1–20.

Mellinkoff, Ruth, *The Horned Moses in Medieval Art and Thought* (Berkeley, CA and London, 1970).

Mendelson, Sara and Patricia Crawford, *Women in Early Modern England 1550–1720* (Oxford, 1998).

Morris, Desmond, Peter Collett, Peter Marsh and Marie O'Shaughnessy, *Gestures: Their Origins and Distribution* (London, 1979).

Muldrew, Craig, *The Economy of Obligation* (Basingstoke, 1998).

‘Interpreting the Market: the Ethics of Credit and Community Relations in Early Modern England', *Social History*, 18 (1993), 163–83.

Mullan, John, *Sentiment and Sociability: the Language of Feeling in the Eighteenth Century* (Oxford, 1988).

Nash, Mary, *The Provoked Wife: the Life and Times of Susannah Cibber* (London, 1977).

Novak, Maximillian, *William Congreve* (New York, 1971).

O'Connell, Sheila, *The Popular Print in England 1550–1850* (London, 1999).

Outhwaite, R. B., *Clandestine Marriage in England, 1500–1800* (London and Rio Grande, OH, 1995).

The Oxford Classical Dictionary, ed. N. G. L. Hammond and H. H. Scullard (Oxford, 1970).

Oxford English Dictionary (Oxford, 1989 edn).

Pagden, Anthony, *The Fall of Natural Man: the American Indian and the Origins of Comparative Ethnology* (Cambridge, 1982).

‘The Savage Critic: Some European Images of the Primitive', *Yearbook of English Studies*, 13 (1983), 32–45.

Parks, Stephen, *John Dunton and the English Book Trade: a Study of his Career with a Checklist of his Publications* (New York and London, 1976).

Parten, Anne, 'Beatrice's Horns: a Note on *Much Ado About Nothing*, II.i. 25–27', *Shakespeare Quarterly*, 35:2 (1984), 201–2.

‘Falstaff's Horns: Masculine Inadequacy and Feminine Mirth in *The Merry Wives of Windsor*', *Studies in Philology*, 82 (1985), 184–99.

Partridge, Eric, *Shakespeare's Bawdy* (London and New York, 1990).

Patterson, Annabel, ‘"Secret History": Liberal Politics and the 1832 Reform Bill', *Literature and History*, 3rd ser., 7 (1998), 33–52.

Paulson, Ronald, *Popular and Polite Art in the Age of Hogarth and Fielding* (Notre Dame, IN and London, 1979).

Payne, Deborah C., 'Reading the Signs in *The Country Wife*', *Studies in English Literature 1500–1900*, 26 (1986), 403–19.

Perry, Ruth, 'Colonizing the Breast: Sexuality and Maternity in Eighteenth-Century England', *Journal of the History of Sexuality*, 2 (1991), 204–34.

Phillips, Roderick, *Putting Asunder: a History of Divorce in Western Society* (Cambridge, 1988).

Pincus, Steven C. A., 'From Butterboxes to Wooden Shoes: the Shift in English Popular Sentiment from Anti-Dutch to Anti-French in the 1670s', *Historical Journal*, 38 (1995), 333–61.

Pointon, Marcia, *Hanging the Head: Portraiture and Social Formation in Eighteenth-Century England* (New Haven, CT and London, 1993).

Pollock, Linda A., 'Living on the Stage of the World: the Concept of Privacy Among the Elite of Early Modern England', in Adrian Wilson (ed.), *Rethinking Social History: English Society 1570–1920 and its Interpretation* (Manchester, 1993), pp. 78–96.

Porter, Roy, 'A Touch of Danger: the Man-Midwife as Sexual Predator', in G. S. Rousseau and Roy Porter (eds.), *Sexual Underworlds of the Enlightenment* (Manchester, 1987), pp. 206–32.

Porter, Roy and Lesley Hall, *The Facts of Life: the Creation of Sexual Knowledge in Britain, 1650–1950* (New Haven, CT and London, 1995).

Quaife, G. R., *Wanton Wenches and Wayward Wives: Peasants and Illicit Sex in Early Seventeenth-Century England* (London, 1979).

Raven, James, *Judging New Wealth: Popular Publishing and Responses to Commerce in England, 1750–1800* (Oxford, 1992).

'New Reading Histories, Print Culture and the Identification of Change: the Case of Eighteenth-Century England', *Social History*, 23 (1998), 268–87.

Rawlings, Philip, *Drunks, Whores and Idle Apprentices: Criminal Biographies of the Eighteenth Century* (London, 1992).

Ribiero, Aileen, *Dress and Morality* (London, 1986).

Richetti, J. J., *Popular Fiction Before Richardson: Narrative Patterns 1700–1739* (Oxford, 1969).

Roberts, David, *The Ladies: Female Patronage of Restoration Drama* (Oxford, 1989).

Roper, Lyndal, *Oedipus and the Devil: Witchcraft, Sexuality and Religion in Early Modern Europe* (London and New York, 1994).

Schlatter, Richard B., *The Social Ideas of Religious Leaders 1660–1688* (London, 1940).

Screech, M. A., *Laughter at the Foot of the Cross* (Harmondsworth, 1997).

Sekora, John, *Luxury: the Concept in Western Thought* (London, 1977).

Shapiro, Barbara J., *'Beyond Reasonable Doubt' and 'Probable Cause': Historical Perspectives on the Anglo-American Law of Evidence* (Berkeley, CA and Oxford, 1991).

Probability and Certainty in Seventeenth-Century England: a Study of the Relationships Between Natural Science, History, Law, and Literature (Princeton, NJ, 1983).

Sharpe, J. A., *Crime in Early Modern England 1550–1750* (London and New York, 1984).

'Domestic Homicide in Early Modern England', *Historical Journal*, 24 (1981), 29–48.

'"Last Dying Speeches": Religion, Ideology and Public Execution in Seventeenth Century England', *PP*, 107 (1985), 144–67.

'Plebeian Marriage in Stuart England: Some Evidence from Popular Literature', *TRHS*, 5th ser., 36 (1986), 69–90.

Sheehan, Bernard W., *Savagism and Civility: Indians and Englishmen in Colonial Virginia* (Cambridge, 1980).

Shevelow, Kathryn, *Women and Print Culture: the Construction of Femininity in the Early Periodical* (London and New York, 1989).

Shoemaker, Robert B., 'The Decline of Public Insult in London 1660–1800', *PP*, 169 (2000), 97–131.

Gender in English Society, 1650–1850: the Emergence of Separate Spheres? (London and New York, 1998).

Prosecution and Punishment: Petty Crime and the Law in London and Rural Middlesex, c.1660–1725 (Cambridge, 1991).

Sinclair, Alison, *The Deceived Husband: a Kleinian Approach to the Literature of Infidelity* (Oxford, 1993).

Slatter, M. Doreen, 'The Records of the Court of Arches', *Journal of Ecclesiastical History*, 4 (1953), 139–53.

Smith, H. Ecroyd, 'Poor Robin', *Notes and Queries*, 6th ser., 7 (28 April 1883), 321–2.

Smith, M. G., *Pastoral Discipline and the Church Courts: the Hexham Court 1680–1730*, Borthwick Papers, 62 (York, 1982).

Solkin, David H., *Painting for Money: the Visual Arts and the Public Sphere in Eighteenth-Century England* (New Haven, CT and London, 1993).

Sommerville, C. John, *Popular Religion in Restoration England* (Gainesville, FL, 1977).
    The Secularisation of Early Modern England: From Religious Culture to Religious Faith (New York and Oxford, 1992).

Spiegel, Gabrielle M., 'History, Historicism and the Social Logic of the Text in the Middle Ages', *Speculum*, 65 (1990), 59–86.

Spufford, Margaret, 'First Steps in Literacy: the Reading and Writing Experience of the Humblest Seventeenth-Century Spiritual Autobiographers', *Social History*, 4 (1979), 407–35.

Spurr, John, *England in the 1670s: 'This Masquerading Age'* (Oxford, 2000).
    'Perjury, Profanity and Politics', *The Seventeenth Century*, 8 (1993), 29–50.
    'Virtue, Religion and Government: the Anglican Uses of Providence', in Tim Harris, Paul Seaward and Mark Goldie (eds.), *The Politics of Religion in Restoration England* (Oxford, 1990), pp. 29–47.
    The Restoration Church of England, 1646–1689 (New Haven, CT and London, 1991).

Squibb, G. D., *Doctors' Commons: a History of the College of Advocates and Doctors of Law* (London, 1977).

Starr, G. A., *Defoe and Casuistry* (Princeton, NJ, 1971).

Staves, Susan, 'Money for Honor: Damages for Criminal Conversation', *Eighteenth-Century Culture*, 11 (1982), 279–97.
    Players' Scepters: Fictions of Authority in the Restoration (Lincoln, NE and London, 1979).

Stone, Lawrence, *The Family, Sex and Marriage in England 1500–1800* (London, 1977).
    'The Residential Development of the West End of London in the Seventeenth Century', in Barbara C. Malamant (ed.), *After the Reformation: Essays in Honor of J. H. Hexter* (Manchester, 1980), pp. 167–214.
    Road to Divorce: England 1530–1987 (Oxford, 1990).
    Uncertain Unions and Broken Lives: Marriage and Divorce in England 1660–1857 (Oxford, 1995).

Straus, Ralph, *The Unspeakable Curll* (London, 1927).

Stretton, Tim, *Women Waging Law in Elizabethan England* (Cambridge, 1998).

Sutherland, James, *The Restoration Newspaper and its Development* (Cambridge, 1986).

Tadmor, Naomi, '"Family" and "Friend" in *Pamela*: a Case Study in the History of the Family in Eighteenth-Century England', *Social History*, 14 (1989), 289–306.

Tanner, Tony, *Adultery and the Novel: Contract and Transgression* (Baltimore, MD and London, 1979).

Tave, Stuart, *The Amiable Humorist: a Study in the Comic Theory of the Eighteenth and Early Nineteenth Centuries* (Chicago, IL and London, 1960).

Thomas, Donald, *A Long Time Burning: the History of Literary Censorship in England* (London, 1969).

Thomas, Keith, 'Cases of Conscience in Seventeenth-Century England', in John Morrill, Paul Slack and Daniel Woolf (eds.), *Public Duty and Private Conscience in Seventeenth-Century England: Essays Presented to G. E. Aylmer* (Oxford, 1993), pp. 27–56.

'Cleanliness and Godliness in Early Modern England', in Anthony Fletcher and Peter Roberts (eds.), *Religion, Culture and Society in Early Modern Britain: Essays in Honour of Patrick Collinson* (Cambridge, 1994), pp. 56–83.

'The Double Standard', *Journal of the History of Ideas*, 20 (1959), 195–216.

History and Literature (Swansea, 1988).

Man and the Natural World: Changing Attitudes in England 1500–1800 (Harmondsworth, 1983).

'The Meaning of Literacy in Early Modern England', in Gerd Baumann (ed.), *The Written Word: Literacy in Transition* (Oxford, 1986), pp. 97–131.

'The Place of Laughter in Tudor and Stuart England', *Times Literary Supplement*, 21 January (1977), 77–81.

'The Puritans and Adultery: the Act of 1650 Reconsidered', in Donald Pennington and Keith Thomas (eds.), *Puritans and Revolutionaries: Essays in Seventeenth-Century History Presented to Christopher Hill* (Oxford, 1978), pp. 257–82.

Religion and the Decline of Magic: Studies in Popular Beliefs in Sixteenth and Seventeenth Century England (Harmondsworth, 1973).

Thompson, E. P., *Customs in Common* (Harmondsworth, 1991).

Thompson, John B., 'Scandal and Social Theory', in James Lull and Stephen Hinerman (eds.), *Media Scandals: Morality and Desire in the Popular Culture Marketplace* (Cambridge, 1997), pp. 34–64.

Thompson, Roger, *Unfit for Modest Ears: a Study of Pornographic, Obscene and Bawdy Works Written or Published in England in the Second Half of the Seventeenth Century* (Basingstoke, 1979).

Tilley, Morris Palmer (ed.), *A Dictionary of the Proverbs in England in the Sixteenth and Seventeenth Centuries* (Ann Arbor, MI, 1950).

Tosh, John, 'What Should Historians do with Masculinity? Reflections on Nineteenth-Century Britain', *History Workshop Journal*, 33 (1994), 179–202.

Trumbach, Randolph, *Sex and the Gender Revolution, Volume I: Heterosexuality and the Third Gender in Enlightenment London* (Chicago, IL and London, 1998).

Turner, David M., 'Adulterous Kisses and the Meanings of Familiarity in Early Modern Britain', in Karen Harvey (ed.), *The Kiss in History* (Manchester, forthcoming).

'"Nothing is so Secret but shall be Revealed": the Scandalous Life of Robert Foulkes', in Tim Hitchcock and Michele Cohen (eds.), *English Masculinities, 1660–1800* (London, 1999), pp. 169–92.

Turner, James Grantham, 'The Properties of Libertinism', in Robert P. Maccubin (ed.), *'Tis Nature's Fault: Unauthorized Sexuality During the Enlightenment* (Cambridge, 1987), pp. 75–87.

Twyning, John, *London Dispossessed: Literature and Social Space in the Early Modern City* (Basingstoke, 1998).

Underdown, David, *A Freeborn People: Politics and the Nation in Seventeenth-Century England* (Oxford, 1996).

Revel, Riot and Rebellion: Popular Politics and Culture in England 1603–1660 (Oxford, 1985).

'The Taming of the Scold: the Enforcement of Patriarchal Authority in Early Modern England', in Anthony Fletcher and John Stevenson (eds.), *Order and Disorder in Early Modern England* (Cambridge, 1985), pp. 116–36.

Underwood, Dale, *Etherege and the Seventeenth-Century Comedy of Manners* (New Haven, CT, 1957).

Van Lennep, William, Emmett L. Avery, Arthur H. Scouten, George Winchester Stone and Charles Beeches Hogan (eds.), *The London Stage, 1660–1800* (5 vols. Carbondale, IL, 1960–8).

Verberckmoes, Johan, *Laughter, Jestbooks and Society in the Spanish Netherlands* (Basingstoke, 1999).

Vickery, Amanda, *The Gentleman's Daughter: Women's Lives in Georgian England* (New Haven, CT and London, 1998).

'Golden Age to Separate Spheres? A Review of the Categories and Chronology of English Women's History', *Historical Journal*, 36 (1993), 383–414.

Waddams, S. D., *Sexual Slander in Nineteenth-Century England: Defamation in the Ecclesiastical Courts, 1815–1855* (Toronto and London, 2000).

Wagner, Peter, *Eros Revived: Erotica of the Enlightenment in England and America* (London, 1990).

'The Pornographer in the Courtroom: Trial Reports about Cases of Sexual Crimes and Delinquencies as a Genre of Eighteenth Century Erotica', in P. G. Boucé (ed.), *Sexuality in Eighteenth Century Britain* (Manchester, 1982), pp. 120–40.

Walker, Garthine, '"Demons in Female Form": Representations of Women and Gender in Murder Pamphlets of the Late Sixteenth and Early Seventeenth Centuries', in William Zunder and Suzanne Trill (eds.), *Writing and the English Renaissance* (London and New York, 1996), pp. 123–39.

'Rereading Rape and Sexual Violence in Early Modern England', *Gender and History*, 10 (1998), 1–25.

'"Strange Kind of Stealing": Abduction in Early Modern Wales', in Michael Roberts and Simone Clarke (eds.), *Women and Gender in Early Modern Wales* (Cardiff, 2000), pp. 50–74.

Wall, Alison, 'For Love, Money, or Politics? A Clandestine Marriage and the Elizabethan Court of Arches', *Historical Journal*, 38 (1995), 511–33.

Wall, Cynthia, *The Literary and Cultural Spaces of Restoration London* (Cambridge, 1998).

Walsh, John and Stephen Taylor, 'Introduction: the Church and Anglicanism in the "Long" Eighteenth Century', in John Walsh, Colin Hayden and Stephen Taylor (eds.), *The Church of England c.1689–c.1833: From Toleration to Tractarianism* (Cambridge, 1993), pp. 1–64.

Walsham, Alexandra, *Providence in Early Modern England* (Oxford, 1999).

Wardroper, John (ed.), *Jest Upon Jest: a Selection from the Jestbooks and Collections of Merry Tales published from the Reign of Richard III to George III* (London, 1970).

Watt, Tessa, *Cheap Print and Popular Piety, 1550–1640* (Cambridge, 1991).

Weatherill, Lorna, *Consumer Behaviour and Material Culture in Britain 1660–1760* (London and New York, 1988).

'Consumer Behaviour, Textiles and Dress in the Late Seventeenth and Early Eighteenth Centuries', *Textile History*, 22 (1991), 297–310.

Weil, Rachel, *Political Passions: Gender, the Family and Political Argument in England, 1680–1714* (Manchester, 1999).

'Sometimes a Scepter is Only a Scepter: Pornography and Politics in Restoration England', in Lynn Hunt (ed.), *The Invention of Pornography: Obscenity and the Origins of Modernity 1500–1800* (New York, 1993), pp. 125–53.

Weiner, Martin J., 'The Sad Story of George Hall: Adultery, Murder and the Politics of Mercy in Mid-Victorian England', *Social History*, 24 (1999), 174–95.

Westermann, Mariet, *The Amusements of Jan Steen: Comic Painting in the Seventeenth Century* (Zwolle, 1997).

Whyman, Susan E., *Sociability and Power in Late-Stuart England: the Cultural World of the Verneys 1660–1720* (Oxford, 1999).

Wickberg, Daniel, *The Senses of Humor: Self and Laughter in Modern America* (Ithaca, NY and London, 1998).

Williams, Carolyn D., '"Another Self in the Case": Gender, Marriage and the Individual in Augustan Literature', in Roy Porter (ed.), *Rewriting the Self: Histories from the Renaissance to the Present* (London, 1997), pp. 91–118.

Williams, Tamsyn, '"Magnetic Figures": Polemical Prints of the English Revolution', in Lucy Gent and Nigel Llewellyn (eds.), *Renaissance Bodies: the Human Figure in English Culture, c.1540–1660* (London, 1990), pp. 86–110.

Wilson, Adrian, *The Making of Man-Midwifery: Childbirth in England 1660–1770* (London, 1995).

'Participant or Patient? Seventeenth-Century Childbirth from the Mother's Point of View', in Roy Porter (ed.), *Patients and Practitioners: Lay Perceptions of Medicine in Pre-Industrial Society* (Cambridge, 1985), pp. 129–44.

Wilson, John Harold, *The Private Life of Mr Pepys* (London, 1959).

Wiltenburg, Joy, *Disorderly Women and Female Power in the Street Literature of Early Modern England and Germany* (Charlottesville, VA and London, 1992).

Wolfram, Sybil, 'Divorce in England 1700–1857', *Oxford Journal of Legal Studies*, 5 (1985), 155–86.

Wrightson, Keith, *English Society 1580–1680* (London, 1982).

'Infanticide in Earlier Seventeenth-Century England', *Local Population Studies*, 15 (1975), 10–22.

'"Sorts of People" in Tudor and Stuart England', in Jonathan Barry and Christopher Brooks (eds.), *The Middling Sort of People: Culture, Society and Politics in England 1550–1800* (Basingstoke, 1994), pp. 28–51.

Wunderli, Richard, *London Church Courts and Society on the Eve of the Reformation* (Cambridge, MA, 1981).

5 UNPUBLISHED THESES

Bailey, Joanne, 'Breaking the Conjugal Vows: Marriage and Marriage Breakdown in the North of England, 1660–1800', PhD thesis, University of Durham (1999).

Berry, Helen, 'Gender, Society and Print Culture in Late Seventeenth-Century England, with Special Reference to the *Athenian Mercury* (1691–97)', PhD thesis, University of Cambridge (1998).

Botica, Allan, 'Audience, Playhouse and Play in Restoration Theatre, 1660–1710', DPhil thesis, University of Oxford (1985).

Childs, Fenela, 'Prescriptions for Manners in English Courtesy Literature 1690–1760, and their Social Implications', DPhil thesis, University of Oxford (1984).

Crouch, Kimberley, 'Attitudes Toward Actresses in Eighteenth-Century Britain', DPhil thesis, University of Oxford (1995).

Dabhoiwala, Faramerz, 'Prostitution and Police in London, *c.*1660–*c.*1760', DPhil thesis, University of Oxford (1995).

Melville, Jennifer, 'The Use and Organisation of Domestic Space in Late Seventeenth-Century London', PhD thesis, University of Cambridge (1999).

Norrel, L., 'The Cuckold in Restoration Comedy', PhD thesis, Florida State University (1962).

Shepard, Alexandra, 'Meanings of Manhood in Early Modern England, with Special Reference to Cambridge, *c.*1560–1640', PhD thesis, University of Cambridge (1998).

Tadmor, Naomi, 'Concepts of the Family in Five Eighteenth-Century Texts', PhD thesis, University of Cambridge (1992).

Turner, David M., 'Rakes, Libertines and Sexual Honour in Restoration England, 1660–1700', MA thesis, University of Durham (1994).

Walker, Garthine, 'Crime, Gender and Social Order in Early Modern Cheshire', PhD thesis, University of Liverpool (1994).

Weil, Rachel, 'Sexual Ideology and Political Propaganda in England, 1680–1714', PhD thesis, Princeton University (1991).

Westhauser, Karl E., 'The Power of Conversation: the Evolution of Modern Social Relations in Augustan London', PhD thesis, Brown University (1994).

Index

Past and Present Publications

General Editor: LYNDAL ROPER, *Royal Holloway, University of London*

Witchcraft Persecutions in Bavaria: Popular Magic, Religious Zealotry and Reason of State in Early Modern Europe, Wolfgang Behringer

Understanding Popular Violence in the English Revolution: The Colchester Plunderers, John Walter

The Moral World of the Law, edited by Peter Coss

Travel and Ethnology in the Renaissance: South India through European Eyes, 1250–1625, Joan-Pau Rubiés

Holy Rulers and Blessed Princesses: Dynastic Cults in Central Medieval Europe, Gábor Klaniczay

Rebellion, Community and Custom in Early Modern Germany, Norbert Schindler

*Also published in paperback

†Co-published with the Maison des Sciences de l'Homme, Paris

U.W.E.L. LEARNING RESOURCES